China Orders the World

China Orders the World

*Normative Soft Power
and Foreign Policy*

Edited by

William A. Callahan and Elena Barabantseva

Woodrow Wilson Center Press
Washington, D.C.

The Johns Hopkins University Press
Baltimore

EDITORIAL OFFICES
Woodrow Wilson Center Press
One Woodrow Wilson Plaza
1300 Pennsylvania Avenue, N.W.
Washington, D.C. 20004-3027
Telephone: 202-691-4029
www.wilsoncenter.org

ORDER FROM

The Johns Hopkins University Press
Hampden Station
P.O. Box 50370
Baltimore, Maryland 21211
Telephone: 1-800-537-5487
www.press.jhu.edu/books/

© 2011 by the Woodrow Wilson International Center for Scholars
Printed in the United States of America

2 4 6 8 9 7 5 3 1

Library of Congress Cataloging-in-Publication Data

China orders the world : normative soft power and foreign policy / edited by William A. Callahan and Elena Barabantseva.
   p. cm
  Includes bibliographical references and index.
  ISBN 978-1-4214-0383-0 (hardcover : alk. paper)
  1. China—Foreign relations—21st century. 2. China—Foreign relations—Philosophy. I. Callahan, William A. II. Barabantseva, Elena.
  JZ1734.C545   2011
  327.51—dc23
                                                2011032035

Woodrow Wilson Center Press
Washington, D.C.

The Woodrow Wilson International Center for Scholars is the national, living U.S. memorial honoring President Woodrow Wilson. In providing an essential link between the worlds of ideas and public policy, the Center addresses current and emerging challenges confronting the United States and the world. The Center promotes policy-relevant research and dialogue to increase understanding and enhance the capabilities and knowledge of leaders, citizens, and institutions worldwide. Created by an act of Congress in 1968, the Center is a nonpartisan institution headquartered in Washington, D.C., and supported by both public and private funds.

Conclusions or opinions expressed in Center publications and programs are those of the authors and speakers and do not necessarily reflect the views of the Center staff, fellows, trustees, advisory groups, or any individuals or organizations that provide financial support to the Center.

The Center is the publisher of *The Wilson Quarterly* and home of Woodrow Wilson Center Press and dialogue television and radio. For more information about the Center's activities and publications, please visit us on the Web at www.wilsoncenter.org.

Jane Harman, Director, President, and CEO

Board of Trustees
Joseph B. Gildenhorn, Chair
Sander R. Gerber, Vice Chair

Public members: James H. Billington, Librarian of Congress; Hillary R. Clinton, Secretary of State; G. Wayne Clough, Secretary of the Smithsonian Institution; Arne Duncan, Secretary of Education; David Ferriero, Archivist of the United States; James Leach, Chairman of the National Endowment for the Humanities; Kathleen Sebelius, Secretary of Health and Human Services; Melody Barnes, Designated Appointee of the President from within the Federal Government

Private citizen members: Timothy Broas, John T. Casteen III, Charles E. Cobb Jr., Thelma Duggin, Carlos M. Gutierrez, Susan Hutchison, Barry S. Jackson

To Sofia

and

To the memory of Yang Yu-wei

Contents

List of Illustrations   xi

Acknowledgments   xiii

1   Introduction: Tradition, Modernity, and Foreign Policy in China   1
    William A. Callahan

Part I   Rediscovering Traditional Concepts

2   Rethinking Empire from the Chinese Concept "All-under-Heaven" (Tianxia, 天下)   21
    Zhao Tingyang

3   The Possibility and Inevitability of a Chinese School of International Relations Theory   37
    Qin Yaqing

4   Xunzi's Thoughts on International Politics and Their Implications   54
    Yan Xuetong

Part II   Mixing Past, Present, and Future

5   Tianxia, Empire, and the World: Chinese Visions of World Order for the Twenty-First Century   91
    William A. Callahan

| 6 | The Enduring Function of the Substance/Essence (*Ti/Yong*) Dichotomy in Chinese Nationalism
Christopher R. Hughes | 118 |
| 7 | Paradoxes of Tradition and Modernity at the New Frontier: China, Islam, and the Problem of "Different Heavens"
David Kerr | 143 |

Part III Tradition and Modernity in Popular and State Discourse

8	Beyond World Order: Change in China's Negotiations over the World *Elena Barabantseva*	183
9	Confucianism, "Cultural Tradition," and Official Discourse in China at the Start of the New Century *Sébastien Billioud*	215
10	Conclusion: World Harmony or Harmonizing the World? *William A. Callahan*	249

| Contributors | 269 |
| Index | 273 |

Illustrations

Table

4.1	The Nature of the State's Power and Its Foundation	72

Figures

4.1	The Nature of Great Powers and International Order	56
4.2	Decisionmakers and the International Order	57
4.3	Relations of Different Variables at Different Levels	59
4.4	Causes of Uneven Power Development	66
4.5	Evil Human Nature, Social Hierarchy, and Their Influence on International Order	77
4.6	The Five Ordinance System	78
4.7	Relations among Concepts of Power Elements	81
7.1	Before Sovereignty: Central Eurasian Empires and Inner Asian Societies, circa 1600	155
8.1	The Logo of the Confucius Institute	197
8.2	Taking Photos in the World Park	207
8.3	The Entrance to the World Park	207
10.1	Olympic Slogan Sign at Beijing's Airport	254

Acknowledgments

This book is the result of a panel, "Tradition and Modernity in China's Foreign Policy," organized by the editors for the launch conference of the British Inter-University China Centre (BICC) in June 2007. BICC is an international center of excellence funded by the Economic and Social Research Council (U.K.) that joins together Oxford, Manchester, and Bristol universities (ESRC R103705). We would like to thank BICC's director, Frank Pieke, its codirector, Robert Bickers, and its administrator, Daniel Holloway, for providing space and time for our discussion of the interplay of ideas and policy. Not all the panel's participants are included in this volume, so we would like to thank these other scholars for their conference contributions and comments. As for the authors who are included, we thank them for their patience; as Chinese leaders often say, this project has gone through many twists and turns. At Manchester, we thank Jonathan Hughes for copyediting many of these chapters and Eduardo Fe-Rodriguez for reproducing Yan Xuetong's tables and figures. At the Woodrow Wilson Center, we would like to thank Joe Brinley for his editing expertise and Bob Hathaway for his interest and support.

The following chapters of this book have been previously published in different versions. *Chapter 2:* Zhao Tingyang, "Rethinking Empire from a Chinese Concept 'All-under-Heaven' (Tian-xia)," *Social Identities* 12, no. 1 (2006): 29–41. *Chapter 3:* Qin Yaqing, "Guoji guanxi lilun Zhongguo pai shengcheng de keneng he biran," *Shijie jingji yu zhengzhi*, no. 3 (2006): 7–13. *Chapter 4:* Yan Xuetong, "Xun Zi's Thoughts on International Politics and Their Implications," *Chinese Journal of International Politics* 2, no. 1 (2008): 135–65. *Chapter 5:* William A. Callahan, "Chinese Visions of World Order: Post-Hegemonic or a New Hegemony?" *International Studies*

Review 10 (2008): 749–61. *Chapter 8:* Elena Barabantseva, "Beyond World Order: Changes in China's Negotiations over the World," *Alternatives: Global, Local, Political* 34, no. 2 (2009): 129–56. *Chapter 9:* Sébastien Billioud, "Confucianism, 'Cultural Tradition,' and Official Discourse in China at the Start of the New Century," translated by Christopher Storey, *China Perspectives*, no. 3 (2007): 50–65.

China Orders the World

Chapter 1

Introduction: Tradition, Modernity, and Foreign Policy in China

William A. Callahan

In September 2005, Chinese president Hu Jintao introduced "harmonious world" (和谐世界) as a new concept of world order to a global audience at the United Nations headquarters in New York.[1] "Harmonious world" is an extension into the arena of foreign relations of Hu's domestic policy of "harmonious society" (和谐社会), which seeks to use state power to "close wealth divide and ease growing social tensions."[2] Officials and scholars in China thus explain "building a harmonious world" as a new—and better—way of seeking "lasting peace and common prosperity," whereby different civilizations can coexist in the global community.[3]

These laudable goals are hardly earth-shattering—who would argue against global peace, prosperity, and harmony? But Beijing's promotion of "harmonious world" as the basis of its foreign policy marks a shift in China's understanding of itself, and of its understanding of the world. For the past thirty years, Beijing has very carefully formulated its economic reform strategy to challenge neither the West nor the current world order: Deng Xiaoping's "peace and development" strategy thus allowed Beijing to take advantage of globalization to develop China's domestic economy. Yet Beijing's active promotion of "harmonious world" suggests that the era of Deng's "lay low" strategy is coming to an end; but what comes next is still not clear.[4]

What is most interesting is that although prominent Western experts have concluded that China is a status quo power that is unlikely to challenge the international system, an idealized version of China's imperial past is now inspiring some Chinese scholars' and policymakers' plans for China's future—and the world's future.⁵ The goal is no longer just to "save China" (救国) but also to "save the world." We can see this in discussions of the Beijing Consensus, the China model of development, and the Chinese School of international relations theory—all of which explicitly challenge the international status quo to think about post-Western world orders. This book's goal is to explain China's intellectual debates in the broader historical and theoretical context of its search for a post-Western world order. Indeed, the book itself is evidence of how Chinese concepts are making an impact beyond issues of East Asian politics and thus influencing broader debates about security and global governance in the West.

There has been much talk since 2009 about how China is now more assertive—and even arrogant—in international affairs in the wake of its successful navigation of the global economic crisis.⁶ But Beijing's more robust foreign policy is not entirely new. Since 2005, China has been making a transition from a generally passive international role to a more active one. With reform and opening, China has made staggering progress in building its economy, becoming the world's factory while successfully fighting poverty at home. Reflecting on this economic success, intellectuals and policymakers in China have been asking "What comes next?" How can China convert this new economic power into enduring political and cultural influence? In an article titled "Interrelating Harmonious World and Harmonious Society Policies," Yan Xuetong, the director of the Institute of International Studies at Tsinghua University (and the author of chapter 4 in the present volume), spoke to this new anxiety of opportunity by asking several questions pointing to China's potential objectives: Should economic interest still be at the top of China's agenda? Should China use its new power to expand its international markets or to expand its friendship relations? Should China increase its international investment or increase its respect for other countries? Should China's main objective be to increase its economic gains or to increase its international influence?⁷

That such a diverse set of potential objectives can fit under the rubric of "harmonious world" underlines how this concept can be used explain anything—and, indeed, everything—that Beijing does.⁸ In other words, something is going on, things are shifting—but no one can confidently say what is going on, and where policy is shifting.

Although the content of Hu Jintao's harmonious world foreign policy is still sketchy, the timing of its announcement is noteworthy. He introduced China's new foreign policy narrative at the United Nations' sixtieth-anniversary summit. Although sixty years is not a milestone in Euro-American

Introduction: Tradition, Modernity, and Foreign Policy in China   3

timekeeping, it represents a natural cycle in traditional Chinese culture, where sixty years mark both the end of one era and the birth of a new era.⁹ Indeed, in 2009 China celebrated the endings and beginnings of eras with the sixtieth anniversary of the founding of the People's Republic of China (PRC). And in 2011, the hundredth anniversary of the Republican Revolution that ended two millennia of empire is likewise provoking discussion of China's past and future. Indeed, for Confucius, this liminal moment is the best time to reflect on the past and plan for the future: "At sixty, my ear was an obedient organ for the reception of truth."¹⁰

With this extended period of transition, China is in the midst of a long millennial moment; intellectuals, policymakers, and even people on the street all are experiencing a heady mix of excitement and uncertainty about the possibilities for the twenty-first century, which they feel is China's century. The opening lines of a 2005 white paper titled "China's Road of Peaceful Development" speak to this special time when past, present, and future are all intertwined with the destiny of China and the world: "Looking back upon history, basing itself on the present reality and looking forward to the future, China will unswervingly follow the road of peaceful development, making great efforts to achieve a peaceful, open, cooperative and harmonious development."¹¹ To understand China's perplexing present, officials and public intellectuals alike have been looking to both the past and the future for ideas, structures, and models.¹²

As we have seen in China's three recent global spectacles—Beijing's Olympic Games in 2008, the PRC's sixtieth-anniversary celebrations in 2009, and Shanghai's World Expo in 2010—China is presenting itself to the world as the source of ancient wisdom and high technology, which together form an alternative model of progress and development. China's challenge to the Euro-American dominance of international politics became even sharper just after the Olympic Games ended when the global financial crisis erupted in the United States in September 2008. Many commentators thus see not just the rise of China—but also the fall of the West.¹³ As the director of a Confucius Institute in the United Kingdom put it, the rapid spread of Confucius Institutes around the world—more than three hundred have opened in five years—shows how people are embracing China's view of the world.¹⁴ The big question now is: What will Beijing do with this new global power? How would China run the world?

China's vibrant intellectual debate about its future has only recently attracted the attention of Western scholars. Interesting books have been published about the debates among liberalism, the New Left, nationalism,

Chinese tradition, and critical theory in China.[15] Although these analyses have tended to focus on the domestic impact of China's fierce ideological polemic, the present volume aims to explain China's intellectual debates in the broader historical and theoretical context of China's search for a post-Western world order. As the chapters that follow show, discussions of "harmonious world" are only the tip of the iceberg. Whereas Hu Jintao's introduction of the harmonious world policy at the UN in 2005 appealed to a global audience, his reinvocation of this concept as a central theme in his "Report to the 17th Party Conference" in 2007 appealed to a domestic audience.[16] Together, these pronouncements have become part of a much broader discussion in China about future world orders and new international relations (IR) theories. Indeed, many of the book's chapters show how the vagueness of Beijing's official harmonious world foreign policy creates a conceptual vacuum that is being filled by a range of unofficial and quasi-official theories, concepts, and grand strategies for the Chinese century.

The call in China for an internationalization of Chinese norms has some resonance outside China as well. Critical IR theorists in both the West and the non-West note how IR theory is Eurocentric, based on European history and European philosophy. They argue that it is necessary to both provincialize Europe and to look for universals outside Europe. Thus people are now talking about what India, Russia, Islam, and South America have to say about global norms and world order.[17] Chinese-style IR theory is attracting the most attention because China has its own long history of global politics and a rich philosophical tradition.[18] As Ole Wæver remarked in his survey of alternative sources of IR theory, "The most obvious candidate for an independent IR tradition based on a unique philosophical tradition is China, though very little independent theorizing has taken place."[19]

Although this new interest in Chinese visions of world order is encouraging, it has its own set of problems. The discussion of Chinese IR theory is now often reduced to a chapter on "the Chinese perspective" in anthologies of alternative traditions. Unfortunately, this treatment of different national and civilizational traditions tends to essentialize them, and their contribution to IR theory. Therefore, this book's analysis of Chinese norms and soft power is important because its chapters, especially those in part I, provide multiple views of "Chinese tradition." The book's goal thus is to offer a rich sense of the complex debates going on in China—debates that are increasingly having an impact on widespread discussions of the future of global politics.

Soft Power, Identity, and China's Foreign Policy

In the past two decades, many concepts have been offered to explain post–Cold War international politics, ranging from "the end of history" to "the clash of civilizations," "globalization," and new understandings of "empire."[20] With the rise of anti-Americanism around the world in the wake of the invasion of Iraq in 2003, the concept of "soft power" took on new relevance. Indeed, Joseph Nye coined this term to rationalize a decline in U.S. hard power in the early 1990s, but when the United States was at the height of its hard power in 2004, he felt it was necessary to clarify and systematize the soft power concept. His purpose in the 2000s thus was different from that in the 1990s: to warn the American leadership of the hazards of "going it alone" as the sole superpower in the twenty-first century.[21] But while American soft power experienced a dramatic decline during the George W. Bush administration, the soft power of the concept itself has increased in value; "soft power" has now spread conceptually beyond explaining the particular cultural influence of the United States to become a new "universal" construct for describing and defining the broad mechanisms of world politics.[22]

Most recently, the concept of soft power has been deployed to explain the rise of China beyond its growing military power and economic clout. Rather than acting as a revolutionary power that challenges the international system, Beijing has been engaging in a "charm offensive" to convince the world of its peaceful status quo intensions.[23] Indeed, starting in 2006, China's political leaders and editorialists themselves began utilizing the term "soft power"; in addition to promoting the harmonious world policy, Hu Jintao spoke enthusiastically about soft power in his "Report to the 17th Party Conference" (2007).[24] Since then, scholars have been busy analyzing the PRC's growing soft power in terms of state policies that have successfully spread China's culture, language, development model, and peacekeeping troops around the world.[25]

Beijing's interest in soft power is therefore quite recent, and constitutes an important foreign policy shift.[26] Since 2001 Beijing's economic policy has pushed its national champions to "go global" to develop global brands that can conquer the world market. The influential philosopher Zhao Tingyang (the author of chapter 2 below) argues that Chinese culture must also go global: China needs to excel not just in economic production but also in "knowledge production" that exploits its own indigenous "resources of traditional thought."[27] Similarly, Chinese scholarly contributions to social science theory, especially theories of development and modernization, are interpreted as an expression of China's growing global influence and as signs of "quality" of the Chinese nation.[28] Thus China needs to do more than develop the institutional soft power of the Confucian Institutes that teach Chinese language and culture around the world; it also needs to develop normative soft power in order to create and export its understandings of the world—such as "harmonious world"—that conceptualize globalization in new and different ways.

One of soft power's most important aspects is the ability of a state to set the agenda of international politics and use its values to define not only world problems but also the range of possible solutions.[29] Although there has been a thorough cataloguing of China's soft power assets in terms of their effectiveness and limitations, much less attention has been paid to the normative aspect of China's soft power.

Investigations of Chinese visions of world order are not new—in 1968, the doyen of American Sinology, John King Fairbank, edited the seminal text on this topic, *The Chinese World Order: Traditional China's Foreign Relations*.[30] Fairbank's idealized description of a hierarchical Sinocentric world order with the Chinese empire at the core and loyal tributary states and barbarians at the periphery has generated considerable debate during the past four decades.[31] The current invocation of this debate in international studies argues that China's traditional hierarchical regional order was much more peaceful than Europe's egalitarian Westphalian world order.[32] The story of the Ming Dynasty admiral Zheng He is presented as emblematic of the guiding distinction between Oriental peace and Occidental violence. Thus, while European imperial fleets smuggled opium and established colonies, Zheng He's massive fleet explored Asia and Africa on seven voyages of peace and friendship (1405–33). Vice Foreign Minister Zhang Yesui explains the contemporary significance of Zheng He's voyages by stressing how they "promoted the peaceful coexistence of various civilizations, demonstrating China's cultural tradition of friendship in international relations."[33]

In the past few years, there has been a traditional culture fever in China and among the Chinese diaspora; this lively debate discusses what ideas and norms should constitute China's "contribution" to world civilization.[34] Rather than simply provide suitably Chinese parallels to "international," "security," or other mainstream IR concepts, many public intellectuals in Greater China have been promoting traditional Chinese concepts like harmony (和谐), great harmony (大同), and All-under-Heaven (Tianxia, 天下) to explain China's visions of world order in ways that go beyond its official policy of peacefully rising within the international system.

Although Chinese scholars have been employing traditional concepts to explain current domestic and foreign policies for more than a decade,[35] recent discussions of Chinese-inspired world order have dramatically shifted these debates from the margins to the mainstream.[36] China's public intellectuals—including contributors to this volume such as Yan Xuetong—are important beyond their academic writings for being popular commentators on China Central Television (CCTV) news programs. Yu Dan took this public role one step further with her prime time explanations of the Confucian *Analects* on CCTV-10's *Lecture Room* program, which became a runaway best seller when it was published in book form in 2007.[37] Like other public intellectuals, Yu has also gone global; her book has been translated and published in English as *Confucius from the Heart: Ancient Wisdom for Today's World*, which has been promoted in Britain through China's network of Confucius Institutes.[38]

In this way, Chinese debates about traditional culture and world order serve as good examples of how soft power takes shape as the romanticization of a particular national culture into "universally desirable values."[39] It is certainly interesting to trace patterns of global hegemony in terms of the spread of a universalized national culture—Americanization, Europeanization, Japanization, and Sinicization.[40] Yet this analytical framework risks limiting our analysis to singular understandings of national cultures as they go global. Rather than comparing the soft power of Americanization with that of Sinicization, this book shows how it is more productive to examine recent Chinese debates in terms of *different* forms of Pax Sinica. In other words, if soft power grows out of a normative view of one's own political culture, the question shifts to ask "which norms" are being revived in China. As the chapters that follow show, Chinese intellectuals are not simply reviving ancient concepts for the twenty-first century; they are mixing different ideas, institutions, and models, and thus often synthesizing a new hybrid of ancient and modern, foreign and domestic. The question thus expands beyond that of "which norms" are being followed to consider what form these new hybrids will take—Confucian Leninism, market socialism, socialist harmonious society, the Chinese School of IR theory, and so on.

This book does not aim to provide a singular description of "the real China" and its soft power. "Chinese tradition" and "soft power" are interesting precisely because they each raise more questions than they answer.

We need to go beyond undertheorized pronouncements about "Chinese tradition" and "soft power" to consider how both emerge from particular theoretical and historical contexts. In this way, we can see how they provide us with various understandings of world order, and sharper understandings of identity and security politics in China.

Therefore, this book takes a broad view of foreign policy; following David Campbell's discussion of America's international politics, we need to understand two distinct but related senses of "foreign policy." On the one hand, foreign policy refers to all practices of differentiation between friend and enemy, self and other. This practice of foreign policy is divorced from the state and applies to encounters with otherness at various sociological sites: ethnicity, race, class, gender, region, and sexuality. On the other hand, the second sense of foreign policy—which Campbell capitalizes as "Foreign Policy"—is a performance by the state that serves to reproduce the construction of identity made possible by the first mode of foreign policy.[41] The job of "Foreign Policy," then, is to guard the cultural and discursive borders inscribed by "foreign policy." And foreign policy, in both senses, is about frontiers of identity and territory.

Thus rather than focusing on the "security dilemmas" of the PRC's interactions with other nation-states, this book explores foreign policy in terms of what Qin Yaqing calls the "identity dilemma" of China's view of itself and the world. Understanding the intellectual debate in China about what it means to be Chinese and how China should lead the world in the twenty-first century thus is crucial because it gives us a sense of the parameters within which new official policies (e.g., "harmonious world") are formulated, implemented, defended—and rejected.

Plan of the Book

To explore these issues, this book is divided into three parts, each of which employs textual analysis to put China's search for a post-Western world order in a historical and theoretical context. Chapters 2 through 4, which make up part I, show how prominent public intellectuals in China, including both social scientists and analytical philosophers, are increasingly looking to traditional Chinese concepts to think about world politics in new and different ways. In addition to their academic expertise, the authors of chapters 2, 3, and 4—respectively, Zhao Tingyang, Qin Yaqing, and Yan Xuetong—are important because they are key players in broader policy debates about China's international role.⁴² Though many like to describe Chinese tradition in terms of an essentialized Confucian pacifism, these chapters offer three different ways of conceiving the Chinese world order.

In chapter 2, Zhao shows how Chinese intellectuals are moving beyond a cultural nationalism that focuses on how Chinese culture should govern domestic politics to a patriotic cosmopolitanism whereby Chinese culture is necessary for governing the globe. He joins the debate about global governance by arguing that only China's concept of Tianxia (All-under-Heaven) is able to generate a world institution that could transcend the violence and division of the present international system. This chapter is important beyond the persuasiveness of Zhao's arguments; his ideas are being widely quoted among scholars and policymakers in China, and increasingly in the West as well.

In chapter 3, Qin shows how the elites who make foreign policy are thinking about how China can use its economic and political success to promote Chinese norms as universal IR theory. He argues that China needs to creatively combine the insights from three sources: traditional culture (including Tianxia), revolution in the modern period, and the past thirty years of reform and opening. His goal thus is not merely to provide a "Chinese perspective" on already existing global debates; in this chapter and other essays, he consciously engages in building theory with the aim of creating a universally applicable scientific IR theory.⁴³ As with Zhao, Qin's views are also important for discursive reasons; he has become the spokesperson, at home and abroad, for the Chinese School of IR theory.

Although Qin argues the case for a Chinese-style IR theory in general terms, in chapter 4, Yan provides a powerful example of how Chinese norms can be employed to think about global politics. He offers a close reading of the work of the ancient philosopher Xunzi—but for a practical purpose, namely, to consider the question "What kind of state should China rise to be?" After concluding that hierarchical systems can be useful, he argues that China needs to employ a combination of hard and soft power to build a hierarchical world system where submission is voluntary rather than coerced. Whereas Zhao and Qin give a general outline of Chinese approaches, Yan's chapter is important because its detailed analysis applies Chinese concepts to current events—showing both the strengths and the weaknesses of this approach. Yan's views are especially noteworthy because he is one of China's top strategists and is actively developing institutional structures to support discussions of its contribution to a post-Western world order.⁴⁴

Part I thus shows the richness of recent IR theorizing in China, which is the product of very deliberate crossover activities: Zhao is an analytical philosopher who has decided to mix ancient thought and public policy, whereas Qin and Yan are political scientists who now study classical texts. These three chapters all agree that Chinese norms should be more prominent in international discourse. But each highlights a different set of norms, which is then applied in quite different ways to solve global problems.

Although versions of these chapters have been published before, this is the first time that the ideas and analyses of these three leading scholars have been presented together as a discussion of different approaches to Chinese world ordering. But these key writings of Zhao, Qin, and Yan are more than primary sources of Chinese theory because they are consciously joining global debates about peace, war, and world order. Most important, jointly publishing these three chapters here reveals the diversity of Chinese tradition. Though many analyses of Chinese IR theory assert that they are presenting "*the* Chinese perspective," these three chapters show how there are many Chinese perspectives. Part I thus serves as a fruitful entry point into the critical view of Chinese IR theory that is elaborated in the balance of the book.

Whereas part I presents three distinct and coherent views of Chinese world ordering, in part II, chapters 5 through 7 take varied approaches to the general theme of how past, present, and future are intermixed in Chinese discussions of concepts and politics. In chapter 5, William A. Callahan takes a critical view of how Zhao and other Chinese intellectuals are promoting Tianxia as a model of world order, which he argues goes against Beijing's stated foreign policy of peacefully rising within the international system. After outlining popular discussion of this "magnanimous" Tianxia system, he examines some of the theoretical problems raised by this reading of Tianxia, in particular how its approach to "otherness" encourages a conversion of difference, if not a conquest of it. Hence, rather than guide us toward a posthegemonic world order, as promised, Tianxia presents a new hegemony whereby imperial China's hierarchical governance is updated for the twenty-first century. Callahan argues that Zhao's notion of global governance is interesting not just as an alternative world order but also because it shows how new ideas emerge in China's foreign policy discussion networks. In other words, he argues that the vagueness of Beijing's official "harmonious world" policy has created discursive space for debate about a range of strategic concepts, including Tianxia.

Although many descriptions of Chinese norms assert an exceptionalism that seeks to revive the superior moral path of Confucian pacificism, in chapter 6, Christopher R. Hughes shows that Chinese thought is most successful when it combines with other thought systems. He argues that the traditional Chinese idea of *ti/yong* (Chinese substance / Western function) emerged as a method for China to survive in the global imperial system of the late nineteenth century, and that it continues to inform how ideology works in the current era of globalization. Rather than assuming that Confucianism is a universal ethical system, he demonstrates how Chinese elites have used Confucianism to stimulate loyalty to the nation in an enduring political strategy of mass mobilization. Rather than providing an alternative utopian world order, Confucianism thus has enabled a popular politics in China that looks to Realism and the national interest.

In chapter 7, David Kerr compares the transnational logics of Confucian China and Turkic-Islamic civilization as a context for analyzing the current political problems that China faces in Central Eurasia. He studies the fluidity of China's relations at this New Frontier (Xinjiang), and suggests that we can learn much about the nature of contemporary Chinese foreign policy from the way that it negotiates between the received ideas of tradition and modernity, and between the temporal and spatial frontiers of China and Turkic Islam. He argues that power is produced each time China reinscribes difference alongside uniformity in both its domestic ethnic politics and its regional state politics. Although most compare China and the West, Kerr offers a close comparative reading of Chinese and Islamic modes of governance that highlights the difficulties that China faces when it must negotiate around the multiple sovereignties of Asian tradition and modernity.

Part III, comprising chapters 8 through 10, moves out of the elite discussions of the academy to consider how tradition and modernity incite popular—and populist—discourse in China. In chapter 8, Elena Barabantseva looks at two examples—a Confucius Institute promotional video and Jia Zhangke's film *Shijie* (*The World*)—to compare different ways of thinking about the globe: Tianxia as a inward-looking system that values order and stability, and *Shijie* as an outward-looking concept that entails an appreciation of change, contingency, and multiple formulations of the world and China's place in it. Barabantseva thus pushes this book's discussion of Tianxia and world order in new directions by arguing that we need to think beyond received understandings of Tianxia and the Westphalian system to be able to critically appreciate the interpretive struggles involved when

China creates itself in the negotiation of its relationships with the world. The chapter shows how these interpretive struggles emerge not just among the elite but also as part of the daily life of China's underclass.

In chapter 9, Sébastien Billioud brings the state back in as he critically describes how Confucianism and traditional culture, broadly conceived, have become more prominent in China's official discourse. Through a close reading of leaders' speeches and a number of policy documents, he shows how the party-state uses cultural tradition to strengthen popular legitimacy in the twenty-first century. But this is much more than an elite instrumentally manipulating the masses through top-down propaganda. Rather, the party-state has allowed a measure of social autonomy for people to discuss "tradition" in intellectual debates and popular practices, while still preserving its levers of control. Billioud concludes by emphasizing how this new situation signifies an exit from the PRC's monological view of history; we are now in a new era where the past is again being seen as meaningful by different groups in China, which are producing and reinventing Chinese tradition according to their different needs.

Chapter 10, the conclusion, examines how traditional Chinese norms are exerting a growing influence on both official and popular foreign policy in the PRC. It summarizes the book's debate by examining the shared yet alternative themes of exceptionalism/syncretism, hierarchy/equality, Westphalian system/Chinese School of IR theory, perfect world/contingent worlds, epistemological optimism/epistemological skepticism, theory/policy, and great harmony/harmony-with-difference. It then develops the book's analysis of theoretical trends in China to consider how Beijing's "harmonious society" and "harmonious world" policies could make an impact on world ordering. Although such norms are a source of soft power for China, ancient ideals like Tianxia and "great harmony" actually challenge Beijing's role as a status quo power. Because these new/old ideals are promoted by academics, public intellectuals, and officials, this book shows how we need to expand our gaze to include a new and diverse set of nongovernmental and non-elite sources to understand the making of foreign policy in China, where identity and security issues are intimately interwoven.

Chinese IR theory is still a new field, so we hope that this book's preliminary survey of this emerging topic will provoke even more discussion of the meaning and impact of Chinese norms as they "go global." To take China seriously as an emerging world power, we need to understand how Chinese scholars and policymakers imagine their future on the international stage. Rather than providing hard-and-fast answers about the trajectory of

Beijing's foreign policy in the twenty-first century, this book raises more questions—which is surely the appropriate approach to a topic that is only growing in importance. As Confucius remarked, "The asking of questions itself is the correct rite."[45]

Notes

1. Hu Jintao, "Nuli jianshe chijiu heping gongtong fanrong de hexie shijie" [Making an effort to build a sustainable, peaceful, and united prosperous harmonious world, speech at the United Nations sixtieth-year celebration], *Renmin Ribao* (*People's Daily*), September 16, 2006.

2. "Harmonious World: China's Ancient Philosophy for New Int'l Order (1)," *People's Daily*, October 2, 2007.

3. See, e.g., Ruan Zongze, "Goujian hexie shijie de Zhongguo waijiao" [China's foreign relations of building a harmonious world], *Liaowang*, no. 46 (November 14, 2005): 13–15; and Liu Jianfei, "Sino-U.S. Relations and Building a Harmonious World," *Journal of Contemporary China* 18, no. 60 (2009): 479–90.

4. Deng's "lay low" strategy was best expressed in the slogan "Bide time, conceal capabilities, but do some things" (韬光养晦有所作为).

5. See Alastair Iain Johnston, *Social States: China in International Institutions, 1980–2000* (Princeton, N.J.: Princeton University Press, 2008); David M. Lampton, *The Three Faces of Chinese Power: Might, Money and Minds* (Berkeley: University of California Press, 2008); and Susan Shirk, *China: Fragile Superpower* (New York: Oxford University Press, 2007).

6. Bonnie Glaser and Brad Glosserman, "China's Cheonan Problem," PacNet 31, Center for Strategic and International Studies, June 18, 2010; Kerry Brown, "Silent Witness," *South China Morning Post*, June 5, 2010.

7. Yan Xuetong, "Hexie shehui yu hexie shijie de zhengci guanxi" [Interrelating harmonious world and harmonious society policies], *Guoji zhengzhi yanjiu*, no. 1 (2006): 14–15.

8. See Yan Xuetong, "China Implementing Harmonious Diplomacy," *China Daily*, January 19, 2007; and Jean-Marc F. Blanchard and Sujian Guo, "'Harmonious World' and China's New Foreign Policy," in *"Harmonious World" and China's New Foreign Policy*, edited by Sujian Guo and Jean-Marc F. Blanchard (New York: Lexington Books, 2008), 8.

9. Sixty years is the combination of the twelve-year cycle of China's zodiac and the five-year cycle of the five elements. See Geremie R. Barmé, "Anniversaries in the Light, and in the Dark," *China Heritage Quarterly*, no. 17 (2009).

10. Confucius, *The Analects*, 2/4.

11. State Council, "China's Road of Peaceful Development," quoted by Xinhua, December 22, 2005.

12. Gan Yang's article "Mainland China: Thirty Years and Sixty Years" is an example of this sixty year / millennial feeling; Gan Yang, "Zhongguo daolu, sanshi nian yu liushi nian" [Mainland China: Thirty years and sixty years], *Dushu* no. 6 (2007): 3–13. The book *China Is Unhappy* is an example of the frustration and disappointment

that often accompany millennial moments; Song Xiaojun et al., *Zhongguo bu gaoxing: Da shidai, da mubiao, ji women de neiyou waihuan* [China is unhappy: The great era, grand objective, and our domestic troubles and foreign calamities] (Nanjing: Jiangsu renmin chubanshe, 2009).

13. See *The Economist*, "How China Sees the World," March 19, 2009; Ye Hailin, "Beijing Aoyun chongji Xifang jiazhi zixin" [Beijing Olympics are a blow to self-confidence of Western values], *Guoji xianqu daobao*, August 28, 2008; Joshua Cooper Ramo, *The Beijing Consensus* (London: Foreign Policy Centre, 2004); Martin Fletcher, "The Chinese Dream Has Replaced America's," *The Times* (London), August 22, 2008; Joshua Cooper Ramo, *Brand China* (London: Foreign Policy Centre, 2007); Martin Jacques, *When China Rules the World: The Rise of the Middle Kingdom and the End of the Western World* (London: Allen Lane, 2009); Fareed Zakaria, *The Post-American World, and the Rise of the Rest* (New York: Penguin, 2009), 87–128; and Liu Mingfu, *Zhongguo meng: Hou Meiguo shidai de daguo siwei zhanlue dingwei* [The China dream: The great power thinking and strategic positioning of China in the post-American age] (Beijing: Zhongguo youyi chuban gongsi, 2010).

14. Hong Liu, Cosmopolitan Cultures in East Asia conference, University of Manchester, Manchester, May 2009.

15. Mark Leonard, *What China Thinks* (London: Fourth Estate, 2008); Daniel A. Bell, *New Confucianism: Politics and Everyday Life in a Changing Society* (Princeton, N.J.: Princeton University Press, 2008); John Makeham, *Lost Soul: "Confucianism" in Contemporary Chinese Academic Discourse* (Cambridge, Mass.: Harvard University Press, 2008); Shiping Hua, *Chinese Utopianism: A Comparative Study of Reformist Thought with Japan and Russia, 1989–1997*) (Stanford, Calif.: Stanford University Press, 2008); and Gloria Davies, *Worrying about China: The Language of Chinese Critical Inquiry* (Cambridge, Mass.: Harvard University Press, 2007). For a think tank report that touches on how these debates discuss foreign policy, see Melissa Murphy, *Decoding Chinese Politics: Intellectual Debates and Why They Matter* (Washington, D.C.: Center for Strategic and International Studies, 2008).

16. See "Full Text of Hu Jintao's Report at 17th Party Congress," Xinhua, October 24, 2007. The CCP Constitution was amended to include the goal of "building a harmonious world": "CPC Constitution Amendment Advocates Building of Harmonious World," Xinhua, October 25, 2007.

17. Two special journal issues are indicative of this multicultural trend in international studies; see J. Ann Tickner and Andre P. Tsyganov, "Responsible Scholarship in International Relations: A Symposium," *International Studies Review* 10, no. 4 (2008): 661–66; and Amitav Acharya and Barry Buzan, "Preface: Why Is There No Non-Western IR Theory: Reflections On and From Asia," *International Relations of the Asia-Pacific* 7, no. 3 (2007): 285–86. The second project has been republished as a book: Amitav Acharya and Barry Buzan, eds., *Non-Western International Relations Theory: Perspectives On and Beyond Asia* (New York: Routledge, 2010). Also see articles like Yiwei Wang, "Between Science and Art: Questionable International Relations Theories," *Japanese Journal of Political Science* 8, no. 2 (2007): 191–208.

18. This is not the first time in recent history that China has been taken as a model for a unified world order; see Arnold Toynbee and Daisaku Ikeda, *Choose Life: A Dialogue* (New York: Oxford University Press, 1976), 228–36, 243–46.

19. Ole Wæver, "The Sociology of a Not So International Discipline: American and

European Developments in International Relations," *International Organization* 52, no. 4 (1998): 687–727, at 696.

20. Francis Fukuyama, "The End of History?" *The National Interest*, Summer 1989; Samuel P. Huntington, "The Clash of Civilizations?" *Foreign Affairs* 72, no. 3 (1993): 22–49; David Held, Anthony McGrew, David Goldblatt, and Jonathan Perraton, *Global Transformations: Politics, Economics and Culture* (Stanford, Calif.: Stanford University Press, 1999); Michael Hardt and Antonio Negri, *Empire* (Cambridge, Mass.: Harvard University Press, 2000); and David Harvey, *The New Imperialism* (Oxford: Oxford University Press, 2003).

21. Joseph S. Nye Jr., *Bound to Lead: The Changing Nature of American Power* (New York: Basic Books, 1991); Joseph S. Nye Jr., *Soft Power: The Means to Success in World Politics* (New York: PublicAffairs, 2004); David Leheny, "A Narrow Place to Cross Swords: 'Soft Power' and the Politics of Japanese Popular Culture in East Asia," in *Beyond Japan: The Dynamics of East Asian Regionalism*, edited by Peter J. Katzenstein and Takashi Shiraishi (Ithaca, N.Y.: Cornell University Press, 2006), 211–33. Although Nye coined the term "soft power," the concept of soft power draws on earlier international politics theorists, e.g., Hans J. Morgenthau, Ray S. Cline, Klaus Knorr, Richard N. Rosecrance, and Robert Cox, as well as sociologists such as Steven Lukes; see Nye, *Bound to Lead*, 29–35, 266.

22. Nye, *Soft Power*, 73–89; Jean-Ives Haine, "The EU's Soft Power: Not Hard Enough?" *Georgetown Journal of International Affairs* 5, no. 1 (2004): 69–77; Leheny, "Narrow Place."

23. See Joshua Kurlantzick, *Charm Offensive: How China's Soft Power Is Transforming the World* (New Haven, Conn.: Yale University Press, 2007).

24. See "Full Text of Hu Jintao's Report"; and Embassy of the People's Republic of China in the United States, "Soft Power, a New Focus at China's 'Two Sessions,'" March 14, 2007. Chinese scholars have also been discussing the PRC's growing soft power; see Shi Yinhong, "'Harmonious World' Is Pragmatic Foreign Policy," *China Daily*, May 7, 2007; Yu Keping, "We Must Work to Create a Harmonious World," *China Daily*, May 10, 2007; Pang Zhongying, "Fazhan Zhongguo ruan liliang" [Develop China's soft power], *Liaowang*, no. 1 (2006): 63; Pang Zhongying, "Zhongguo ruan liliang de neihan" [The content of China's soft power], *Liaowang*, no. 45 (2005): 62; and Wei Zongyou, "Quanli, ruan quanli yu guojia xingxiang" [Power, soft power and national image], *Guoji guancha*, no. 5 (2005): 39–45.

25. Bates Gill and Yanzhong Huang, "Sources and Limits of Chinese 'Soft Power,'" *Survival* 48, no. 2 (2006): 17–36; Kurlantzick, *Charm Offensive*; Esther Pan, *China's Soft Power Initiative* (New York: Council on Foreign Relations, 2006); Joseph S. Nye Jr., "The Rise of China's Soft Power," *Wall Street Journal Asia*, December 29, 2005.

26. Han Bo and Jiang Qingyong, *Ruan shili: Zhongguo shijiao* [Soft power: China's perspective] (Beijing: Renmin chubanshe, 2009). This book is the product of an officially sponsored soft power research institute based at Peking University.

27. Zhao Tingyang, *Tianxia tixi: Shijie zhidu zhexue daolun* [The Tianxia system: A Philosophy for the World Institution] (Nanjing: Jiangsu jiaoyu chubanshe, 2005), 1.

28. He Chuanqi et al., *China Modernisation Report Outlook (–2007)* (Beijing: Peking University Press, 2007), 152.

29. Nye, *Soft Power*, 7.

30. John King Fairbank, ed., *The Chinese World Order: Traditional China's Foreign Relations* (Cambridge, Mass.: Harvard University Press, 1968).

31. Ibid.; Morris Rossabi, ed., *China among Equals: The Middle Kingdom and Its Neighbors, 10th–14th Centuries* (Berkeley: University of California Press, 1983); Mark Mancall, *China at the Center: 300 years of Foreign Policy* (New York: Free Press, 1984); Paul Cohen, *Discovering History in China: American Historical Writings on the Recent Chinese Past* (New York: Columbia University Press, 1986); James Hevia, *Cherishing Men from Afar: Qing Guest Ritual and the Macartney Embassy of 1793* (Durham, N.C.: Duke University Press, 1995); Lydia H. Liu, *The Clash of Empires: The Invention of China in Modern World Making* (Cambridge, Mass.: Harvard University Press, 2004); David C. Kang, *China Rising: Peace, Power and Order in East Asia* (New York: Columbia University Press, 2007); Feng Zhang, "Chinese Primacy in East Asian History: Deconstructing the Tribute System in China's Early Ming Dynasty," PhD dissertation, London School of Economics and Political Science, 2009; and William A. Callahan, *China: The Pessoptimist Nation* (Oxford: Oxford University Press, 2010). Hevia summarizes much of this debate; *Cherishing Men from Afar*, 7–15. Fairbank's view also informs understandings of China's traditional foreign policy among many current international relations scholars in the PRC; see Yan Xuetong, *Zhongguo guojia liyi fenxi* [An analysis of China's national interest] (Tianjin: Renmin chubanshe, 1995); Dan Xingwu, "Liang daguoji tixi de chongtu yu jindai Zhongguo de shengcheng" [The clash of two international systems and the formation of modern China], PhD dissertation, Chinese Academy of Social Sciences, International Politics Department, 2005; Zhang, "Chinese Primacy in East Asian History."

32. Kang, *China Rising*; Li Shaojun, *Guoji zhengzhixue gailun* [An introduction to international politics] (Shanghai: Renmin chubanshe, 2002), 526–34; Yan Xuetong "The Rise of China in Chinese Eyes," *Journal of Contemporary China* 10, no. 26 (2001): 33–40; Zhang Tiejun, "Chinese Strategic Culture: Traditional and Present Features," *Comparative Strategy* 21, no. 2 (2002): 73–80; Liu Zhiguang, *Dongfang heping zhuyi: yuanqi, liubian ji zouxiang* [Oriental pacificism: Its origins, development and future] (Changsha: Hunan chubanshe, 1992).

33. "Anniversary Highlights China's Peaceful Growth," *China Daily*, July 12, 2005. Also see Callahan, *China*, 20–21.

34. Wang Gungwu, "Tianxia and Empire: External Chinese Perspectives," Inaugural Tsai Lecture, Harvard University, Cambridge, Mass., May 4, 2006; Fei-Ling Wang, "Heading Off Fears of a Resurgent China," *International Herald Tribune*, April 11, 2006; Xiang Lanxin, "Jieyan quqi, shenyan hexie" [Give up talking about China's rise, be careful discussing world harmony], *Lianhe zaobao* (Singapore), March 26, 2006.

35. See Dan, "Liang daguoji tixi de chongtu," 23–38; Shi Bin, "Guoji guanxi yanjiu 'Zhongguo hua' de lunzheng" [The debate over Sinicization in international relations research], in *Zhongguo gouji guanxi yanjiu (1995–2005)* [International Relations Research in China (1995–2005)], edited by Wang Yizhou and Yuan Zhengqing (Beijiing: Beijing daxue chubanshe, 2006), 518–45; Zhang Lidong and Pan Yihe, "Traditional Chinese Thoughts Resources of International Organization Construction," in *Construction within Contradiction: Multiple Perspectives on the Relationship between China and International Organizations*, edited by Wang Yizhou (Beijing: China Development Publishing House, 2003), 259–87; Li Shaojun, "Lun Zhongguo wenmingde heping neihan: Cong chuantong dao xianshi—dui 'Zhongguo weixie' lun de huida" [The peaceful orientation of Chinese Civilization: From tradition to reality—a response to "China

Threat" Theory], *Guoji jingji pinglun*, no. 19 (1999): 30–33; Sheng Hong, "Shenme shi wenming" [What is civilization?], *Zhanlüe yu guanli*, no. 5 (1995): 88–98; Liu, *Dongfang heping zhuyi*; and William A. Callahan, *Contingent States: Greater China and Transnational Relations* (Minneapolis: University of Minnesota Press, 2004), 30–33.

36. See Liu, *Zhongguo meng*; Hu Jintao, "Build Towards a Harmonious World of Lasting Peace and Common Prosperity," speech at the High-Level Plenary Meeting of the United Nations Sixtieth Session, New York, September 17, 2005; Qin Xiaoying, "Harmonious Society to Be a Model for the World," *China Daily*, October 13, 2006; Yu, "We Must Work."

37. Yu Dan, *Lunyu xinde* [Insights from *The Analects*] (Beijing: Zhonghua shuju, 2007).

38. Yu Dan, *Confucius from the Heart: Ancient Wisdom for Today's World*, translated by Esther Tyldesley (London: Macmillan, 2009).

39. Leheny, "Narrow Place," 223.

40. See Peter J. Katzenstein, *A World of Regions: Asia and Europe in the American Imperium* (Ithaca, N.Y.: Cornell University Press, 2006); and Peter J. Katzenstein, ed., *Civilizations in World Politics: Plural and Pluralistic Perspectives* (New York: Routledge, 2010).

41. David Campbell, *Writing Security: United States Foreign Policy and the Politics of Identity*, rev. ed. (Minneapolis: University of Minnesota Press, 1998), 68–70.

42. A Baidu search of Zhao Tingyang shows how this philosopher's ideas about world order are widely quoted and widely discussed. Qin Yaqing has worked hard to present his ideas in popular as well as scholarly outlets—see, for example, his op-ed essay pieces that were republished in *Lilun cankao*: Qin Yaqing, "Hexie shehui yu hexie shijie" [Harmonious society and harmonious world], *Lilun cankao*, no. 1 (2006): 57; and Qin Yaqing, "Hexie shijie: Zhongguo waijiao xinlinian" [Harmonious world: China's new diplomatic concept], *Lilun cankao*, no. 5 (2007): 22–23.

43. See Qin Yaqing, "Relationality and Processual Construction: Bringing Chinese Ideas into International Relations Theory," *Social Sciences in China* 30, no. 3 (2009): 5–20; and Qin Yaqing, "Why Is There No Chinese International Relations Theory?" in *Non-Western International Relations Theory*, ed. Acharya and Buzan, 26–50.

44. This is discussed in more detail in chapter 10 of the present volume. Also see Yan Xuetong and Xu Jin, eds., *Wangba tianxia sixiang ji qidi* [World leadership theories and their implications] (Beijing: Shijie zhishi chubanshe, 2009).

45. Confucius, *The Analects*, 3/15.

Part I

Rediscovering Traditional Concepts

Chapter 2

Rethinking Empire from the Chinese Concept "All-under-Heaven" (Tianxia, 天下)

Zhao Tingyang

"Empire" is not only a geographical concept but also a cultural institutional one. There have been great empires in the past, always reminding us of their splendid victories and fatal collapse. The modern age has been mainly an age of nation-states, in which the concept of empire has been distorted in terms of the imperialism that should assume responsibility for the most terrible wars recorded in history.

As is now realized, because of penetrating globalization and astonishing technological developments, the modernity of the nation-state system has been weakened, while a still-vague new age emerges,[1] an age of globality as the consequence of globalization. But what is the most likely form of global governance? Personally, I feel as if the steps toward a new empire could be now be heard, and indeed it has already been discussed.[2] What ideal of empire could we expect for a new empire? This seems an important and serious question. So in this chapter I would like to introduce the Chinese traditional conception of world governance, which is quite different from the usual understanding of empire, and which might offer a more constructive and positive way to rethink the best idea of an acceptable empire.

This chapter was originally published as "Rethinking Empire from a Chinese Concept 'All-under-Heaven' (Tian-xia)," *Social Identities* 12, no. 1 (2006): 29–41.

The Concept of "All-under-Heaven"

In contrast to the Western concept of empire, China has a three-thousand-year-old traditional concept, "All-under-Heaven," that is very relevant to the *idea* of empire. We are led to think that a thing always has, in Platonic philosophy, its *idea* that essentially makes it *as it is*. And an *idea* also implies, if further interpreted, the perfect conception for a thing to be *as it is expected*. This means that a perfect idea turns out to be the ideal of a thing. Here, the concept of All-under-Heaven could be considered the supposed ideal of a perfect empire.

The term "All-under-Heaven" (Tianxia, 天下), found in almost the oldest Chinese texts, means first the Earth, or the whole world under heaven.[3] It is almost equivalent to "the universe" or "the world" in Western languages. Its second meaning is the "hearts of all peoples" (*minxin*, 民心), or the "general will of the people." The world is always the home-for-people, that is, the Earth *as it is ours* more than the Earth *as it is*. All-under-Heaven therefore consists of both the Earth and its people. Consequently, an emperor does not really enjoy his Empire of All-under-Heaven, even if he conquers an extraordinary vastness of land, unless he receives the sincere and true support from the people on the land. As the philosopher Xunzi (313–238 BC) said in his essay "On Kingship and Supremacy,"

> Enjoying All-under-Heaven does not mean to receive the lands from people who are forced to give, but to satisfy all people with a good way of governance.[4]

All-under-Heaven's third meaning, the ethical and/or political meaning, is a world institution, or a universal system for the world, a utopia of the world-as-one-family. This political-ethical ideal of the world boasts of its very distinctness in its philosophical and practical pursuit of world governance ensured by a world institution. The ideal of All-under-Heaven as the philosophical concept of a world institution essentially distinguishes itself from the pattern of the traditional military empire—for instance, the Roman Empire—or that of an imperialist nation-state—for example, the British Empire. The conceptually defined Empire of All-under-Heaven does *not* mean a country at all but instead *an institutional world*.[5] And it expects a *world-society* instead of nation-states. All-under-Heaven is a deep concept of the world, defined by the trinity of the geographical, psychological, and political worlds. From the viewpoint of this political ontology, our supposed world is now still a *nonworld*, for the world has not yet been completed in its full sense. World institution and full popular support are still missing. We are talking nonsense about the world, for the world has not yet been fulfilled with its worldness.

The concept of All-under-Heaven shows its uniqueness in its political and philosophical worldview, which creates the *worldwide measure*, or the worldwide viewpoint, of seeing the affairs and problems of the world in the measure of worldness. It defines the world as a categorical *rethinking unit* of viewing and interpreting political life, constitution, and institution. This methodology is essentially different from the Western approach. In Western political theory, the biggest political unit is found to be a country or nation-state, whereas in Chinese theory, it is the framework of "world-society." States have always been seen as subordinate units inside the framework of the world-society that are regarded as a necessary and the highest political unit. Chinese political philosophy defines a political order in which the world is primary, whereas the nation-state is primary in Western philosophy. Certainly, Westerners do think about the world, but the Western imaginations of the world are nothing higher and greater than international alliances or unions of nation-states, not going beyond the framework of nation-states. Such projects have essential difficulties in reaching the real integrality of the world, for they are limited by the perspectives of nation-states, due to the lack of a vision of worldness. To see the world from its worldness is different from seeing it from part of it.

All-under-Heaven should be understood together with another closely related concept, the "Son of Heaven" (Tianzi, 天子), that is, structurally pertaining to All-under-Heaven. The concepts of All-under-Heaven and the Son of Heaven make a philosophical foundation for the system of empire. The Son of Heaven, analogous to an emperor,[6] is entitled to "enjoy his reign of the world under the Heaven" (see *The Poems*).[7] He is born to have "All-under-Heaven as his home," just as naturally as a man has a home of his own according to his natural rights, and "nothing left there out of his world of home." Although not even the strongest empires have controlled the entire world, it is not difficult to conceive of the world being controlled by a conceptual empire. Of most importance is what a Son of Heaven *does* rather than *is*. In other words, one could self-claim one's destiny as the mandate of Heaven to be, but must be reconfirmed the Son of Heaven if and only if there is evidence to justify his qualification—that is, as the Confucian master Mencius argued, one's being supported by the peoples.[8] The people's choice is conceived as the final evidence or examination of the legitimacy or justification of governance. The Chinese theory of political legitimacy allows two ways to prove the rightness of the reign; one of them is the *legitimacy* of the establishment of an empire—that is, to save peoples from a terrible situation when, and only when, welcomed by most of the people—and the other is the *justification* of enjoyment of the reign, which is to keep the world in the order that most of the people want.

According to Confucius' theory of justification, "*p* is *p* if *p* does as *p* is conceptually meant to do"; thus, we do not say that a king, an institution, or a political system *is* better but rather *does* better, as evidenced.[9] However, what is considered evidence in the Chinese way is not always based on statistics, or on a democratic election, but rather what is collected by means of observation of social trends or preferences, and especially by the obvious fact that people autonomously choose to follow and pledge their allegiance, instead of voting for one of several dubious politicians. In fact, careful and sincere observations can better detect truth and come to a better reflection of public choice than do democratic elections, which become spoilt by money, misled by the media, and distorted by strategic votes. The autonomy of people *to follow or not to follow* is regarded as a fundamental question in Chinese political philosophy as the matter of the "people's heart" (*minxin*, 民心), and it is considered closer to the truth of political reality than democracy. The problem of the people's heart (it might better be translated in the Western way as "demo-allegiance") must, theoretically, be a better representation than democracy of the problem of public choice. If we follow the facts, it seems to be the case that the masses always make the wrong choices for themselves through a misled democracy.

The knowledge of public preference has never been an epistemological problem to Chinese minds, for evidence of public preference is thought to be apparent. Instead, the Chinese have taken the ethical problem of the "sincerity" of concern for the people most seriously. The unspoken theory is that most people do not really know what is best for them, but that the elite do, so the elite ought genuinely to decide for the people. In the late nineteenth century, many Chinese began to think, influenced by Western discourse, that the best way of carrying out the Chinese principle of the "people's heart" was democracy. But the problem of public choice remains unsolved today, and has become an even greater difficulty, for democracy represents misled minds much more than independent ones, false wants much more than true needs, and illusive advantages much more than real goods and virtues.

In Chinese philosophy, the legitimacy of All-under-Heaven is asserted as *absolute*, whereas a Son of Heaven is not, which indicates three implicative principles: (1) The political legitimacy of reign of All-under-Heaven is independent of and prior to any ideology or religion; (2) the reign of All-under-Heaven is open to any qualified candidates who best know the Way (*Dao*, 道) to improve the happiness of all peoples universally; and (3) this will not be a dictator or a superpower, but one who has the right and power to justify the governance of All-under-Heaven. Laozi, the founder of Daoism, pointed out that

> a king could rule a state by his orders, win a war by strategies, but enjoy All-under-Heaven only by doing nothing to decrease the freedom and to deny the interests of people.[10]

The appeal to the evidence of the people's support has become the justified reason for another political group to launch a revolution, a "rewriting of the mandate of Heaven" in Chinese terms. In fact the justification of revolution has become four-thousand-year-old tradition. And the theory of All-under-Heaven has no discriminating rule to deny the opportunity for any nation to be in charge of the governance of All-under-Heaven. Historically, the Mongolians and the Manchus governed China for four hundred years, and their governance was considered as representing legitimate dynasties of China. More interestingly, both the Mongolian and the Manchu emperors adopted the theory of All-under-Heaven in establishing their legitimate reign.[11]

In the Chinese system of ideas, "familyship" is very powerful in interpreting ethical-political legitimacy, for familyship is thought to be the naturally given ground and resource for love, harmony, and obligations, and thus a full argument that "exhausts the essence of humanity."[12] Chinese philosophy has developed the very consciousness of the virtue of familyship.[13] The essence of humanity, fundamentally constituted as familyship, is claimed as the "first thing with which a lord is concerned most" and the only thing "impossible to be altered forever," whereas all other rules and knowledge are alterable.[14] Familyship is the minimal and irreducible location of harmony, cooperation, common interests, and happiness, so it is arguably the universal framework for interpreting all possible cases of harmony, cooperation, common interests, and happiness.

The virtue of the-world-as-All-under-Heaven is always understood and interpreted in terms of familyship. And it analytically implies the claim for the wholeness and harmony of the world to be a world, for the necessary conditions for family happiness are always its wholeness and harmony. And as also implied logically, anything against the wholeness and harmony of the world is defined as politically unacceptable (the interference in the liberty of an individual might be an unacceptable political mistake, whereas the damage to harmony is the first political mistake). Thus the principle of harmony, originating in the ideal of familyship, is made a paradigm applied further to the explanations of the possibility of any kind of harmony in the world. All-under-Heaven is nothing but the greatest family, a world-family; that said, all political levels, defined as "All-under-Heaven, states, and families," should be essentially homogenous or homological so as to create a harmonious system. This is the key to understanding Chinese political theory. The world's effective political order must progress from All-under-Heaven, to state, to families, so as to ensure universal *consistency and transitivity* in political life, or the *uniformity of society* (just like the uniformity of nature), whereas an ethical order progresses from families, to states, to All-under-Heaven, so as to ensure ethical consistency and transitivity. It implies that a world is in order if and only if it is ordered with the highest world institution, whereas the world institution must reflect the virtue of familyship. According to this principle, Chinese political and ethical theories are made one. We all have reason to highlight the importance of political-ethical consistency and transitivity, because any inconsistency or contradiction in the system will be a disaster. For instance, democracy, equality, and liberty have been developed in Western domestic society but have never extended to international society. This case of political inconsistency and intransitivity could greatly damage the reputation of democracy, equality, and liberty.

The Chinese system of families, states, and All-under-Heaven, which differs fundamentally from the Western system of individuals, nations, and internationals, is often criticized for its neglect of the individual along with individual rights, but this is a misunderstanding of Chinese philosophy and a poor understanding of political society. There is no Chinese denial of the value of the individual, but rather a denial of the individual as a political foundation or starting point, because the political makes sense only when it deals with "relations" rather than "individuals," and the political is meant to speak for coexistence rather than a single existence. In a very Chinese way, politics aims at a good society of peaceful "order" (*zhi*, 治), which is the first condition for any possible happiness of each and all, and at keeping a society from the "disorder" (*luan*, 乱) that destroys all possibilities of individual happiness. This political conception could find a strong argument in Chinese ontology, the *ontology of relations*, instead of the Western *ontology of things*.

According to the grammar of Chinese philosophy, the political philosophy focusing on the absoluteness of individual or nation misleads political questions and logic, for it encourages conflicts and consciousness of the enemy, which creates more problems than solutions. Carl Schmitt's wonderful theory of recognition of enemy/friend could be an example. It rightly reflects the typical error in Western political consciousness, or subconsciousness, whereby a political impulse divides and breaks up the world. In contrast, one of the principles of Chinese political philosophy is said "to turn the enemy into a friend," and it would lose its meaning if it were not to remove conflicts and pacify social problems—in a word, to "transform" (*hua*, 化) the bad into the good. Today, some investigations into game theory seem to support Chinese philosophy because in a game, maximizers will find a limit to improving their own interests, given that Pareto efficiency for common happiness would be impossible without trusted cooperation.

The concept of All-under-Heaven is meant to be an empire of worldness responsible for the common happiness of all peoples. It refers to a theoretical or *conceptual* empire that has never really existed. I do not say that Chinese dynasties, for instance the Qin (秦) Dynasty, were not empires. Quite the opposite; China had been an empire in its usual sense for a long time. Every dynasty of Chinese empire had tried to apply the concept of All-under-Heaven but had never been able to realize it because of practical limitations. All-under-Heaven means a very different empire, which is not necessarily a world superpower but a world under a commonly agreed-on institution, a plan to make the world a place of worldness. The ancient Chinese empires had no power to accomplish the plan of worldness, but had tried to be an exemplar empire of familyship. The comprehensive view of the world as All-under-Heaven surely takes the whole world as a single political system that is much greater and higher than a single country or nation-state. Consequently, the empire of All-under-Heaven highlights the problem of time rather than of space, that is, the problem of its duration rather than of its territory; and it has been apparent in the Chinese concern for the legitimacy of its dynasties rather than actual territorial conquest.

The ancient Chinese practical project of the Empire of All-under-Heaven had many substates (*guo*, 国) that were *institutionally* loyal to the empire, which were institutional centers but independent in their governance. These substates were not nation-states at all but were ruled by kings or noble families and were politically recognized by the emperor. Before the centralized government of the vast Chinese Empire was set up in 221 BC, China had been an "ideal" empire, close to the concept of All-under-Heaven, consisting of many "substates," which were independent in their economies, military powers, and cultures but were politically and ethically dependent on the empire's institutional center.[15] There was a tributary system between the suzerain center and the substates. The suzerain center enjoyed its authority in recognizing the legitimacy of the substates, but it never interfered unless a substate declared war on another member of the family of All-under-Heaven.

The Chinese institution of empire experienced revolutionary reform in 221 BC, when the Qin emperor conquered China and created a country with centralized governance over many provinces, instead of substates. But this institutional reform did not change the ideal of All-under-Heaven. On the contrary, it seemed to lead the Chinese to the idea of an even wider understanding of the world, a nearly "global" picture of the world in which all foreign countries, near and far, were seen as the theoretically taken-in substates. So the former smaller picture of All-under-Heaven had been just mapped onto the enlarged one. And the *legal tributary system* had also been redefined and transformed into the *voluntary tributary system*, in which foreign countries volunteered to decide whether to join.

The voluntary tributary system expresses much of the diplomatic strategy of the ancient Chinese Empire. It developed stipulated reciprocity into the voluntary practice in a tributary system, and always ran it in a pattern of much greater returns to any tributary gifts. Reciprocity has been a leading idea in Chinese thinking. And it has been performed within the norms of practical life to express mutual respect. The *Interpretation of Rites* says: "The reciprocal repays is mostly preferred in the rites. And no pay or no repay no respect."[16] Reciprocity is a truer echo of the other's heartfelt respect than an economically equal exchange. And it has been argued that the ideal of social relations is rooted in the essence of reciprocity as heart-for-heart, much more than the reciprocity of interests-for-interests. The primary concept or principle in Confucian theory is *ren* (仁), literally meaning the best relationship "of-two-persons."[17] And even more interesting, the oldest literal meaning of *ren* was the best relationship of "thousands of hearts." *Ren* had been considered the only fundamental principle whereby the harmony of peoples could be developed. Reciprocity understood in the Chinese way has less to do with the reciprocal utilitarianism or balance in commercial exchange and much more to do with the *reciprocity of hearts*.

The principle of voluntariness is key to the Chinese understanding of "relations" from the viewpoint of otherness. Some scholars have argued that the general Chinese ethical principle appears the same as the Western Golden Rule.[18] But it differs essentially in the philosophical presuppositions whereby Western philosophy sees in terms of subjectivity but the Chinese in terms of otherness. The Bible's Golden Rule, "Do unto others as you would have them do to you" sounds promising, but it would encounter challenges and difficulties when other hearts are taken into account. The otherness of the other heart is something absolute and transcendent, so the other heart might reasonably want a different life. In terms of otherness, the Chinese ethical principle thus runs: "Let others reach their goals if you reach yours." It is easy to see the subtle difference between the Western and Chinese rules. I have rewritten the Bible's rule in a negative representation to be a better representation of the absoluteness of otherness: "Never do to others what the others would not want you to do to them." When facing the problem of the irreducible diversities of the hearts of others, Chinese philosophy found a solution in the highlighting of voluntariness. The two-thousand-year-old *Interpretation of Rites* says that harmony can be developed under two conditions:

> To be heart to heart closed when congenial to each other; to respect reciprocally when different from each other. . . . Rites differ in forms but are equal in essence as the expression of respect, just as in the same way, music differs in styles but is equal in essence as the expression of heart.[19]

This means that to love what is the same as ours is not a problem at all, and thus it proves nothing of the essence of humanity. And our brilliant virtue of humanity could show its excellence only in respecting the dissimilar forms of life. And to respect the other in his or her otherness is at least to respect their voluntariness or rights in developing their culture:

> It is proper to learn values from others whereas unjust to impose one's values onto the others. Or to say, the values are to be learnt by rather than to be taught to the others.[20]

Accordingly, an Empire of All-under-Heaven could only be an exemplar passively in situ, rather than positively become a missionary. Here we see the difference between the Western and Chinese ethics: Western philosophy sees humanity through the eyes of subjectivity, whereas the Chinese sees it through the eyes of otherness. And this is a clue for distinguishing cultural empire from cultural imperialism.

The Relevance to Contemporary Problems

The All-under-Heaven pattern of all-states-in-a-family reminds us of the similarities with the United Nations pattern, one of which is that they are both world organizations dedicated to solve international problems and to ensure peace and order in the world. But their differences might be more important, taking into account the successes that the All-under-Heaven pattern has had in Chinese history in bringing long periods of peace and stable society in many dynasties, in contrast with the inability of the UN pattern to deal with international conflicts. Furthermore, we might be encouraged to find in the All-under-Heaven pattern the theoretical potential to resolve international and intercultural problems.

The comparison of the All-under-Heaven pattern with the United Nations might still sound a little farfetched for the United Nations is not an empire system, but it would also be a mistake to neglect the flexibility and inclusiveness of the concept of All-under-Heaven. One factor that could reduce the unreasonableness of this comparison is that the utopia of All-under-Heaven is not a narrowly defined empire but an extensively defined world society with harmony, communication, and cooperation for all nations, guaranteed by a commonly agreed-on institution.

In spite of history's uncontrollable causes and conditions, the successes and failures of these two patterns—All-under-Heaven and the United Nations—are due to the different philosophical presuppositions upon which their world system concepts are built. All-under-Heaven presupposes the oneness of the world, and this oneness shows itself in all the world's diversities.[21] The oneness of the world is also reflected in the political principle of "inclusion of all" in All-under-Heaven in terms of familyship. Oneness means the denial of the existence of any pagan, so that nothing in the world can be defined unacceptable, no matter how strange it might seem. But, slightly differently, the pattern of the UN relies on two divergent presuppositions: pluralism and universalism. The pluralism is of the reluctant "political correctness" to please the developing countries, and the universalism is to satisfy the developed countries, especially the major Western powers. To reconcile this divergence, the UN has made great efforts to validate rational dialogue to replace conflicts. There is no doubt that rational dialogue has had an impact in reducing wars and fighting, but not in conflict reduction, and instead has encouraged the strategic game of noncooperation, thus universally enhancing the personality of the selfish maximizer. And, worse, the UN has no power to stop a superpower from universalizing itself alone in the name of globalization. The UN is more of a political market for nations and less of an institution for the world itself.

The consequential difference between these two patterns is rooted in their different understandings of the oneness of the world. The concept of All-under-Heaven commits us to the oneness of the world as the intact wholeness that implies the acceptance of the diversities as they are and are meant to be in the world. The concept of the United Nations has taken oneness as a mission of Western modernity to be accomplished. It is apparent and not surprising that oneness as a mission has been developed from universalism. And unfortunately, universalism is a type of fundamentalism. The reason is quite simple: Universalism means to universalize something rather than everything, and to universalize the self instead of others, which thus means a sort of fundamentalism that insists on the ideology of making others the pagan. Political modernity has inherited from Christian ideology and never gone beyond this ideology's format, which invented unacceptable others, cultural clashes and wars, ideological dogmas and propaganda, and so on. The worst is the universalism that tries to universalize others in a way they do not want.

The theoretical problems of understanding oneness as a mission to be accomplished have already been shown. The United Nations is an international organization mapping onto an individualist society. It inherits and enlarges the problems of an individualist society; for instance, international conflicts copy social conflicts. And worse, it does not enhance international democracy over social democracy. As has been observed, a superpower has every opportunity to invalidate an international organization such as the United Nations. Furthermore, the All-under-Heaven system, instead of an international organization, would be a more effective channel to the ideal of the world-as-one, because of the logical impossibility of an always-justified international choice through democracy, according to Arrow's theorem. I am not criticizing the United Nations; it has tried its best. What I am discussing are the given limitations in the potentiality of the UN pattern. The UN is supposed to be an international organization, conditioned by the interests of every nation-state, dealing with international problems in the age of the nation-state rather than in the age of globality. And it seems to enhance rather than weaken, as Giddens pointed out, the system of nation-states as the modern political form.[22] To be fair to the United Nations, it is not designed to take care of the world but of nations; and it is of, not beyond, modernity. In short, internationality *is not* and *cannot be* worldness. The question of *world institution* has now become more urgent since the world has plunged into globalization.

It is interesting to consider the pattern of the European Union, and perhaps the United European States in the future. The EU is an excellent invention of a real and institutionally organized region. But it is still not a system that could be extended to the world, for it is just a company of nation-states, and it is difficult to form and give priority to a European common interest over the interests of each of its member nation-states, let alone a world interest. Theoretically speaking, the EU has gone not as far as Kant's idea. A well-organized region such as the EU is essentially something of an enlarged nation-state meant to compete with other world regions or powers, rather than an ideal for the world, given its lack of a worldview of worldness. The EU pattern enhances the integration of a region but also deepens its separation from the world.

Globalization is breaking the world system of nation-states. It is not new. It is a combination of universalism and fundamentalism, in which fundamentalism—whether through capitalism, modern industry, postmodern technologies, self-claimed world religions, or ideology—tries to universalize itself.[23] And within the process of globalization itself, it is likely that one or more nation-states will transform themselves into new empires, different from the imperialism of nation-states. Will there be an age of new empires to come? Will be there a new form of empire, or just a postmodern return to the old ways? We should consider whether there is a more reasonable and commendable concept of empire. Comparative study would help to clarify the concept of empire, though this is beyond the scope of this chapter. The differences among the ideas or patterns of empires can be detailed as follows:

1. *The pattern of the Roman Empire:* This is the typical ancient empire, not referring only to the Roman Empire but also to others. It is considered a military superpower with territorial expansion. It would encompass the whole world if it were possible in its claimed or hidden ideal. Consequently, it always has temporary frontiers instead of clearly settled boundaries. We know that this pattern has not worked since the age of nation-states.
2. *The pattern of the British Empire:* This is the typical modern empire

based on a nation-state under the mixed ideals of nationalism, imperialism, and colonialism. It has definitely divided boundaries, except in disputed areas. The definite boundaries do not indicate the self-restraint of imperialism, but the safeguard of their national interests against the free entry of others. Instead of territorial expansion, imperialism has created colonies to develop and maintain its control of the world and the division of the world into the developed and the undeveloped countries and regions. This pattern has become impossible since World War II because of the universalizing of the system of nation-states, together with nationalism and the consciousness of independence.

3. *The new pattern of the American "empire":* This is a new imperialism, inheriting many characteristics of modern imperialism but transforming direct control into the hidden, yet totally dominating, world control by means of hegemony, or "American leadership," as Americans prefer to call it.[24] This hegemonic imperialism is occurring not only in political and economical spheres but also in knowledge, especially through globalization, in which it has the greatest power to universalize its own.[25] This new imperialism differs from the traditional empire in that it is much more than a game winner, because it also defines the rules. The world would become disordered if a player in the game also became the rule maker.

4. *The pattern of All-under-Heaven:* All-under-Heaven appears much like globalization, but is essentially different because it contains no such sense of the "-ization." All-under-Heaven indicates globalism instead. It means an *institutionally ordered world* or a *world institution* responsible for confirming the political legitimacy of world governance as well as local governance, and to allow the justification of systems. Its political goal is to create "All-under-Heaven," the trinity of the geographical world (the Earth), the psychological world (the hearts of all people), and the political world (the world institution). It is a grand narrative, perhaps the grandest narrative in political philosophies. The very virtue of the All-under-Heaven pattern is its worldview of worldness, which could let us understand world problems correctly and discover solutions for them. Worldness is a principle higher than internationality.

My conclusion is that the most important political problem today is not the so-called failed states but the *failed world*, a disordered world of chaos. This is why I maintain that our world is not yet a world, but is still a nonworld. And there are so many world problems too challenging to be resolved by a nation, a region, or any international contract. International theory in the framework of internationality finds its limitation in dealing with world problems, the shared problems of the world. Worldness cannot be reduced to internationality, for it is of the wholeness or totality rather than the between-ness. Our globe needs a world theory, rather than an international theory, to speak for the world. And All-under-Heaven as a world theory could provide a better view for political philosophy and political science.

Notes

1. However, not all think so. E.g., Anthony D. Smith insisted that the system of nation-states would not be broken up as many think, because no new system could be stronger than nationalism in the coming future. See Anthony D. Smith, *Nations and Nationalism in a Global Era* (Cambridge: Polity Press, 1996).

2. See Michael Hardt and Antonio Negri, *Empire* (Cambridge, Mass.: Harvard University Press, 2001).

3. Two thousand years ago, the popular Chinese imagination of the so-called All-under-Heaven was interesting in its square division of the world into "nine regions" (*jiuzhou*, 九州) spreading from the central region to the rest in eight directions. And the land consisting of the nine regions was the area of ancient China, while the oldest capital city in China is rightly in the central region. But Zou Yan (邹衍), one of China's earliest geographers, exceptionally had a much wider sight of the land that was thought to comprise eighty-one "nine regions"—reckoned by multiplying by nine—and he said ancient China was "just the one of the eighty-one" in the world. See Sima Qian, *Shiji*, 74 (91 BC), 2344.

4. Xunzi, "On Kingship and Supremacy," in *The Book of Xunzi* (c. 200 BC).

5. The Chinese philosopher Liang Shuming thought that ancient China had been developing itself as a "world" rather than a "country." See Liang Shuming, *The Collected Works of Liang Shuming* (Beijing: Beijing Normal University Press, 1992), 332.

6. In Chinese history, before King Qin Shi Huang the Great self-nominated as "the first emperor" in 221 BC, the king in general was called the Son of Heaven, and this was kept as the interpretive name for the emperor.

7. *Poems* (c. 1000 BC).

8. Mencius argued that people were of greater weight than the government and that the support from people was the final confirmation of the reign. And he insisted that the king would lose his reign if he lost his people's support, and he lost his people's support because he was against the people's hearts. The *Interpretation of Rites* also said: "Enjoying the reign when receiving the support from the people, and losing the reign when losing the support of the people." See Mencius, *The Book of Mencius* (c. 220 BC), as well as *Interpretation of Rites* (c. 500 BC).

9. Confucius had claimed his famous theory of justification as "p is p if p does as p is meant to do"; for instance, a king should do as the concept of king requires. See Confucius, *The Analects* (c. 500 BC).

10. See Laozi, *Daode jing* (c. 500 BC).

11. In 1271, the Mongolian emperor changed the empire name "Mongolia" to the Chinese name "Da-yuan" (大元), meaning "as vast as the vastest," for he thought that "Mongolia" was rather local and thus not good for his empire of All-under-Heaven; see Liang Song, *The History of Yuan Dynasty* (c. 1370), section 4 of Yuan-shi-zu, vol. 7. The Manchu nation ruled China successfully for nearly three hundred years with the support of the people. The Manchu king wrote an interesting letter to the Chinese emperor of the Ming Dynasty before its declaration of a war on it, in which the Manchu king took advantage of the theory of All-under-Heaven to speak for his justice: "All kinds of things from insects to humankind in the world are created and nurtured by the nature itself, not by your empire, so that nothing is your private property. And Heaven is always so fair that your empire will be blamed and punished for your abusing the governance. . . . All-under-Heaven will be given to one who has greater virtues." See Pang, Sun, and Li, eds., *The Early History of the Qing Dynasty* (Beijing: Press of the People's University of China, 1984), 289–96).

12. *Interpretations of Rites* (c. 500 BC), chapter on Da-zhuan.

13. Only a few Chinese philosophers had the opposite opinion to the principle of familyship. For instance, Shang Yang said that the ethics of familyship encouraged selfishness and evils rather than kindness and goodness, and he thought laws were the most important things. See Shang Yang, *The Book of Shang Yang* (c. 300 BC).

14. *Interpretations of Rites* (c. 500 BC), chapter on Da-zhuan.

15. A Chinese substate in ancient times appeared similar to a Greek city-state in many but not all aspects. The oldest word for state in Chinese is *huo* (或), meaning "a militarily guarded city," whereas the land outside is called the "field" (ye, 野), and later added a wall or border around the city to make a new word, *guo* (國). A substate was considered a member in a family-like empire.

16. *Interpretations of Rites* (c. 500 BC), chapter on Qu-li.

17. Ren has often been translated as "humanity" or "kindness." These are not good translations.

18. See Hans Kung and Karl-Josef Kuschel, eds., *A Global Ethic: The Declaration of the Parliament of the World's Religions* (New York: Continuum, 1993).

19. *Interpretations of Rites* (c. 500 BC), chapter on Yue-ji.

20. Ibid., chapter on Qu-li.

21. Laozi said: "The Way of the world produces the Oneness of its own. And the Oneness has its two-ness. Then the two-ness self-develops into three-ness. And the three-ness is the minimal base for the diversities in the world." See Laozi, *Daode jing.*

22. Anthony Giddens, *The Nation-State and Violence* (Cambridge: Polity Press: 1985).

23. *The Communist Manifesto* was one of the earliest texts discussing something of globalization. It says: "The bourgeoisie has, through its exploitation of the world market, given a cosmopolitan character to production and consumption in every country." And "as in material, so also in intellectual production, the intellectual creations of individual nations become common property. National one-sidedness and narrow-mindedness become more and more impossible, and from the numerous national and local literatures, there arises a world literature."

24. Hardt and Negri, *Empire*, argue that the new empire of today is different from European imperialism and is mainly evident in American constitutionalism, which is more akin to the Roman Empire than to European imperialism.

25. However, the American empire seems still not satisfied with its "leadership." Nye calls upon the United States to enhance its "soft power" as complement to its "hard power," for the United States is still not powerful enough to "go it alone," even though it is the strongest power since Rome. See Joseph Nye Jr., *The Paradox of American Power: Why the World's Only Superpower Can't Go It Alone* (Oxford: Oxford University Press, 2002).

Chapter 3

The Possibility and Inevitability of a Chinese School of International Relations Theory

Qin Yaqing

Is it possible for us to create a Chinese School of international relations (IR) theory? The answer to this question is related to the existence of two perspectives in social science. The first view is monism, which considers that both natural science and social science belong to the same scientific tradition, such that their ontology, epistemology, and methodology are the same. The objective of both natural science and social science is to discover laws. The underlying assumption is that laws exist in the natural world that await human discovery; the same is true for the social world. As such, there is no difference between the study of natural science and social science. The second view is dualism, which sees the natural world and the social world as fundamentally different, because humans are both the subject and the object of social science research. Because human beings conduct social science research, it can never be value neutral; and because the research is about humanity, it cannot be treated simply as a physical phenomenon like metals or machines. According to this view, the objective of social science, in addition to discovering laws as in natural science, is to understand the meaning of the social world. This is something that does not concern natural science.

This chapter was translated by Kelvin Chi-kin Cheung. It was originally published as "Guoji guanxi lilun Zhongguo pai shengcheng de keneng he biran," *Shijie jingji yu zhengzhi*, no. 3 (2006): 7–13.

The Geocultural Birthmark of Social Science Theory and the Possibility of a Chinese School

Max Weber posited this specific objective of social science—that social science can exist as an independent system of knowledge because it has different objectives than natural science. Humans have the ability to project meanings onto the social world that do not exist in the physical world. In researching the social world, the first thing we need to know is the social meaning of any human action. Meaning constitutes the content of a conception, which is the core idea of the social world, and it is something that is absent in the study of the physical world. The objective existence of physical matter forms the ontological basis of natural science, which aims to discover laws in the world, with explanation as its epistemology. Such a clear distinction, however, does not apply to social science. Social science is unavoidably subjective; its aim is not merely to discover laws in the social world but also to understand the social world's meaning. As such, its epistemology consists of "explaining" as well as "understanding."[1] Besides, in many cases, "understanding" is the main concern in social science, and the interpretative approach is an important way to constitute "understanding" because social facts are themselves products of social practice.[2] In view of this, social science, either for understanding or interpretation, will inevitably involve human subjectivity instead of simply discovering and explaining the linear causal relationship of objective phenomena.

Those who hold the monistic view think that there are no national boundaries in IR theory because a proper theory must be universal. This is because laws transcend the limits of time and space. The universal nature of scientific theory lies in its ability to generalize and replicate results. There can be different schools of theory; however, they would not be distinguished on the basis of nationality. The same is true for social science. Hence any attempt to establish theory based on national boundaries must be in vain, and indigenous propositions are necessarily false propositions.

Those who hold a dualistic view believe that although natural science has no national borders, it is possible for social science to have national distinctions. The reason is that understanding is an important way of knowing in social science, and understanding is very much delimited by geocultural differences. For instance, the different colors used in wedding gowns in the West (white) and China (red) are the results of different understandings of the meanings of color in these two cultures. Differences in geography, culture, history, ways of thinking, and collective memory are among the factors that constitute the differences in people's understanding. That is to say, the social practice and interaction of people from different geocultural settings will create different social phenomena and meanings, which will result in the formation of unique ways of understanding, knowledge systems, and thus different theories. According to Marx, "Men make their own history, but they do not make it as they please; they do not make it under self-selected circumstances, but under circumstances existing already."[3] These circumstances are closely related to the geocultural histories of individual nations, which provide the basis for national distinctions in social science theory. In this sense, the national label of IR theory is not only possible but also inevitable.

I follow the dualistic view of social science, and think that the indigenous character of social theory is natural and inevitable because the essence of social science theory is found in the geoculture in which it is embedded,[4] for three main reasons. First, social structure and institutions are delimited by time and space, and therefore are restricted by history and geography. Second, the limit of time and space determines the context of social practices, within which humans interact, and where the shared knowledge system is thus created. Third, because interactions at the micro level have a clear geocultural character, it is difficult for different societies to follow the same path from the micro level to the macro structure.[5]

Different cultures form in the diversity of geographical and historical conditions, and these cultures form the basis of the national character of social knowledge. As such, social science theory must be based in a particular geoculture and must consist of certain indigenous conceptions in its rudimentary stage. For instance, the theory of traditional Chinese medicine regards a human being as a holistic system, and different people constitute different wholes. This holistic conception emphasizes restoring the internal balance of the whole body, thus allowing practitioners to treat a person's illness without directly attending to its symptoms. Western medicine, conversely, sees human beings as the composition of separate units that can be treated individually; as such, practitioners of Western medicine treat illness by directly treating its symptoms. Moreover, the meridian system in traditional Chinese medicine and anatomical theory in Western medicine have developed from very different philosophical foundations, each with its respective strengths and weaknesses.[6] In terms of IR theory, the traditional Chinese worldview is "Tianxia" (All-under-Heaven), which does not contain any concept of sovereignty. The Western worldview, however, focuses on individual sovereign states in an anarchical logic, which relies on dualistic competition and coexistence between self and other that are legalistically equal. In the absence of the concept of sovereignty and dualistic oppositions, Tianxia understands the world according to distance in terms of geography and social relationships.

Nevertheless, if a theory from a specific geoculture does not have a certain universal sense, it will never become a mainstream theory in the world. Because human nature is universal, theories concerning humanity should share certain commonalities, which form the basis of the universal nature of social theory. Rational choice theory, which is commonly adopted in social science studies, is an example of this universalization of theory. Emphasizing the geocultural birthmark of social science theory does not mean that we need to have one culture replace another, or that we have to use theories developed in one culture to subvert theories from other cultures.

My aim here is to point out that it is inevitable for social science theory to have a geocultural birthmark. Thus the English School, which originated in Britain, is rooted in the diplomatic history of European states and the legal conventions of European societies. The emergence of the English School would not have been possible without these unique collective memories.[7] In the case of the postwar United States, the development of IR theory did not need a national label because it used the world as a reference model. Nevertheless, the thought and practice of mainstream IR theory in the United States are still based on the collective memories in the United States, particularly the memories of postwar America.

Moreover, because the United States is the sole hegemon to emerge from World War II,[8] it could develop its IR theory in order to maintain its hegemony and the related international system. As such, theories like hegemonic stability theory, power transition theory, and neoliberal institutionalism all derive from these concerns, and hence bear America's indigenous character.[9] This is why Stanley Hoffman stated that IR is an American social science and that IR theory is American theory.[10] At the same time, because the United States has been the sole hegemon since World War II, IR theories developed in the United States have benefited from its global influence to become "universal" theories. During the Cold War, the English School did not receive its due recognition in the IR discipline. But it was widely accepted after the Cold War due to changes in international affairs: Competition in the international system diminished, and the need for an international society has grown, while Europe has more closely integrated by constructing an international society beyond nation-states. Thus there is a general acceptance of the English School, which has the notion of "international society" as its core, and this trend in turn has affected the development of IR theory in the United States.

On the basis of this analysis, a Chinese School of IR theory should possess two characteristics: (1) The theory must originate from the Chinese geocultural discourse, and (2) its development must acquire universal value. For instance, the notion of Tianxia in Confucian culture is different from the anarchical (international) system in Westphalian culture. During the heyday of the nation-state system, the hierarchical order advocated by Confucianism was rejected. In today's globalized world, this hierarchal order based on inequality is still not accepted. However, should Confucian moral and regulatory concepts like benevolence (*ren*, 仁), ritual (*li*, 礼), virtue (*de*, 德), harmony (*he*, 和), and the doctrine of the mean (*zhongyong*, 中庸) have universal value?[11] Furthermore, the foundation of the Enlightenment is to use knowledge to achieve certainty in life, whereas traditional Chinese thought looks to the ideas of change and uncertainty. With growing uncertainty in the globalized world, would such ideas have important systemic effects?

These are the questions that need serious consideration for the development of the Chinese School of IR theory. Certainly, we need to pay particular attention to two factors. First, learning from other cultures is necessary in the process of developing a universal theory from a specific geocultural discourse. Hybridity in social science theory is probably a positive attribute for acquiring universal status. Second, there should not be only one school of Chinese IR theory; it is possible to have competing schools of thought emerge—although it is likely that only one would exist at the beginning. Moreover, such knowledge-oriented theory could be the result of a collective intellectual endeavor, as in the case of the Frankfurt School or the English School. It could also be the result of the creative ingenuity of one individual's theory. In any case, those who develop such a theory need to be socialized in the same cultural context.

Three Sources of Thought and Practice in the Chinese School

Social science theory is rooted in a specific nation's geocultural discourse; therefore, it will consist of a thick precipitation of that nation's thought and practices. Carr, Wright, and Wendt have demonstrated this in their classification of IR theory.[12] The intellectual resources of Realism come from the thoughts of Thucydides and Hobbes, and its practical source is IR during

World War II and the Cold War. Liberalism draws on Lockean and Kantian humanism, and its practical source is the modern capitalist system. The English School inherits the legacy of Hugo Grotius, and its development is inspired by the diplomatic experience of eighteenth- and nineteenth-century Europe. It also learns from the experience of European integration.[13] So what would be the intellectual and practical sources of a Chinese School of IR theory? Three pairs of sources of intellectual and practical experience need to be seriously considered.

The first paired sources of Chinese IR theory are the Confucian idea of "Tianxia" and the practice of China's tributary system, both of which function according to hierarchical order.[14] Hierarchy implies social strata, and order is the fundamental condition of the system's existence and function. Since the Qin and Han dynasties (221 BC–AD 220), China's "international" system has been the tributary system, which follows the Imperial Court's "Ritual Order." This is different from West's notion of the international system. According to John K. Fairbank, China's tributary system is a world system rather than an international system or an interstate system.[15] Fairbank thus discusses the important differences between the traditional Chinese worldview and the Western view of the international system; in China the world is a holistic unit that is based on order, rather than Hobbesian culture's battlefield of nation-states.

This difference is inherent in the notion of "Tianxia." The core of the notion of Tianxia revolves around the idea of a "Chinese system." According to the Chinese understanding, the word "Tian" includes the concept of nature, god, and ethics. As such, Tianxia is not merely a material concept but also a social and cultural concept. The notion of Tianxia is infinite in terms of space and time; it also prescribes a utopian order. Tianxia is where nature and humanity intersect, a space where political authority and social order interact. It is thus the core concept underlying the tributary system.[16] Tianxia is a holistic concept, manifested in the form of concentric circles. According to Fei Xiaotong, Chinese social structure is similar to the ripples created when one drops a stone in water, which extend infinitely. This structure weakens the absolute subjectivity of the "self," and thus cancels the binary opposition between self and other.[17] "What is different from the local is something that is unfamiliar, remote, and distant, instead of something that is in opposition, intolerable, or needs to be conquered."[18] As such, anarchy does not exist in the Tianxia system.

Order is always intrinsic in the system envisioned by the notion of Tianxia. Within the Tianxia system, structure is hierarchical because only such an arrangement could sustain its stability and harmonious order. Order could only be achieved when there is a clear stratification of classes and there is likewise an orderly relationship between them. The institution of "Five Ordinance Zones" (*wu fu*, 五服) established the social and political relationships and different roles for individuals within society, where order is achieved through such hierarchical relationships. The extension of this hierarchical structure to the world forms the Tianxia system. This is the characteristic of the social structure in China as well as the basis of its worldview. This system makes no distinction between inside and outside, and therefore is not anarchical. Accordingly, the Tianxia system is not a Hobbesian culture because the units within it do not fight with each other; it is not a Lockean culture because units do no compete with each other; and it is not a Kantian culture because units do not relate as equal friends.

The ideal manifestation of this hierarchical structure is the relationship between father and son, which not only reflects hierarchical difference but also involves responsibility. On the one hand, the hierarchical structure does not see the Hobbesian culture of "war of all against all" as the fundamental characteristic of the international system; on the other, it does not acknowledge the equality between units that is a common principle among the Hobbesian, Lockean, and Kantian culture. Within the anarchical system, nation-states are equal in the legalistic sense. The conception and structure of sovereignty comes from the recognition of equal rights among units. International society, as defined by Hedley Bull, is based on the fundamental principle of equality among states; in other words, international society could only be formed by sovereign states.[19] This could not be acknowledged in the Tianxia system.

The principle of "ritual" that sustains this hierarchical order is different from the anarchical culture; it comes from China's specific historical experience and cultural construction. This principle could not be expressed in terms of the binary oppositions of Western discourse, nor could it be represented in Western phenomenological structure. The ideal mode of Tianxia is harmony (*hexie*, 和谐) and great unity (*datong*, 大同), as well as a harmonious relationship with the world. The tool for maintaining order in the Tianxia system is the principle of "ritual," and the rule of ritual formed the basis of governance. Within this hierarchical structure, international order is the extension beyond the domestic level of the Confucian regulatory framework of ritual.[20] Order is sustained by the rule of ritual, which can be seen as a combination of governance by institutions and norms because ritual forms a normative and institutional structure that governs political and social behavior. The core of the rule of ritual is "benevolence" (*ren*), which is an important moral concept in Chinese philosophy; in this sense, the fundamental concern of the rule of ritual is morality. As such, the rule of ritual is different from the mainstream perspectives of the Western international order in the past three hundred years, particularly the one envisioned by Realism. It is also different from instrumental rationality, the epistemological foundation of the Western scientific and philosophical concepts since the Enlightenment.

The second paired sources of Chinese IR theory are the contemporary idea of sovereignty and revolutionary practice in China. The core of contemporary Chinese thought and practice is "revolution." Modern thought in China—from Kang Youwei, Yan Fu, and Sun Yat-sen to Mao Zedong—developed when China was forced to open itself to the world. It is also the product of collective memory and deep reflection in China. China began to have a new self-consciousness after being invaded by the imperialist powers. This self-consciousness forced the Chinese people to reflect upon their existence in the past, to search for a new position, and to strive for a new way of existence. Following the failure of the Hundred Days Reform (1898), revolution replaced reform as the dominant ideology of contemporary Chinese thought and practice. The main objective was to break away from the old world in order to create a new one.

As mentioned above, the Tianxia system is based on a hierarchical structure with unequal members. If we consider the quest for equality in the modern world and the dominant thought in the West during the past three hundred years, we will notice that people's sense of equality has been growing steadily since the Renaissance and the Enlightenment. Equality thus has now become a universal value and norm. There is resistance to all kinds of inequality in the social world—for example, anticolonialism, antislavery, and feminism. Because it is not in accordance with the universal norm of equality, the Tianxia concept and the tributary system that it legitimized both became targets of attack.

Ever since the principle of sovereignty was established in the Westphalian system, sovereign equality not only became the norm in the international system but also became a widely accepted institution. When China encountered the West in the nineteenth century, the institution of sovereignty overwhelmed China's Tianxia system. This made the Chinese people question Chinese technology, institutions, and even culture.[21] The Tianxia system and Confucian moral doctrine failed to meet this challenge. China's revolutions aimed to remove this backward technology, institutions, and culture. The Chinese people began a grand learning process in the international domain, and they began to accept Western concepts such as sovereign equality.

As such, revolutionary thought and practice in contemporary China have developed through a critique of traditional Chinese culture and a learning process from the West, with input from the elite intelligentsia and the participation from the wider population. The idea and practice of revolution has run through the Hundred Days Reform to the Nationalist Revolution (1911) and the Communist Revolution (1949), and the transition from reform to revolution was the destiny of this period. The concept of revolution is the most important idea that China's intellectual elite learned from the West. In particular, Marxism-Leninism has become the intellectual foundation of China's modernization, which followed the model of the Russian Revolution. The Republican Revolution, the Land Reform, and Mao's thought and practice together indigenized revolutionary thought to form China's stunning collective experience in that period.[22] Thus the intellectual and practical experience of revolution must be one of the sources for the Chinese School of IR theory.

Because revolutionary thought and practice were learned from the West, it could be argued that Western knowledge has subverted Chinese thought to a certain extent. Moreover, the encounter between Chinese and Western civilization has made China suffer from severe identity anxiety.[23] For international relations, the Chinese people began to understand the concepts of sovereignty, equality, and, more important, nationalism in its modernist sense. At the same time, the people's understanding of the term "*guo*" (国, state) was already different from that of Confucianism and the tributary system. The contemporary Chinese people wished for China to be able to join the Western international system as an equal member among other modern nation-states like Britain, France, Germany, and Japan. But they failed to achieve this, and thus the question of China's identity in international society was not resolved by China's revolution or by revolution's China. Yet the collision between China and the West, and China's revolutionary practice, both have left an indelible legacy for the Chinese people.

The third paired sources of Chinese IR theory are the intellectual resources of China's reform and opening and the practical experiences of China's integration into international society. The core thinking and practice of China's reform, which began in the late 1970s and resulted in enormous social change, is related to the goal of integrating with international society. The intellectual source of reform and opening comes from Deng

Xiaoping's understandings of Chinese society and his wish to improve the Chinese people's living standard. This unprecedented social transformation began with the initiative of several peasants in the village of Xiaogang in Anhui Province. Their motivation was simple: to feed themselves. Since then, China has begun to genuinely open its door to the world. The difference between Deng Xiaoping's and Nikita Khrushchev's reform programs is that Deng's consisted of opening up—opening up to the world is part of economic reform, and both are complementary to each other. The failure of Khrushchev's reforms in the USSR had much to do with that nation's closed-door policy and a lack of a global perspective. In some respects, the Tianxia concept and traditional China's worldview have an implicit bearing on China's reform and opening, which have once again made the Chinese people directly face the international system.

These changes have had important implications. Since 1840, China's most salient problem has been its relation to the international system, which has never been resolved. The Tianxia concept, and the tributary system it legitimized, were crushed by Western and Japanese weapons. China was left not knowing how to interact with the world. After two thousand years of effective governance, all the rituals, institutions, morality, and conceptions seemed to lose their regulatory capacity overnight. New China was born in 1949; however, despite spectacular development in the 1950s, China had not yet resolved the pressing problem of its relationship with the international system. The Cold War extended this situation, and people's ideology also contributed to this impasse. Things only began to change in the era of reform and opening.

China now has irrevocably entered the world system and international society. If we look to the current international system—where capital is the economic foundation, international institutions have become the governing rule, and the relative strength of individual states regulates the distribution of power—then in all these dimensions China has already entered this world system. And China's identity has experienced a significant change since it entered the international system. In the century after 1840, China was in a state of confusion and suffered internal turmoil and external threats; thus, its hope to become an equal member of the international system was not fulfilled. The half century that followed was China's revolutionary period, where it isolated itself from the rest of the international system. But since reform and opening began in 1978, China has started to integrate and thus to become a responsible member of international society; at the same time, it has been expected to become a "stakeholder."[24]

This process of reform and opening has led China to address its self-positioning in the international system. One can identify at least three forms of practical activities during the process of China's integration into the international system during the past three decades. First, China has developed from a revolutionary state outside the international system to become a responsible member within it.[25] Second, the Chinese Communist Party has transformed itself from a revolutionary party into a ruling party. And third, the level at which China identifies with the international system has surpassed those of all preceding eras. This not only concerns economic development. More important, there have been fundamental conception changes; in particular, China has experienced a fundamental change in the perception of its self-identity. This change is not limited to instrumental calculations at the strategic level, but also concerns a common understanding at the identity level.

China's history of integration into the international system and international society is short, and the process is still at the adjustment stage. Nonetheless, China has begun to address its relationship with the world, which, as noted, is a problem that has remained unresolved for the past century. This engagement with the world is important for both the concepts and practice of reform and opening, and is also central to the collective experience and memory of the Chinese people in this era. There is no doubt that the Chinese School of IR theory will learn from these experiences, and the theories and practices of IR will also be enriched as China continues to rise and integrates with the international system. From this perspective, the emergence of a Chinese School is theoretically inevitable.

Theoretical Core, Core Problematic, and the Identity Dilemma

A coherent knowledge system requires a theoretical core. Above, I have discussed three pairs of intellectual and practical resources for the Chinese School of IR theory. Now we need to see how these resources can form the theoretical core that is necessary for developing a Chinese School that is both universally applicable and rooted in Chinese geocultural discourse.

According to Lakatos, a scientific research program is formed by a theoretical core and a protective belt. The fundamental difference that separates one theory from another is the difference in their theoretical core. For instance, the theories of gravity, quantum mechanics, and relativity are distinct theories because their theoretical cores are incompatible with each other. A theory has not been falsified unless its theoretical core has been shattered.²⁶ In other words, the theoretical core is the life and soul of a theory. Although Lakatos has not discussed the formation of theoretical core in detail, he explains that a research program begins with a primitive "model," which later develops into a more sophisticated theoretical system. This process is similar to the phenomenon of "nucleation" in systems theory, whereby a system is formed by the multiplication and extension of its primary parts.

Because problem solving is an important objective of a theory, the formation of the theoretical core should directly related to a core problematic; thus, a new theoretical paradigm is built on a theoretical core, and the core is developed on the basis of a core concept, which in turn is created from a core problematic.²⁷ The core problematic usually comes from nativistic concerns. For instance, mainstream IR theory in the United States is concerned with U.S. hegemony after World War II and the problem of how to sustain it. In the case of postwar Britain, hegemony was not its main concern; instead, the process of European integration made the question of international society more pressing. The problems concerning countries in the developing world were poverty and development, which led to the creation of dependency theory. Contemporary China's core problematic is how to peacefully integrate into international society. If we extend and generalize it, China's core problematic is its relationship with the international system; at the level of ontology, the problem becomes one of China's identity in relation to the international system.

"What is China?" This question reflects the identity dilemma that China experienced when it began to face the international system. In the two thousand years of Chinese history following the Qin and Han dynasties, China did not need to consider its relationship with the international system. China had not faced any system that needed its serious consideration other than the tributary system, within which its identity was clear and indisputable. In the last century, however, it began to experience anxiety regarding its identity in the international system, and it fell into the dilemma of its role in the process of achieving modernity. The Chinese people were forced to consider the question "Who are we?" In the past, China regarded those who had not been civilized by Chinese culture as barbarians; but now, it seems that the Chinese themselves have become barbarians. The critique of Chinese culture since the May 4th Movement and the adoption of Western civilization is a contest between Chinese and Western technology, institutions, and culture. More fundamentally, it is a process whereby

China tries to reestablish its position and identity in the international system. In the process of modernization, China has yet to resolve this problem, and this is the identity dilemma that it experienced when facing the international system.

The current international system was constructed by the West, and it is formed on the basis of equality among sovereign nation-states. In the past, Chinese lacked a self-conscious understanding of the concepts and practice of such a system because China was outside the international system, primarily having an antagonistic relationship with it. Revolutionary thought and practice in contemporary China have led the Chinese people to wish for a new state of affairs that breaks away from the old; the rise of nationalism also has led them to feel the oppression of the existing system. China wanted to join the international system, but its effort was not acknowledged; at the same time, China also found it impossible to change the existing system. This situation began to change when China started its reform and opening. On the one hand, China finally has decided to integrate into international system; on the other, the rest of the world acknowledges the necessity of China's participation. This interaction has facilitated the transformation of China's economy, society, and the general ideas of its people. In the process of integrating into the world, the rapid development and transformation of China, with its vast population of more than 1.3 billion people, makes the emergence of the Chinese School of IR theory not only possible but also inevitable.

Recently, "the rise of China" has become an important academic topic both inside China and abroad. The question of "China's rise" remains a problem of the identity dilemma China faces in the process of integrating into the international system. China has begun to address this identity problem in this era of reform and opening, but the process has not been smooth. Guo Shuyong discusses three external environment scenarios for China's rise—an adverse external environment, an optimistic external environment, and an in-between external environment—and three strategies for China's rise—rise through military conflict; peaceful rise; and rise through a mixture of military and peaceful strategy, depending on the international environment.[28] The interaction of the three external environment scenarios and the three strategies for China's rising will influence how people think about the form of China's rise. The antagonistic relationship anticipated in Hobbesian culture will lead to a violent rise; the competitive Lockean culture would allow a country to rise either peacefully or violently; and Kantian culture will see the rise of a country as necessarily nonviolent. The question remains one of China's relations with the international system, which is fundamentally the question "What is China?" China has been addressing this question in the process of reform and opening, however, the heated debate engendered by this identity dilemma suggests that China has not completely resolved this problem. How could China's traditional culture, its contemporary revolutionary tradition, and the ideas behind its reform and opening all be integrated to form the theoretical core of the Chinese School of IR theory? The question itself is exciting and challenging for both theory and practice.

Conclusion

This chapter has raised three points. First, it is possible to have a Chinese School of IR theory; the geocultural characteristic of every social science theory is an indelible birthmark. Second, the Chinese School has three paired rich intellectual sources of theory: the two-thousand-year history of the Tianxia concept, and the corresponding practice of the tributary system; the hundred year history of revolutionary thought and practice; and the ideas and experiences of reform from the past three decades. Third, the emergence of the Chinese School is not only possible but is also inevitable. China is experiencing rapid development, huge social transformations, and deep conceptual change. These changes can lead China to address the problem of its integration with international society, and the process of negotiating its relationship with the world will inevitably lead to the emergence of the Chinese School of IR theory.

The development of the Chinese School of IR theory is different from the idea of indigenizing existing Western IR theory. Although indigenization involves the development of native theoretical content, to a certain extent it consists of backward societies learning and borrowing from the existing theories of advanced societies to explain native phenomena. For instance, we could talk of a Chinese-style Realism, a Chinese-style Liberalism, a Chinese-style Constructivism, and so on, where the result would be a localized explanation that verifies Western theories. By contrast, native consciousness and characteristics in social theories have different meanings that emphasize how theory can emerge from the native culture, and can develop through interaction with other cultures. Thus, its development not only transforms the self and other but also fuses them together to achieve universality. This is the true nature of the Chinese School of IR theory.

Notes

1. John Gerard Ruggie, "What Makes the World Hang Together? Neo-Utilitarianism and the Social Constructivist Challenge," in *Exploration and Contestation in the Study of World Politics*, edited by Peter J. Katzenstein, Robert O. Keohane, and Stephen D. Krasner (Cambridge, Mass.: MIT Press, 1999), 215–46.
2. See E. H. Carr, *The Twenty Years' Crisis, 1919–1939: An Introduction to the Study of International Relations* (New York: Harper & Row, 1964); and Hayward A. Alker, *Rediscovering and Reformulations: Humanistic Methodologies for International Studies* (Cambridge: Cambridge University Press, 1996).
3. Quoted by Ruggie, "What Makes the World Hang Together?" 236.
4. This is different from indigenization. The indigenous consciousness and character of social science theories emphasize that social theories originate in local culture. The universality of indigenous social theories is built upon interacting with theories from other cultures.
5. Qin Yaqing and Alexander Wendt, "The Development Space of Constructivism," *Shijie jingji yu zhengzhi*, no. 1 (2005): 11–12. For a similar discussion regarding the different pathways connecting micro and macro structure, see Alexander Wendt, *Social Theory of International Politics* (Cambridge: Cambridge University Press, 1999), 139–65.
6. *Translator's note:* In this comparison of traditional Chinese medicine and Western medicine, I have translated the meaning of the metaphor rather than the literal meaning of the source text because a direct translation would not convey the meaning implied in the Chinese context.
7. See Tim Dunne, *Inventing International Society: A History of the English School* (New York: St. Martin's Press, 1998).
8. Stephen Ambrose, *Rise to Globalism: American Foreign Policy since 1938*, 4th ed. (New York: Penguin Books, 1985).
9. Qin Yaqing, "Guoji zhengzhi lilun de hexin wenti yu Zhongguo xuepai de shengcheng" [The core problem of international relations theory and the emergence of the Chinese School], *Zhongguo shehui kexue*, no. 3 (2005): 165–76.
10. Stanley Hoffman, "American Social Science: International Relations," in *International Theory: Critical Investigations*, edited by James Der Derian (New York: New York University Press, 1995), 212–41.
11. This question has been noticed by scholars outside the IR discipline in China. From the perspective of nativism, these scholars raise the question of (post)modernity and universality of Confucianism in the era of globalization. This is very instructive to the scholars of IR. However, in their attempts to popularize the notion of Tianxia in Chinese culture, they fail to take into consideration its a priori assumption that legitimizes inequality. Although the modern world, to a certain extend, still exists in a state of de facto inequality, de jure equality has already become a universal norm. See Zhao Tingyang, *Tianxia tixi: Shijie zhidu zhexue daolun* [The Tianxia system: Introduction to the philosophy of world institution] (Nanjing: Jiangsu jiaoyu chubanshe, 2005); see also Wang Mingming, "Zuowei shijie tushi de Tianxia, [Tianxia as the configuration of the world], in *Xixue "Zhongguo hua" de lishi kunjing* [The historical impasse of the Sinicization of Western knowledge] (Guilin: Guangxi shifan daxue chubanshe, 2005), 214–88.

12. E. H. Carr divides IR theory into idealism and realism, and their related practical experiences are the international relations in Europe between the two world wars. Martin Wight divides it into Realism, Rationalism, and Revolutionism, and their related practical experiences are the history of international relations and diplomatic history in contemporary Europe. And Alexander Wendt distinguishes between Hobbesian culture, Lockean culture, and Kantian culture, using medieval European international relations, Westphalian international relations, and the international relations of the North Atlantic region as the practical sources. See Carr, *Twenty Years' Crisis,* 12–21, 62–83; Martin Wight, *International Theory: The Three Traditions* (Leicester: Leicester University Press and Royal Institute of International Affairs, 1991); and Wendt, *Social Theory.*

13. See Dunne, *Inventing International Society.*

14. Regarding hierarchical order, see Fei Xiaotong, "Chaxu geju" [Hierarchical structure], in *Xiangtu Zhongguo* [From the soil: The foundations of Chinese society], by Fei Xiaotong (Beijing: Beijing chubanshe, 2005), 29–40. *Translator's note:* In referring to to Fei Xiaotong's work, I have used the terms from the English translation of *Xiangtu Zhongguo,* except that for "chaxu geju," I use "hierarchical structure" instead of "the differential mode of association" because it makes more sense in the context of IR theory; see Fei Xiaotong, *From the Soil: the Foundation of Chinese Society,* translated by Gary G. Hamilton and Wang Zheng (Berkeley: University of California Press, 1992).

15. See John Fairbank, *China: A New History* (Cambridge: Cambridge University Press, 1992); and John Fairbank and Edwin O. Reischaner, *China: Tradition and Transformation* (Boston: Houghton Mifflin, 1989).

16. Dan Xingwu, "Liangda tixi de chongtu yu jindai Zhongguo de shengcheng" [The conflict between two systems and the birth of contemporary China], PhD dissertation, Graduate School of the Chinese Academy of Social Sciences, 2005, 24–25.

17. See Fei Xiaotong, "Chaxu geju," 29–40.

18. Zhao, *Tianxia tixi,* 51.

19. Hedley Bull, *The Anarchical Society: A Study of Order in World Politics* (New York: Palgrave Macmillan, 2002), 8–19.

20. Fei Xiaotong, "Xiweizhe siren de daode" [The morality of personal relationships], "Jiazu" [Patrilineages], and "Lizhi zhixu" [Ritual order], all in *Xiangtu Zhongguo,* 41–50, 51–59, 68–76.

21. See Li Zehou, *Zhongguo jindai sixiang shilun* [Contemporary Chinese intellectual history] (Tianjin: Tianjin Shehui kexue yuan chubanshe, 2003).

22. Robert Jervis, *Perception and Misperception in International Politics* (Princeton, N.J.: Princeton University Press, 1976), 262–70. Jervis considers that revolution and war are two types of events that have the most significant impact on collective entities like states. The most significant events in China since 1840 have been revolutions and wars.

23. See Le Daiyun, "Shijie wenhua yujingzhong de 'Xuehengpai'" [The "Xuehengpai" in world cultural discourse], *Xinhua wenzhai,* no. 16 (2005): 92–94.

24. Robert Zoellick, "Whither China? From Membership to Responsibility," *Washington File,* September 23, 2005.

25. Qin Yaqing, "Guojia shenfen, zhanlüe wenhua he anquan liyi" [Identity of state, strategic culture and security interest], *Shijie jingji yu zhengzhi,* no. 1 (2003): 10–15.

26. Imre Lakatos, *The Methodology of Scientific Research Programmes* (Cambridge: Cambridge Unviersty Press, 1978).

27. Robert Cox, "Social Forces, States and World Order: Beyond International Relations Theory," in *Neorealism and its Critics*, edited by Robert Keohane (New York: Columbia University Press, 1986), 204–54; Qin, ""Guoji zhengzhi lilun de hexin wenti," 165–76.

28. Guo Shuyong, "Guanyu Zhongguo jueqi de ruogan lilun zhengming ji qi xueshu yiyi" [Certain theoretical debates and their academic implications regarding the rise of China], *Guoji guancha*, no. 4 (2005): 31–38.

Chapter 4

Xunzi's Thoughts on International Politics and Their Implications

Yan Xuetong

There is considerable depth and breadth of research on the ancient Chinese philosophy of Xunzi. These studies, however, usually explain his ideas from the perspective of domestic politics and governance. This article explores Xunzi's thoughts on international politics from the perspective of international politics.[1] Xunzi's expositions of international politics were few, and were diffused over different books. His most pertinent views are expounded in book 11, "Of Kings and Lords-Protector"; book 9, "On the Regulations of a King"; and book 18, "Rectifying Theses." Although they contain no systemic ideas or formal theories on international politics, Xunzi's thoughts from two thousand years ago are nonetheless relevant to current explanations of international political phenomena; certain of his ideas in this context offer plausible and sensible rationales. This chapter discusses Xunzi's analytical methodology and ideas on international politics and how it may have provided inspiration for contemporary China's "rising strategy."

Methodology for Analyzing International Politics

Main methodological approaches in modern international relations theory employ either system-level or unit-level analysis, consist of three determination theories, and can be divided into strict and comprehensive analysis.

This chapter is a revised version of "Xun Zi's Thoughts on International Politics and Their Implications," *Chinese Journal of International Politics* 2, no. 1 (2008): 135–65.

This section discusses each of the three methodological aspects of international relations theory in Xunzi's writings.

System-Level and Unit-Level Analysis

The two key analytical variables in modern international political theory used to explain international political phenomena are those of the unit actor and the international system. Unitary analysis focuses on change in the unit actor; systemic analysis focuses on change in the international system. Xunzi discusses the function of international norms and the Five Ordinance System (*wufu*, 五服), and their role in preventing international conflict, according to the Universal Unification Idea. His analyses of achieving stability in the international order are primarily from the point of view of great powers. It was his belief that it is the inner nature of great powers that determines the stability of the international system, and not the system that modifies the behavior of great countries.

Xunzi's first analysis is of the three changes of situation that states undergo: rise, decline, and destruction. His conclusions reflect the causes of transformation in the international order. The dependent variable in this case has two key values: *anning* (安宁) or *zhi* (治) (peace, order, and stability), and *hunluan* (混乱) or *luan* (乱) (disorder and chaos); the independent variable has three values: *wang* (王, true kingship), *ba* (霸, hegemony or, according to the actual Xunzi text, lord-protector), and *qiang* (强, might or power). Xunzi uses these terms in both the verbal and nominal senses. The verb *wang* means to lead the world, *ba* means to wield hegemony in certain areas of the world, and *qiang* means to exert greater power than other states. The nouns *wang*, *ba*, and *qiang* also reflect these different behaviors by states and leaders.[2] Xunzi, therefore, treats state nature, type of leader and nature of policy as three systemically consistent, compatible manifestations of one thing. In other words, stability in the international system depends on the nature of great states. States of true kingship bring stability to the international order; mighty states bring chaos; and hegemon relations are stable with hegemon allies and chaotic with nonallied states (see figure 4.1).

The system, state, and individual are the three general levels of analyses in international politics theory. Xunzi's analysis could be interpreted at the individual level, because to him the ruler is the fundamental independent variable and the nature of state is the intermediate variable. He regards the state as the instrument with which the ruler governs and manages society. When the mores and beliefs of rulers differ, so too do the principles and

Figure 4.1. The Nature of Great Powers and International Order

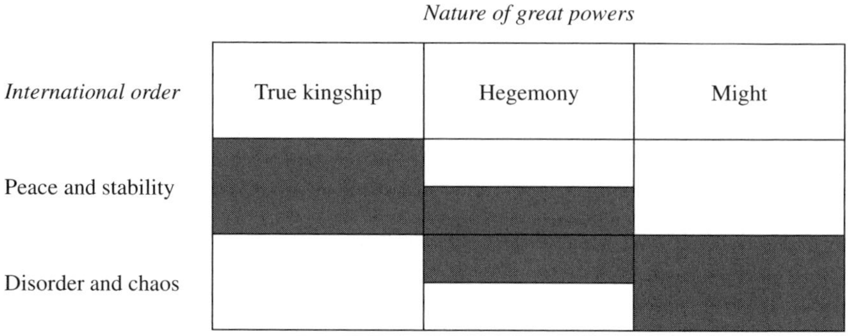

	Nature of great powers		
International order	True kingship	Hegemony	Might
Peace and stability	■	■	
Disorder and chaos		■	■

tactics involved in the use of the state as an instrument, and hence its nature. The differences in the mores and ethics of leaders of great world powers, moreover, determine the nature of states and of the international order as either peace-stability or disorder-chaos. Xunzi says: "The state is the most powerful instrument for benefit in the world. The ruler of men is the most influential position of authority for benefit in the world. If a ruler employs the Way to maintain these two—the state and his position—then there will be the greatest peace and security, the greater honor and prosperity, and the wellspring for accumulating what is beautiful and fine. If a ruler does not employ the Way to maintain them, then there will be the greatest danger and peril and the greatest humiliation and adversity. It would be better not to have these two than to have them."[3]

But Xunzi's individual-level analysis is not restricted to the ruler; it emphasizes ministers as an intermediate variable of importance equal to the nature of the state, because it is that between state and ruler (see figure 4.2). The core function of the ruler, therefore, is not solely that of governance but also of selecting ministers best suited to administering the country. He says: "Those who are to maintain the state certainly cannot be so alone. Since this is the case, the strength, defensive security, and glory of country lie in the selection of its prime minister. Where a ruler is himself able and his prime minister is able, he will become a True King. Where the ruler is personally incapable, but knows it, becomes apprehensive, and seeks those who are able, then he will become powerful. When the ruler is personally incapable, but neither realize[s] it, nor becomes apprehensive, nor seeks those who are able, but merely makes use of those who fawn over him and flatter him, those [who] form his entourage of assistants, or those who are

Figure 4.2. Decisionmakers and the International Order

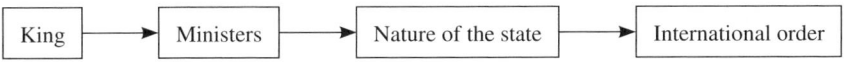

related to him, then he will be endangered and encroached upon, and, in the extreme case, annihilated."[4]

When comparing rulers and ministers, Xunzi sees the function of the ruler as deterministic, because the type of minister, as an intermediate variable, depends upon the changing variable of the nature of the ruler. In Xunzi's belief system, there is no scarcity of decent ministers; whether or not they are selected and used by rulers is the main matter. There are various types of minister; the key to able governance is the type of minister the ruler seeks. As Xunzi says, "Thus, the relation between King Cheng and the Duke of Zhou was that he heeded the duke's advice on everything that transpired, for he realized what was valuable. The relations of Duke Huan to Guan Zhong were that in the business of state he used Guan for everything that developed, for he knew what was beneficial. The kingdom of Wu had Wu Zixu but was incapable of using him, so ultimately the country was destroyed, for it turned against the Way and lost this worthy man. Thus, those who honored sages became king; those who valued the worthy became lords-protector; those who respected the worthy survived; and those that scorned them were destroyed."[5]

Ideational and Internal Determination of Cause

International politics theory can be divided into three determination theories: material determination, idea determination, and idea-material concurrent determination. Realist theory, which sees a state's hard power as the determining factor, is normally a material determination theory; constructivism, which sees human ideas as the determining factor, is normally an idea determination theory; and institutionalism takes a compromise position, according equal importance to material power and institutional norms. Xunzi does not deny the importance of material power, but his analysis, in viewing ideas as the original driving force behind human behavior, concurs with constructivism. In his discussion of behavioral norms, Xunzi's concepts of "True King, Hegemon, and the Mighty" compare with Alexander Wendt's concepts of Kantian culture, Lockean culture, and Hobbesian culture. Xunzi argues: "The True King tries to win men; the lord-protector to acquire allies; the powerful to capture land."⁶ In his view, winning talented people depends on ethics and mores, winning the support of allies depends on trust and honesty, and capturing land depends on hard power. Wendt, conversely, believes that the three cultures have different structures and reflect "three different degrees to which a norm can be *internalized*, and thus as generating three different pathways by which the same structure can be produced—force, price, and legitimacy."⁷ When comparing the conceptualizations of Xunzi and Wendt, the True King and Mighty concepts are respectively similar to the Kantian and Hobbesian cultures, but the Hegemon concept differs from Lockean culture.

Xunzi believed that it is rulers' and ministers' ideas, rather than capabilities, that cause change in a state's change of power status. In his view, the different ideas that rulers have cause them to select ministers with different political principles, whose different policies on administrating the country have different results. In his words: "If the ruler is guided by the model of a True King and associates with men who are proper companions for a True King, then the ruler himself will also be a True King. If he is guided by the model of a lord-protector and associates with men who are proper companions for a lord-protector, then he himself will also be a lord-protector. If the model by which he is guided is proper for a doomed country and he associates with men who are proper for a doomed country, then the ruler himself will be doomed as well."⁸

Xunzi's idea of ruler and ministers as constituting the original state behavior dynamic correlates with internal factor determination theory. He argues: "With these instruments (of government) he can be king, or with them he can be mere lord-protector. With these instruments he can survive, or with them he can perish. In a country of ten thousand chariots, it is the ruler who establishes its majesty and strength, who makes finer its fame and reputation, and who bends its enemies to submission. What makes a country secure or endangered, good or bad, is determined exclusively by its ruler and not by others. Whether he is a king or a mere lord-protector, whether he is secure and viably existing or in imminent peril and faced with utter destruction—these are determined by the ruler himself and not by others."⁹ In other words, world leadership, hegemony, and protecting the state's security depend on no other person than the ruler.

Strict and Comparative Analysis

International politics phenomena are the result of multiple factors. Analytical methodology can therefore be divided into the two categories of strict and comprehensive analysis, according to how many independent variables an analysis takes into account. Comprehensive analysis places multiple variables in parallel and explains the value change in causal variables without discussing the relationship between them. Strict analysis, in contrast, uses a single variable to explain changes in causality through logic chains, which requires analyzing the relationship between each independent variable. Kenneth N. Waltz's use of the structure of great powers as an independent variable to explain whether war occurs in the international system is an example of strict analysis. Hans J. Morgenthau, conversely, uses many independent variables—such as power, interest, culture, law, mores, and diplomatic tactics—to explain changes in the international system. This is comprehensive analysis.

Xunzi's work comes under the strict analysis category. He uses the ideas of rulers as the fundamental independent variable to explain the nature of ministers responsible for making a state's policies. He therefore uses the nature of ministers to explain the nature of the state, and the nature of the state to explain order or disorder in the international system (see figure 4.2). Figure 4.3 shows the structure of this analytical logic, whereby the strategic orientation between ministers and the nature of the country is the intermediate factor, and the extent of power and foreign relations are the two intermediate variables between the nature of the country and international order. Variables at different levels in Xunzi's thought thus have clear logical connections in consistent relationship.

Comparative analysis is the opposite approach to that of single case analysis. Single case analysis uses a case study to argue from a positive viewpoint, whereas comparative analysis uses both positive and negative viewpoints to prove or disprove the argument. As Xunzi uses both positive and negative examples to make his point, his analysis is comparative. The

Figure 4.3. Relations of Different Variables at Different Levels

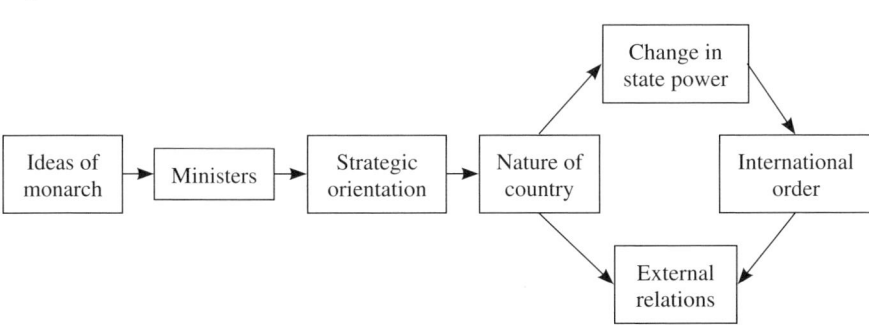

positive examples Xunzi uses include Shang Tang, duke of Zhou, and King Wen; Jie and Zhou are usually his negative examples. In his argument that true kingship authority is not arbitrarily seized but naturally formulated, for instance, Xunzi says: "Tang and Wu did not seize the whole world. Rather, they cultivated the Way, carried out their moral duty, caused whatever benefited the empire in common to flourish, and removed whatever did harm to the whole world, so that the empire offered allegiance to them. Jie and Zhou Xin did not abandon the world. Rather, they turned against inner power of (their forebears) Yu and Tang, brought chaos to the divisions of social functions inherent in ritual and moral principles, behaved like wild beasts, gathered up their own ultimate catastrophe, completed their own evil, so that the world abandoned them. The empire offering allegiance to you is what is meant by King. The whole world abandoning you is what is meant by ruination."[10]

Xunzi's understanding of international politics has strong logical basis, but his analytical method is not scientific, according to modern scientific standards. Neither do the examples he uses to make his point strictly accord with the positivist model. As most of his analytical examples are historical legend, the backgrounds to and general processes of events that he cites are absent. Finally, not all the sources of his pertinent knowledge can be given and therefore proved. His case study analysis also lacks the necessary control mechanism over variables, which places it under the inductive school simple enumeration method. Simple enumeration, although acknowledged as the most commonly used of methodologies, is of low scientific credence. Cases studies so conducted, therefore, lack positivistic strength and persuasiveness.

Understanding the Power of a State

The meanings of state and state power in Xunzi are consistent with their conceptualizations in modern political science. This section examines Xunzi's dual understanding of the state, highlighting the relationship between political and military-economic power, and the reasons for the uneven development of state power.

A State's Dual Function as Actor and Instrument

In Xunzi's works, the concept of the state refers to both polity and governing instrument. As such, it is consistent with modern political science's conceptualization of the state, from the international politics perspective, as a type of unit actor, and from the perspective of domestic politics as an instrument with which to order and govern the people.[11]

As regards power differentials, Xunzi differentiates between Son of Heaven and feudal lord states. He says: "In antiquity, the Sons of Heaven had a thousand offices in his government and the feudal lords each had a hundred. To use these thousand offices to execute orders in all the countries of the Xia Chinese traditions is what is meant by being 'King.' To use these hundred offices to execute orders within the boundaries of the states so that although there might be unrest in the state, it does not reach the point where the lord might be displaced, or destroyed—this is what is meant by being a lord."[12] The states in this quotation are obviously political units, but the Son of Heaven is sovereign and considerably larger in size and strength than the feudal lord, and therefore has far greater power.

From a functional perspective, Xunzi sees the state as a political instrument. He says: "Since the state is the greatest implement and heaviest burden in the world, it is impermissible that he who rules the state should not be good first at determining the right position and then placing (the state) there, for if he locates it in a precarious place, danger will result."[13]

The Relationship between Political and Military-Economic Power

Xunzi's concept of the functions of political, military, and economic power, and the relationships among the three, is quite different from that of modern times. Modern understanding generally sees economic power as the foundation of political power; Xunzi holds a directly opposing view.

Political power, in Xunzi's opinion, is the foundation of economic and military power, because no matter how immense, they lack meaning without a solid basis of political power. Xunzi's ideas in this regard are similar in logic to former chief of the U.S. Central Intelligence Agency, Ray Cline's, comprehensive power formula—$Pp = (C + E + M) \times (S + W)$—where Pp is perceived power, C is critical mass, E is economic capability, M is military capability, S is strategic purpose, and W is the will to pursue national strategy. According to this formula, comprehensive power is the multiplied product of both hard and soft power. When soft power is zero, comprehensive power is also zero, and hard power has no function. Xunzi points out: "King Wen had carried it out in a territory only 100 li square [square kilometers], and the world was unified. Jie Gui and Zhou Xin cast it aside and although they possess the much more substantial power of the whole empire, they were unable to obtain the status of a commoner and grow to a ripe old age. Hence if one makes good use of the Way, then a state only 100 li square is sufficient to establish an independent rule. But if one does not make good use of it, then like Chu, 6,000 li in extent, it will become the servant of its adversary."[14] The collapse in 1991 of the mighty Soviet Union illustrates Xunzi's point. The Soviet Union's military power at that time was equivalent to that of the United States, and its economic capability was number three in the world. But hard power was insufficient to sustain the state's survival upon the Soviet government's losing the capability for internal and external political mobility.

Xunzi also believed that political power is the basis for hard power growth and that the correctness, as regards morals and ethics, of state national policy determines the state's core strength and prosperity or weakness. If policy is ethically correct, national power increases; morally incorrect policy leads to its destruction. Xunzi says: "If the ruler does not exalt ritual principles, then the army will be weak. If he does not love his people, then the army will be weak. If when he prohibits or approves something he is untrustworthy, then the army will be weak. If his commendations and rewards do not penetrate down to the lower ranks, then the army will be weak. If the generals and marshals are incapable, then the army will be weak. If the ruler is fond of achievement, then the country will be impoverished. If he is fond of profits, then the country will be poor . . . Thus, although under Yu there were ten years of flood and under Tang there were seven years of drought, there were no vegetable-colored people in the world. Yet after this ten-year period when the grain ripened again, there was still an accumulated surplus of old grain. This was due to no other cause than that they knew the application of the principle of root and branch and of source and outflow."[15]

In Xunzi's view, therefore, that people did not starve to death during the ten years of floods in Yu's time or in the ten years of drought in Tang's time, and the yearly abundant harvests and food surpluses that followed these two decades were for reasons none other than Yu and Tang's knowledge of what actually constitutes the state's foundation and what are merely superficial factors. Similarly, the United States' checking and balancing of the three powers, Japan's Meiji Restoration, and the Soviet Union's socialist system gained for those states tremendous increases in national power. These historical examples confirm Xunzi's view that political power is the basis on which to strengthen hard power.

Xunzi thus believed that rapid economic growth depends upon the state's political system, and not that economic development forms the basis of the political system. He explains: "Hence, one who cultivates ritual principles becomes a king; one who effectively exercises government become strong; one who wins over the people will be secure; and one who merely collects tax levies will perish. Accordingly, the True King enriches the people; the lord-protector enriches his scholar-knights; a state that can barely manage to survive enriches its grand officers; and a state that is doomed enriches only the ruler's coffers and fills up his storehouses."[16] This brings to mind that since 1978, when China implemented the reform and opening policy replacing that based on "class struggle," the Chinese economy has raced ahead. It is an event in history that endorses Xunzi's view of the political system as the basis for economic growth.

Xunzi also regarded principled foreign relations as a basis of national security. In his opinion, whether a state is secure is determined by its good relations with other states as well as its military power. He says: "A humane man would keep in good order the obligations between small and large countries, between the strong and weak, and would sedulously maintain them. The important point of ritual would be observed with the extreme of good form. The *gui* jade baton and the *bi* jade insignia would be very sumptuous. The presents and contributions would be very munificent. The means he uses to persuade others must be those of a gentleman who is elegantly correct in form and of discriminating intelligence. Should others have designs against him, who among them could become angry with him? This being so, those who act out of anger will not commit aggression against him. If for the sake of a reputation, or for the sake of profit, or because of anger, others do not commit aggression against him, then his country will be as secure as a boulder and as long-lived as the Winnowing Basket and Wings constellations."[17]

A historical comparison that confirms Xunzi's view of principled foreign relations as the basis for national security is that of China's foreign policy. In the 1960s, China was in simultaneous opposition to the United States and the Soviet Union. By the beginning of the twenty-first century, however, China had implemented a policy of good-neighborliness and friendly relations with both these hegemonic powers. This policy change transformed China's situation from one of military confrontations in Vietnam with the United States and Soviet military pressure to its north during the 1960s to China's, the United States', and Russia's (since the fall of the Soviet Union in 1991) maintenance of normal great power relations in the early twenty-first century. As such, it represents a considerable improvement in China's security environment.

Xunzi also believed that political power is more effective than economic power in the event of diplomatic confrontations. Using wealth to buy other countries' support, he says, is pointless; the most effective way of strengthening the state is through moral and ethical principles. He says: "If I attempt to serve the state by using valuable and precious goods, then these costly objects will be depleted, yet friendly relations will not be secured. If I trust in treaties and solemnly swear to covenants, then although the terms of the agreement are firmly settled, they will be overturned without a single day elapsing. If I cede territory bit by bit, then although the amount to be ceded has been settled, the desire will not be satiated. The more I acquiesce to their demands, the more they will encroach, the inevitable end being that at the depletion of my resources, they will not stop until they have taken the whole country.... Thus, the intelligent ruler does not proceed along this path. He invariably cultivates ritual principles in order to arrange the court in an orderly fashion, rectifies the laws in order to make the governmental bureau uniformly arranged, and adjusts the operating of the government in order to handle the people uniformly. It is only after this has been done that emergencies and reports are uniformly disposed of by the court, the various tasks and duties uniformly handled by the bureaus, and the multitude of commoners uniformly handled by their subordinates, ... In such a situation, those who are nearby zealously try to become close to the ruler and those who are in distant regions long to reach him. The ruler and his subjects will be of one mind, and the three armies will make a common effort. When his fame and reputation are sufficient to sear and scorch them and his majesty and strength enough to thrash and flog them, he simply folds his hands before his breast in salute and signals with his finger. Then not one of the strong and aggressive states will fail to come in haste to serve him. The situation would be like the case of Wuhuo, the Crow Catcher (a big and powerful fellow), battling the Jiao Pygmies (a small and short guy)."[18]

Xunzi's wisdom is again demonstrated in the cases of Japan in 2005 and China in 1971. Japan, in an attempt to obtain permanent membership in the United Nations Security Council, invested $16 billion in developing countries in 2005 as a means of buying their support. But it failed.[19] The United States in 1971, a time when American foreign aid to the developing world was much higher than that from China, opposed Beijing's application for UN membership. With the support of African countries, however, Beijing successfully restored its UN membership. These two historical events prove Xunzi's theory that political power is more important than economic power in global diplomatic affairs.

Reasons for the Uneven Development of Power

Xunzi believed that it is the failed governance of other countries that makes a country powerful. He says: "In this way, while for my enemy the accumulated effect of each day is further decay, for me it is greater preservation in good order; while for him the accumulated effect of each day is greater impoverishment, for me it is greater wealth; while for him the accumulated effect of each day is greater burden, for me each day brings greater ease. While the relationship between ruler and subject, superior and subordinate, for him is increasingly pervaded by stern oppression and is marked by mutual estrangement and hostility, for me it's increasingly pervaded by liberality and is marked by closeness and affection. On account of this, I can merely await the imminent decay of my enemy. Anyone who can make his country like this could become lord-protector."[20] Xunzi's idea is identical to the current concept of relative power in modern international relations (IR) theory, whereby one state's power status is relative to that of other states; widening the gap between it and others, therefore, is the key to strengthening its power. The main result of widening this gap is that it decreases the power status of others. If the power of all states increases at the same rate, their power status relationship does not change.

Xunzi also argues: "All others are given to anarchy, I alone am controlled. All others face peril; I alone am secure. All others fail and are destroyed; I alone succeed and control them. Thus, when a humane man has control of the state, he does not want merely to maintain what he possesses and nothing more, but instead wants to unite all people."[21] Xunzi is thus not against annexation. In his view, different types of annexation bring different results, insofar as annexation based on the power of morals and principles strengthens, but that more rudely accomplished can weaken. As he says, "One who uses moral power to annex people will become a True King; one who employs raw power to annex them will become weak; and one who employs wealth to annex them will become poor. In this regard, antiquity and today are one and the same."[22]

The conclusion that Xunzi reaches in his ideological determination of why there is uneven development of power among states, therefore, is that it is the result of the different ideas of their respective rulers. He says: "There are sham ministers, presumptuous ministers, meritorious ministers, and sage ministers. . . . Accordingly, one who employs sage ministers will become a king; one who employs meritorious ministers will be strong; one who employs a presumptuous minister will be endangered; and one who

Figure 4.4. Causes of Uneven Power Development

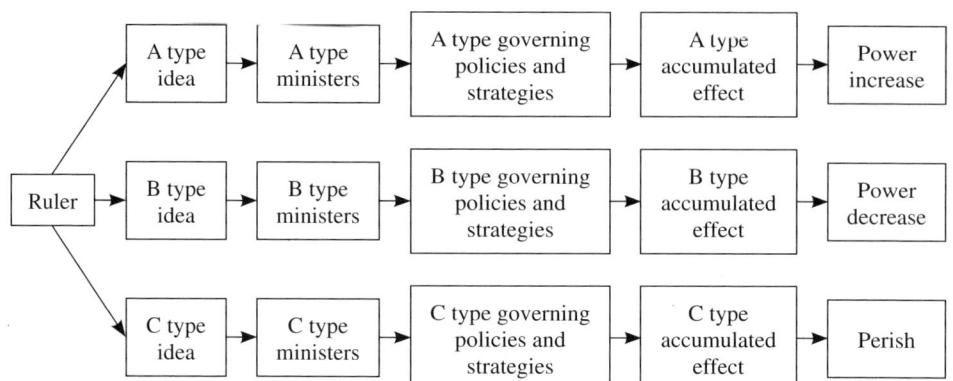

employs a sham minister will be doomed."[23] This argument sets out a logical relationship: The change in a state's power status is caused by change in a state's policy, made by the ministers who supervise the state, who are selected according to the ruler's idea (see figure 4.4).

Xunzi says, "Without exception all who exercise rulership desire strength and have an aversion to weakness. They all desire security and have an aversion to danger. They desire honor and have aversion to disgrace. In this both Yu and Jie were the same. What way is convenient to bring the fruition the three things all men desire and allow them to avoid the three aversions? I say that there is not way more direct than relying on the careful selection of a prime minister."[24] In his summary of the historical lessons of doomed states, Xunzi points out: "In antiquity there were ten thousand countries; today there are only ten odd."[25] In other words, the reason why states failed is, without exception, because they did not select the right ministers.

Xunzi believed that the appointment of different qualities of official relates directly to the increase or decrease in state power. He consequently emphasizes the selection of suitable officials as a core state-strengthening strategy. He says: "If he should desire to gain the harmonious unification of the world, controlling the likes of Qin and Chu, then he could do not better than an astute and intelligent gentleman. His use of knowledge penetrates into the smallest crevices. His actions and undertakings are not toilsome, yet his accomplishments and reputation are extremely grand. His management of affairs is extremely easy and reaches the ultimate of what is enjoyable. Accordingly, an intelligent lord will consider him a precious treasure, and a stupid one will consider him a vexatious difficulty."[26]

Xunzi also emphasizes merit-based principles as the guideline for selecting officials. He says: "What possible reason could there be for the lord of men not to search wide and far without regard for consanguinity or nobility and rank, being concerned solely to seek out those who are genuinely able? If a man were like this, then his servants would consider official positions less vital. They would yield to those who are more worthy and able and would be content to follow after them. In such a situation, it would be as though Shun or Yu had returned again and that the undertakings of True King had just recommenced. To accomplish the splendid achievement of unifying the world and gaining a reputation the equal of that of Shun or Yu—what could possibly give pleasure of equal refinement?"[27]

Xunzi's understanding of how changes in national power occur represents the traditional "wise ruler—virtuous minister" concept espoused by ancient Chinese political thinkers, whereby talented political officials constitute the basis for strengthening the state. But Xunzi sees institutions as humanly determined, as opposed to the concept of modern democratic electoral systems, wherein unsuitable officials are removed from office on the principles of self-correction and self-adjustment. During the time of Xunzi, it was not generally believed that institutional innovation is the fundamental reason for a state's change in power status. As Xunzi regarded unification of the world as True Kingship's highest goal, he is not unconditionally against state annexation, and he uses the nature of annexation as the criterion on which to judge whether or not it is justifiable. This idea is obviously not consistent with post–World War II international norms. Xunzi may also have had an exaggerated idea of the importance of political power as regards preserving national security. The foreign policy of one small state, no matter how ethical and moral, does not necessarily protect it from the aggressive ambitions of larger powers. The 1990 Iraqi invasion and annexation of Kuwait is an apposite example.

Understanding International Authority

Discussions of power in modern IR theory are on three dimensions. The first is that of power relations: whether international relations are cooperative, competitive, or confrontational. The second is power differentiation:

whether the kind of power a country holds is dominant, supplementary, or participatory. Third is the content of power: whether the accent of a country's power is on its politics, economy, or security. Xunzi's discussion of international power, however, concentrates on the different natures of power. This is an area of scant research in contemporary IR theory.

The Definition of Tianxia (World) and You Tianxia (Having the World)

The concept of Tianxia is at the foundation of Xunzi's analysis of the nature of international power. Clarification of his view of Tianxia gives a better understanding of Xunzi's thoughts on kingship, hegemony (lord-protector), and might (power).

In Xunzi's view, Tianxia is "world" and You Tianxia is "having the world" or achieving leadership of the world. But the power status of "having the world" is gained through peoples' and other states" voluntary submission, rather than through use of force. He says: "Since the world is the weightiest burden, only the strongest person will be able to bear it. Since it is the largest thing, only the most discriminating will be able to allocate social responsibilities properly. Since it is the most populous entity, only the most enlightened will be able to make it harmonious. Only a sage is capable of fully meeting these three conditions. Thus, only a sage is capable of being a true king. A sage thoroughly perfects himself in the Way and is a person of complete refinement, so he can be the balance scale of judgment for the whole world. . . . The empire is the greatest of all, and only a sage can possess it."[28] He refutes the idea that Jie and Zhou did once "have world leadership" in the clarification: "In accord with popular opinion, persuaders offer the thesis: Jie and Zhou Xin truly possessed the empire; Tang and Wu usurped it and stole the throne. This is not so. If one means that by the normal rule Jie and Zhou Xin would have possessed formal title to the empire, then it would be so. If 'empire' refers to the fact that the world was with Jie and Zhou Xin, then it would not be so."[29] Xunzi, therefore, rejects the proposition that Jie and Zhou once possessed world leadership.

Xunzi differentiates titular and actual world leadership. He says: "In the descendants of sage kings who inherited the empire in later generations is vested the position of political power and authority and in them is contained spiritual authority over the empire. Although all this is so, when a descendant is untalented and does not hit the mark, the Hundred Clans, on the one hand, will loathe him, and the feudal lords, on the other, will desert him. Nearby those within his own borders will not be united; far away the feudal lords will not heed him. His commands are not carried out even within his own borders, and in the worst case the feudal lords first encroach on him, slicking off territory, then they openly attack and invade. Given such a situation, although he might not yet perished, I would say that he no longer really possessed the empire."[30] A current example of this differentiation is that of the Afghan government's titular governance from 2002 to 2006 of the country, when its real power was actually restricted to the capital city of Kabul. This example, although not of world leadership, is helpful to an understanding of what Xunzi means by You Tianxia (having the world).

Xunzi also distinguished between state power and world leadership. He believed it was possible to seize state power, but not world leadership, which is organically achieved: "Accordingly, although it is possible for a state to be taken by force, it is impossible for the whole empire to be taken by force."[31] In other words, it may be possible to seize the power to govern the state, but there is no possibility of seizing world leadership. A historical example is that of Nazi Germany's military and economic power surge in the early stages of World War II and its military expansion abroad, which enlarged Germany's presence in global affairs. But rather than achieving world leadership, Germany, to the contrary, became the enemy of many more states. This is a valid example of Xunzi's proposition that state governance and world leadership require different qualities of power.

Kingship Based on Political-Moral Principles

Xunzi believed that the power of true kingship is the highest in the world, and that it is based on kingship's ethical and moral principles. He says: "There is the ancient saying: They uniformly applied moral principles throughout the land, and in a single day it was plainly evident. Such were Tang and Wu. Tang began with Bo and King Wu with Hao, both territories only 100 li square, yet they unified the world, made the feudal lords their servants, so that wherever news of them penetrated there were none who did not submit to them and follow after them. This was due to no other cause than that they perfected moral principles. This is what is called 'moral principles being established and becoming a universal king.'"[32] A current example is that of the Vatican: It is smaller than Singapore, of far lower economic power, and has no army. But Singapore cannot match the Vatican's powerful influence on global affairs. This example endorses Xunzi's belief that respected ethical and moral principles are the basis for world leadership.

Xunzi believed True Kingship is defined by its moral principles. He says: "The Way of a True King is not like this. His humanity is the loftiest in the world, his justice the most admirable, and his majesty the most marvelous. His humanity being the loftiest is the cause of none in the world being estranged from him. His justice being the most admirable is the cause of none failing to esteem him. His majesty being the most marvelous is the cause of no one in the world presuming to oppose him, his majesty permitting no opposition coupled with a way that wins the allegiance of others is the cause of his triumphing without having to wage war, of his gaining his objectives without resort to force, and of the world submitting to him without his armies exerting themselves."[33]

Xunzi believed that for the "True King, . . . the empire is the greatest of all, and only a sage who thoroughly perfects himself in the Way and who can possess it."[34] In other words, the sage is morally and totally perfect, thus fit to possess the world. Finding a leader that meets Xunzi's high standard is unlikely. But the moral principles of the individual leaders to which Xunzi refers, as regards the role that moral leadership plays in the establishment of international norms and effecting change in the international system, become obvious when comparing President Franklin Roosevelt's deportment during World War II and that of President George W. Bush. Roosevelt's ideal of world peace promoted and helped to establish the United Nations after World War II, while Bush's Christian fundamentalist beliefs prevented U.S. compliance with international norms and led directly to the decline and fall of global nuclear nonproliferation.

Hegemony Based on Hard Power and Strategic Candor

Xunzi regarded hegemonic power as inferior to that of True Kingship. In his view, states willingly submit to kingship's world leadership, while the hegemon wins it through formidable power and strategic candor. In other words, the sage organically ascends to True Kingship, while hegemony is won by a ruler's hard efforts.

Hegemony is nonetheless hardly achieved. Although of a lower moral order than True Kingship, the hegemon must nonetheless display at least candor in its efforts toward supremacy. Xunzi thus describes the hegemon: "Although the moral force of their inner power had not yet reached perfection and although moral principles had not yet been fully attained, yet, in a general way, they displayed rational principles for ordering the world. Their punishments and rewards, their prohibitions and assents, were believed by the world. Their ministers and subjects fully and clearly knew that they were capable of exercising constraints over them. When the rules and edicts of government had been set forth, then although they might see opportunity for profit or danger of loss, they would not deceive their people. When agreements had already been settled, then although they might see the opportunity for profit or danger of loss, they would not deceive their allies. Since they behaved in this fashion, their army was strong, their cities well defended, and hostile countries stood in awe of them. Then the unity of their own countries was a brilliantly evident beacon, and their allies had faith in them. Although from despised and backward countries, their majestic authority shook the whole world. Such were the five lords-protector ... Thus, that Duke Huan of Qi, Duke Wen of Jin, King Zhuang of Chu, King Helu of Wu, and King Goujian of Yue, all of whom were of despised and backward countries, held majestic sway over the world and [that] their might held peril for all the Central States was due to no other cause than that they were in the main trustworthy. This is what is called 'established trust and becoming a lord-protector.'"[35]

But Xunzi believed that although strategic candor wins the trust of allies, hegemony cannot succeed without the backing of hard power. Without it, the state is not acknowledged as a lord-protector. Xunzi says of the hegemon: "The way of the lord-protector is quite different. He opens up wilderness lands to cultivation, fills the granaries and storehouses, and provides useful implements. On the basis of careful recruitment and assessment, he selects scholar-knights of genuine talent and ability and then gradually encourages them with commendations and rewards or strictly disciplines them with rebukes and punishments. He offers survival to those who face destruction; he provides for the continuation of those whose lineage faces extinction; he guards the weak and forbids aggressive behavior. Yet if he has no mind to annex territory of other states, the feudal lords will draw close to him. If he cultivates a way that treats them as friends and equals and strictly observes forms of respect in his dealing with them, the other feudal lords will be pleased with him.... Hence by making clear in his conduct that he has no intention to annex lands and by inspiring trust in his friendship and his sense of equality with them, if there happens to be no True King ruling the world, he will invariably triumph. Such is one who knows the way of a lord-protector."[36]

Might Based on Military Strength and Strategy

Xunzi regarded might as a type of power inferior to that of lord-protector (or hegemony), because it depends entirely on military strength and strategy.

Table 4.1. The Nature of the State's Power and Its Foundation

	Nature of the State's Power		
Power's Foundation	True Kingship	Hegemony (Lord-Protector)	Might (Powerful)
Mores and ethics	Strong	Fair, honest	None
Power and strength	Strong / weak, possible	Strong	Strong

As might is expanded by military aggression and occupation of other states' territory, a powerful state makes many enemies. This creates greater potential for arbitrary incursions that weaken the state's power status. Xunzi says: "When others defend the ramparts of their cities and send out knights to do battle with me and I overcome them through superior power, then the number of casualties among their population is necessarily very great. Where casualties have been extreme, the population is bound to hate me with vehemence. If the population detests me, then each day their desire to fight with me will grow. Where other defends the ramparts of their cities and sends out knights to do battle with me and I overcome them through superior power, then the number of casualties among my own people is certain to be very great. If the number of casualties among my own people has been great, they are certain to have a fierce dislike for me. If my own people hate me, then each day they will have less desire to fight for me; so as others grow more willing to fight, my own people will grow less willing to defend me. In this way, the cause of my former strength is reversed and produces weakness. Lands may be acquired, but their inhabitants will flee. As involvement become more numerous, accomplishments decrease. Although there is more to defend, the wherewithal to defend it diminishes. In this way the basis of my former greatness is reversed and is taken piece by piece from me."[37] Table 4.1 sets out the three different natures and bases of power according to Xunzi: True Kingship, hegemony, and might.

Xunzi's analysis, however, underestimates the importance of hard power to True Kingship. Although the Tang and Wu territories of Hao and Gao comprised only 100 li, other lords and kingdoms of the time were even smaller and weaker. States during the Spring-Autumn Period were much larger, and as Qi and Qin were at one time actually bigger than Chu, it was not always the most powerful country. Xunzi's mention of the state of Chu's superior size to that of Tang and Wu in his argument about the extent of importance to True Kingship of morality and just principles, therefore, is not entirely convincing. It is less so when recalling the end of World War I, when U.S. president Woodrow Wilson was internationally accorded high respect for his proposition of the just and moral "Fourteen Points" on which to establish a League of Nations. The United States' isolationist policy, however, precluded the Wilson administration's adequate participation in international affairs. This prevented the United States from achieving world leadership.

This example suggests that a leader's moral and ethical background is a necessary but insufficient condition for achieving world leadership. A state without big power, or that does not wholly participate in world affairs, cannot obtain world leadership solely on the grounds of high morals and ethics. Hard power is thus of equal importance to both True Kingship and hegemony. As Hans Morgenthau notes, the domestic ethics, mores, and laws limiting the struggle for domestic power do not function in international politics, as the ethical norms of domestic and international society differ.[38] But Xunzi, in his insistence that domestic social norms also apply to international society, obviously makes no such distinction.

Understanding International Order

Xunzi's understanding of the effect of ideas concurs with Constructivist theory, but his views on international conflict and stability are more aligned to Realist theory, whereas his ideas about preventing conflict and maintaining international order and stability are compatible with institutionalist theory.

Human Nature as the Root Cause of Conflict

Xunzi believed that human nature inclines naturally toward evil, and that competing for selfish interests is a natural social phenomenon that leads inevitably to violent conflict. He says: "Now, the nature of man is such that he is born with a love of profit. Following this nature will cause its aggressiveness and greedy tendencies to grow and courtesy and deference to disappear. . . . This being the case, when each person follows his inborn nature and indulges his natural inclinations, aggressiveness and greed are certain to develop. This is accomplished by violation of social class distinctions and throws the natural order into anarchy, resulting in a cruel tyranny."[39] It is interesting to note that the first of Hans Morgenthau's six principles of political realism is also that of human nature: "Political realism believes that politics, like society in general, is governed by objective laws that have their roots in human nature. . . . Human nature, in which the laws of politics have their roots, has not changed since the classical philosophies of China, India and Greece endeavored to discover these laws."[40]

Xunzi makes a specific analysis of human nature: "Mencius contended that 'since man can learn, his nature is good.' I say that this is not so. It shows that Mencius did not reach any real understanding of what man's inborn nature is and that he did not investigate the division between those things that are inborn in man and those that are acquired. As a general rule, 'inborn nature' embraces what is spontaneous from Nature, what cannot be learned, and what required no application to master. Ritual principles and moral duty are creations of the sage. They are things that people must study to be able to follow them and to which they must apply themselves before they can fulfill their precepts. What cannot be gained by learning and cannot be mastered by application yet is found in man is properly termed 'inborn nature.' What must be learned before a man can do it and what he must apply himself to before he can master it yet is found in man is properly called 'acquired nature.' This is precisely the distinction between 'inborn' and 'acquired' natures.'"[41]

Xunzi also believed that man's evil nature is the root cause of international conflict. Because humanity's desires have no limits and it is impossible to satisfy unlimited desires by material means, he says: "Men are born with desires which, if not satisfied, cannot be lead men to seek to satisfy them. If in seeking to satisfy their desires men observe no measure and apportion things without limits, then it would be impossible for them not to contend over the means to satisfy their desire. Such contention leads to disorder. Disorder leads to poverty."[42]

The Constraining Function of Social Norms

Xunzi did not believe that increasing social wealth resolves the conflicts arising from human competitiveness. He defines human beings' desires as a natural emotive reaction: "Inborn nature is the consequence of Heaven. Emotions are the substance of that nature. Desires are the resources of nature. Seeking what is desired is the responses of the emotions."[43] Xunzi, based on this reasoning, believed that strengthening the ability to reason constrains desire and therefore avoids social disorder. He says: "What men desire most is life, and what they hate most is death. Be that as it may, men sometimes pursue life and end up with death. It is not that they do not really desire life and rather desire death; it is that it proved impossible to continue living and it was possible to die. Thus, when desires run to excess, actions do not reach that point because the mind stops them. If what the mind permits coincides with reason, then although the desires are not strong enough the mind has ordered them to do so. If what the mind permits conflicts with what is reasonable, then although the desire[s] be few, how could it stop at disorder! Thus, order and disorder lie in what the mind permits and not with the desires that belong to our essential natures. Although you claim to have succeeded in finding the cause of order and disorder, if you do not seek it where it lies but instead seek it where it does not lie, then you will miss the truth."[44]

Xunzi is thus convinced that strengthening mental reasoning is a way of establishing social norms, and particularly ritual principles. He makes a point of discussing the content of ritual: "Ritual principles are the guiding ropes that pull the government. Where the exercise of government does not make use of ritual principles, the government will not succeed. . . . The relationship of ritual principles to the correct governance of the nation is like that of suspended balance and steelyard to the determination of weight or that of the darkened marking line to straightness. Thus, a man without ritual will not live, an undertaking without ritual will not succeed, and a nation without ritual will not be tranquil."[45] He also says: "Now, since human nature is evil, it must await the instructions of a teacher and the model before it can be put aright, and it must obtain ritual principles and a sense of moral right before it can become orderly. Nowadays, since men lack both teacher and model, they are prejudiced, wicked, and not upright. Since they lack ritual principles and precepts of moral duty, they are perverse, rebellious, and disorderly."[46]

Xunzi explains, from a supply-demand balance perspective, how social norms constrain a state's behavior, avoid violent conflicts and maintain international order. He believed that norms make human desires reasonable and so help to achieve satisfaction. In other words, that they achieve the balance between decreased human desires and increased satisfaction. He says: "The Ancient Kings abhorred such disorder; so they established the regulations contained within ritual and moral principles in order to apportion things, to nurture the desire of men, and to supply the means for their satisfaction . . . . In this way the two of them, desires and goods, sustained each other over the course of time. This is the origin of ritual principles."[47] His ideas regarding norms as a means of preventing violent conflict between states shares certain common assumptions with modern institutionalism;

both hold that certain norms exist in the human mind that in some way control and constrain the temptation to pursue individual self-interest. Robert Keohane and Joseph Nye say: "All these regimes were designed to resolve common problems in which the uncontrolled pursuit of individual self-interest by some governments could adversely affect the national interest of all the rest."[48] "Over time, governments develop reputations for compliance, not just to the letter of law but to the spirit as well. These reputations constitute one of their most important assets."[49]

The Hierarchical Foundation of Social Norms

Xunzi believed that social norms enact two functions in their prevention of state conflicts. The first, as discussed above, is that of achieving balance between temptation and satisfaction; the second is the design of a social hierarchy within which human behavior is accordingly regulated, thus preventing conflict. He says: "It is of the inborn nature of human beings that it is impossible for them not to form societies. If they form a society in which there are no class divisions, strife will develop. If there is strife, then there will be social disorder; if there is social disorder, there will be hardship for all. Hence, a situation in which there are no class divisions is the greatest affliction mankind can have. A situation in which there are class divisions is the most basic benefit under Heaven. And it is the lord of men who is the indispensable element wherewith to 'arrange the scale' of the classes of men."[50] He also says, in his explanation of how social norms prevent social chaos or disorder: "The Ancient Kings abhorred such disorder. Thus, they instituted regulations, ritual practices, and moral principles in order to create proper social and class divisions. They ordered that there be sufficient gradations of wealth and eminence of station to bring everyone under supervision. This is the fundamental principle by which to nurture the empire."[51]

Xunzi believed, therefore, that international violent conflict is inevitable unless there is a social hierarchy in place that constrains human temptation to pursue material interests. He says: "Two men of equal eminence cannot attend each other; two men of the same low status cannot commend each other—such is the norm of Heaven. When power and positions are equally distributed and likes and dislikes are identical, and material goods are inadequate to satisfy all, there is certain to be contention. Such contention is bound to produce civil disorder, and this disorder will result in poverty."[52]

Xunzi's beliefs regarding the benefits to international norms of social hierarchy are based on his observations of the Western Zhou Dynasty's Five

Figure 4.5. Evil Human Nature, Social Hierarchy, and Their Influence on International Order

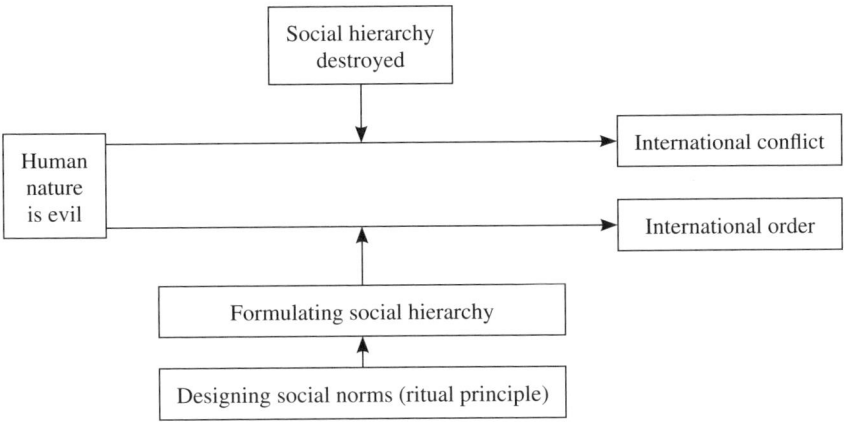

Ordinance System.⁵³ He says that the Tang and the Wu decided on different ordinances because they "observed the qualities inherent in the land forms and regulated with ordinances the vessels and implements. They judged the various distances and so differentiated grades of tribute and offerings."⁵⁴ In other words, the king decided upon a social hierarchy, according to distance and contribution, whereby no one was exactly the same. The United Nations has a similarly hierarchical membership, for example, in that of its Security Council, which has permanent, nonpermanent, and ordinary members. The International Monetary Fund also allots voting powers according to the extent of shares and contributions of each member. The World Trade Organization applies different tax and tariff levels according to a state's category of national development. All provide examples of the validity of Xunzi's belief in hierarchical order as the basis for effective international norms. Figure 4.5 portrays his definition of the logical relationships among human nature, social hierarchy, social norms, and international order.

Xunzi describes the Five Ordinance System thus: "Accordingly, all states of Xia Chinese have identical obligations for service to the king and have identical standard of conduct. The countries of the Man, Yi, Rong, and Di barbarians perform the same obligatory services to the king, but the regulations governing them are not the same. Those who are enforced within [the royal domain] do royal service. Those who are enforced without [the royal domain] do feudal service. Those who are in the feudal marches zone do guest service. The Man and Yi nations do service according to treaty obligations. The Rong and Yi do irregular service. Those who do royal service provide offerings for the sacrifices of thanks; those who do feudal service provide for the drinking ceremonies; those who do service according to treaty present tribute offerings; and those who do irregular service come to pay their respects at the succession of the new king. This is just what is meant by they observed the qualities inherent in the land forms and regulated with ordinances the vessels and implements; they judged the various distances and so differentiated grades of tributes and offerings—for such is the perfection of true kingship."[55] Figure 4.6 shows the Five Ordinance System.

Figure 4.6. The Five Ordinance System

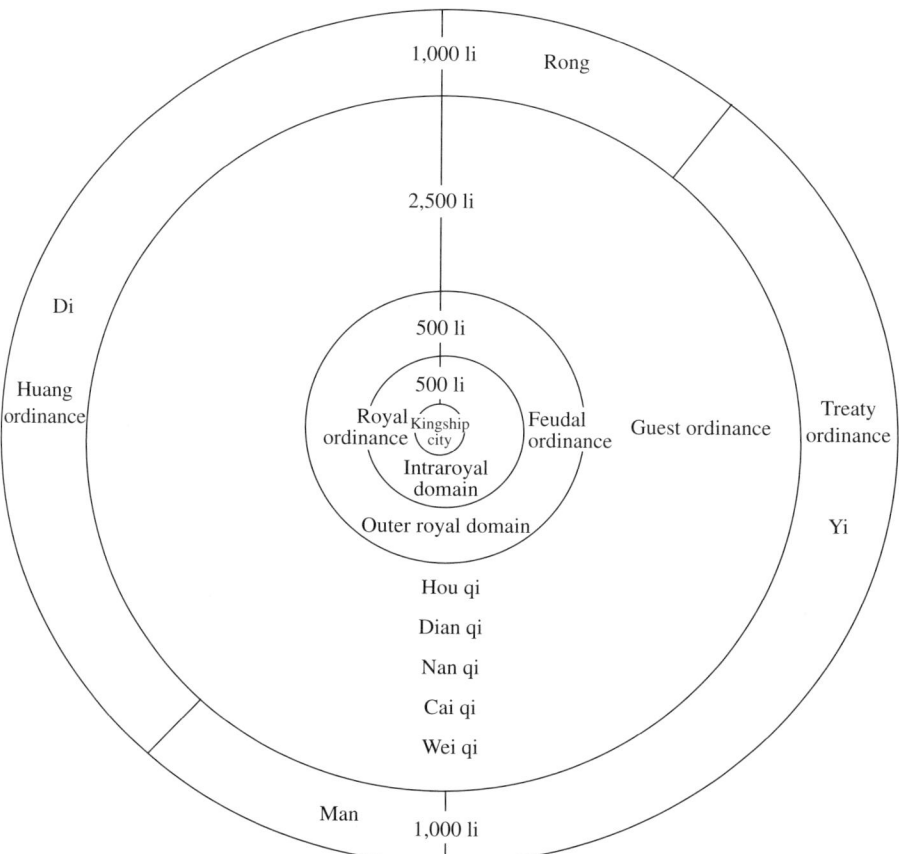

Xunzi's views on the causes of war are basically consistent with Realist theory, that is, that international war is caused by anarchy in social systems. Xunzi, however, does not expand on the concept that a hierarchical system inhibits international conflict, failing to take into account that changes in power relationships also result in changed relations within the social hierarchy. If states whose power relationships change do not accordingly adjust their perceptions of one another, as regards relative power status, war remains possible. Xunzi's analysis does not discuss how the hierarchical order can be adjusted to deal with changes in the power relationship among states. The reason for this is his emphasis on internal factor determination; he considers only how state policies influence a state's power relationship, not how changes in power relationship influence a state's behavior.

Inspirations Offered by Xunzi's Thoughts on China's Rising Strategy

The purpose of my discussion of Xunzi's thoughts on international politics is not only to present the views of an ancient thinker on international relations but, more important, to offer enlightenment on China's rising strategy.

THE OBJECTIVE OF THE RISING STRATEGY

Xunzi believed that true kingship is a higher form of world leadership than hegemony, because Tianxia (Heaven, or the world) is attained through voluntary submission, rather than force. This understanding prompts the thought: What kind of state should China rise to be? A superpower could be either a hegemon or a true kingship. The different natures of the two are expressed not just in their power differential but also in their moral and ethical level. If China wants, in contrast to the contemporary leadership role enacted by the United States, to be a "True Kingship" state, its strategic goal must, in addition to narrowing the power gap between China and the United States, be to present to the world a better social role model.

International society pays ever greater attention to the kind of superpower China might become. It obviously does not want China to become another Nazi Germany or Imperial Japan. Yet it also would not want China to become another United States, for this would lead to one of two things: a world dominated by two hegemonic powers, which would trigger resumption of the Cold War; or China's simply replacing the United States and the world order remaining the same. International society wants neither scenario. If China becomes a True Kingship country—a superstate grounded in high morals and ethics—it should bring about a world order that would be more peaceful and secure than that of today. True Kingship may not be the perfect international system but, compared with the current hegemonic system, would be one imbued with greater cooperation and security. To become a superstate of a True Kingship nature, China must make itself a role model state.

Academia has proposed two competing social models: the "Beijing Consensus" and the "Washington Consensus." If China could build a state deemed worthy of duplication by others, it would organically become a True Kingship state. Beijing has since 1978, when China began implementing the reform and opening policy, focused on economic construction. Increasing material wealth strengthens China's power position, but does not gain it respect from the world. This is because a superstate that perceives national wealth as its highest interest is generally a harbinger of disaster, and not blessing, to other countries. The Chinese government in September 2005 proposed the new foreign policy of "a harmonious world," whose emphasis is on building friendly relations as matter of key foreign policy objective.[56] Yet the August 2006 Central Foreign Affairs Meeting Report again specified: "Foreign affairs must center on economic construction."[57] Two months later, the Sixth Plenum of the Chinese Communist Party Sixteenth Congress reconfirmed construction of a harmonious society as the long-term task of socialism, raising social equality and justice as the basic conditions for social harmony.[58] The level of inconsistency in these propositions implies that the Chinese government gives building a harmonious society priority over maximizing national wealth. Political inertia, as a result of long-term emphasis on economic construction, however, has impeded the government in its conscious formulation of this objective within its rising strategy to build a True Kingship state.

THE POWER BASIS FOR THE RISING STRATEGY

The Chinese government has already established the strategic principle of the country's peaceful development path,[59] but whether its main purpose is to increase material power or strengthen operational power (political power) remains unclear. Economic development as the fundamental means of strengthening comprehensive national power is the prevailing idea in China today. But Xunzi's belief that political power is the basis on which hard power considers comprehensive national power brings to mind China's experience, since 1949, of political change followed by strengthened economic development and military power. The Chinese Communist Party established a completely new political system in 1949, which from 1949 to 1956, greatly expanded China's comprehensive national power. Implementation of the reform and opening policy in 1978 then created almost thirty years of rapid economic growth, and the 2002 policy of parallel development of national defense and economic construction rapidly strengthened China's defense capability.[60] Ill-advised government policies, such as during the Great Leap Forward and the Cultural Revolution, conversely, caused a tremendous weakening in national economic and military power.

Xunzi's concept of *yi* (义, moral and ethical principles) is different from the contemporary concept of "soft power," because soft power does not distinguish between cultural and political power, Zi's *yi* concept regards a ruler/leader's ideas as political power, and as such constituting the element of comprehensive power. Moreover, if the soft power formula is divided into cultural and political power, it is obviously the latter of the two that is crucial to the functioning of other power elements. For example, America's military, economic, and cultural power grew steadily from 2003 to 2006, but its political mobilization, or political power, seriously weakened after the George W. Bush administration's illegal launch of the Iraq War. During these three years, the comprehensive national power of the United States displayed a shrinking trend and its international status declined. Both this example and that of the disintegration of the former Soviet Union imply that political power is operational, while military, economic, and cultural power are material; the latter cannot function properly without the former. Figure 4.7 shows the relationships among various elements of power.

It is useful to take the elements portrayed in figure 4.7 and convert them to variables, whereby *CP* means comprehensive national power, *M* means military power, *E* means economic power, *C* means cultural power, and

Figure 4.7. Relations among Concepts of Power Elements

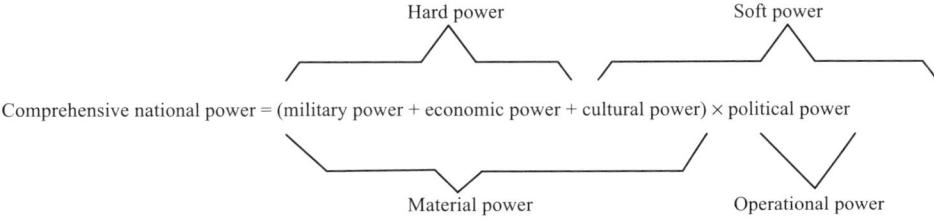

P means political power. Figure 4.7 thus enables a simplified comprehensive national power formula:

$$CP = (M + E + C) * P$$

This formula implies, on the assumption that China's current military, economic, and cultural power remains constant, that if China greatly increases its political power, as regards strengthening strategic trust and honesty, it stands to dramatically increase its comprehensive power and international status. Taking the 2006 China-Africa Forum as an example, although the total amount of aid from China to African countries in the coming three years does not surpass that of the European Union and the United States, the African reaction to Chinese aid is nevertheless much warmer and stronger than to EU and U.S. aid. The Chinese aid program, unlike that of the EU and the United States, carries no political preconditions. The honesty and trust reflected in China's aid program, therefore, greatly strengthens the political impact of its economic assistance. This implies that although the correct strategy for strengthening China's soft power includes both political and cultural power, its central focus should be on political power.

THE TACTICS OF THE RISING STRATEGY

If China's rising strategy is indeed based on strengthening political power, then the approaches to the strategy popularly proposed by Chinese academics are clearly inappropriate. The idea, for example, of economic construction as the central task makes materialism the dominant ideology in Chinese society, and also influences discussions of "strategies for the rise of great powers." Discussions within China's academia outline four main strategies: reform strategy (multipolarity or resistance), avoidance strategy (independence or isolationism), entry strategy (free-rider or bandwagon) and follow strategy (multilateral cooperation). All, other than the reform strategy, are logically based on the idea of increasing China's economic wealth.

Xunzi proposes, in contrast, a great power, talented-people-oriented strategy. He sees change in international politics as the result of leaders' ideas, whose main focus is on selecting talent. Stalin said in 1935: "Cadres decide everything." In 1938, Mao Zedong also stated: "When the political line is decided, cadres are the determining factor."[61] These views concur with Xunzi's ideas. The human resource strategy in China is still mainly directed at enterprise development, and not viewed on the same level as strategies designed specifically for China's rise. Talent is still regarded in terms of technical workers, rather than politicians or high-ranking officials. Xunzi's idea of talented people gives inspiration in this respect, in that it demonstrates that the strategy of recruiting talented people is beneficial to more than just enterprise development, having since ancient times been used to effect the rise of great powers. The most needed people in this case are not technical workers but politicians and government officials with institutional innovation ideas. Innovative strength and capability in institutions, therefore, provides the fundamental impetus for the rise of a great power.

If the rise of great powers two thousand years ago during the agrarian period depended on talented people, then it is also the main requirement for economic development in today's information economy era. It can thus be assumed that talented people are still the determining factor in the rise of a great power. Xunzi's idea of talent is that of competent individuals of high moral fiber. Many such are available; the key is whether rulers select them. This idea raises two aspects of the human resource strategy for the rise of great powers. The first is a high level of openness, as regards the selection of people from all over the world, based on high competence and moral standards; this enhances a government's ability to make the right decisions. The administrations at work during the golden age of China's Tang Dynasty and India's Moslem states, for example, owed their competence and high quality to the talented foreign bureaucrats that the administrative authorities employed, according to historical records. It is estimated that 70 percent of the Indian Moslem states' bureaucracy comprised Persians and Afghans.[62] The United States' rise to its hegemonic position is also largely attributable to its absorption of foreign elites and talented peoples. The second aspect of the human resource strategy is that of the need for rapid adjustment and corrective action to remove unqualified officials and reduce the probabilities of decisionmaking errors. All politicians and officials potentially stand to lose the ability to make the right decisions, for reasons of bribery and corruption, out-of-date knowledge, reduced thinking capacity, or poor health. Establishing a system that removes and replaces officials provides more opportunities for talented people, reduces decisionmaking errors, and, in the end, strengthens political power.

Fair and Equitable International Norms

After the signing in 1648 of the Westphalia Treaty, the equality of state sovereignty became a universal international norm. It is one in direct opposition to Xunzi's belief that a differentiated, hierarchical norm helps prevent conflict between states. Certain countries worry that a rising China might revive the old East Asian tributary system. But any such renewal would inevitably lessen China's international political mobilization. Objectively, however, big and small states are not equal in power. Establishing a hierarchical norm, therefore, could help maintain a balance of power and responsibility, thereby reducing international conflict and strengthening cooperative relationships.

"Hierarchy" is a negative term in modern political language, synonymous with inequality. Because, however, the power status between states objectively differs, only a normative hierarchical order maintains fairness. The principle of absolute equality actually promotes unfairness. In a boxing match, for example, boxers are classed according to weight—a kind of normative hierarchical order intended to uphold fair play. Without differentiated weight ranking, a fair match is obviously impossible. As regards international norms, differentiation depends on the concerned state's position in international society, according to Xunzi's explanation of the Five Ordinance System. The closer a state's power status to the world center, the more closely it should follow strictly designed international norms. International norms applied to peripheral states, conversely, should be more relaxed and flexible. This is an unequal but fair international norm. In the free trade area "10+1" (China and the ten members of the Association of Southeast Asian Nations, ASEAN), for example, China will be the first to levy zero tariffs on the agricultural products it imports from the ASEAN countries. This unequal regulation will enhance 10+1 development. Japan, in its pursuit of economic cooperation with the ASEAN countries, however, demands parallel tariff levels, which impedes the ASEAN's development.

Historically, neither hierarchical orders nor those based on equal sovereignty have prevented large-scale international wars. But when comparing eras of modern IR history, interstate peace has been more widespread in areas in where a hierarchical system, rather than one based on equal sovereignty, is in place. During the Cold War era, for example, equal status between the United States and the Soviet Union forced them to launch proxy wars, but American and Soviet special status, respectively, within NATO and the Warsaw Pact enabled them to prevent military conflict between the member states of these two organizations. A rising China will inevitably influence the international security system. What kind of international norm should China propose to maintain international peace? Protecting international peace requires the level of power possessed only by a superpower. China should propose, according to Xunzi's understanding, a normative hierarchical order that helps prevent conflict, whereby different countries bear different international security responsibilities, and promote a system wherein different countries abide by different security norms. For example, big and small states in international peace-keeping missions have different security responsibilities and possess different levels of authority; and, as regards nuclear nonproliferation, nuclear states stringently abide by their nonproliferation responsibilities while providing nuclear security guarantees to nonnuclear states.

This author believes that Xunzi's ideas on statecraft can be summed up in one of his main statements: "One who uses the state to establish justice will be king; one who establishes trust will be a lord-protector; and one who establishes a record of expediency and opportunism will perish."[63] The inspiration that Xunzi's thoughts provide for formulating China's rising strategy, therefore, comprises the following points: If China bases itself upon political power and persistently pursues institutional innovation, then it will rise to become the world's leading state; if China balances the development of political, military, and economic power, then it will become a strong global power; if China takes economic construction as the central priority, then it will gradually become a medium-level developed country; if China takes political struggle as the guideline, then it will perish. Xunzi's ideas represent one school of thought on international politics among many expounded by various ancient Chinese thinkers. Exploration of his and other ancient's ideas and thoughts could be of help in both developing and constructing modern IR theory, and providing guidelines for reasonable strategies that promote China's rise. When exploring Xunzi's ideas and thoughts, however, it should be borne in mind that their reasoning and rationale include certain irrational elements that call for prudent judgment.

Notes

1. This chapter analyses Xunzi's thoughts solely from an international politics perspective; it has no intention of participating in the academic debate concerning historical and documentary studies of this ancient philosopher. In explaining Xunzi's ideas, the author of this chapter consulted Yang Liuqiao's *Xunzi guyi* [Interpretation of Xunzi];

Wang Tianhai's (edited and annotated) *Xunzi jiaoshi* [Correction and annotation of Xunzi's works]; Jian Nahua and Yang Hanqing's *Xunzi quanyi* [Interpretation of the complete works of Xunzi]; and Gao Changshan's *Xunzi* [Xunzi]. In the field of history, Wang Xianqian's *Xunzi jijie* [Collection and interpretation of Xunzi's works] is widely acknowledged as the seminal work for the study of Xunzi. All citations of Xunzi's works in this chapter, therefore, are from Shen Xiaohuan and Wang Xingxian's edited version. The article's English translations of Xunzi's works are from John Knoblock, *Xunzi: A Translation and Study of the Complete Works*, vols. 1–3 (Stanford, Calif.: Stanford University Press, 1990).

2. It should be noted that in Xunzi's works, *ba* is similar to the linguistically neutral "hegemony," which has no negative. The word "hegemony," therefore, is also used neutrally in this article, and does not imply external aggression or bullying of small countries.

3. Shen Xiaohuan and Wang Xingxian, eds., *Xunzi jijie* [Collection and interpretation of Xunzi's Work], book 11, "Of Kings and Lords-Protector," 202; Knoblock, *Xunzi*, vol. 2, 149.

4. Shen and Wang, *Xunzi jijie*, book 11, 209; Knoblock, *Xunzi*, vol. 2, 154.

5. Shen and Wang, *Xunzi jijie*, book 24, "On the Gentleman," 452–453; Knoblock, *Xunzi*, vol. III, 167.

6. Shen and Wang, *Xunzi jijie*, book 9, "On the Regulation of a King," 154; Knoblock, *Xunzi*, vol. 2, 98.

7. Alexander Wendt, *Social Theory of International Politics* (Cambridge: Cambridge University Press, 1999), 250.

8. Shen and Wang, *Xunzi jijie*, book 11, "207; Knoblock, *Xunzi*, vol. 2, 153.

9. Shen and Wang, *Xunzi jijie*, book 9, 171; Knoblock, *Xunzi*, vol. 2, 108.

10. Shen and Wang, *Xunzi jijie*, book 18, "Rectifying Theses," 324; Knoblock, *Xunzi*, vol. 3, 35.

11. Yan Xuetong, *Zhongguo guojia liyi fenxi* [Analysis of China's National Interest] (Tianjin: Tianjin renmin chubanshe, 1997), 4–6.

12. Shen and Wang, *Xunzi jijie*, book 18, 323; Knoblock, *Xunzi*, vol. 3, 34.

13. Shen and Wang, *Xunzi jijie*, book 11, 207; Knoblock, *Xunzi*, vol. 2, 153.

14. Shen and Wang, *Xunzi jijie*, book 7, "On Confucius," 109; Knoblock, *Xunzi*, vol. 2, 59.

15. Shen and Wang, *Xunzi jijie*, book 10, "On Enriching the State," 194–95; Knoblock, *Xunzi*, vol. 2, 134–35.

16. Shen and Wang, *Xunzi jijie*, book 9, 153–54; Knoblock, *Xunzi*, vol. 2, 98.

17. Shen and Wang, *Xunzi jijie*, book 10, 198; Knoblock, *Xunzi*, vol. 2, 136–37.

18. Shen and Wang, *Xunzi jijie*, book 10, 199–201; Knoblock, *Xunzi*, vol. 2, 137–38.

19. Lu Yang, "Feizhou nasheme zhengjiu ziji?" [How can Africa save itself?], http://news.xinhuanet.com/world/2005-07/22/content_3252643.htm.

20. Shen and Wang, *Xunzi jijie*, book 9, 173–74; Knoblock, *Xunzi*, vol. 2, 111.

21. Shen and Wang, *Xunzi jijie*, book 10, 199; Knoblock, *Xunzi*, vol. 2, 37.

22. Shen and Wang, *Xunzi jijie*, book 16, "Debate on the Principles of Warfare," 290; Knoblock, *Xunzi*, vol. 2, 234.

23. Shen and Wang, *Xunzi jijie*, book 13, "On the Way of Ministers," 247–48; Knoblock, *Xunzi*, vol. 2, 197–98.

24. Shen and Wang, *Xunzi jijie*, book 12, On the Way of a Lord," 240; Knoblock, *Xunzi*, vol. 2, 185.

25. Shen and Wang, *Xunzi jijie*, book 12, 242; Knoblock, *Xunzi*, vol. 2, 187.
26. Shen and Wang, *Xunzi jijie*, book 11, 216; Knoblock, *Xunzi*, vol. 2, 159–60.
27. Shen and Wang, *Xunzi jijie*, book 11, 218; Knoblock, *Xunzi*, vol. 2, 161.
28. Shen and Wang, *Xunzi jijie*, book 18, 324–26; Knoblock, *Xunzi*, vol. 3, 35–36.
29. Shen and Wang, *Xunzi jijie*, book 18, 322–323; Knoblock, *Xunzi*, vol. 3, 34.
30. Shen and Wang, *Xunzi jijie*, book 18, 323; Knoblock, *Xunzi*, vol. 3, 36.
31. Shen and Wang, *Xunzi jijie*, book 18, 326; Knoblock, *Xunzi*, vol. 3, 36.
32. Shen and Wang, *Xunzi jijie*, book 11, 204; Knoblock, *Xunzi*, vol. 2, 151.
33. Shen and Wang, *Xunzi jijie*, book 9, 158; Knoblock, *Xunzi*, vol. 2, 100.
34. Shen and Wang, *Xunzi jijie*, book 18, 325; Knoblock, *Xunzi*, vol. 3, 36.
35. Shen and Wang, *Xunzi jijie*, book 11, 204–5; Knoblock, *Xunzi*, vol. 2, 151–52.
36. Shen and Wang, *Xunzi jijie*, book 9, 156–57; Knoblock, *Xunzi*, vol. 2, 99–100.
37. Shen and Wang, *Xunzi jijie*, Book 9, 154–55; Knoblock, *Xunzi*, vol. II, 98–99.
38. Hans J. Morgenthau, *Politics among Nations: The Struggle for Power and Peace* (New York: Alfred A. Knopf, 2005), 247–49.
39. Shen and Wang, *Xunzi jijie*, book 23, "Man's Nature Is Evil," 434–35; Knoblock, *Xunzi*, vol. 3, 151.
40. Morgenthau, *Politics among Nations*, 4.
41. Shen and Wang, *Xunzi jijie*, book 23, 435–36; Knoblock, *Xunzi*, vol. 3, 152.
42. Shen and Wang, *Xunzi jijie*, book 19, "Discourse on Ritual Principles," 346; Knoblock, *Xunzi*, vol. 3, 55.
43. Shen and Wang, *Xunzi jijie*, book 22, "On the Correct Use of Names," 428; Knoblock, *Xunzi*, vol. 3, 136.
44. Shen and Wang, *Xunzi jijie*, book 22, 428; Knoblock, *Xunzi*, vol. 3, 135.
45. Shen and Wang, *Xunzi jijie*, book 27, "The Great Compendium," 492, 495; Knoblock, *Xunzi*, vol. 3, 213, 217.
46. Shen and Wang, *Xunzi jijie*, book 23, 435; Knoblock, *Xunzi*, vol. 3, 74.
47. Shen and Wang, *Xunzi jijie*, book 19, 346; Knoblock, *Xunzi*, vol. 3, 55.
48. Robert O. Keohane and Joseph S. Nye, *Power and Interdependence* (New York: Longman, 2001), 294.
49. Ibid., 295.
50. Shen and Wang, *Xunzi jijie*, book 10, 179; Knoblock, *Xunzi*, vol. 2, 123.
51. Shen and Wang, *Xunzi jijie*, book 9, 152; Knoblock, *Xunzi*, vol. 2, 96.
52. Shen and Wang, *Xunzi jijie*, book 9, 152; Knoblock, *Xunzi*, vol. 2, 96.
53. The Five Ordinances System, according to Shen and Wang's *Xunzi jijie*, was an international system with the Zhou King's kingship city at the center and a broad core and periphery. The *dian* ordinance, which occupied the 500 li surrounding the kingship city, was for planting various grains and acted as the King's food supplier. The surrounding 500 li surrounding was the *hou* ordinance, which mainly provided the king with labor and territorial protection. The 2,500 li surrounding that was the *bin* ordinance, which comprised the vassal states of which China consisted. This area was subdivided into five 500-li *qi*—in the order *hou qi*, *dian qi*, *nan qi*, *ai qi*, and *wei qi*—that were mostly responsible for cultural education and military support. The next areas contained the *yao* ordinance and the *huang* ordinance, each of 1,000 li, but their distance from the center is uncertain. The *yao* ordinance was further divided into the *man* and *yi* ordinances, each of 500 li, of similar political order but reduced taxation. The *huang* ordinance was further divided into the *zhen* ordinance and *fan* ordinance, each

also covering 500 li, which had simple political systems and norms, and where population mobility was high. There are, however, various other academic explanations of the five ordinances system. See Ye Zicheng, *Chunqiu shiqi de Zhongguo waijao sixiang* [Chinese ideas and thoughts of diplomacy during the spring–autumn period] (Hong Kong: Hong Kong shehui kexue chubanshe, 2003), 28.

54. Shen and Wang, *Xunzi jijie*, book 18, 329; Knoblock, *Xunzi*, vol. 3, 38.

55. Shen and Wang, *Xunzi jijie*, book 18, 329–30; Knoblock, *Xunzi*, vol. 3, 38–39.

56. Hu Jintao, "Nuli jianshe chijiu heping gongtong fanrong de hexie shijie" [Making an effort to build a sustainable, peaceful, and united prosperous harmonious world, speech at the United Nations sixtieth-year celebration], *Renmin Ribao* (*People's Daily*), September 16, 2006.

57. "Zhongyang waishi gongzuo huiyi zai jing juxing" [Central foreign affairs meeting held in Beijing], *Renmin Ribao*, August 24, 2006.

58. "Zhonggong zhongyang guanyu goujian shehui zhuyi hexie shehui ruogan zhongda wenti de jueding" [Chinese Communist Party Central Committee's decision on construction of socialist harmonious society], *Renmin Ribao*, October 19, 2006.

59. Hu, "Nuli jianshe chijiu heping gongtong fanrong de hexie shijie."

60. Zhu Rongji, "*Zhengfu gongzuo baogao*" [Government report], in *Shiliu da yilai zhongyao wenxian xuanbian* [Selection of important documents since CCP 16th Congress] (Beijing: Zhongyang wenxian chubanshe, 2005), 188.

61. Mao Zedong, *Mao Zedong xuanji* [Selected works of Mao Zedong] (Beijing: Renmin chubanshe, 1991), 526, 535.

62. L. S. Stavrianos, *The World since 1500: A Global History* (London: Prentice Hall International, 1966), 36–37.

63. Shen and Wang, *Xunzi jijie*, book 11, 202; Knoblock, *Xunzi*, vol. 2, 150.

Part II

Mixing Past, Present, and Future

Chapter 5

Tianxia, Empire, and the World: Chinese Visions of World Order for the Twenty-First Century

William A. Callahan

As the chapters in part I of this book have shown, there is increasing interest in Chinese thought, both as an alternative to Eurocentric international relations (IR), and because the People's Republic of China (PRC) as an emerging power will soon have the institutional might to promote its view of the world. Although prominent Western experts have concluded that China is a status quo power that is unlikely to challenge the international system,[1] the preceding three chapters clearly demonstrate how an idealized version of China's imperial past is inspiring its scholars' and policymakers' plans for its future—and the world's future. Rather than simply provide suitably Chinese parallels to "international," "security," or other mainstream international relations concepts, these and other public intellectuals in Greater China have been looking to ancient concepts like "Tianxia" (天下)

This chapter is a revised and extended version of "Chinese Visions of World Order: Post-Hegemonic or a New Hegemony?" *International Studies Review* 10 (2008): 749–61. For funding fieldwork in China, I would like to thank the British Inter-University China Centre (RES-580-28-0008), funded by the Economic and Social Research Council; the University of Manchester's Centre for Chinese Studies; the British Academy / Chinese Academy Social Sciences visiting fellowship (2007); and the Universities China Committee in London (2009). I received helpful comments at the International Studies Association's 2007 symposium on responsible scholarship, and from Elena Barabantseva, David Blaney, Sumalee Bumroongsook, Paul A. Cohen, Dan Xingwu, Victoria Tin-bor Hui, Li Shaojun, Mustapha Kamal Pasha, Chih-yu Shih, J. Ann Tickner, Andrei P. Tsygankov, and Wang Yizhou.

to understand Chinese visions of world order. As chapter 1 argues, understanding this intellectual debate is important because public intellectuals have a growing voice in Beijing's foreign policy; current IR debates thus can give us a sense of the parameters of the self/other relations within which new official policies (e.g., "harmonious world") are formulated, implemented, defended—and rejected.

Tianxia is interesting both because it was key to the governance and self-understanding of more than two millennia of Chinese empire, and also because discussion of Tianxia is becoming popular again in the twenty-first century as a Chinese model of world order that is universally valid—but in ways that go against China's official policy of peacefully rising within the international system. On the one hand, the premier historian of overseas Chinese, Wang Gungwu, chose "Tianxia and Empire" as the topic for his inaugural Tsai Lecture at Harvard in 2006.[2] On the other, in April 2005 a prominent philosopher at the Chinese Academy of Social Sciences, Zhao Tingyang, published *Tianxia tixi: Shijie zhidu zhexue daolun* (The Tianxia system: A philosophy for the world institution) to describe a Chinese model of world order that is universally valid.[3] *Tianxia tixi* became a best seller in China because it caught a wave of interest in Chinese-style solutions to world problems, and especially an interest in how the traditional concept of Tianxia combines the seemingly contradictory discourses of nationalism and cosmopolitanism.

Although Chinese scholars have been employing traditional concepts—including Tianxia—to explain current domestic and foreign policies for more than a decade,[4] Zhao's plan for a Chinese-inspired world utopia provides an exemplary case of the workings of normative policymaking because it dramatically shifted these discussions from the margins to the mainstream.[5] The popularity of Zhao's very singular understanding of Tianxia thus powerfully demonstrates a broader trend that will outlive the considerable impact of his particular book: "Chinese-style IR" has become a topic of conversation not just among public intellectuals and IR scholars but also in the much broader arenas of popular culture and state policy as a sort of patriotic cosmopolitanism.

In this way, the Tianxia system is the current answer to the perennial question that transfixes intellectuals and policy elites in Beijing: "What is China's proper role in the world?" Many Western scholars and policymakers likewise increasingly are asking "What does China want?"[6] Hence, if the predictions about China overtaking the United States to become the dominant superpower in the next few decades are true,[7] it is important to see how China will order the world.

To examine China's alternative worldview, I first consider Zhao's discussion of how the all-inclusive Tianxia system would solve the world's problems through a world institution that embraces difference according to a "magnanimous" (大度) social grammar. Because Zhao is looking to the positive aspects of Chinese thought, the chapter's first section summarizes his argument. This is more difficult than it may appear. *Tianxia tixi* contains three long chapters that utilize many of the same arguments and examples in sometimes contradictory ways. In a way, this book was not written as a single narrative but as a collection of Zhao's thoughts about Tianxia. Because Zhao's key English-language essay is a chapter in this book,[8] it is helpful to describe the Chinese-language materials because they inform the broader debate over foreign policy in Greater China.[9]

The second section of this chapter examines some of the philosophical and historical problems posed by this romantic understanding of Tianxia, in particular how its approach to an ethical world order encourages a "conversion" of difference, if not a conquest of it. This is in line with popular understandings of Chinese culture and ethnicity that take for granted that China's national minorities need to be assimilated into Han civilization, while at the same time overseas Chinese must resist assimilation to their host countries' cultures.[10] The chapter finds that Tianxia's most important impact is not on the world stage but in China's domestic politics. The power of Tianxia comes less from the sophistication of its theoretical argument than from its strategic placement in China's discursive networks of power. The chapter examines how Tianxia recently has been redeployed by both China's state intellectuals and public intellectuals among the Chinese diaspora in ways that blur the conceptual boundaries between empire and globalism, and hierarchy and cosmopolitanism. The chapter concludes that rather than guide us towards a posthegemonic world order, Tianxia presents a new hegemony that reproduces China's hierarchical empire for the twenty-first century. This chapter thus has two objectives: (1) to critically describe a non-Western worldview as a model of world order, and (2) to examine how ideas get put into play in making China's foreign policy.

The Tianxia System

The problem in international politics today, according to Zhao, is not "failed states" like Afghanistan but a "failed world." Indeed, he declares that our world is actually a "nonworld."[11] Here Zhao is appealing to Chinese philosophy's guiding normative logic: Though "world" *should* refer to a peaceful order, what we have is a disordered world of chaos. And whereas many would see world disorder as a political or economic problem (that would be solved by a better political or economic system), Zhao argues that world chaos is a conceptual problem: "To order the world we need to first create new world concepts which will lead to new world structures."[12] Because he feels that Western concepts (especially those from the Westphalia system) have gotten us into this mess, he boldly states that only the Chinese concept of Tianxia—literally translated as "All-under-Heaven"—can do the conceptual work that is necessary for world order.

Throughout Zhao's discussion, he plays with the definition of this ancient and often vague term, sometimes reading Tianxia as "the World," and other times understanding it as "Empire." Either way, Tianxia is presented as a legitimate world order that is very different from Western imperialism. This new way of thinking of global problems on a global scale presents a utopia that orders political relations in quite different ways from popular understandings of globalization and cosmopolitanism; rather than looking to hybridity or "glocalization"—a combination of globalization and localication (as do chapters 6, 7, and 8 in this book)—Zhao's Tianxia is a unified, single-ordered system.[13] He thus offers Tianxia as a utopia that sets the analytical and institutional framework necessary for solving the world's problems. In other worlds, Tianxia is presented as a utopia that has practical applications.

Tianxia: Three Interwoven Meanings

In its most basic sense, Tianxia is a geographical term. Literally speaking, *tian* (天) is the heavens, the sky, and what is on top, whereas *xia* (下) is an indexical term meaning below, lower, inferior.[14] "Tianxia" thus refers to everything below the sky, and thus is commonly used in classical texts to refer to "the Earth" and "the (Chinese) world."

But Zhao argues that in addition to this material and geographical sense, Tianxia also contains two other important meanings that are not just descriptive but normative: (1) Tianxia as "all the people," the people's heart (*minxin*, 民心), the people's will; and (2) Tianxia as the "world institution."[15] Each of these three meanings of Tianxia—geographical, psychological, and institutional—is necessary and interdependent in Zhao's normative world. Here he is elaborating on Chinese thought—Tianxia is actually *not* the focus of much contemporary or historical debate in Chinese philosophy—to engage with a much wider audience to tackle problems not just in political philosophy but also in political science.¹⁶ In this way, he seeks to unify not only the world but the world of thought as well.

Tianxia as "the World" Geographically

Zhao argues that world chaos emerges from using the improper perspective to view the world, conceptualize its problems, and thus formulate solutions. Arguing that the present Westphalian world order leads to conflict because it is based on competing national interests, he tells us that we need to think about world order in terms of a truly global view. The world's problems are too big for any one nation, superpower, region, or international organization. Although the United Nations and the European Union are good ways of thinking beyond the state that come from good intentions, he feels that they are still limited by their reliance on the analytical framework of international relations that is based on thinking from the nation-state.

To counter the mainstream way of framing "the international," Zhao looks to an ancient passage from Laozi's *Daode jing* (chap. 54) that instructs us to "use the world [Tianxia] to examine the world [Tianxia]." Zhao uses this important passage to argue that Tianxia is more than a place; it is a method for looking at world problems and world order from a truly global perspective—thinking *through* the world in an "all-inclusive" (*wuwai*, 无外) way, rather than thinking *about* the world from an inferior national or individual perspective.¹⁷ Though existing theories provide a "view from somewhere," Zhao's Tianxia presents a holistic "view from everywhere."¹⁸ To create world order, we need to use this holistic view to measure the world according to a world standard, rather than according to national interests.

By thinking through the world with a "view from everywhere," Zhao argues that we can have a "complete and perfect" understanding of problems and solutions that is "all-inclusive."¹⁹ World unity thus leads to world peace and a harmonious world.

Tianxia as "All the People"

The all-inclusive nature of Tianxia is more than geographical. Zhao uses it ethically to define the second notion of Tianxia as "all the people." Here he underlines how a proper Tianxia system does not have an "outside" either geographically or ethically because China's "magnanimous thought" does not reject "the Other."²⁰ In China's all-inclusive Tianxia system, distinctions between inside and outside, and even friends and enemies, are more relative than absolute. Whereas the West, according to Zhao, starkly divides the world according to racial distinctions, Chinese thought unites it according to an ethical logic that is cultural.[21] The goal of the Tianxia system is "transformation" (*hua*, 化) that changes the self and the other, normatively ordering "chaos" by transforming the "many" into "the one."[22] Though Carl Schmitt (like Mao Zedong[23]) defines politics as the practice of publicly distinguishing between enemies and friends, Zhao tells us that "Tianxia theory is a theory for 'transforming enemies into friends,' where 'transformation' seeks to attract people rather than conquer them."[24] In later writings, Zhao elaborates on the enemy/friend transformation by arguing that the goal of Chinese philosophy is improvement not just of the self but also of all the nations/peoples of the world; against the liberal ethic of "live and let live," Zhao promotes a Confucian ethic of "improve if let improve."[25]

Thus Tianxia as "the world" includes "all peoples." Zhao glosses the famous classical passage "Tianxia belongs to all" (Tianxia *wei gong*, 天下为公) to argue that "Tianxia is the people of Tianxia's Tianxia. The people of Tianxia all think in terms of Tianxia. Of course this is the superior ideal."[26] Likewise, Zhao quotes another famous classical passage, "Tianxia is one family" (Tianxia *yi jia*, 天下一家) to argue that the world is one family.[27]

The philosophical and political problem for Zhao is how to represent the interests of the people of Tianxia as a truly world interest. He argues—at length—that democracy is illegitimate for representing the world's interest because (1) it is based on individual desires, which are manipulated in both elections and surveys, and (2) although democratic institutions may work in domestic politics, they do not (and he argues cannot) work on a global scale. Because he feels that democracy is an "erroneous" way of determining the people's will, he reasons that the people's general will needs to be determined by a "careful observation of social trends" by a Confucian-Leninist elite.[28] Thus, the criterion for judging the people's heart is not "freedom" but "order"—which is one of the main themes of traditional Chinese thought (i.e., order/chaos).[29] Tianxia, Zhao reminds us, refers to the greatest and highest order.[30]

Tianxia as the World Institution

Because the Tianxia system is defined by order, Zhao argues that this alternative world order needs to be established and maintained through a world institution. As he concludes the book: "Tianxia theory is the core philosophy . . . that provides the deepest theoretical plan for the world institution."[31] Because Tianxia refers to the greatest order, its structure as the world institution has fundamental legitimacy.[32] Again, he tells us that although the European Union and the United Nations seem to be superstate regional and world institutions, they are limited by a worldview that is based on nation-states. Although the West organizes political life in terms of the three levels of "individual, community, and nation-state," Zhao tells us that Chinese political thought looks to the levels of "Tianxia, state, and family." And though the Western world prioritizes the individual and works in terms of the nation-state, the Tianxia system starts at the largest level, Tianxia, and orders political and social life in a top-down manner.[33]

The legitimacy of the Tianxia world system does not come from procedural measures such as those that define liberal democracy (e.g., elections or the outcome of rational debate in civil society) but from two substantive criteria: universal effectiveness and complete transitivity.[34] The political rules and ethical judgments that apply at one level need to effectively apply at all levels; remember that democracy is "erroneous" because it applies only at the domestic level of the state but not at the world level of Tianxia. To argue these points about effective transitivity, Zhao uses a famous passage from the Confucian "Great Learning—*Daxue*, 大学" that links pacifying Tianxia, governing the state and properly ordering families.[35] For Zhao, this shows the "priority and primacy of world governance by a world institution," with order "descending down to states and families."[36] Both ends of this social-political continuum are important—but for different reasons: Whereas Tianxia provides political order for "inferior" levels, family (*jia*, 家) morality sets the ethical standard for superior levels.[37] As a way of shifting our attention away from statecentric views of order and world politics, Zhao stresses that the family and Tianxia are the two pillars of his world institution.

Zhao concludes one of the core chapters of *Tianxia tixi* with a comparative analysis of historical empire systems, arguing that the Tianxia system is the most appropriate empire for the twenty-first century.[38] The Roman Empire, the British Empire, and America's new empire all have fatal flaws. The Roman Empire was a universal empire that expanded its territory through military conquest and thus had no natural borders. The British Empire, conversely, is an example of modern imperialism that is based on the logic of the nation-state, which integrated the illegitimate ideas and practices of nationalism, imperialism, and colonialism. This conjunction of capitalism and imperial colonialism resulted in an unbalanced world system that followed the divisive logic of the nation-state by imposing territorial borders between peoples. America's "new empire" of globalization has transformed modern imperialism's direct control into a more hidden domination of the world's politics, economics, and culture. This globalization of American values means that the United States not only plays the game but also sets the rules—which Zhao feels is "disastrous."[39] Although Zhao's works are often seen as a call for China to promote its "soft power," he is particularly—and repeatedly—critical of Joseph Nye's discussions of soft power.[40]

Lastly, Zhao presents the "Tianxia model" as the solution to both modern imperialism and new imperialism.[41] Whereas previous empires have taken a particular nation-state as the model and universalized its particular values, criteria, and standards, Tianxia is the only system that thinks through the world. When we take Tianxia as an a priori and complete concept for the world institution, then we can distinguish a positive globalism from a negative globalization.[42] Still, Zhao stresses that he is not advocating the resurrection of ancient China's imperial practice; his objective is to sketch out a utopia, with Tianxia theory providing only a "theoretical plan" that utilizes the resources of China's tradition thought. Indeed, he spends the bulk of this five page description of Tianxia criticizing other people and other places: the U.S.-UK war in Iraq, Habermas's communicative rationality, Nye's soft power, Hardt and Negri's new understanding of empire, the international politics of human rights, the limits of liberalism, and so on.[43]

Hence Zhao does not dwell on the details of how the world institution would work in the twenty-first century, or how we would get from the present international system to his utopian Tianxia system, except to note that participation is voluntary.[44] At other times, he states that though the Tianxia institution is shared, each locality would be independent economically, politically, and culturally as substates in the Tianxia system rather than autonomous nation-states in the Westphalian international system.[45] In later works, he employs the historical example of the Zhou Dynasty (1045–256 BC) to elaborate on the workings of the Tianxia system, which has a large central imperial state (天子之国; 宗主国) surrounded by smaller aristocratic vassal states that pay tribute and corvée; the centralized military force is strong enough to launch punitive expeditions against wayward tributaries, and vassal states' armies are large enough for them to combine to overthrow an oppressive emperor.[46] Yet this idealized historical description tends to raise more questions than it answers about Tianxia's contemporary relevance.

Thus, on the last page of *Tianxia tixi*, Zhao opines that "what we have discussed here is merely limited to the philosophical questions of Tianxia theory, and the realization of the future's world institution model certainly poses very complicated questions, which philosophy cannot yet answer."[47]

To sum up, Zhao tells us that the world has serious political problems that need to be solved first conceptually, and then institutionally. His arguments grow out of a more general feeling among China's intellectuals that its ethical system of domestic and international order was destroyed by the violent tendencies of selfish (Western) nation-states that operated (and continues to operate) in the Westphalian world system. He provides the Tianxia system as the solution to the world's problems, arguing that we need to think through the world to understand it, and thus effectively and legitimately govern it.

Tianxia is a hierarchical system that values order over freedom, ethics over law, and elite governance over democracy and human rights. It is literally a "top-down" (i.e., *tian-xia*) prescription for the world's ills. Employing a mixture of tradition and modernity, the book uses ancient texts to propose a very modernist solution to the very modern problems of world order. Tianxia is presented as *the* proper, all-inclusive master narrative of world order that will solve all the world's problems through a single master institution that has "no outside" and operates according to a "view from everywhere." Rather than being like contemporary philosophical debates that characteristically question such master narratives, Zhao's reasoning is like popular strands of theoretical physics that seek the final "theory of everything."

Philosophical and Social Criticism

Tianxia tixi is both an ambitious and an ambiguous work. Before proposing the Tianxia system as the solution to the world's problems in the body of the book, in his "Introduction," Zhao clears the scholarly terrain of rival theories from both China and the West. He quickly goes through the history of contemporary Chinese thought, arguing most strongly against a group of scholars who give a robustly self-critical view of China's struggles with modernity and the West.[48]

Zhao feels that their obsession with "digging up skeletons" from China's past and looking to the West for answers makes the Chinese people lose hope, and thus damages China's "social cohesion and unity."[49] He quotes

Michel Foucault's power/knowledge argument,[50] but argues that "at the same time we also must stress the relations of 'knowledge/responsibility' as the theoretical meaning of knowledge." He concludes that "truth is not the highest judgment, for truth must be good, truth must be responsible, because in the end what humanity needs is life, not truth."[51]

Zhao's project thus is concerned more with public policy rather than with critical theory. His aim is to explore the theoretical possibilities offered by Chinese thought for dealing with the China's—and the world's—current political problems.[52] Rather than dwelling on his country's "past mistakes," he very deliberately takes what he calls a "positive view" of Chinese tradition: "Simply put, we must discuss the positive meaning of the concept of 'China.'"[53] In this way, he is able to revive a three-thousand-year-old ideal like Tianxia by looking to "its conditions of possibility" and "potential beyond history."[54] The goal thus is not criticize China (whose problems are all figured as in "the past" rather than the present) but to "rethink China" in order to "rethink the world."[55]

Although Zhao is certainly striking out in a new direction by exploring the theoretical possibilities of Tianxia, his argument is based on a cavalier use of a few key passages from Chinese thought, which upon closer consideration actually *do not* support his Tianxia worldview. His argument for thinking through the world is based largely on his reading of chapter 54 of Laozi's *Daode jing*: "Use the world [Tianxia] to examine the world [Tianxia]." This passage is cited numerous times in each chapter; but Zhao usually takes it out of context. The larger passage is "use the self to examine the self, use the family to examine the family, use the neighborhood to examine the neighborhood, use the world to examine the world. How do I know that the workings of the world [Tianxia] are like this? From this."[56] Thus although there is nothing in this passage that prioritizes Tianxia over other spaces of activity—and actually suggests that we start with the self, not with the world—Zhao reads it as a top-down hierarchy where "the superior levels have to exist, and where common interest comes from them more than from the units at the inferior levels."[57] He thus uses the *Daode jing* in very odd ways to support his argument for a hierarchical world order, and he likewise plays fast and loose with other key classical Chinese texts to support his Tianxia system.

Criticisms of *Tianxia tixi* by Chinese scholars tend to focus on these problems, and argue that Zhao does not provide the proper historical and philosophical understanding of the Tianxia concept.[58] Though he presents himself to international audiences as "the Chinese Perspective,"⁵⁹ his Chinese critics argue that this Tianxia system is merely his own individual perspective, which is full of errors.⁶⁰ Yet "Tianxia" itself is an empty term—it refers to everything *except* the heavens—that demands to be explained and interpreted in various different ways.⁶¹ Hence, to dwell on Zhao's textual problems would miss the point of the book. He is very clear that he is *not* interested in joining the standard philosophical debate about the true meaning of ancient texts. Thus, he does not mind that his book has generated much criticism—as I argue in this chapter's conclusion, feeding off critical commentary is actually the secret of his success. His project is actually to "transcend the historical limits" of Chinese tradition in order to explore the theoretical possibilities offered by Chinese thought for dealing with contemporary problems.⁶² As noted above, his Tianxia system is a utopia that has practical applications. Hence it is most important to focus on the political ethics of his Tianxia system.

Social Theory

In discussing the benefits of the Tianxia system, Zhao employs contemporary social theory's concept of self/other relations to compare how analytical borders are drawn in China and the West. Here he is following thinkers like Emmanuel Levinas and Gaston Bachelard in seeing social relations and space as ethical and normative practices.⁶³ William Connolly and R. B. J. Walker applied this mode of analysis to international relations to question how foreign policy emerges when the national self performs its identity as a mode of exclusion of the other as a foreign enemy.⁶⁴ The critical aim of these theorists is to resist the urge to convert difference into otherness, and thus allow diverse modes of life exist.

Zhao's most important argument, then, is that Chinese thought and the Tianxia system provide a productive form of self/other relations that does not exclude difference. But upon scrutiny, Zhao's statement that China and Tianxia are "all-inclusive" runs into problems. His argument concentrates on how the West has absolutely excluded otherness and has dealt with difference through conquest. Yet Tzvetan Todorov's analysis of early European encounters with America shows how violent conquest is only one mode of dealing with difference; conversion to the conqueror's worldview is another technique of imperial violence.⁶⁵ In other words, although exclusion certainly is an important issue, it is also important to examine how self/other relations work to *include* difference in hierarchical ways. Thus although Zhao's all-inclusive Tianxia system may not have an outside, its institutionally backed "self" utilizes both absolute exclusion and hierarchical inclusion to marginalize three social groups: the West, the people, and other nations along China's frontier.

Excluding "the West"

Zhao's master narrative is based on a fundamental and absolute distinction between a moral China and an immoral West whose individualist thought system and Westphalian world system he feels need to be transcended. Although he is very interested in how analytical frameworks set the terms of debate,[66] he is going in a different direction from scholars such as Wang Hui who argue that to understand China it is essential to question such absolute distinctions: "So, just what are China's problems? Or, what methods or even language should be used to analyze them? . . . [Because] the binaries of reform/conservatism, the West/China, capitalism/socialism, and market / [state] planning are still hegemonic concepts, . . . problems can hardly be brought to light."[67] Hence even though Zhao is very critical of how Western thought employs absolute binaries, he uses the same analytical framework of China/West to construct and exclude "the West" as the other in ways similar to European Orientalism.

Zhao thus is able to ignore the vibrant explorations of cosmopolitanism since Kant revived this discussion in the late eighteenth century. Recent discussions of "cosmopolitan democracy" and "actually existing cosmopolitanisms" are particularly interesting because their decentered participatory ethos runs counter to the Tianxia system's unitary, hierarchical world institution governed by elites.[68] Zhao likewise treats international relations theory as nothing but statecentric realism, and thus does not consider how postpositivist IR theory is self-critically considering many of the same questions that interest him. In other words, he is not interested in critically understanding Western thought so much as creating an Occidentalized West as the other, so as to reaffirm the identity of Tianxia as the all-inclusive self that presents the globe's *only* alternative for a peaceful world order. In this sense, his Pax Sinica mission of "improve if let improve" is quite similar to that of the Western imperial scholars whom he criticizes; he is likewise aiming to integrate culture and power, in what some now call China's "yellow man's burden" of using its ethical mode of governance to pacify and civilize the world.[69]

Guiding the Masses

As noted above, Zhao's main argument against democracy is that the world's masses are incapable of thinking through the world. Because "the masses always make the wrong choices," they cannot be trusted to act in a truly world interest.[70] He goes on—at length—to criticize common people as "blind followers, selfish, irresponsible, foolish, and vulgar." He likewise worries about the legitimacy of a society that is dominated by "swindlers, petty people, whores, idiots, and scoundrels."[71] And he concludes that "most people do not really know what is best for them, but the elite do, so the elite ought genuinely to decide for the people."[72] His solution thus is not to totally exclude the people but to include them in a hierarchical way that is guided by the Confucian-Leninist elite.

Conquering and Converting Other Nationalities

Zhao does not give much historical evidence for the utility of the Tianxia model; he is more interested in the possibilities of pure thought than in the messy experience of history. Even so, at times he does elaborate on what he means by an all-inclusive Tianxia that seeks to transform enemies into friends. But rather than stress how inside and outside are "intimately" interwoven,[73] he argues that Tianxia describes a place that is all part of the normatively good "inside," and thus lacks an outside (*wuwai*). Though there are inside/outside distinctions within the Tianxia system, he feels that these relations are not of absolute otherness but of relative cultural difference. To explain these contingent social relations, he appeals to imperial China's "tribute system" of concentric circles with the civilized imperial capital at the center flowing out to embrace the various "barbaric" peoples at the periphery.[74] Rather than criticizing imperial China's "civilization/barbarism distinction" (华夷之辨) as a tool of imperial governance,[75] he argues that it is still useful, with "barbaric lands and tributary states serving as beneficial competitors" for Chinese civilization.[76]

Although Zhao stresses that these were not racial distinctions, this is a moot point. If we accept that "race" is a pseudoscientific concept deployed to explain cultural differences, then the category of "racism" did not exist before modern science and social Darwinism. When Zhao says that the benefit of this "civilization/barbarism" interaction was an "objective discussion of the long term advantages and disadvantages of different cultures," it certainly sounds like a hierarchy of cultures analogous to modern racism and the PRC's current concern with the "population quality" of its national minorities.[77] More to the point, these hierarchical cultural relations whereby the goal is to transform enemies into friends follow the logic of the other technique of imperial violence discussed above: conversion. Though Zhao suggests that we need to transform peoples by "improving their interests,"[78] Shapiro reminds us that community building always entails community destroying.[79] In other words, "improve if let improve" seems to only go one way, in what Zhao calls "Confucian Improvement" (孔子改进).[80]

In current discussions of world order, it is popular to see traditional China as a benevolent and magnanimous empire that provided peace and stability for centuries before the arrival of Western imperialism in the nineteenth century. This narrative is now used in Chinese and Western international relations texts to explain why China is not a threat to world order in the twenty-first century.[81] Yet this comparison of a war-mongering Westphalian Europe with a peace-loving imperial China employs a very narrow definition of "war" as an interstate phenomena, and a very shallow understanding of China's historical experience.[82] Actually, the Chinese state has often engaged in violent interactions with states and semi-states along its frontiers. According to China's Academy of Military Science, in its long imperial history (770 BC–AD 1912), China engaged in 3,756 wars,[83] for an average of 1.4 wars per year. In its first century, the Qing Dynasty (1644–1911) expanded massively in the West, including a struggle over the northwest frontier with Tsarist Russia and the Mongolian Zunghar state that lasted into the 1770s. Rather than being a case of Western imperial incursion into China (as it is presented in China's modern history textbooks),[84] this episode is better understood as a violent struggle between three empires—the Manchu Qing, Tsarist Russia, and the Mongolian Zunghar—that resulted in the annihilation of the Zunghar as a people.[85] A key classical phrase that Zhao does not mention is instructive: "The Tianxia is united" (Tianxia *yitong*, 天下一统) describes "uniting the Tianxia through conquest."[86] This reflects how the Chinese Empire at times had a para bellum policy where, as Johnston argues, war was a constant occurrence in a zero-sum game that employed both pure violence and absolute flexibility.[87]

Hence Zhao's argument that Tianxia is all-inclusive seems to miss the point that not everyone wants to be included. Rather than be "improved" on Beijing's terms, some people want to stay different, and outside. China's imperial and contemporary history in Tibet, Taiwan, and Xinjiang is instructive for what happens to difference that prefers to stay outside and not be transformed into a "friend"—it is redefined as a terrorist separatist threat that warrants military action. China's *legal* claim to these territories is strong, but Zhao's point is to stress the *ethical* legitimacy of the Tianxia model, which is lacking. The main question then is not whether China has a pattern of self/other relations that is similar to the West (or not), but how the Tianxia system addresses difference.[88] Because Zhao figures his Tianxia system as "all-inclusive," any difference risks being converted/improved into the sameness of the overarching (Chinese) self. Indeed, the clashes of 2008–9 in Tibet and Xinjiang show how Zhao's "ethical possibilities" are being violently applied by the Chinese state through the violent exclusion (which employs a grossly racialized language that demonizes whole populations) of people who want to maintain a different social system.

To sum up, this section has shown how Zhao's Tianxia utopia has serious theoretical problems both in terms of its cavalier reading of classical Chinese texts and its odd use of contemporary social theory's vocabulary of ethical relations in a way that promotes "conversion" rather than "conquest." Last, it is necessary to point out the irony of one of Zhao's main arguments. Each imperial system that he criticizes—Roman, British, and American—has had its own utopian ideal to inspire its governance regime: Pax Romana, the civilizing mission, white man's burden, free world, and so on. Hence all the "Western" empires discussed in *Tianxia tixi* have likewise argued that they are best for the world as the manifestation of an altruistic philosophical project that is not only just but also inevitable.

Although Zhao understandably criticizes the West for universalizing its particular worldview at the considerable expense of other ones, is he doing anything different? Is he not trying to universalize the very particular Chinese concept of Tianxia in order to apply it to the world? And does not his Pax Sinica risk creating the very problems of an intolerant world order that he seeks to solve, by simply replacing Eurocentrism with Sinocentrism? Rather than a posthegemonic world order, does not Tianxia offer a new hegemony?

This leads us to the next section's argument that the real meaning of the Tianxia system is not found in its alternative world order but in what it can tell us about current debates in Beijing about identity, security, and China's role in the world. In this way, Tianxia is a strong example of how domestic and international politics inform each other as part of a broader struggle over the meaning of "China," which is closely linked with the meaning of "the world" (on this point, also see chapter 8 in this volume).

Conclusion: Rethinking China and Rethinking the World

Although Zhao does not discuss it, the meaning of Tianxia is even more complex than the empire/world dynamic. According to classical and modern dictionaries, "Tianxia" also means "China." This is one reason why Zhao's book is so popular: Tianxia is about China, and China's global role in the twenty-first century—which are very hot topics in the PRC and among overseas Chinese. According to many scholars, imperial China's Tianxia system of governance worked very well—until it was challenged by Western imperialism. Thus, in modern times, China was forced to build a nation-state to defend itself from these foreign challenges. The question that many Chinese scholars are now asking is whether it is time for China (which is now a strong nation-state) to engage in promoting, establishing, or constructing Tianxia. Chinese identity thus emerges through a curious combination of modern victimization and ancient civilization.[89] Tianxia here is promoted not just for China's benefit but also for the benefit of the world. As chapter 10 of this book shows, this is one of the arguments for Beijing's current "harmonious world" foreign policy.

Whereas, in the early twentieth century, imperial China's hierarchical world order was seen as the problem, now many Chinese scholars see it as the solution to the world's ills. Because Chinese culture is taken to be superior, many feel that it is the duty of patriotic Chinese to spread Chinese values, language, and culture not just in Asia but also around the world.[90] Tianxia thus provides a heuristic device for understanding how Chinese elites view their role in the world, and the world itself.[91] This is where we come to the second objective of the chapter: to examine how new ideas emerge in China's making of foreign policy. Zhao's *Tianxia tixi* is meaningful not just as a philosophical or an academic text. Its power and influence thus emerge not necessarily from its arguments—which one critic describes as "pale and weak"[92]—but from its position in a network of debates among public intellectuals, state intellectuals, and political leaders about China's role in the world as a major power.

Among public intellectuals, Zhao's Tianxia theory is embedded in China's political culture that, on the one hand, has an enduring anxiety about unity and disunity (including order and chaos), and, on the other, has a strong tradition of utopian thought that seeks to address these perennial issues with the "complete and perfect world."[93] Thus, Zhao is not alone in looking to the past for China's future strengths: Zhang Yimou's film *Hero* (英雄)

(2002) concludes with the assassin being transformed into a hero when he decides *not* to kill the emperor, which is much like Zhao's goal of transforming enemies into friends. The lesson drawn from this historical parable is that the individual must sacrifice himself and his kingdom for the greater good of the Tianxia empire, because as the hero reasons, "Only the King of Qin can stop the chaos by unifying Tianxia" through conquest.[94]

Hence Zhao's book is part of the broader discussion of *how* China will be a world power: the "Introduction" to *Tianxia tixi* is called "Why We Need to Discuss China's Worldview." Zhao feels that to be a true world power, China needs to excel not just in economic production but also in "knowledge production."[95] And to become a knowledge-producing power, China needs to stop importing ideas from the West and to start exploiting its own indigenous "resources of traditional thought." Thus, the aim of his book is to "rethink China" so as to "restructure China." But because China's problems are the world's problems, we then need to rethink and restructure the world in terms of Tianxia.

Here Tianxia is embedded in an important debate about how China can fit into the world system as a "responsible great power" that has emerged via a network of liberal Chinese IR scholars during the past decade.[96] China is trying to prove to the world (and especially the West) that it is no longer a revolutionary state that challenges international order but is a "responsible" member of international society. The PRC has demonstrated this by pursuing a more multilateral foreign policy that includes expanding its membership in international organizations at both the regional and global levels.

Zhao's "Introduction" also talks about China's "responsibility" to the world, but he adds a theoretical twist to argue that it will become a responsible great power not merely by amassing economic and military capabilities but also by "creating new world concepts and new world structures":

> Bearing responsibility for the world, and not just for one's own country, this is China's philosophical perspective. In practice it provides totally new possibilities, especially if we use "Tianxia" as the primary analytical unit for understanding political/economic interests. When we use Tianxia to understand the world, then we can use "the world" to analyze problems, and transcend the Western mode of thought that relies on nation-state, and then we will be able to take responsibility for the world as our own responsibility, and thus create new world concepts and new world structures.[97]

Here the notion of a "responsible China" shifts dramatically from that of a conservative state that is responsible to the current world order to Zhao's Tianxia that is responsible for creating a totally new world order.

Although "responsible China" appealed to a network of liberal IR scholars in China, the chapters in part I of the present volume show that an important group of Chinese IR theorists is also very interested in Zhao's Tianxia system. This network is engaged in promoting a "Chinese style" of international relations theory.[98] With China's recent economic growth, Chinese scholars have sought to carve out space for their own unique research in a transnational academic market. Thus, many key IR scholars are hailing Zhao's Tianxia system as a way to create space for a "Chinese School" of IR in an intellectual environment dominated by Western IR.[99] Indeed, the editors of China's top international studies journal, *World Economics and Politics*, invited Zhao to write the editorial page essay for its September 2006 issue; and then in 2008, they invited him back to respond to a critical view of *Tianxia tixi*.[100] Another group of elite IR scholars reprinted one of *Tianxia tixi*'s chapters as the lead chapter in their edited volume *Chinese Scholars View the World: International Order*.[101]

But again, Zhao is doing more than contributing to this debate that sees the "Chinese School" as an assertion of cultural sovereignty to protect China's unique way of understanding the world. He is interested in transcending this chaotic (and nationalistic) intellectual scene by unifying the world of thought under the banner of the Tianxia system.

Finally, Zhao's writings are embedded in the discursive network of China's top political leaders; Tianxia's utopian themes resonate with Beijing's latest foreign policy narrative, "harmonious world." Just five months after *Tianxia tixi* was published, President Hu Jintao outlined his four-point plan for a harmonious world at the United Nations in September 2005.[102] Since then, the harmonious world formulation has dominated China's explanations for its responsible engagement with the world, including an important section of the December 2005 white paper "China's Peaceful Development Road."[103] (This policy is analyzed in greater detail in chapter 10 of this book). In later works, Zhao elaborates on the conceptual importance of "harmony" in the Tianxia system, while praising the Chinese government for "once again utilizing the resources of China's traditional thought" in its twin policies of building a "harmonious society" and a "harmonious world."[104] Though "harmonious society" refers to Beijing's policy of using centralized state power to "rebalance" China's economy and society, the Tianxia system's world institution suggests that China would use strong centralized power to rebalance the world.[105] Yu Keping, who is a close adviser to Hu, very directly relates the concepts of harmonious world and Tianxia, seeing "harmonious world" as a "new take on the development of the ancient Chinese dream of Tianxia Datong (the great harmony of the world)."[106] The relation of scholarship and government policy—especially the ties between philosophers and the Foreign Ministry—is certainly opaque in China. But recent studies have shown how broader social networks, including think tank scholars and university professors, are having an increasing impact on foreign policy debates in Beijing.[107]

Tianxia is thus embedded in a broad discussion of Chinese visions of world order that includes a feature film like *Hero*, dozens of articles in prominent IR journals, and even the Chinese president's harmonious world foreign policy narrative. Zhao's ideas are *not* influential in the standard sense of everyone agreeing with his proposed Tianxia system; actually the film, academic articles, and state policy all disagree with him on many important issues. Rather, his ideas are indirectly influential according to the normative logic of soft power: He has been able to set the agenda, and thus productively generate a powerful discourse that sets the boundaries of how people think about China's past, present, and future. And he does this by employing familiar vocabularies; for the general reader, he talks of "sacrifice for Tianxia"; for liberal IR scholars, he talks of China as a "responsible great power"; for IR theorists, he discusses how China has its own "worldview" that is different from the West's; and for Beijing's political elite, his ideas resonate with China's "harmonious world" policy.

Zhao actually has very different understandings of these key phrases from each of these groups, but he uses this familiar language to position himself at the center of these core discursive networks, and thus present his contrary views as the mainstream view. By rethinking China in this way, he is also able to rethink the world, and thus set discursive boundaries to control popular understandings not just of the past and the present but of the future as well.[108] In this way, the Tianxia system is part of China's assertion of its normative soft power, but in a way that complements its hard power of economic and military strength. In other words, Tianxia is not a post-hegemonic ideal so much as a proposal for a new hegemony.

Although Zhao's book was reviewed alongside Habermas's work,[109] perhaps the best way to understand the role of *Tianxia tixi* is to compare it with Samuel Huntington's high-profile writings on the clash of civilizations.[110] The point is not whether Huntington's articles and book are intellectually sophisticated (or not), or whether U.S. policy is dictated or influenced by them (or not). Rather, the texts are powerful as polemics that define problems in specific ways that actually serve to limit the range of possible solutions. In this way, Huntington set the terms of the debate about post–Cold War international politics that in turn generated a certain range of responses. Even when these responses are critical of the clash of civilizations argument, they add to its influence by recirculating the idea that "civilization" is the key topic of debate for international politics.[111] Indeed, Beijing's harmonious world policy is a prominent example of a foreign policy that employs "civilization" to frame international politics.

Zhao was already famous among intellectuals in the humanities before he put together his thoughts on Tianxia in 2005. *Tianxia tixi* worked to grow the market for a politically inflected discussion of Chinese utopia, and it is provoking responses from both IR scholars and political leaders in China. By inserting his discussion of a Chinese utopia into powerful discursive networks, Zhao has asserted himself as the "mainstream" for discussions of China's future—and of the world's future. He mainstreamed Tianxia not by making arguments with which all would agree; rather, he was successful because he described this exotic idea in terms of already-existing vocabularies and debates. People now must respond to his arguments, even when they are discussing something else—nationalism, globalization, socialism, empire, world peace, and so on.[112] His recent writings thus present an exemplary case study of how new ideas emerge in the making of Chinese foreign policy.

Although *Tianxia tixi* has serious theoretical and ethical problems, the book has quite successfully generated considerable social capital for Zhao as well as enhancing China's soft power as a source of a universally valid model of world politics. The power of Tianxia thus comes less from nuanced argument than from its strategic placement in China's discursive networks of power. Rather than guide us toward a utopian world order that will solve global problems, Tianxia is an example of the workings of normative power, in the sense that it recenters Chinese understandings of world order as a patriotic activity in domestic politics. It helps us understand how ideas about foreign policy—including those that chafe with the official view—get put into play in Beijing as part of the domestic politics of China's national image.

Beijing says that China will peacefully rise as a responsible power within the present international system, and not challenge the structures and norms of world order. But the success of books like *Tianxia tixi* shows that there is a hunger in China for "Chinese solutions" to world problems, and a craving for nationalist solutions to global issues, especially when they promote a patriotic form of cosmopolitanism.[113] This is the main significance of *Tianxia tixi* for China's foreign policy. Indeed, it is not an isolated example but the sign of a broader trend where China's imperial mode of governance is increasingly revived for the twenty-first century. It shows how popular views of self/other relations that draw on concepts from China's historical empire are increasingly informing Beijing's official policy.[114]

In a broader sense *Tianxia tixi*'s rise to prominence in China can serve as a cautionary tale for IR theorists. Though it is popular to argue that the Westphalian system is flawed, it does not necessarily follow that alternative worldviews are any better. And though it is admirable to engage in a "dialogue of civilizations," it is important that it does not become a clash of empires in the sense of promoting revived versions of British, Chinese, Indian, Islamic, Russian, and any other imperial regimes.

Indeed, though the Westphalian system is rightly criticized for being statecentric, the Tianxia example shows how non-Western alternatives can be even more statecentric. Although many IR theorists caution us to resist the urge to convert difference into otherness to allow diverse modes of life exist, Zhao's Tianxia system requires an even stronger policing of social, cultural, and political boundaries. Proposals for a "posthegemonic" system thus often contain the seeds of a new—and often violent—system of inclusion and exclusion: Tianxia presents a popular example of a new hegemony, whereby imperial China's hierarchical governance is updated for the twenty-first century.

Notes

1. Alastair Iain Johnston, *Social States: China in International Institutions, 1980–2000* (Princeton, N.J.: Princeton University Press, 2008); Susan Shirk, *China: Fragile Superpower* (New York: Oxford University Press, 2007); David M. Lampton, *The Three Faces of Chinese Power: Might, Money, and Minds* (Berkeley: University of California Press, 2008); Bates Gill, *Rising Star: China's New Security Diplomacy* (Washington, D.C.: Brookings Institution Press, 2007).

2. Wang Gungwu, "Tianxia and Empire: External Chinese Perspectives," Inaugural Tsai Lecture, Harvard University, May 4, 2006.

3. Zhao Tingyang, *Tianxia tixi: Shijie zhidu zhexue daolun* [The Tianxia system: A philosophy for the world institution] (Nanjing: Jiangsu jiaoyu chubanshe, 2005).

4. See Dan Xingwu, "Liang daguoji tixi de chongtu yu jindai Zhongguo de shengcheng" [The clash of two international systems and the formation of modern China], PhD dissertation, International Politics Department, Chinese Academy of Social Sciences,

2005, 23–38; Li Shaojun, "Lun Zhongguo wenming de heping neihan: Cong chuantong dao xianshi—dui 'Zhongguo weixie' lun de huida" [The peaceful orientation of Chinese Civilization: From tradition to reality—a response to "China threat" theory], *Guoji jingji pinglun*, no. 19 (1999): 30–33; Sheng Hong, "Shenme shi wenming" [What is civilization?] *Zhanlüe yu guanli*, no. 5 (1995): 88–98.

5. Zhao's book provides an excellent case study because it is popular beyond the humanities in social science and policy discussions. According to the China Knowledge Resource Integrated Database, the combination of "Zhao Tingyang" and "Tianxia" is mentioned in 2,028 articles since *Tianxia tixi* was published in 2005, and in 386 articles in 2009 alone. Zhao's view of Tianxia dominates discussions in high-profile journals as well, most notably *World Economics and Politics* (Shijie jingji yu zhengzhi), *International Survey* (Guoji guancha), *International Political Science* (Guoji zhengzhi kexue), *Social Scientists* (Shehui kexuejia), *World Philosophy* (Shijie zhexue), *Reading* (Dushu), *Central Party School Journal* (Zhonggong zhongyang dangxiao xuebao), *Social Science Front* (Shehui kexue zhanxian), and *Social Sciences in China* (Zhongguo shehui kexue bao).

6. Jeffrey W. Legro, "What China Will Want: The Future Intentions of a Rising Power," *Perspectives on Politics* 5, no. 3 (2007): 515–34; Allen Carlson, "China's Conflicted Olympic Moment," *Current History*, September 2007, 252–56, at 253ff.

7. See, e.g., Martin Jacques, *When China Rules the World: The Rise of the Middle Kingdom and the End of the Western World* (London: Allen Lane, 2009).

8. Zhao Tingyang, "Rethinking Empire from a Chinese Concept 'All-under-Heaven' (Tian-xia)," *Social Identities* 12, no. 1 (2006): 29–41; Zhao Tingyang, "All Under Heaven," *China Security* 4, no. 2 (2008): 15; Zhao Tingyang, "A Political World Philosophy in Terms of All-under-Heaven (Tian-xia)," *Diogenes* 56, no. 1 (2009): 5–18.

9. My analysis also includes Zhao's revised and refined views for the Chinese audience: Zhao Tingyang, "Tianxia tixi de yige jianyao biaoshu" [A brief explanation of the Tianxia system], *Shijie jingji yu zhengzhi*, no. 10 (2008): 57–65; and Zhao Tingyang, *Huai shijie yanjiu: Zuo wei diyi zhexue de zhengzhi zhexue* [Investigations of the bad world: Political philosophy as first philosophy] (Beijing: Zhongguo renmin daxue chubanshe, 2009), esp. 76–124.

10. See William A. Callahan, *China: The Pessoptimist Nation* (Oxford: Oxford University Press, 2010), 127–60; and Elena Barabantseva, *Overseas Chinese, Ethnic Minorities and Nationalism: De-Centering China* (London: Routledge, 2011).

11. Zhao, *Tianxia tixi*, 21, 110.

12. Ibid., 21.

13. Ibid., 35.

14. See Xu Shen, *Shuowen jiezi zhu* [Explaining simple and analyzing compound characters, with annotations] (Shanghai: Shanghai guji chubanshe, 1981), 1, 2.

15. Zhao, *Tianxia tixi*, 41, 123–24.

16. Ibid., 32, 30.

17. For a discussion of imperial China's transition in the late nineteenth century from a Tianxia-based world order to a state-centric view, see Joseph R. Levinson, *Confucian China and Its Modern Fate* (Berkeley: University of California Press, 1968), 95–108.

18. Zhao, *Tianxia tixi*, 108.

19. Ibid., 108, 40.

20. Ibid., 14, 30, 13.

21. Ibid., 51–54.
22. Ibid., 13.
23. Zhao, *Huai shijie yanjiu*, 3, quotes Mao Zedong's famous passage: "Who are our enemies? Who are our friends? This is a question of the first importance for the revolution"; Mao Zedong, "Analysis of the Classes in Chinese Society (March 1926)," *Selected Works of Mao Tse-tung*, vol. 1 (Beijing: Renmin chubanshe, 1967), 13.
24. Carl Schmitt, *The Concept of the Political* (Chicago: University of Chicago Press, 1996); Zhao, *Tianxia tixi*, 33.
25. Zhao, *Huai shijie yanjiu*, 119–20; Zhao, "Tianxia tixi de yige jianyao biaoshu," 63.
26. Zhao, *Tianxia tixi*, 30.
27. Ibid., 41, 77.
28. Ibid., 19.
29. Zhao elaborates on the order/chaos theme in Zhao, *Huai shijie yanjiu*, esp. 125–83.
30. Zhao, *Tianxia tixi*, 31.
31. Ibid., 160.
32. Ibid., 31.
33. Ibid., 17.
34. Ibid., 19.
35. See *Confucian Analects: The Great Learning and the Doctrine of the Mean*, translated by James Legge (New York: Dover, 1971), 357–59.
36. Zhao, "Rethinking Empire," 8.
37. Ibid.
38. Zhao, *Tianxia tixi*, 102–9.
39. Ibid., 102–5.
40. Ibid., 157.
41. Ibid., 105–9.
42. Ibid., 105.
43. Ibid., 106–9.
44. Zhao "Rethinking Empire," 36.
45. Zhao, *Tianxia tixi*, 78.
46. See Zhao, *Huai shijie yanjiu*, 87–88; Zhao, "Tianxia tixi de yige jianyao biaoshu," 61–62.
47. Zhao, *Tianxia tixi*, 160.
48. For an interesting discussion of debates in contemporary Chinese thought, see Wang Hui, *China's New Order: Society, Politics, and Economy in Transition* (Cambridge, Mass.: Harvard University Press, 2003), 140–87; Gloria Davies, *Worrying about China: The Language of Chinese Critical Inquiry* (Cambridge, Mass.: Harvard University Press, 2007); and John Makeham, *Lost Soul: "Confucianism" in Contemporary Chinese Academic Discourse* (Cambridge, Mass.: Harvard University Press, 2008).)
49. Zhao, *Tianxia tixi*, 4–5.
50. See Michel Foucault, *Power/Knowledge: Selected Interviews and Writings, 1972–1977*, edited by Colin Gordon (New York: Pantheon, 1980).
51. Zhao, *Tianxia tixi*, 5–6. Of course, Foucault would argue that you cannot separate "life" from truth claims about it.
52. Zhao, *Tianxia tixi*, 16.
53. Ibid., 3.

54. Ibid., 46.
55. Ibid., 10–11.
56. Chen Guying, *Laozi: Zhu, yi, ji pingjie* [Laozi: Text, notes, and comments] (Beijing: Zhonghua shuju, 1985), 273–75.
57. Zhao, *Tianxia tixi*, 62.
58. See Zhang Shuguang, "Tianxia lilun he shijie zhidu: Jiu 'Tianxia tixi' wenxue yu Zhao Tingyang xiansheng" [Tianxia theory and world order: Questions about Mr. Zhao Tingyang's *Tianxia tixi*], *Zhongguo Shuping*, no. 5 (2006); and email correspondence from Dan Xingwu, June 14, 2007. I heard this criticism of Zhao's textual errors many times when I presented this research in Beijing in April 2007.
59. See Jan Nederveen Pieterse, "Emancipatory Cosmopolitanism: Towards an Agenda," *Development and Change* 37, no. 6 (2006): 1247–57, at 1255; Zhao, "Rethinking Empire"; Zhao, "All under Heaven"; Zhao, "Political World Philosophy."
60. In a 2008 essay, Zhao responded to his critics (including the author); but many of his explanations were unpersuasive because they were inconsistent with points made in *Tianxia tixi*; see Zhao, "Tianxia tixi de yige jianyao biaoshu."
61. For interesting alternative notions of Tianxia, see Chih-yu Shih's recent essays and Geremie R. Barmé's special issue on Tien-hsia/Tianxia in *China Heritage Quarterly*. Chih-yu Shih, *Negotiating Ethnicity in China: Citizenship as a Response to the State* (New York: Routledge, 2002); Geremie R. Barmé, "Everything in the World," *China Heritage Quarterly* no. 9 (September 2009).
62. Zhao, *Tianxia tixi*, 16.
63. Emmanuel Levinas, "Ethics as First Philosophy," in *The Levinas Reader*, edited by Sean Hand (Oxford: Blackwell, 2000), 75–88; Gaston Bachelard, *The Poetics of Space* (Boston: Beacon Press, 1994).
64. William Connolly, *Identity/Difference: Democratic Negotiations of Political Paradox* (Ithaca, N.Y.: Cornell University Press, 1991), 36–63; R. B. J. Walker, *Inside/Outside: International Relations as Political Theory* (Cambridge: Cambridge University Press, 1993).
65. Tzvetan Todorov, *The Conquest of America: The Question of the Other* (New York: HarperCollins, 1984).
66. Zhao, *Tianxia tixi*, 1, 7.
67. Wang, *China's New Order*, 146.
68. See Daniele Archibugi and David Held, *Cosmopolitan Democracy: An Agenda for a New World Order* (Cambridge: Polity Press, 1995); and Pheng Cheah and Bruce Robbins, *Cosmopolitics: Thinking and Feeling Beyond the Nation* (Minneapolis: University of Minnesota Press, 1998).
69. Edward Said, *Orientalism* (New York: Vintage Books, 1978); Pal Nyiri, "The Yellow Man's Burden: Chinese Immigrants on a Civilizing Mission," *China Journal* 56 (2006): 83–106, at 106.
70. Zhao, "Rethinking Empire," 31.
71. Zhao, *Tianxia tixi*, 27.
72. Zhao, "Rethinking Empire," 32.
73. Bachelard, *Poetics of Space*, 217–18.
74. This is discussed further by Zhao, *Huai shijie yanjiu*, 88–89; and Zhao, "Tianxia tixi de yige jianyao biaoshu," 61–62.
75. See Callahan, *China*, 19–28.

76. Zhao, *Tianxia tixi*, 53, 59–61. Strangely, in a response to his critics, Zhao dismisses the "civilization/barbarism distinction" as a "mistake," with no explanation for why he promoted it previously; see Zhao, "Tianxia tixi de yige jianyao biaoshu," 58, while reinvoking it in his later work, *Huai shijie yanjiu*, 88–89.

77. Zhao, *Tianxia tixi*, 54.

78. Zhao, "Rethinking Empire," 36; Zhao, "Political World Philosophy."

79. Michael J. Shapiro, *Methods and Nations: Cultural Governance and the Indigenous Subject* (New York: Routledge, 2004), 126.

80. Zhao, "Tianxia tixi de yige jianyao biaoshu," 62; Zhao, *Huai shijie yanjiu*, 119.

81. Li, ""Lun Zhongguo wenming"; Yongjin Zhang, "System, Empire and State in Chinese International Relations," *Review of International Studies* 27 (December 2001): 43–63; David C. Kang, *China Rising: Peace, Power and Order in East Asia* (New York: Columbia University Press, 2007).

82. David C. Kang, "Getting Asia Wrong: The Need for New Analytical Frameworks," *International Security* 27, no. 4 (2003): 57–85, at 65–66. For a more critical view, see Victoria Tin-bor Hui, "How China Was Ruled," *The American Interest*, Spring 2008, 53–65.

83. Fu Zhongxia et al., eds., *Zhongguo lidai zhanzheng nianbiao* [Historical chronology of warfare in China] (Beijing: Jiefangjun chubanshe, 2002); cited by Yuan-kang Wang, "The Chinese World Order and War in Asian History," paper presented at American Political Science Association annual conference, Toronto, September 2009, http://ssrn.com/abstract=1451551.

84. See Callahan, *China*, 31–60.

85. Peter C. Perdue, *China Marches West: The Qing Conquest of Central Eurasia* (Cambridge, Mass.: Harvard University Press, 2005), 256–89.

86. Wang, "Tianxia and Empire," 3.

87. See Alastair Iain Johnston, *Cultural Realism: Strategic Culture and Grand Strategy in Chinese History* (Princeton, N.J.: Princeton University Press, 1995), 249–54; and Hui, "How China Was Ruled."

88. Chih-yu Shih, "The West that Is Not Western: Self-Identification in the Oriental Modernity," paper presented at forty-eighth annual meeting of International Studies Association, Chicago, March 2007.

89. See Callahan, *China*, 1–30.

90. Edward Friedman, "Where Is Chinese Nationalism? The Political Geography of a Moving Project," *Nations and Nationalism* 14, no. 4 (2008): 721–38; Nyiri, "Yellow Man's Burden," 106.

91. David Leheny, "A Narrow Place to Cross Swords: 'Soft Power' and the Politics of Japanese Popular Culture in East Asia," in *Beyond Japan: The Dynamics of East Asian Regionalism*, edited by Peter J. Katzenstein and Takashi Shiraishi (Ithacam N.Y.: Cornell University Press, 2006), 211–33.

92. Zhang, "Tianxia lilun."

93. Zhao, *Tianxia tixi*, 40; Shiping Hua, *Chinese Utopianism: A Comparative Study of Reformist Thought with Japan and Russia, 1989–1997* (Stanford, Calif.: Stanford University Press, 2008); William A. Callahan, "Remembering the Future: Utopia, Empire and Harmony in 21st-Century International Theory," *European Journal of International Relations* 10, no. 4 (2004): 569–601.

94. For an explanation of the use of film in political analysis, see chapter 8 in the

present volume, by Elena Barabantseva; Shapiro, *Methods and Nations*, 141–72; and Sheldon Hsiao-peng Liu, ed., *Transnational Chinese Cinema* (Honolulu: University of Hawaii Press, 1997).

95. Zhao, *Tianxia tixi*, 1.

96. Wang Yizhou, "Mianxiang 21 shijiede Zhongguo waijiao: sanzhong xuqiude xunqiu jiqi pingheng" [Towards a Chinese diplomacy for the 21st century: Pursuing and balancing three needs], *Zhanlüe yu guanli*, no. 6 (1999): 18–27; Xia Liping, "China: A Responsible Great Power," *Journal of Contemporary China* 10, no. 26 (2001): 17–25; Chih-yu Shih, "Breeding a Reluctant Dragon: Can China Rise into Partnership and Away from Antagonism?" *Review of International Studies* 31, no. 4 (2005): 755–74.

97. Zhao, *Tianxia tixi*, 3.

98. See Shi Bin, "Guoji guanxi yanjiu 'Zhongguo hua' de lunzheng" [The debate over Sinicization in international relations research], in *Zhongguo gouji guanxi yanjiu (1995–2005)* [International Relations Research in China (1995-2005)], edited by Wang Yizhou and Yuan Zhengqing (Beijiing: Beijing daxue chubanshe, 2006), 518–45; Zhang Lidong and Pan Yihe, "Traditional Chinese Thoughts Resources of International Organization Construction," in *Construction within Contradiction: Multiple Perspectives on the Relationship between China and International Organizations*, edited by Wang Yizhou (Beijing: China Development Publishing House, 2003), 259–87; Liang Shoude, "Constructing an International Relations Theory with 'Chinese Characteristics,'" *Political Science* 49, no. 1 (1997): 23–49; Liang Shoude and Hong Yinxian, *Guoji zhengzhixue lilun* [International Politics Theory] (Beijing: Beijing daxue chubanshe, 2000); and Song Xinning, "Building International Relations Theory with Chinese Characteristics," *Journal of Contemporary China* 10, no. 26 (2001): 61–74.

99. In addition to the other chapters in this book, see Wang Yiwei, "Tanxun Zhongguo de xin shenfen: Guanyu minzu zhuyi de shenhua" [Exploring China's new identity: The myth of nationalism], *Shijie jingji yu zhengzhi*, no. 2 (2006): 1–13.

100. Zhao Tingyang, "Guanyu hexie shijie de sekao" [Some thoughts about the harmonious world], *Shijie jingji yu zhengzhi*, no. 9 (2006): 1; Zhao, "Tianxia tixi de yige jianyao biaoshu," which was a response to Ke Lan'an [William A. Callahan], "Zhongguo shiye xia de shijie zhixu: Tianxia, diguo he shijie" [Chinese visions of world order: Tianxia, empire and the world], *Shijie jingji yu zhengzhi*, no. 10 (2008): 49–56.

101. Zhao Tingyang, "Tianxia gainian yu shijie zhidu" [The Tianxia concept and the world system], in *Zhongguo xuezhi kan shijie: Guoji zhixu chuan* [Chinese scholars view the world: International order], edited by Qin Yaqing (Beijing: New World Press, 2006), 3–35.

102. Hu Jintao, "Nuli jianshe chijiu heping gongtong fanrong de hexie shijie" [Making an effort to build a sustainable, peaceful, and united prosperous harmonious world, speech at the United Nations sixtieth-year celebration], *Renmin Ribao*, September 16, 2006.

103. Wu Jianmin, "'Harmonious World' Helps Rebut 'China Threat,'" *People's Daily*, March 20, 2006; State Council, "China's Peaceful Development Road," Beijing, December 22, 2005.

104. Zhao, "Guanyu hexie shijie de sekao," 1; Zhao, ""Tianxia tixi de yige jianyao biaoshu," 63; Zhao, *Huai shijie yanjiu*, 110–20.

105. This argument is explored in chapter 10 of the present volume. For more about harmonious society and harmonious world, see Jean-Marc F. Blanchard and Sujian Guo, "'Harmonious World' and China's New Foreign Policy," in *"Harmonious World" and*

China's New Foreign Policy, edited by Sujian Guo and Jean-Marc F. Blanchard (New York: Lexington Books, 2008), 1–20.

106. Yu Keping, "We Must Work to Create a Harmonious World," *China Daily*, May 10, 2007. Yu is famous for his liberal essay "Democracy Is a Good Thing," first published in the *Beijing Daily News* on October 23, 2006; see Yu Keping, *Democracy Is a Good Thing: Essays on Politics, Society, and Culture in Contemporary China* (Washington, D.C.: Brookings Institution Press, 2008).)

107. Linda Jakobson and Dean Knox, *New Foreign Policy Actors in China*, SIPRI Policy Paper 26 (Stockholm: Stockholm International Peace Research Institute, 2010); Bonnie S. Glaser and Evan S. Medeiros, "The Changing Ecology of Foreign Policy-Making in China: The Ascension and Demise of the Theory of 'Peaceful Rise,'" *China Quarterly*, no. 190 (2007): 291–310.

108. See Shapiro, *Methods and Nations*, 48.

109. Sun Shu, "Shijie, yihuo tianxia?" [The world, or Tianxia?], *Boyan yangshu*, no. 11 (2005): 4–10.

110. Samuel P. Huntington, "The Clash of Civilizations?" *Foreign Affairs* 72, no. 3 (1993): 22–49.

111. See Peter J. Katzenstein, ed., *Civilizations in World Politics: Plural and Pluralistic Perspectives* (New York: Routledge, 2010).

112. This, of course, includes the author. See Fei-Ling Wang, "Heading Off Fears of a Resurgent China," *International Herald Tribune*, April 11, 2006; and Xiang Lanxin, "Jieyan quqi, shenyan hexie" [Stop talking about China's rise, be careful discussing world harmony], *Lianhe zaobao* (Singapore), March 26, 2006.

113. For an enthusiastic endorsement of Zhao's *Tianxia tixi*, which is described as an "exceedingly beautiful utopia," see Feng Zhang, "The Tianxia System: World Order in a Chinese Utopia," *Global Asia* 4, no. 4 (Winter 2010).

114. See Callahan, *China*; and Ma Rong, "Lijie minzu guanxi de xinselu: Xiaoshu zuqun wenti de 'qu zhengzhihua'" [New perspectives on nationalities relations: The "depoliticization" of the ethnic minority question], *Beijing daxue xuebao* 41, no. 6 (2004): 122–33.

Chapter 6

The Enduring Function of the Substance/Essence (*Ti/Yong*) Dichotomy in Chinese Nationalism

Christopher R. Hughes

Since the advent of "globalization" as a widely used concept in the 1990s, the impact of transnational processes on national identity has become a central theme in the debate between those categorized as "hyperglobalists," who believe in the withering away of the state, "skeptics," who deny that there is anything qualitatively new occurring, and "transformationalists," who see the state as an important actor that both shapes and is shaped by globalizing processes.[1] Yet such a discussion is far from new in China, where the impact of imperialism on identity has been at the center of intellectual life and policymaking since the mid–nineteenth century in the form of a discourse on what is known as the "*ti/yong*" dichotomy.

The immediate meaning of "*ti/yong*" can be gained from its two Chinese ideograms: The word "*ti*" (体) can be translated as "body," and the word "*yong*" (用) as "use." Due to the pioneering work of the intellectual historian Joseph Levenson, however, the terms are usually rendered into English as "essence" and "function."[2] The meaning of the formula becomes clearer when we are told that it is the abbreviated form of the longer prescription to take "Chinese studies as essence, Western studies as function" (*zhong xue wei ti, xi xue wei yong,* 中学为体西学为用). In other words, the *ti/yong* dichotomy is presented as a call to use Western functional knowledge and technology to preserve Chinese identity.

The enduring significance of the *ti/yong* formula at the beginning of the twenty-first century can be seen when China's leaders advocate using a "scientific outlook" on development that is premised on engagement with the global system and will result in the "great rejuvenation of the Chinese nation" and "the thriving of Chinese culture," at the center of which is the building of a "harmonious society."[3] Its position in popular discourse in a variety of forms can even be seen when the director of the opening ceremony of the 2008 Beijing Olympic Games, the filmmaker Zhang Yimou, explains the value of his use of digital technology by borrowing an aphorism from Mao Zedong: "Use the ancient to serve the present, use the foreign to serve China. We have to use the splendid culture that makes us most proud, and use modern audiovisual equipment to package it."[4]

Within the dominant narrative of Chinese intellectual history, however, the use of *ti/yong* has been marginalized and dismissed as a philosophical absurdity by historians, revolutionaries, and reformers alike. The complaint is best summed up by the remark made by Yan Fu, the first translator of social-Darwinist works into Chinese, who ridiculed the formula as being about as feasible as combining the function of a horse with the body of an ox.[5] This view has been taken up and reproduced by the international narrative on Chinese modernity, primarily through the monumental story of the transition from Confucianism to modernity in the work of Levenson, who describes *ti/yong* as a "philosophical attenuation" because it proposes that you can separate scientific knowledge from culture.[6] Such a judgment must be questioned when the idea of using foreign know-how to protect Chinese identity has remained at the center of the Chinese Communist Party's (CCP's) ideology, state policy, and popular discussion down to today.

This chapter argues that the reason for this cannot be found in searching for its logical consistency. Instead, it needs to be understood as a political act that goes back to the attempt by Qing Dynasty officials to mobilize the population by making tradition capable of harnessing the forces of nationalism as they entered China in the late nineteenth century. This makes possible the grouping together of certain discourses on the syncretism of knowledge and identity, mass mobilization through "national humiliation," and the creation of a form of nationalist legitimacy. In the process, the concept of Chinese national essence is reduced from Confucian universalism to become a malleable object of political loyalty for the nation, making possible a variety of options for the formation of nationalism and the making of foreign policy.

Putting *Ti/Yong* into Nationalist Discourse

In the *Archaeology of Knowledge*, Michel Foucault proposes that "providing one defines the conditions clearly, it might be legitimate to constitute, on the basis of correctly described relations, discursive groups that are not arbitrary, but remain invisible."[7] It is proposed here that the *ti/yong* formula makes possible just such a discursive grouping through a process of erasure that goes back to the political strategies used by activists in the late Qing Dynasty and is reproduced in the orthodox international narrative on Chinese modernity.

Probably the most influential text in this process of erasure is the influential *Qing dai xueshu gailun* (General discussion of Qing Dynasty studies), published by the political writer Liang Qichao in 1921.[8] It is here that the phrase "study China as essence, study the West as function" is first used.[9] However, Liang coins the phrase only to dismiss it by attributing it to the figure of Zhang Zhidong (1837–1909), governor general of the central Chinese provinces of Hubei and Hunan. For Liang, Zhang and *ti/yong* are condemned because he presents them as representative of a type of mistaken thinking that denies that Europe and the United States have any worthwhile knowledge beyond manufacturing, measuring, and navigation.

That this is no more than a political strategy by Liang, however, can be seen from the fact that Zhang does not actually state the formula "study China as essence, study the West as function." The nearest he gets to this is in his most influential text, the 1898 *Quan xue pian* (Exhortation to study), where he uses the phrase "Chinese as inner, Western as outer" (*zhong xue wei nei, xi xue wei wai*, 中学为内 西学为外).[10] But even this is only mentioned as part of a general discussion on the nature of comparative studies, rather than raised to a prominent position in his work. In fact Zhang rarely uses the terms "*ti*" and "*yong*."

This imposition of the *ti/yong* formula on Zhang begins to make sense when we realize that Liang's views on Zhang emerge from a position of exile and exclusion from state power after he had to flee China as a member of the disbanded Hundred Days Reform movement. Zhang, however, remained at the imperial court and sought to maintain stability through the throne. In the years that followed, Liang launched a bitter campaign against Zhang from Tokyo, publishing a series of articles that have been described as "notable for their lack of coherent content, being largely emotional denunciations."[11]

Liang's substitution of the terms "*ti*" and "*yong*" for Zhang's "*nei*" (inner) and "*wai*" (outer) might be traceable to his familiarity with the nationalist discourse of Meiji Japan. There, the discussion of the "national structure" (*guo ti*; Japanese *kokutai*) had taken place in the seventeenth century when the Bakufu administration had encouraged scholars to think about enhancing social stability by nativizing Confucianism in a way that would legitimize the hierarchical social order, at the head of which was the emperor. This helped to lay the foundations for the emergence of Japanese nationalism in the nineteenth century, but looked to the past and to native traditions.[12] It looks remarkably conservative in comparison with the discourse on "national essence" (*guo cui*, 国粹) that emerged after the samurai class was disenfranchised by the Meiji reforms and was accelerated by the national humiliation that swept the country after negotiations with the Western powers to revise the Unequal Treaties broke down in 1887.[13]

By imposing the vocabulary of the older Japanese *kokutai* movement on Zhang, Liang could make himself appear radical in comparison with the establishment bureaucrat he portrayed as introducing Western knowledge without properly understanding it. This allows Liang to present himself, along with his fellow constitutional reformers Kang Youwei and Tan Sitong, as bringing new life to what he describes as the "intellectual famine" (学问饥荒) left by Zhang.

Yet this dismissal of Zhang is little more than a caricature. Zhang was actually an advocate of "self-strengthening," the belief held by radical Confucian administrators since the defeat by Britain in the Opium War that the secret of building state power lay in the construction of railroads, heavy industry, and modern armaments. He was also at one with this movement in advocating a foreign policy based on the power-balancing principle of "use barbarians to control barbarians." His plan for the modernization of the education system was approved by the Court in 1904 and became the foundation for policy in the last years of the Qing Dynasty and even in the early Republic.[14] Even Mao Zedong, who also condemns Zhang Zhidong for not understanding that functional change transforms cultural essence, admits that the maintenance of steel output under Chiang Kai-shek's rule would not have been possible "had he not benefited from what Zhang Zhidong and others did in the late Qing period."[15]

The success of Liang's use of *ti/yong* to erase the importance of a figure like Zhang can be seen in the way it is reproduced by historians like Levenson. In this version of the story, the *ti/yong* formula is dismissed as a "philosophical attenuation" on the grounds that treating "essence" and "function" as separate entities was never the intention of the Southern Song Dynasty philosopher Zhu Xi, who first began using the concepts "*ti*" and "*yong*."[16] Such an analytical appraisal, however, misses the point that the formula was born as an essentially political act, evident above all in the fact that the *Quan xue pian* was produced in large quantities as one of the first political pamphlets for mass consumption. It was issued complete with an imperial rescript commanding that it be distributed to the viceroys, governors and "literary examiners" of the whole empire, so that it could be extensively published and widely circulated in the provinces.

The erasure of Zhang's contribution to the narrative of the long Chinese revolution by caricaturing *ti/yong* is thus due not to any particular philosophical acumen on the part of Liang. After all, even he works within *ti/yong* by ending his history of Qing thought with an argument for populating China with "scientific people" for whom the "spiritual famine" is filled by a metaphysics developed from nativized Buddhism.[17] The success of his erasure is thus more likely to be due to Liang's iconic position as a father of the anti-Manchu nationalist discourse that discredited the Qing Dynasty. Zhang, conversely, is on the losing side not due to a lack of rigor in his thinking but because he supported reform through the Manchu Qing Court until his death. Yet, despite this erasure, an analysis of Zhang's text shows that it produces a remarkable discussion of the relationship between cultural identity and the importation of foreign knowledge in a way that brings together discursive themes that remain central to Chinese politics down to the present.

Ti/Yong as Syncretism

The first of these themes is the ability to bring together concepts from different systems of thought through a process of syncretism. In this respect, it is in fact quite wrong to propose that nineteenth-century Chinese reformers like Zhang ever really imagined that the dynastic system could be maintained without fundamental reforms to the cultural base by which it was legitimized. Instead, neo-Confucianism proves to be a remarkably flexible discourse because it provides a language that has been shaped over many centuries by strategies to accommodate the impact of rival foreign cultures without undermining China's domestic political system. This was certainly obvious to the Chinese elite of Zhang's time, who were well versed in the way that philosophers like Zhu Xi had met the challenge of foreign ideas.

Buddhism, for example, was a particularly difficult challenge after it arrived from India during the Eastern Han Dynasty. Though it enriched the Chinese vocabulary and brought with it new astronomical, calendrical, and medical studies, it also posed a challenge to the social values that legitimated the Confucian order and established new centers of political influence in the monasteries. China's only woman empress, Wu Zetian of the Tang Dynasty, even legitimated her position by claiming to be a living Bodhisattva.[18]

Politically, the thinking of the Southern Song philosophers may also have been attractive to the late Qing because it too was a weak dynasty surrounded by powerful neighbors. Zhu Xi's ontological distinction of *ti* from *yong* was in fact devised as part of his project to bring together the threads of neo-Confucianism at a time when Buddhism was experiencing a revival under the patronage of a sympathetic court. This entailed matching the metaphysical claims of Buddhism by appropriating some of its concepts, and going one better by proposing that it was possible to derive knowledge of the "principles" of reality (*li*) from the Confucian texts. This merging of elements of Confucianism, Daoism, and Buddhism established the neo-Confucian vocabulary that was used to legitimate political power until the end of the dynastic system in 1911.

After the trauma of the Mongol occupation of the Yuan Dynasty, this conceptual division of knowledge proved to be useful as the Ming and Qing dynasty thinkers began to rebuild a sense of Chinese identity. It also played an important role when dealing with the impact of Christianity, when the "new learning" (*xin xue*, 新学) was divided into desirable and undesirable elements. The *Annotated Catalogue of the Imperial Library* (1782) thus defined "Western learning" (*xi xue*, 西学) by separating its desirable fields such as astronomy and mathematics from the undesirable Christian "principles" (*li*).[19] From a Chinese perspective, this was merely disentangling the two kinds of knowledge that the Jesuits had erroneously mixed in their plan to put science into the service of propagating their religion.

When syncretism was ruptured, rebellion and revolution were the result. This was what occurred when a disaffected official, Hong Xiuquan, discovered a Christian missionary pamphlet that gave him a vocabulary to challenge the Confucianist legitimation of the Qing Dynasty and launch the Taiping Rebellion that almost overthrew the empire in the mid–nineteenth century. Faced by this kind of domestic upheaval, syncretism had to be rebalanced. Qing reformers did so by initiating radical attempts to appropriate foreign knowledge, sometimes even working with foreign militaries, as when their forces fought alongside the British and French under the command of General Charles Gordon in 1862 to suppress the Taipings.

At the same time, the Zongli Yamen (literally the "Office for the General Management of Affairs and Trade with Every Country") was established, as was the first school of Western languages and sciences (同文馆) in Beijing. Ambassadors began to be sent abroad to gather knowledge and negotiate treaties, and were soon supplemented by the sending of selected students overseas to learn about the secrets of national power, starting with the United States and then going on to Europe. Moreover, the use of foreign loans to subsidize military campaigns against domestic rebellions, the suppression of Yakub Beg's secession in East Turkestan, and for the defense of Taiwan created new pressures to join the world financial system.

The awareness of a need to adapt to transnational processes can even be seen in Liang's own intellectual and political leader, the constitutionalist Kang Youwei, who began his 1897 memorial to the emperor on political reform by stating:

> China is one country in a world of 800,000 li; China is one country among more than fifty. The globe [*diqiu*] has been connected since the end of the Ming Dynasty, transportation has boomed since the reigns of Jiaqing and Daoguang [1796–1851]. The new events of the past hundred years represent change that is unprecedented in the preceding 4,000 years.[20]

Although the transactions between the Qing Empire and the rest of the world to which Kang alludes were not on the scale as what has occurred for the People's Republic of China under "reform and opening," the impact of transnational processes on domestic identity politics is clearly visible at this time. In 1820, in fact, China accounted for 30 percent of global gross domestic product.[21] By the 1870s, the Jiangnan arsenal had become one of the largest in the world, the China Merchants' Steam Navigation Company had been established, and telegraph cables were being laid to link Hong Kong, Guangzhou, and Shanghai with London and San Francisco. As Kang's language demonstrates, such developments were sufficient to force people interested in the "self-strengthening" of the Qing Dynasty to discuss local military, political, and economic issues in terms of "world order," a phenomenon that sociologists claim is typical of a globalistic mentality.[22]

This historical development meant that nationalism entered the Qing

Empire at the end of the nineteenth century within what was already a lively discourse on the relationship between the Chinese cultural essence and the impact of transnational processes. Reformers like Zhang Zhidong were certainly discussing the impact of transnational processes long before Liang Qichao introduced the vocabulary of "nationalism" into the Chinese vocabulary via the medium of Japanese neologisms. Even the Dowager Empress could see the value in reforming the state's basic institutions.

Lacking the vocabulary of nationalism, "self-strengtheners" had to draw on the concepts of neo-Confucianism to articulate a response to this global challenge. In this respect, they had already generated a number of dichotomies that could be used to explain the relationship of Chinese orthodoxy to the new learning. These included formulas such as "Self-sufficiency as essence, promote sincerity as function"; "Defense as essence, war as function"; "Rely on industry for essence, rely on commerce for function"; and "Metaphysical study [*li xue* of the Song Dynasty] for essence, economics for function."[23]

When considering the potentials of the current Confucian revival, it is important to bear in mind the syncretic nature of this discourse to which Zhang Zhidong contributed. In terms of ontological logic, Levenson is no doubt right to point out that Zhu Xi never proposed the separation of essence from function. Yet such a judgment overlooks the way in which change in neo-Confucianism is explained by an understanding of reality as a "balanced inequality" between the eternally opposing forces of "yin" and "yang."[24] When the rather static view of culture that is implicit in Levenson's appraisal is discarded, the potential for the tension between Chinese *ti* and foreign *yong* to generate a new type of mass politics through the propagation of the theme of "national humiliation" (*guo chi*, 国耻) becomes clearer.[25]

Ti/Yong and National Humiliation

The way in which the transformation of Confucianism into a symbol of resistance against imperialism puts the tension between the Chinese essence and Western knowledge at the heart of mass politics can be seen very clearly in Zhang Zhidong's *Quan xue pian*. This radical turn was enabled by the defeat of the Qing forces in Korea by Japan and the concession of Taiwan in 1895, a trauma that unleashed new political forces by radicalizing politics and triggering the establishment of the first real nationalist political parties. At the same time, defeat led to the eruption of antiforeign movements rooted in folk practices that eventually mushroomed into the Boxer Rebellion. Faced by rising popular anger over the impotence of the Qing state, Zhang sought a formula that could unite the population by providing a bridge between what appeared to be the incommensurable positions of dogmatic conservatism on the one side and revolutionary reform on the other. His answer amounts to one of the first attempts to promote mass mobilization by propagating what he called "knowing shame" (*zhi chi*, 知耻).

The source of this "knowing shame" can be found in an aphorism in chapter 12 of the Confucian text *The Doctrine of the Mean*, where it is stated that "love of study leads to knowledge, acting strongly leads to benevolence, knowing shame leads to courage" (*hao xue jinhu zhi, li xing jinhu ren, zhi chi jinhu yong*; 好学近乎知，力行近乎仁，知耻近乎勇).[26] Zhang claims that this passage is his greatest source of inspiration, drawing attention to the fact that it was delivered by Confucius as advice on how to seek state power to the duke of Ai, the leader of the weak Kingdom of Lu during the period of the Warring States that preceded the Qin unification of China in 221 BC.

For Zhang, "knowing shame" is of such importance that he makes it the first of "five types of knowing." He reinforces this when he draws attention to the weakness of the empire, already evident in the metaphorical use of the Kingdom of Lu, by insisting on the need to know the "shame" of China's failing to be like nations that have maintained their independence, such as Japan, Turkey, Siam, and Cuba. This rendering of the nation as the referent object for shame is then further strengthened when Zhang makes "knowing fear" (*zhi ju*, 知惧) the second of his five types of knowledge, insisting that it is necessary to propagate the fear that the empire could share the fate of colonized nations like India, Annam, Burma, Korea, Egypt, and Poland.[27]

Commentators who look for logical consistency in the *ti/yong* dichotomy tend to overlook the psychological importance of the prominence that Zhang gives to "knowing shame" and "knowing fear." From this perspective, however, Zhang's thinking on the use of emotions to mobilize the population is actually more radical than that of Liang Qichao's constitutionalist comrades, such as Kang Youwei and Tan Sitong, who mine the classics to find an ultimate resolution of differences between cultures and races (*zhong*) under a doctrine of "great harmony" (*datong shijie*). The shock of the defeat by Japan in Korea leads Zhang to a point where he rejects this utopianism in favor of using Confucianism as an object to stimulate loyalty within a world perpetually driven by the struggle for survival.[28]

This radical departure from the Sinocentric vision of the world is further developed through appropriation of the modern conception of the international system when Zhang explores the theme of "uniting hearts" (*tong xin*) in the first chapter of *Quan xue pian*. It is here that he establishes that the three tasks that must be completed to save China are to protect the state (*bao guojia*), protect the sacred teachings (*bao sheng jiao*), and protect the Chinese race (*bao hua zhong*). In this formula, the state exists to protect the teachings of Confucius, but both are only needed to protect the Chinese race. Little doubt is left that the state is more important for racial survival than the possession of a superior culture when Zhang cites the example of Turkey to show how an irrational religion like Islam can survive when the nation is strong and warlike, whereas India shows that a sincere philosophy like Buddhism can perish when the nation is stupid and foolish.[29]

Zhang in fact devotes the entire fourth chapter of *Quan xue pian* to a racial categorization of humanity through "knowing categories" (*zhi lei*). Tracing the division of the world into competing races (*zhonglei*), back to the Chinese classics, he modernizes the fivefold division of humanity according to color that he takes from "foreigners."[30] This allows for the development of a historicist vision, according to which the Chinese race has been sapped of its vitality due to the lack of competition from powerful neighbors, whereas the countries of Europe have grown strong through desperate competition and the fight to avoid destruction. In the past fifty years especially, the Chinese officials and people are condemned for a pride and indolence that has left their country almost irredeemably stupid and weak.[31]

Within such a vision, Confucianism clearly ceases to be presented as a universal culture but becomes the particular possession of the Chinese nation that might be taken away by superior force. It is thus a misreading of Zhang to suggest that he makes the universalist claim that Confucian culture is superior to other cultures or that it is an unchanging entity. The principles of Confucian social hierarchy (*san wang*) remain important as a code of domestic cohesion in his overall vision, but they are no longer extended to the whole of humanity.

Moreover, the need to survive means that his delimitation of the sphere of orthodox culture can be quite progressive, going far beyond importing science and technology from the West. This is clear when Zhang lists "knowing change" (*zhi bian*, 知变) and "knowing necessity" (*zhi yao*, 知要) as the third and fourth of his five modes of knowing. Without changing the customary way of doing things, he explains, it is not possible to change the "laws" (*bian fa*, 变法), which is the prerequisite for transforming "tools" (*bian qi*, 变器). He specifically states that studying the West should focus on knowing government and not on the arts.[32]

It is in the fifth type of knowing, namely "knowing the root" (*zhi ben*, 知本), that the discourse of humiliation is completed. Zhang explains this as follows:

> When overseas do not forget the country, when you see alien customs do not forget your relatives, know lots of techniques but do not forget the Sage.[33]

Aside from this being a remarkable paraphrasing of the educational policies developed in the 1980s, when China began to send large numbers of students overseas for technical training,[34] it shows how Zhang's model of knowing amounts to a defense of Confucianism as the most appropriate ethical system for Chinese society. Most significant, though, is the way that this opens the door to his most revolutionary achievement, which is the reduction of ethics from the status of universal principles to the level of core values that define the nation, give it strength, and need to be defended.

Embedded in the classical texts, ethics thus takes on a new role not as a guide to daily conduct but as providing symbols that must be protected and disseminated so that any transgression will stimulate shame and fear. This is delineated in a chapter on "sequence" (循序), where Zhang explains how students should understand the Chinese classics, customs, and history, then "later on Western learning can be used to make up for our shortcomings and Western government used to heal our ailments, thus gaining its benefits and not its harm."[35] That this does not imply a universal validity for Confucianism is made even clearer when he goes on to liken this approach to the Western practice of learning Christianity in church and Latin at school; first learning the map of one's own country and then learning the map of the world; and learning patriotism (*ai guo*, 爱国) by studying the virtuous rulers in one's own history. If Chinese scholars did not study China, he asked, then how could the country use them?

Writing in the aftermath of the defeat by Japan, it appears that Zhang Zhidong had come to the realization that making Confucianism a token of resistance to foreign rivals was a price worth paying if it was to have a role in political life. It is argued below that, in the longer term, this representation of a national essence (*ti*) has proven to be an enduring political strategy that has been more effective for engaging in the politics of mass mobilization than mining Confucian tradition to find alternative visions of modernity based on harmony and cosmopolitanism.

Ti/Yong and Political Legitimacy under Nationalism

Given that the main function of the *ti/yong* formula is to stimulate popular emotions of shame and fear by reifying a Chinese national essence, it would be a mistake to look for its longer-term significance in the preservation of Confucianism alone. Because the syncretic logic assumed by the formula allows competing systems of ideas to exist in an unresolved yet dynamic and politically productive tension, it becomes possible to combine Confucianism with any orthodoxy that signifies Chinese "essence" (*ti*). The possibility of a new theory of political legitimacy is thus opened up for any actor who can successfully claim to be the guardian of the national essence. Representations of Confucianism have thus waxed and waned as political actors claiming state power have sought to represent the national essence in modern terms.

This dynamic can be seen in the deployment of Confucianism by Yuan Shikai, the first president of the Republic of China, who had been the most modern of the Qing Dynasty generals. When Yuan attempted to roll back the Republican Revolution by creating a constitutional monarchy with himself as emperor, he turned to Confucianism for a state ideology, revising the new republic's plans for educational reform by restoring the worship of Confucius and bringing study of the classics back into elementary school. The stress was on combining the themes of developing strength and self-discipline as found in Confucius and Mencius, emphasizing patriotic education, duty to the state, public spirited action, industrial training, and military preparedness.[36] Yuan's plans were aborted with his death in 1916, the year before his projected enthronement as the new emperor.

When the Kuomintang (KMT) came back into power, however, it maintained the same tension between *ti* and *yong* by replacing Confucianism with the new orthodoxy of Sun Yatsen's "Three Principles of the People," namely "nationalism, people's rights, and people's welfare." Looking at the general view of the world in Sunism, we are again confronted with the picture of China as a nation facing annihilation in the struggle for survival among competing races (*zhong*) because it lacks national spirit (*minzu de jingshen*). National salvation is to be achieved partly by importing foreign know-how, especially from the Soviet Union after the Bolshevik Revolution. Yet the ideology of Communism remains anathema.

Sun Yatsen himself never envisioned that importing technology from abroad would be allowed to erode his belief that all the peoples of China could be united to form a great Chinese ("Zhonghua") nation on the basis of ancient Chinese cultures.[37] He is prepared to borrow political ideas from the democracies, yet it is the institutions of ancestor worship, reverence for the family, and religion that are the foundations out of which a nationalist sentiment is to become a force that can bind together the "plate of loose sand" that is China. This conception of the Chinese essence must be rendered in a way that allows for a rejection of what is seen as the enfeebling influence of the new cosmopolitanism being developed out of the "Tianxia" worldview.

Zhang Zhidong, of course, could only make this departure from "Tianxia" implicit in his conception of a world of competing races, because it remained the foundation of Qing Dynasty legitimacy. Sun, as leader of the anti-Manchu revolution, faced no such inhibitions. Sun's Three Principles doctrine is also certainly different from Zhang Zhidong's political program insofar as it promotes democratization under the principle of "people's rights" (*min quan*). In his reaction to the promotion of this idea by Kang Youwei, Zhang had condemned it as a foolhardy devolution of power to a self-centered gentry and generally uninformed citizenry that would only accelerate the process of national disintegration.[38] Even this difference over rights narrowed, however, after the KMT expanded its military power to much of China in the 1927 Northern Expedition and the promotion of its ideological orthodoxy meant that the new Chinese essence took precedence over the democratic project.

Looking at the field of education, the KMT's nation building can be understood as a continuation of the basic dynamic of trying to achieve the right balance between *ti* and *yong* that had begun when Zhang Zhidong persuaded the Dowager Empress to allow the Confucian classics to share a place with other branches of knowledge in the reforms that he made to the civil service examinations in 1902.[39] The KMT similarly paid attention to the *yong* side of the dichotomy by emphasizing vocational training. More science colleges were established at universities and enrollment in the arts, social sciences, and law was not allowed to exceed their intake. Academia Sinica was established to undertake national research in 1928, and the Beijing Research Academy the following year.[40]

Strengthening of the *ti* is even clearer as Chaing Kai-shek made the teaching of the Three Principles compulsory for schools and proclaimed the celebration of days of national humiliation. When the Japanese invaded Northeast China in 1931, more emphasis was given to military and physical training in schools, and textbooks included details on the armaments of foreign countries in social studies and methods of preventing gas attacks in chemistry. Committees were established to strengthen national cohesiveness by administering education in Mongolia and Tibet and overseeing the teaching of 10 million Chinese overseas. Teachers had to attend courses in anticommunism and the Three Principles.[41] Attention was given to party training in 1932 when the KMT founded the Chungshan Memorial Cultural and Educational Institute in Nanjing, to promote advanced study and training in ideology.

Chiang's increasing tendency to legitimate his dictatorship by combining the Three Principles with Confucian morality reached a peak with the New Life Movement that was launched in 1934 to combat the spread of Communism. This strategy of presenting the KMT dictatorship as the guardian of the true national essence even survived under the KMT in Taiwan until the late 1980s, when it began to be made unsustainable by the island's democratization.

Ti/Yong and the Sinification of Marxism

As with the KMT, the CCP effectively maintained the basic dynamics of the *ti/yong* formula by replacing Confucianism with its own version of the Chinese essence, claiming the "Sinification of Marxism" to be one of the greatest achievements of "Mao Zedong Thought." Despite Mao's dismissal of Zhang Zhidong, his appropriation of *ti/yong* can in fact be seen in the way that he divides cultural essence and functional knowledge in his prescription to "use the ancient to serve the present, use the foreign to serve China" (*gu wei jin yong, yang wei zhong yong*; 古为今用洋为中用),[42] used more recently by Zhang Yimou in the context of the Beijing Olympics.

The more that is learned about Mao's personal life, the clearer it becomes just how much value he attached to classical learning. For the pre-Marxist Mao, the model to be followed for those who wished to save the nation was Zeng Guofan, the self-strengthening contemporary of Zhang Zhidong. Rather than leaving this attachment to tradition behind after turning to Communism, he continued to see the works of Han Yu, the Tang

Dynasty opponent of the impact of Buddhism on Chinese orthodoxy, as the model for Chinese linguistic style. Sima Guang's *Mirror of Government* (资治通鉴) was one of his main sources for understanding political change and military strategy until the end of his life.[43] It might also be added that in the mature Mao, the dialectical understanding of reality as an uninterrupted revolution driven by a creative tension between opposites, in which "one divides into two," has more in common with the yin/yang understanding of change that underpins the neo-Confucianism of Zhang Zhidong than with the formal Aristotelian logic implicit in Levenson's criticism of *ti/yong* as a "philosophical attenuation."

Just as the trauma of defeat by Japan had reinforced the need for both Zhang Zhidong and the KMT in previous years to use the dynamics of *ti/yong* to mobilize the population through propagating shame, the presentation of Mao as the person who could use foreign knowledge to preserve the Chinese essence became particularly salient when he claimed leadership of the United Front in the war against Japan in the 1930s. The propagation of national "shame" to mobilize the masses in this process is continued as he reminds his audience at this time of how the imperialists occupied "many neighboring powers formerly under her [China's] protection" and seized or leased parts of Chinese territory, such as Port Arthur (Lüshun), Taiwan and the Penghu Islands, Hong Kong, and the territory of Guangzhouwan leased to France.[44]

It was in this context that the CCP began to be cast as the true inheritor of what Mao considered to be the essence of "a splendid old culture" that had been created during the long period of Chinese history and that could be drawn on selectively to develop the "new national culture."[45] When Mao advocated learning from both socialist cultures and the various capitalist countries in the Age of Enlightenment, he graphically described the process of acculturation as follows:

> We should not gulp any of this foreign material down uncritically, but must treat it as we do our food—first chewing it, then submitting it to the working of the stomach and intestines with their juices and secretions, and separating it into nutriment to be absorbed and waste matter to be discarded—before it can nourish us.[46]

Before the Cultural Revolution, there was even an attempt to explicitly cast CCP members as followers of Confucian ethics. In 1954, the CCP organ *Guangming Daily* raised the topic of Confucianism by publishing a short debate on the subject. Many students learned the classics indirectly through literature lessons, easily equating Confucian and Communist principles. As one language professor explained: "For instance, Confucius tells you to value humanity, sympathy, and tolerance; and he teaches you love of country, and respect for your teachers, parents, and the aged. You should be a faithful husband, he says, and true to your friends, loving to your children, and a modest person. All this is the same as Communism expects and teaches."[47]

In 1961, the 2,440th anniversary of Confucius' death was celebrated, and a conference was held that insisted on his progressive class views.[48] Liu Shaoqi's *How to Be a Good Communist*, originally presented in the CCP base area of Yanan during the war against Japan, was also revived at this time and used to promote the idea of "self-cultivation," effectively nativizing the Communist call for the absolute subordination of the individual to the "Party spirit" as an alternative to the liberal democracy that might enter the nation along with foreign technology.[49]

The radicals of the Cultural Revolution also worked within the structure of *ti/yong* insofar as they saw education as a way to build character through the immersion of young people in Mao Zedong Thought. As Unger points out, they were not only "redder" than the moderates, they were more traditional too, seeming almost Confucian in their belief that the principal purpose of schooling lay in the teaching of morals. For them, labor had a special significance as a morally purifying activity when linked to political teachings and conducted in the proper group environment.[50] Their belief that learning was a highly practical activity that could be divorced from Marxist theory can also be seen as mirroring the division of knowledge into *ti* and *yong* inherited from the late Qing.

Ti/Yong and "Reform and Opening"

After the Cultural Revolution, *ti* and *yong* had to be reformulated in a way that was suitable for what was to become the period of "reform and opening." The appearance of previously unpublished works by Mao, such as his 1956 speech "On the Ten Major Relationships," provided legitimacy for his post–Cultural Revolution successors to learn from foreign countries with "an analytical and critical eye, rather than "copy everything indiscriminately and transplant mechanically."[51] The vocabulary of *ti/yong* was even explicitly used when the Ministry of Industry attacked isolationist policies just after the fall of the Gang of Four in an article in *People's Daily* that recommended the study and use of "good" foreign experience and technology under the title "Self-Sufficiency, Use the Foreign to Serve China" (*zili gengsheng, yang wei zhong yong*; 自立更生, 洋为中用).[52]

As the leadership moved toward opening China to more foreign investment and sending students overseas, the conception of a national essence was again increasingly filled by a revival of the pre–Cultural Revolution emphasis on Confucian morality. Mao's immediate successor, Chairman Hua Guofeng, in many ways mirrored the late Qing modernizers when he tried to boost his charisma by cultivating an image of himself and his family as the embodiment of the Confucian ideals of frugality and humility. After Hua was deposed and Deng Xiaoping took the reins of power in December 1978, the rehabilitation of figures such as Liu Shaoqi and the publication of the works of the conservative moralist and economic planner Chen Yun further prepared the ground for a revival of this kind of moralizing as an essential counterpoint to the functional knowledge of "reform and opening."

This can be seen in Deng, the main architect for the adjustment of *ti* and *yong* under "reform and opening," who as early as August 1977 calls for a restoration of the balance between morality, knowledge, and physical education.[53] Throughout the 1980s, he is always careful to balance the importation of investment and know-how from abroad with a call to build "socialism with Chinese characteristics," being adamant that the nation should combat the tendency of "worshipping things foreign, or fawning on foreigners."[54] This is then developed into the project to build both "material civilization" and "socialist spiritual civilization."[55]

The revival of tradition within this discourse begins to enter education policy as early as 1979, when a national conference in the city of Taiyuan accepted that the past had its place in contemporary society, reaffirmed the legacy of tradition that Mao had recognized in 1940, and pointed out that he had always appreciated the rationality and concepts of loyalty, benevolence, merciful authority, and respect for the aged in Confucius.[56] Throughout the following decade, the education and propaganda organs of the state and party struggled to reconcile the teaching of political thought and ethics with the movement towards the market, creating an elite that is not only technologically "expert" but also ideologically "red."

Experts were to be produced by decentralizing the management and financing of the education system and by sending more students overseas to satisfy the demands of the economy. As this increased the tension between *ti* and *yong*, they were to be made "red" through more emphasis on the use of patriotic education to prevent undesirable influences from abroad from polluting their national character, combining "love of the motherland, love of the party, and love of socialism" into one body of thought.[57]

This call to strengthen the Chinese essence was taken up by local cadres with the support of conservative CCP elders with such enthusiasm that it erupted into the "anti–spiritual pollution" and "anti–bourgeois liberalization" campaigns of the early to mid-1980s, which saw Western cultural mores trashed at the same time that investment and management know-how was being increasingly imported. Just as with Zhang and the Boxers, such outbreaks reveal the difficulty for reformers of trying to maintain the "balanced inequality" between the yang of Chinese *ti* and the yin of foreign *yong*, presenting a dilemma that generates many of the arguments over political change in the 1980s. The reformist position was presented in 1985 in the CCP Central Committee's key document for education reform, which looks to a future when China will require a range of technical and administrative personnel who understand the culture of modern science but also have the right ideals, morality, culture, discipline, and "ardent love" of the socialist motherland and socialism. Yet the national *ti* still must be protected by instilling a spirit of sacrifice and the will to struggle to create a wealthy and strong country and people in the rising generation of technicians.[58]

When this attempt to maintain a balance between *ti* and *yong* was challenged by prominent CCP intellectuals in the late 1980s, crisis ensued and discipline was meted out. The Marxist historian Li Zehou, for example, was frozen out of academic life and eventually had to leave China after he compared would-be historical materialists with those nineteenth-century Confucian reformers who had failed to realize that objects such as ships and trains were manifestations of the cultural substance of modern society. Inverting the *ti/yong* balance, he argued that formulas such as "the Sinification of Marxism," "the Chinese-style road to modernization," and "Chinese-style socialism" do in fact amount to taking the West as "substance" and China as "function" (*xi ti zhong yong*).[59]

Yet while a critic like Li rejected the crudities of the cultural campaigns of the 1980s, he was never able to bring himself to accept the idea that modernization means "Westernization." Instead, he meant that national cultures could perform the "function" (*yong*) of adapting science and technology to local conditions, as demonstrated by the case of Japan. His punishment was thus relatively short-lived, with rehabilitation coming in the mid-1990s, and thus since then his works have been republished in China.

Those members of the CCP who called for "comprehensive Westernization," however, were expelled from the party, the most prominent being the writer Wang Ruowang, the journalist Liu Binyan, and the astrophysicist Fang Lizhi. The stresses in the *ti/yong* dichotomy at this time are best represented by the fact that one of the main charges against Fang was that he had failed to live up to the standard of "socialist spiritual civilization" because he had advocated the view that science should be the standard of truth. After the suppression of dissent in 1989, such figures fled into permanent exile. Since then, the process of "reform and opening" has continued to seek an optimal balance between preserving the CCP's version of the Chinese essence through patriotic education and the propagation of "national humiliation" on the one hand, while opening up the economy to globalization and training personnel who can create the wealth and power necessary to save the nation on the other.

Although most observers stress the nationalistic content of the patriotic education that was strengthened after the 1989 repression, they tend to overlook that this has always been balanced by attempts to make the content of education relevant to the development of modern science and technology. The 1995 Education Law makes clear that teachers are supposed to produce personnel who can not only "uphold the guidance of Marxism-Leninism, Mao Zedong Thought, and the theory of building socialism with Chinese characteristics" but can also contribute to economic development. Balancing the old *ti/yong* dichotomy of using foreign learning to preserve the Chinese essence, these new personnel are supposed to continue "the excellent historical cultural tradition of the Chinese nation (*minzu*), [and] absorb all the excellent results of the development of human civilization." The mission of teachers and schools is to "develop education, raise the quality of the whole nation (*minzu*), and facilitate the building of socialist material and spiritual civilization."[60]

Within this context, "establishment intellectuals" can present "tradition" as useful for satisfying the "irrational" (*fei lixing zhuyi*) demands of the people, while advocating the use of Western ideas as necessary for economic management.[61] This prescription of a revival of "tradition" to satisfy the irrational demands of a population that is being dislocated by globalization has now been taken to a new stage (or back to the Qing) by Hu Jintao's call to build a "harmonious society." Just as Zhang Zhidong had the Confucian classics taught alongside more applied knowledge, now they have been included in the curriculum for secondary schools.

The Endurance of *Ti/Yong*: From the Domestic to the International

The survey given above shows that although revolutionaries and reformers since the end of the Qing Dynasty have distanced themselves from the *ti/yong* formula, it constitutes what Foucault would describe as an "invisible discourse," revealed by an analysis of the coexistence, succession, mutual functioning, reciprocal determination, and the correlative transformation of certain themes.[62] It is within this process that modern politics becomes possible by allowing the articulation of a Chinese "essence" that is threatened by the necessary process of importing foreign knowledge, creating a symbol of resistance that can stimulate a mass psychology of shame that can be harnessed by political actors seeking legitimacy.

Given the centrality that this gives the *ti/yong* formula in Chinese politics, it can be expected to have important implications for those areas where the domestic intersects with international relations. A recent example can be found when the intensification of globalization in the late 1990s necessitates the formulation of the "going out" (*zou chuqu*) strategy (usually called "going global" in English translations), which constitutes the logic for making China a world power under the World Trade Organization's rules and procedures when it is presented in the context of the competition between nations in a world situation characterized by "economic globalization and political multipolarity."[63]

The relationship between transnational processes, the system of states, and nationalism on which this is based is elaborated at some length by former CCP general secretary Jiang Zemin, in his work report to the CCP's Sixteenth National Congress in November 2002, where he states:

> The trends toward political multipolarization and economic globalization are developing amidst twists and turns. Science and technology are advancing rapidly, competition in overall national strength is becoming increasingly fierce. Given this pressing situation, we must move forwards or will fall behind. Our Party must stand firm in the forefront of the times and unite and lead the Chinese people of all ethnic groups in accomplishing the three major historical tasks: to propel the modernization drive, to achieve national reunification to safeguard world peace, and promote common development, and in bringing about a great rejuvenation of the Chinese nation on its road to socialism with Chinese characteristics.[64]

Coming after this, the combination of "Confucian" concepts such as a "harmonious society" with the prescription to have a "scientific outlook" for development in Hu Jintao's report to the CCP's Seventeenth National Congress in October 2007 can be seen as a continuation of the attempt to adjust the balance between *ti* and *yong*. Though this revival of harmony as one half of the *ti/yong* dichotomy is plainly directed against growing domestic inequality and corruption and closing the possibility of introducing liberal-democratic reforms, the extension of the idea of a "harmonious world" to foreign policy is problematic. As Daniel Bell points out, the limitations become particularly clear when the United States–led invasion of Iraq must be reconciled by Confucian intellectuals with a policy of reintegrating Taiwan into the Mainland by threatening the island with invasion and bloodshed.[65]

Yet the argument presented in this chapter shows that there is no need to assume that a Confucian ethics in the internal (*nei*) sphere should mean leading by moral example and opposing the use of force in the external one. Iain Johnston has illustrated very well how just war doctrines taken from the Chinese classics can be used to legitimize the use of violence against barbarians through a process of dehumanization.[66] Zhang Zhidong himself was an advocate of a foreign policy based on power balancing drawn from principles in the classics of Chinese statecraft, such as "use barbarians to control barbarians" and "engage the distant to attack the near." A type of neo-Confucianism that is based on using Western knowledge to save the Chinese essence can thus be made fully compatible with a Realist style of foreign policy.

More important for the nature of the Confucian revival is how it can be presented in a way that allows it to continue to be used for the purposes of mass mobilization behind the CCP. From this perspective, the alternative dynamics of national humiliation that are generated by the *ti/yong* formula can again be seen, as when Hu Jintao promotes the concept of "socialist honor and disgrace" (*shehuizhuyi rongru guan*, 社会主义荣辱观) in his 2007 work report. The official Xinhua News Agency explains that this consists of the "eight glories and eight shames" (*ba rong, ba chi*; 八荣八耻), of which "take upholding ardent love of the motherland as glory, take harming the motherland as shame " is the first in the list.[67]

Similarly, when Premier Wen Jiabao drummed up support for China during a tour of the overseas Chinese communities in Asian countries in 2006, he preferred to refer to the aphorism in the *Yi Jing* that explains that "the heavens move, the gentleman never rests from self-strengthening." Xinhua explains the significance of this by pointing out that "only if our Chinese nation relies on self-strengthening without rest, relies on uniting and embracing, relies on bitter toil and hard effort, can it stand up in its own state and all over the world."[68] That such themes continue to have a resonance with the wider population can be seen in the way that they also appear in a text such as the best-selling novel *Lang tuteng* (Wolf totem), where the prescription for self-strengthening in the *Yi Jing* is repeated as part of the search for a revitalized Confucianism in the nomadic spirit of the founders of the great Chinese dynasties that invaded the Central Plains from the north.[69]

Confucianism as a system of ideas is thus compatible with the promotion of the vision of the Chinese race in a predatory world that has been described as a kind of "fascism,"[70] just as it is compatible with doctrines of harmony and cosmopolitanism. By allowing the national essence to be imbued with multiple significances according to the political strategies for which it is mobilized, this reduction of Confucianism from a universal ethical system to an object of national loyalty that is enabled by the *ti/yong* dichotomy goes well beyond mere "romanticism."

Notes

1. David Held et al., *Global Transformations: Politics, Economics and Culture* (Cambridge: Polity Press, 1999); Anthony Smith, *Nations and Nationalism in a Global Era* (Cambridge: Polity Press, 1995).
2. Joseph R. Levenson, *Confucian China and Its Modern Fate* (Berkeley: University of California, 1965), 59–79.
3. Hu Jintao, "Hu Jintao's Report at the 17th Party Congress: Hold High the Great Banner of Socialism with Chinese Characteristics and Strive for New Victories in Building a Moderately Prosperous Society," October 15, 2007, http://www.china.org.cn/english/congress/229611.htm.
4. Xinhua, "Langmang de zhongguo, mengxiang de shijie: Zong daoyan Zhang Yimou zhuanfang" [Romantic China, dream world: A special interview with General Director Zhang Yimou], August 8, 2008, http://news.wenxuecity.com/messages/200808/news-gb2312-671284.html.
5. Cited by Jerome Ch'en, *Yuan Shih-k'ai (1859–1916)* (Stanford, Calif.: Stanford University Press, 1961), 246.
6. Levenson, *Confucian China*, 59–79.
7. Michel Foucault, *The Archaeology of Knowledge* (London: Routledge), 32.
8. Liang Qichao, *Qing dai xueshu gailun* [General discussion of Qing Dynasty studies] (Shanghai: Shanghai guji chubanshe, 2006).
9. Liang, *Qing dai xueshu gailun*, 97.
10. Zhang Zhidong, *Quan xue pian* [Exhortation to study] (1898), in *Zhang Wenxiang gong (Zhidong) quanji*, vol. 203 (Taipei: Wenhai chubanshe, 1970), 14429–626.

11. Daniel H. Bays, *China Enters the Twentieth Century: Chang Chih-tung and the Issues of a new Age, 1895–1909* (Ann Arbor: University of Michigan Press, 1978), 98.

12. Delmer M. Brown, *Nationalism in Japan: An Introductory Historical Analysis* (Berkeley: University of California Press, 1955), 47–61.

13. Ibid., 112–47.

14. Li Xizhu, *Zhang Zhidong yu qing mo xinzheng yanjiu* [Research on Zhang Zhidong and new government in the Late Qing] (Shanghai: Shanghai shudian chubanshe, 2003), 125.

15. Mao Zedong, "On Ideological Work (Talk at a Conference Attended by Party Cadres from People's Liberation Army Units under the Nanjing Command and from Jiangsu and Anhui Provinces, 1957)," in *The Secret Speeches of Chairman Mao: From the Hundred Flowers to the Great Leap Forward*, edited by Roderick MacFarquhar, Timothy Cheek, and Eugene Wu (Cambridge, Mass.: Harvard University Press, 1989), 334.

16. Levenson, *Confucian China*, 59–79.

17. Liang, *Qing dai xueshu gailun*, 178.

18. Ch'en, *Yuan Shih-k'ai*, 1964.

19. Ding Weizhi and Chen Song, *Zhong xi ti yong zhi jian* [Between China and the West, essence and function] (Beijing: Zhongguo shehui kexue chubanshe, 1995), 156–62.

20. Kang Youwei, "Shang Qingdi di wu shu" [Fifth memorial to the Qing emperor], in *Wushu bianfa* [The Wushu reforms], vol. 2, edited by Zhongguo shixue hui (Shanghai: Shanghai renmin chubanshe, 2000), 191.

21. World Bank, *China 2020: Development Challenges in the New Century* (Washington, D.C.: World Bank, 1997), 2.

22. Malcolm Waters, *Globalization* (London: Routledge, 1995), 42.

23. Lee Kuo-chi [Li Guoqi], *Zhang Zhidong de waijiao zhengce* [Zhang Zhidong's foreign policy] (Taipei: Zhongyang yanjiuyuan, 1984), 34.

24. Derk Bodde, "Harmony and Conflict in Chinese Philosophy," in *Studies in Chinese Thought*, edited by Arthur F. Wright (Chicago: University of Chicago Press, 1953), 19–80.

25. On "national humiliation," see William A. Callahan, *China: The Pessoptimist Nation* (Oxford: Oxford University Press, 2010); and Paul A. Cohen, "Remembering and Forgetting National Humiliation in Twentieth Century China," in *China Unbound: Evolving Perspectives on the Chinese Past* (London: RoutledgeCurzon, 2003), 148–84.

26. Chinese and English versions in James Legge, trans., *The Chinese Classics* (Taipei: Southern Materials Center, 1985), 407. Legge's Victorian translation, "To possess the feeling of shame is to be near to energy," fails to capture the force of this line.

27. Zhang, *Quan xue pian*, 14437.

28. Lee, *Zhang Zhidong's Foreign Policy*, 21–22.

29. Zhang, *Quan xue pian*, 14444–45.

30. Ibid., 14473.

31. Ibid., 14472–73.

32. Ibid., 14437.

33. Ibid., 14437.

34. Christopher R. Hughes, *Chinese Nationalism in the Global Era* (London: Routledge, 2006), 69–79.

35. Cited by Li, *Zhang Zhidong yu qing mo xinzheng yanjiu*, 70.

36. John Cleverly, *The Schooling of China* (London: George Allen & Unwin, 1985), 43.

37. Shao Chuan Leng and Norman D. Palmer, *Sun Yat-sen and Communism* (London: Thames & Hudson, 1961), 93.

38. Zhang, *Quan xue pian*, 14485–92.

39. William Ayers, *Chang Chih-tung and Educational Reform in China* (Cambridge, Mass.: Harvard University Press, 1971), 215.

40. Cleverly, *Schooling of China*, 57.

41. Ibid., 59–61.

42. This was an aphorism (*ci*) produced by Mao on September 27, 1964. For an analysis of the formula and its relevance to the revival of tradition in recent years, see Liu Wenquan, "Yi ren wei ben, gu wei jin yong: Hong yang yi ren wei ben de renwen jingshen" [Use the the human as the root, use the ancient for the present: Expand the humanistic spirit of taking the human as the root], *Zhongguo gonchangdang xinwen wang* [News net of the CCP], August 30, 2007, http://theory.people.com.cn/BIG5/49154/49156/6192462.html.

43. Liu Hanmin, ed., *Mao Zedong shici hua shu hua ji guan* [Collected views on Mao Zedong's poetry and prose] (Wuhan: Changjiang wenyi chubanshe, 2002), 349–51, 356–62.

44. Mao Zedong, "The Chinese Revolution and the Chinese Communist Party," in *Selected Works of Mao Tse-tung*, vol. 2 (Beijing: Foreign Languages Press, 1967), 311.

45. Mao Zedong, "On New Democracy," in *Selected Works of Mao Tse-tung*, vol. 2, 381.

46. Ibid., 380.

47. Cited by Cleverly, *Schooling of China*, 124.

48. Ibid., 153.

49. Liu Shaoqi, *How to Be a Good Communist* (Beijing: Foreign Languages Press, 1964).

50. Jonathan Unger, *Education under Mao: Class and Competition in Canton Schools, 1960–1980* (New York: Columbia University Press, 1982), 140–41.

51. Mao Zedong, "On the Ten Major Relationships," in *Selected Works of Mao Tsetung*, vol. 5 (Beijing: Foreign Languages Press, 1977), 303.

52. "Zili gengsheng, yang wei zhong yong: Pipan 'Si Ren Bang' waiqu he pohuai duli zizhu, zili gengsheng fangzheng de zuixing" [Self-sufficiency, use the foreign to serve China: Criticism of the evil activities of the "Gang of Four" to distort and destroy the orientation of independent establishment, self-sufficient development], *People's Daily*, November 16, 1976.

53. Deng Xiaoping, *Build Socialism with Chinese Characteristics* (Beijing: Foreign Languages Press, 1985), 3.

54. Deng Xiaoping, "On the Reform of the System of Party and State Leadership," in *Selected Works of Deng Xiaoping (–1982)* (Beijing: Foreign Languages Press, 1984), 320.

55. Hughes, *Chinese Nationalism*, 22–49.

56. Cleverly, *Schooling of China*, 269.

57. Education Ministry of the People's Republic of China, "Guanyu jiaqiang aiguo zhuyi xuanchuan jiaoyu de yijian (tongzhi)" [CCP center opinions on strengthening patriotic propaganda education (notification)], August 24, 1983.

58. Central Committee of the CCP, *Zhonggong zhongyang guanyu jiaoyu tizhi gaige*

de jueding [Central Committee of the CCP's decision on reforming the education system], May 27, 1985.

59. Li Zehou ""Xi ti zhong yong" jian yi" [Simple explanation of "western substance Chinese function"], *Zou wo ziji de lu* [Taking my own road] (Taipei: Sanmin shuju, 1996), 195–99. Originally published in *Zhongguo wenhua bao*, July 9, 1986.

60. National People's Congress, "Zhonghua renmin gongheguo jiaoyufa" [Education law of the People's Republic of China], in *Shisi da yilai zhongyao wenxian xuanbian* [edited and selected important documents since the Fourteenth National Congress of the CCP, vol. 2] (Beijing: National People's Congress, 1995), 1293–94.

61. Li Fan, "Shichang jingji fazhan de zhengzhi huangjing ji qi dui Zhongguo xiandaihua de yingxiang" [The political environment of the development of the market economy and its influence on China's modernization], *Zhanlue yu guanli*, no. 1 (1994): 20–26.

62. Foucault, *Archaeology of Knowledge*, 32.

63. Hu, "Hu Jintao's Report at the 17th Party Congress."

64. Jiang Zemin, "Full Text of Jiang Zemin's Report at 16th Party Congress," November 17, 2002, http://www.china.org.cn/english/features/49007.htm.

65. Daniel A. Bell, "From Marx to Confucius: Changing Discourses on China's Political Future," *Dissent Magazine*, Spring 2007.

66. Alastair Iain Johnston, *Cultural Realism: Strategic Culture and Grand Strategy in Chinese History* (Princeton, N.J.: Princeton University Press, 1995).

67. Xinhua, "Shehuizhuyi rongru guan: Yimian yinling shehui fengshang de qizhi" [The concept of socialist glory and shame: One aspect of the banner of leading social mores], April 3, 2006, http://news.xinhuanet.com/politics/2006-04/03/content_4376620.htm. The advocacy of "socialist honor and disgrace" appears in the section on cultural development in Hu Jintao's report to the Seventeenth CCP National Congress. The eight glories and eight shames and is explained in the Chinese media as "take upholding ardent love of the motherland as glory, take harming the motherland as shame; take serving the people as honor, take leaving the people as shame; take advocating science as honor, take stupidity and ignorance as shame; take hard work as honor, take love of leisure and dislike of work as shame; take working together as honor, take using others for personal gain as shame; take sincerity and trustworthiness as honor, take seeing profit and forgetting virtue as shame; take discipline and obeying the law as honor, take breaking the law and disorderliness as shame; take hardship and struggle as honor, take wallowing in luxury and pleasure as shame.

68. Xinhua, "Tian xing jian, junzi yi ziqiang bu xi: Wen Jiabao huijian huaqiao huaren zeji" [Wen Jiabao tells the meeting of overseas Chinese: The heavens move, the gentleman never rests from self-strengthening], April 9, 2006, http://news.xinhuanet.com/newscenter/2006-04/09/content_4402033.htm.

69. Jiang Rong, *Lang tuteng* [Wolf totem] (Taipei: Fengyun shidai chubanshe, 2005), 594. Jiang's theory can be derived from his novel, but it is stated systematically in the appendix he attached to the Chinese version and that is not included in the English version published by Penguin in 2008.

70. This is the judgment of *Lang tuteng* by leading German sinologist, Wolfgang Kubin, expressed in an interview with Deutsche Welle, "Macht nichts, wenn sie sich ärgern" [Never mind if they are annoyed], December 27, 2006, http://www.dw-world.de/dw/article/0,2144,2290638,00.html.

Chapter 7

Paradoxes of Tradition and Modernity at the New Frontier: China, Islam, and the Problem of "Different Heavens"

David Kerr

China has never had a consistent strategy for the Islamic world. Although it may have believed that it could subdue the Mongol peoples or befriend the Tibetans, it has never been confident in the face of the world's most dynamic religious force. This is partly due to China's unusual view of religion itself. China treats religion as a form of ideology that is acceptable as a system of individual belief but should not be turned into an ethic of community, especially if this is an alternative to being Chinese. Yet Islam can be interpreted as commanding the opposite: that the community of the faithful is superior to, and binding upon, that of political community. This has resulted in a long struggle to establish a system for the government of relations between China and the Islamic world that has still not been decisively concluded.

China's term for the point at which it meets the Islamic world—Xinjiang or New Frontier—is doubly ironic, therefore. This frontier is hardly new, being the result of many centuries of struggle; but it might also be asked: What is the nature and substance of this frontier? That is, without an agreed system of governance for relations between the Chinese and Islamic worlds, how well established is the frontier, and how do we know where it lies?[1] Indeed, the fact that some people refer to the frontier by an entirely different name—East Turkestan (Ch. *Dong tujuesitan guo*, 东突厥斯坦国)—suggests continuing doubt about these questions. This is both a very old and an immediate question, therefore, given that both Islam and China are perceived to be resurgent. These revivals have some similarity in that they pit an older, traditional Chinese or Islamic world against their modern equivalents. Thus, both China and Islam are in some senses in a struggle between tradition and modernity: to defend the uniqueness of the past at the same time as they embrace the universality of modernity. Clearly, then, China needs a stable system of relations with the Islamic world; yet concerns remain about the compatibility of practices of governance in the two communities, and this is reflected in China's fears about Xinjiang as its frontier with Islam.

This chapter examines certain paradoxes of China's relations with the Islamic world, both looking back at the formation of the New Frontier and forward to China's prospects for emerging as a significant influence in the international relations of the Islamic world in this century. Precisely because of the problems of how to put communities, governance, and frontiers together, this may represent a more significant challenge for China's peaceful emergence than its role in East Asia.

In its first section, the chapter considers comparatively the nature of government in the Chinese and Islamic civilizations, including the governance of frontiers. In the second, section it sets out a historical interpretation of how a boundary was established between the Chinese and Islamic worlds. In the third section, it looks at China's ordering of its boundary in the era after the revolution of 1949. And in the fourth section, it examines contemporary China's efforts to advance its modernist notions of government and governance toward the Islamic world.

Comparative Government of Chinese and Islamic Civilizations

Social theory has long recognized that one of the fundamental markers of the arrival of modernity is the way its transforms social identities. All classical civilizations were notable for the embedding of collective identities in a totalizing worldview that encompassed natural, social, and spiritual existence. Habermas puts this as:

> Worldviews establish an analogical nexus between man, nature, and society which is represented as a totality in the basic concepts of mythical powers. Because these worldviews project a totality in which everything corresponds with everything else, they subjectively attach the collective identity of the group or the tribe with the cosmic order and integrate it with the system of social institutions. In the limit case, worldviews func-

tion as a kind of drive belt that transforms the basic religious consensus into the energy of social solidarity and passes it on to social institutions thus giving them a moral authority.²

In this way, humanity in the traditional world stands at the point that nature, society, and faith meet, and collective identities are derived from a fusion of all three. What occurred in the axial age—perhaps a thousand years either side of the beginning of the Common Era—was that humanity moved further from nature and closer to God, or rather God was seen as having raised humanity above nature. The term used for this shift was civilization—the shift from natural to civil existences and identities—though of course not all civilizations made this shift in the same way or with similar consequences. The Chinese civilization is considered notable in perhaps three ways. First, it was one of the earliest of the axial age civilizations. Second, its conception of civilization is strongly grounded in humanistic practices rather than spiritual law (anthropraxy versus orthodoxy). And third, its concept of Heaven lacks two features common to other civilizations, particularly the Abrahamic faiths: a personal God and a potential for transcendence. These features are, of course, strongly connected to Confucian thought. The *Lun Yu* notes how reluctant Confucius was to discuss the ways of Heaven unless pressed:

> The Master said, I would much rather not have to talk. Tzu-kung said, If our Master did not talk, what should we little ones have to hand down about him? The Master said, Heaven does not speak; yet the four seasons run their course thereby, the hundred creatures, each after its kind, are born thereby. Heaven does no speaking!³

As Schwartz notes:

> Here Heaven is indeed associated with the "impersonal processes" and cycles of nature as well as with the generative processes, which do not suggest deliberate thought or discrete, finite "decisions." The passage does, in fact seem to suggest that nature is, at it were, an "emanation" of Heaven. Unlike the God of the Hebrew Bible, Heaven does not speak.⁴

Of course, Confucianism is not agnostic. There is an assumption that the Way (Dao) exists both in the affairs of men and in the order of Heaven, and the Confucian ideal of Harmony, exists when these prevail and are aligned.

Yet because the order of Heaven cannot be altered Confucian and neo-Confucian thought became preoccupied with a this-worldly Heaven of social-moral equilibrium, rather than an otherworldly Heaven of spiritual transcendence.[5] One further difference was in the nature and location of revelation. The Dao assumes the alignment of human morality with "impersonal processes" that do not command "finite decisions"; therefore righteousness is primarily internal and "self-adjusting." The Abrahamic faiths took a fundamentally different route. Judaism, Christianity, and Islam are not only constructed around a personal God and a transcendent Heaven but also upon the power of revelation. Not only does Heaven speak, but God also directs lawful commandments through prophecy and scripture. This revelation by prophecy, which was external and "world-adjusting," was to have distinctively different consequences for the collective identities of these civilizations, as is most apparent in the youngest of the axial age faiths—Islam.

In some senses, it is an error to consider Islam as simply a civilization. The religious community that was constructed around the revelation given to the Prophet Muhammad certainly adopted many of the civilizational features of traditional Middle Eastern societies, including parts of the Judaic and Christian traditions. But if we are to assume that civilizations are to some extent discrete human communities differentiated by language and culture, social and political practice, and even historical and spatial boundedness, then this has been neither the intent nor the experience of Islam. Islam—submission to the will of God—creates a community of the faithful (*umma*) that transcends all difference. The Qur'ān says:

> Mankind was a single community, then God sent prophets to bring good news and warning, and with them He sent the Scripture and the Truth, to judge between people in their disagreements. It was only those to whom it was given who disagreed about it after clear signs had come to them, because of rivalry between them.[6]

Abdulaziz Sachedina says this citation reveals three things:

> the unity of humankind under one God; the particularity of religions brought by the prophets; and the role of revelation, i.e., "the book," in resolving the differences that touch communities of faith.[7]

Thus one reason why Muslims believe that the Qur'ān supersedes and completes the revelation of the earlier Abrahamic faiths is that it allows for religious and communal pluralism, including across civilizational boundaries. At the same time, the Qur'ān is uncompromising in stating that God's will is absolute[8] and sovereign:[9] that it will brook no challenge. Therefore, the authority of the new pluralistic community of "the book" (*al-kitāb*) was founded on, and sustained by, the absolute and sovereign authority of God over humankind.

If we then turn back to Habermas's categories of the "energy of social solidarity" and the "moral authority of institutions," we see how different the legacies of the "old civilization" of Confucian China and the "new community" of Islam were to become. Confucius is rightly considered a political conservative, both because of his belief that civility (*ren*) was founded on ritual (*li*) and because his vision of the ideal state is backward-looking to the world of the Ancients.[10] Yet this state should not be considered conservative in the sense of a Hobbesian Leviathan—one that imposes its authority on a barely civilized society. When Tzu-kung asks what is required of government, Confucius replies:

> Sufficient food, sufficient weapons, and the confidence of the common people. Tzu-kung said, Suppose you had no choice but to dispense with one of these, which would you forego? The Master said, Weapons. Tsu-kung said, Suppose you were forced to dispense with one of the two that were left, which would you forgo? The Master said, Food. For from old, death has been the lot of all men; but a people that no longer trusts its rulers is lost indeed.[11]

Rather, the Confucian state is perhaps most like Plato's benevolent despotism: "When the Way prevails under Heaven all orders concerning ritual, music and punitive expeditions are issued by the Son of Heaven himself. . . . When the Way prevails, policy is not decided by Ministers; and commoners do not discuss public affairs."[12] Confucius does not say what should occur when Dao does not prevail, perhaps to the point where legitimacy—as expressed in the Will of Heaven (*Tian ming*)—is lost. In this again, he is fundamentally conservative, eschewing the politics of rebellion through confidence in the power of *li* ritual to bring rectification. The social solidarity of traditional China was comparatively weak, therefore, and dependent on a consensus around ritual and a system of legitimacy that placed the moral authority of government in the same context as the natural order of Heaven.

In considering the social solidarity of Islam and the moral authority of its institutions, one must first dispense with some half-truths—the notions of Pan-Islamic or theocratic government. As can be seen from even the brief outline above, the "Pan" in Pan-Islamic is somewhat redundant. Islam recognizes two communities—the human community, and the community of the faithful within it—and the nominal boundaries of polities are viewed as contingent arrangements within the greater history of the revelation. Yet Islam does not mandate theocratic government. In Islamic societies the state, like any other institution, can be judged on how far it conforms to the revealed will of God, but the state may exist for purposes other than those set out in scripture. The problem in both instances—the boundedness and government of the Islamic world—is that if sovereignty and authority reside ultimately with God, then they can hardly be embodied in the state as an *alternative*. Therefore, the Islamic state lay between two ideal conceptions: a Caliphate, where faith and state were indivisible; and a Sultanate, which was bicephalous with mutually regarding religious and political leaderships.[13] In history and in doctrine, therefore, there was a potential for conflict between these two conceptions of the relationship between state and community. But in either case, Islam created a strong bond of social solidarity beyond the locus of the state, while at the same time investing the states of Islamic societies with a considerable potential for moral authority.

These differing conceptions of the solidarity of the community and the authority of its institutions necessarily translated not only into contrasts in collective identity, but perceptions of other communities and the frontiers between them. Thus one of the clearest markers of these civilizations became the frontier between those under the will of Heaven and those without. The Chinese way to manage this frontier was dualistic: drawing the uncivilized toward civility by submission to ritual and recognition of the superiority of the Middle Kingdom; at the same time as conducting a variety of punitive missions against those who resisted. This strategy is too often debated in terms of its offensive or defensive features; it was rather a complex system of reward and punishment. Rewards lay not only in the cultural artifacts of Chinese civilization but also in its wealth, technologies, and the possibility of marriage into Chinese lineages. Punishments included not only war or enslavement but also ostracism—as prevalent as assimilation or punishment was the urge to quarantine China, a policy conducted through defensive infrastructures and migratory controls. But this complex and pragmatic system of assimilation, punishment, and quarantine, and the resulting fluidity of the frontier between civilization and barbarism at many points in Chinese history, stand in contrast to the official ideology of the Confucian state, which wished always to emphasize the positive power of attraction. Poo cites the section from the *Lun Yu* that reads "If the foreign people are not submissive, then we should cultivate our virtue to entice them to come," and notes:

> Here we find an expression of the official programme of cultural assimilation, which also reflected confidence in the superiority of Chinese culture. As long as the foreigners are "transformed [*bian*, 变]" or "acculturated [*hua*, 化]," then there is no problem with them being "Chinese." Race or physical characteristics did not seem to have been a concern in the open discourses.[14]

This, of course, was only in the realm of official discourse. Outside this realm, the physical and ethical otherness of the barbarians predominated in both Chinese representations of the foreigner and Chinese policy. Indeed, those eras that actually resembled the ideal of cultural and ethnic toleration— of a China that was central but also cosmopolitan—became historically notable. The most obvious example was Tang China, whose elite was of mixed heritage. As Abramson notes:

> Intermarriage and assimilation often confounded efforts to clearly distinguish Chinese from barbarian lineages after families had resided for several generations in China, and, most of the time, Tang people were not interested in making the effort. Much of the official rhetoric, particularly in the expansionist first half of the dynasty, stressed ethnic tolerance. In 647 Emperor Taizong explained his success in the following way: "Since antiquity, all have honored the *Hua* [Chinese] and despised the barbarians; only I have loved both as one."[15]

Saying where the frontier lay between China and barbarism, what the boundary was made of, and in consequence how it should be governed, has clearly altered considerably across historical time. This leads Chih-yu Shih to conclude that it is better to think of traditional China as a temporal-historical construct than a territorial-geographical one;[16] or put another way, it was the temporal frontiers of civilization that predominated in Chinese thought rather than the spatial boundaries of the empire, which tended to be politically contingent. Poo is clear, however, in arguing that however the boundary is established—spatially or temporally—its driving force in the long term was the insecurity of Chinese civilization in the face of an uncivilized and threatening periphery.[17]

The Islamic community was born not out of the concern of a conservative dynasty for the security of civilization but from revolutionary upheaval. In the lifetime of the Prophet Muhammad, the main goal was to create a political order centered on Mecca, where Abraham had founded the House of the monotheistic faiths. This struggle faced the three problems encountered by other revolutionary creeds: how to overcome the established order, how to deal with the divisions of the old society, and how to make the change from seizing power to governing. With regard to the first problem, the Qur'ān divides the world into two parts, the Abode of Faith and the Abode of Disbelief (Dār al-Iman and Dar al-Kufr), the frontier between which is established by persuasion and preaching (*da'wah*); that is, by the study of, and compliance with, the Qur'ān itself.[18] Since it could not be assumed that the meeting of the worlds of faith and disbelief could always be conducted in peaceful ways, the Qur'ān also provides rules on the conduct of conflict, for example:

> Fight in God's cause against those who fight you, but do not overstep the limits: God does not love those who overstep the limits. Kill them wherever you encounter them, and drive them from where they drove you out, for persecution is more serious than killing.[19] Fight them until there is no more persecution, and worship is devoted to God. If they cease hostilities, there can be no hostility, except toward aggressors.[20]

Thus, the Qur'ān establishes certain principles for the conduct of just war (*jihād*), namely, the struggle (*jahd*) against persecution or oppression (*fitnah*) of Muslims, but also of proportionality and discrimination. The question of how far the Abode of Faith could be established and maintained by conversion, and how far and in what circumstances, there could be a resort to arms remains a matter of interpretation within Islamic teaching, just as it does in other faiths.

In examining these comparative concepts of government as they emerged in China and Islamic societies, similarities and differences can be identified. Both were concerned with establishing a moral frontier for the civilization, and called on human beings to submit to the rightness of certain ethical codes and forms of behavior. Indeed, both assumed that being fully human—"ren" or "muslim"—required such submission. Differentially, Confucianism advanced a hierarchical order that placed the state next to Heaven and required a passive adjustment to this supermoral order, in a way that treated politics, including the legitimacy of government, as being comparable to the forces of supernature. Islam in contrast created a community of faithful in which each was equal before a personal God, who issued lawful commandments, including the struggle to achieve the realization of the faith itself. This was not intentionally political, but in a world where other communities and civilizations were already established at the point that the Prophet Muhammad received the revelation, it necessarily became so. The potential of this union of personal and political transformation is ably conveyed by Mohammed Arkoun, who argues: "Islam is theologically Protestant but politically Catholic."[21]

In this way Islam questions, if not openly challenges, the separation of authorities and legitimacies typical of government—by unifying Muslims within the world of faith, it makes it difficult to separate them within the world of government. It is hardly surprising, therefore, that a frontier between China and Islam was established as much by political struggle as spiritual conversion.

The Temporal Construction of a New Frontier

In the three hundred years following the Prophet Muhammad's death in 632, the commandment to extend the frontiers of the Islamic community saw both dramatic successes and repeated conflict and fragmentation, as the divisions of Middle Eastern societies and problems of establishing centralized authority continually resurfaced. Under the Arab Empires (Ummayad, 661–750; and Abbasid, 750–945) a common religious and social identity was established in the lands between Spain and Central Asia, opening up this area to shared cultural, economic, and technological exchange. This was achieved in particular by exploiting the traditional trade routes that connected Europe and Asia. By 950, however, the attempt to establish a single political order had failed and the Islamic world entered a period of pluralization in which different converted peoples vied for the right to develop an Islamic society sustained by their own political and cultural traditions. Yet without Islam's capacity to bridge political and cultural boundaries, it is unlikely that the Chinese and Islamic civilizations would have established a common frontier. That they did so was primarily the responsibility of the Turkic peoples of Inner Asia.

The ethnogenesis of the Turks (Ch. tujue, 突厥) is notoriously difficult to establish, not least because sedentarization and historical record seem to support one another. Rather pre-Islamic Turkic communities were notable for their preference of the movable over the immovable: culture, language, and nomadic economy were shared to some degree by a diverse group of peoples who traversed the steppe belt from the Pacific Ocean to the Black Sea; but there was limited movement toward territorialization and a centralized state.[22] The three pre-Islamic Turkic orders—Xiongnu, Kök Turk, and Uyghur—were loose confederations that had their origin in what we now call Mongolia. But Turks were as likely to be found fighting in the ranks of other empires as building their own. This was one of the first means for the transmission of Islam to Inner Asian societies. At the time of the death of the Prophet Muhammad, Tang China had succeeded in extending suzerain relations as far as the Tarim Basin but had had much less success against the Kök Turk Empire, which stretched across the Northern Steppe from Transoxania to the eastern reaches of the Orkhon.[23] The advancing Islamic forces found similar difficulty, and it was to take close to eighty years after the fall of Persia in 637 before the capitals of Transoxania—Bukhara and Samarqand—were incorporated into the Abbasid Empire in 712 and 713. There then followed one of the decisive events in Chinese–Inner Asian relations. A dispute between the Turkic and Iranian peoples of the Ferghana region prompted the intervention of Tang forces based at Kashgar and the newly established forces of the Abbasid Empire at Samarqand. The Battle of Talas in 751, in which the Islamic forces, commanded by Persians but manned by Turks, vanquished the Tang army, was the last occasion on which a Chinese army ventured beyond the Pamirs.[24]

Thereafter, the Chinese position in Inner Asia collapsed as Turkic forces from the north and Tibetan forces from the south took advantage of the mutiny of the Tang general An Lushan in North China (755–63) to seize control of Tarim and Zhungaria. The Tang emperor was forced to seek assistance from the Turks against An Lushan, and those who stayed after the rebellion are held to be the founders of the Muslim communities of Central China.[25] Even after the reestablishment of Tang control, there was no attempt to return to Inner Asia, and it was to be a thousand years later in the time of the Qing Dynasty before China reestablished itself as a power to the west of the Yellow River.[26] As a result, the eastern gateway linking the Islamic world to the steppes was kept open, and the power of the Islamic vision in uniting peoples of different cultures had been vigorously demonstrated. As Frye notes, the proselytizing power of Islam was a fundamental aspect in its military victories:

> The Arabs brought not only a new religion, but also a message of social equality, the end of classes, and the solidarity of belonging together in a great family of Muslims, the *ummah*.... When non-Arabs converted to Islam they were given Arabic names and, according to our sources, they were said to have become Arabs.[27]

The land route in Inner Asia thus became one path for the transmission of Islam into China, complementing the sea route to Canton, which had been established as early as the seventh century. Indeed, the steppe world constructed and traversed by the Turks can be said to have ocean-like characteristics:

> For the steppe world as a whole, the "elongated steppe zones, the isolated oases, and the major mountain passes and corridors of Inner Asia have been the overland equivalents of ocean routes, ports-of-call, and canals," the site of countless journeys in all directions, rivalling in length the maritime ventures of the European age of exploration.[28]

For more than two centuries after Talas Turks served as soldiers in the Arab Empire; but following the dissolution of the Abbasids, Inner Asia was dominated by a succession of empires that were predominantly Turkic and Islamic, though other ethnicities and faiths were intermixed: Qarakhanid, Chaghatay, Timurid, and Shaybanid (999–1218; 1227–1370; 1370–1500; 1500–98). The boundary between China and Islam might therefore have been permanently formed by two major empires: a Chinese imperium based on Confucian culture and feudal agriculture; and a Turkic imperium based on Islamic culture and control of the Inner Asian "ocean routes." That this did not occur was due to the interaction of two long-term factors: first, the continued fragmentation of the Inner Asian world and the movement of the Turks from Inner Asia toward Europe, where they were to found the Ottoman Empire; and second, the corresponding movement of the landed empires of Eurasia to enclose Inner Asia.

With regard to the first factor, it can be noted that both the Chinese and Islamic worlds were forms of *imperium et emporium*—a system of military-political order interlocked with a cultural-technical mode of economy. Both *imperia* had considerable difficulty establishing continuity of political order, but in the case of China, the cultural-technical mode was more stable and less prone to external shocks. In the case of Islamic societies, there were profound divisions in the cultural-technical mode; so that the very openness of the territory between Africa and China, between Europe and India, which had facilitated the transmission of the new faith, also served to pluralize this world and leave it vulnerable to intervention. The Central Asian core of Inner Asia emerged as a microcosm of this historical pattern, forming as it did the meeting point of three related but different societies. Lapidus notes:

> The advent of Islam in this region led to the formation of three types of Islamic society. Among the Kazakhs, Islam became part of popular identity and belief, but not the basis for social organization. Among other tribal peoples and in some oasis communities such as Kashgar, Sufi masters and Sufi lineages mediated, organized, and sometimes governed. In large-scale urbanized societies such as Transoxania, state-organized Islamic societies of the Middle Eastern type were developed.[29]

Such was the strength of Turkicization and Islamicization in Central Asia that the government of the region by the Mongol Chaghatay khans had limited impact, and a hundred years into Mongol rule, these khans themselves began to convert to Islam and enter into marriage with Turks (see figure 7.1).[30]

At the same time, though the Chaghatay and Timurid khanates were important for the creation of Turkestan, and fundamental to establishing Islam as an element in social and political identity, the linkages between this world and the Turkic empires elsewhere weakened. Turkic Empires were established under the Ottomans (1300–1928) and Moghuls (1526–1858), but rivalry with Safavid Iran (1501–1722) created a barrier between the Central Eurasian empires and post-Timurid Turkestan. In essence, the period in which Inner Asia generated the great empires of Central Eurasia reached its peak in the seventeenth century. Thereafter, fundamental changes to the organization of society, economy, and warfare saw a reverse process in which the landed and maritime empires of Europe and Asia expanded at the expense of the Turkic world. In Inner Asia, this process was conducted by Romanov Russia (1613–1917) and Ming and Qing China (1368–1644; 1644–1911), which between them absorbed much of Western and Eastern Turkestan into their empires by the end of the eighteenth century, with the

Figure 7.1. Before Sovereignty: Central Eurasian Empires and Inner Asian Societies, circa 1600

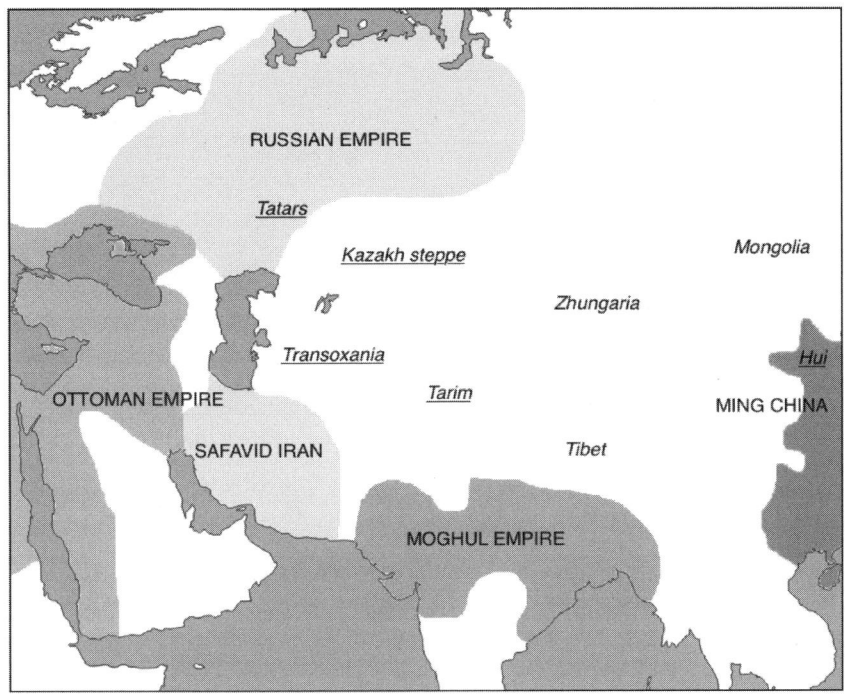

Source: Outline map available at http://d-maps.com.
Note: Islamic societies are underlined.

states of Transoxania falling to Russia in the following century. In doing so, they altered both the ethnoracial characteristics of their empires but also the basic assumptions on which their social solidarities were constructed. The terms commonly applied to the new empires, such as "multiethnic" and "multiconfessional," disguise the problems that the emerging modern states encountered when seeking to incorporate alternative social solidarities and institutions.

The great expansion of the Chinese state in the early modern era would most likely have necessitated a reconfiguration in any case of what it meant to be Chinese; but precisely because the Qing were an Inner Asian dynasty, the perception and formulation of the identity of the new multiethnic empire was highly distinctive. Gang Zhao notes:

An excellent example of the Qing rulers' dexterity and creativity in employing the Han concept of China is Qianlong's 1755 pronouncement: "There exists a view of *China* (*Zhongxia*), according to which non-Han people cannot become *China*'s subjects and their land cannot be integrated into the territory of *China*. This does not represent our dynasty's understanding of *China*, but is instead that of the earlier Han, Tang, Song, and Ming dynasties." As the Qing rulers adopted the idea, they invested it with a new meaning that represented the multiethnic nature of the Qing state. We thus are left with two important questions: how did the Qing court adjust the concept of *China* to the development of the Qing multiethnic empire? And what role did that concept play in the formation of modern Chinese national identity?[31]

The Qing promulgated the notion of the five-nation empire—Man, Han, Meng, Zang, and Hui—and the nationalist accounts of the late nineteenth and twentieth centuries were to endorse the view that the peoples of the Chinese state had always been related to one another, so the creation of a multinational polity was a natural reflection of this. However, this Confucian discourse of harmonious ethnic relations was at odds with the actual conquest of the Inner Asian societies from the seventeenth century onward. Perdue notes that the Qing destruction of the Western Mongol empire—Zhungharia—that barred the route to Turkestan involved practices that were more typical of Central Eurasian warfare.[32] Qianlong justified his decisions by the perfidiousness of the Mongols, saying that he "did not formerly have the intention [of eliminating the Zhunghars]. It was only because they repeatedly submitted and then rebelled that we had to wipe them out."[33]

The expansion into Turkestan proved less onerous than the hundred-year-long campaign against the Western Mongols. The sedentary populations of the oasis cities were much less able to mount sustained resistance to Qing expansion, particularly because they did not constitute a single political unit in themselves. Hami and Turfan had fallen before the final assault against the Zhunghars, and the remaining cities of the Tarim were subdued by 1765. Significant revolts against Chinese rule did, however, take place in 1825, 1830, 1846, and 1857; in each instance with external aide and encouragement from Western Turkestan, either in the form of an attempt to reestablish the religious rule of the Khojas (Naqshbandi sufists who had governed the Tarim oases before the Qing conquest) or Russian imperial interest. The intervention of Yaqub Beg in 1864–77 was sufficiently threatening to require a change to the government of the New Frontier, which ceased to be a private estate of the Manchu Dynasty and became formally incorporated into China as a province in 1884.

Certainly in the first period, 1765–1857, the Qing faced considerable problems of integrating the new frontier into the empire. In material terms, the precarious economy of the region would not support a significant garrison, prompting the Qing to develop various forms of state-led development. Yet there was no real attempt at Sinicization either. Though the peoples of Chinese Turkestan were no longer regarded as barbarians, there was no state-imposed drive to impose a single Chinese identity. As Newby notes, Qing policy was directed toward "creating ties of loyalty, not of identity."[34] Indeed the incomers—soldiers, administrators, exiles, and literati—showed little interest in the values of the new members of the empire:

> On the one hand the Qing—specifically the Qianlong emperor—designated the Turkic-Muslims as possessors of culture, while the Chinese narrative, official and unofficial alike, continued to confine that culture to the status of *fengsu* (风俗). This is nowhere more apparent than in the descriptions given to Islam. Most Qing exiles were not concerned or able to give anything but a superficial account of Islamic teaching and practice, it being highly unlikely that any were familiar with the Koran. . . . Even the obvious signs of orthodox Islamic practice, such as performing the *namaz*, fasting at Ramadan, circumcision, going on *hajj*, and the design of Muslim tombs, are all recorded with little suggestion that they are more than the symbols and rituals of a local cult.[35]

As such, the Qing approach to its new territories was not significantly different to that of other imperial powers of the early modern era; comparisons can be made with the British in India, the French in North Africa, or the internal colonizers of nineteenth-century America.

In contemporary assessments of China's expansion into Central Asia, convention requires that this history is not read forward from an early-modern-era construction of China's place in the international order to the present; but rather backward through China's century of humiliation by imperialism into the past:

> Under the Qing, in the flourishing times of the Kang emperor, the armed rebellion of the Zhunghar state was repeatedly suppressed, and following on, many ethnic splittist movements were suppressed. The Kazakh

and Bulute (Kyrgyz) tribal areas north and south of the Tianshan were combined, and brought under the administration of the Qing government. In 1876 the Qing government smashed the foreign encroachment of Yaqub and overturned the rebellion in South Xinjiang. In 1884 Xinjiang became a province. This safeguarded the integrity of the country, promoted unity of nationalities, and gave significant vigor to the development of Xinjiang. The founding of Xinjiang as a province and the integration of the north and south Tianshan complied with the yearning of all the clans people of the Western regions to end divisions and be incorporated within the national peoples, and the need to realize the aspiration of the motherland's unity and the development trends of the day; it also signified the development and inevitable return to unity of all parts of the Western regions and the motherland's hinterland after more than two thousand years.[36]

In this way, China's encounter with imperialism still acts as a pivot for its historical interpretation of the creation of the Inner Asian boundaries. Foreign encroachment, ethnic division, and armed rebellions were all problems that had to be overcome to permit a national unity that is now considered preordained. Nevertheless, the robustness of this nation-building discourse, which links the politics of the Qing era to that of the People's Republic of China (PRC), disguises the reality that the relationship between China and its frontier regions was at many times one of benign neglect and, between its peoples, mutual disinterest.

Chih-yu Shih supports the view that the confrontation with imperialism generated a decisive discontinuity in the Chinese understanding of world order, centered most particularly on the alien concept of sovereignty. In the traditional world of "All-under-Heaven" China, both the government and frontiers of civilization could be ordered around moral principles; following the encounter with imperialism, there was an enforced shift to geopolitical principles and, most important, the sovereignty "revolution." This necessarily transformed not only China's foreign policy but also its approach to the government of the frontier:

> The sovereignty discourse did not allow the Han and non-Han to be governed by spontaneous exchanges, as in pre-sovereign China. Once China was enclosed within sovereign borders, the Confucian values that once guided emperorship could not survive the call to patriotism. Since then

the non-Han people became officially both Chinese and members of minorities. Hence it is easy to see that any foreign attempts to speak on behalf of these minorities will be regarded as intrusive by all peoples of sovereign China. This is ironic: What imperialism was supposed to have destroyed was the Son of Heaven's emphasis on people's hearts and his inattention to physical borders and territory. Protecting this Celestial Empire now led to its destruction.[37]

Shih's argument is that "Tianxia China" was replaced by "Sovereign China" and that this required a revolutionary shift in the politics of both inside and outside China (*guonei, guowai*). Under Tianxia, the most important frontier was the temporal one between civilization and barbarism; the physical boundary of the state, which changed considerably with each dynasty, was much less important. The relationship between the empire and the frontier societies was also diverse: The concept of suzerainty was used to disguise the fact that there was not a single system of governance for Inner Asia but rather varied interactions aimed at sustaining bonds of loyalty and deference.

The fact that modern international relations came to Asia in the form of imperialism had a decisive impact on the end of this traditional order. China underwent a dual revolution as socialism replaced feudalism in class structure and sovereignty replaced suzerainty at the frontier. For the first time, China had "international relations," a term that assumed that everything within the boundaries of the PRC now constituted a single political nation. However, this chapter questions how far the shift between tradition and modernity in international relations was final and decisive in this way. First, from the history given above, it can be seen that the Qing emperors were well aware of geopolitical imperatives, and particularly those emanating from Inner Asia, and that this had long-term consequences for the construction of a multiethnic empire. Second, we might argue that China's commitment to socialism after 1949 was both a means to achieving sovereignty and also a renewed commitment to the civilizational project; revolutionary socialism gave China a temporal mission in world order as well as the means through sovereign power to achieve this. It is impossible to explain fundamental post-1949 events, such as China's breach with the Soviet Union, without recognizing this. So it is important not to overemphasize the discontinuity between the moral ordering of traditional China and the geopolitical ordering of sovereign China. This also suggests that the

PRC carried forward certain aspects of the Tianxia world, though these were now submerged within the revolutionary discourse of sovereignty and socialism.

In this sense, modern China (Xiandai Zhongguo) referred to something that was still to be achieved as a historical project within modern Asia. This standard version of a modern China that is still to be completed exists in state policies such as that for the reunification with Taiwan and in the new concept of "scientific development"; but the nonstandard also persists in the continued problems of governance at the Inner Asian frontiers. Since 1949, modern China has sustained a drive for transformation and acculturation (*bian*, 变; *hua*, 花), which has not dimmed with the shift from the revolutionary state proclaimed in 1949 to the era of reform and opening begun in 1979. As China has pursued radical modernity from the center, this has provoked reactive transformations and acculturations in others, and notably at the frontier with other parts of the international order. This also suggests some continuity between the eras of tradition and modernity. Thus, Perdue notes that

> the Sinicization thesis, like the civilizing mission thesis, ignores how the Qing continually *reinscribed* difference alongside uniformity in its subject populations. The tension between difference and uniformity applies as much to the Han as to the non-Han populations, but it was on the frontier that it became most evident. Here cultural diversity was not just inherited but constructed.[38]

China's membership of the international world has gone through various modes, therefore, of which Sovereign China is only one. Each has generated its own reinscription of uniformity and difference; and though this was true of "China at the center," it was particularly evident for "China at the margin." Since 1949, though modernity has become the unchallengeable driver of this reinscription, the mode of transformation and acculturation, and the nature of uniformity and difference, have continued to evolve. Thus, I next consider the mode that predominated in the years of Maoist socialist construction.

New China and the Inner Asian Frontier

Tianxia China in its traditional and early modern modes presented changing forms of governance between China and the Inner Asian Islamic world.

With the arrival of New China, a new cycle began. As with many aspects of socialist construction, China chose to draw heavily on Soviet doctrine and practice; so it is worth considering briefly what this was like. Geiss says that nationality policy in Soviet Central Asia

> was "national" in form but "socialist" in content. In this way they included culturally similar population groups in newly created administrative units, created literary languages for each of these units, promoted them by establishing compulsory education on the basis of these languages, and established cultural institutions for the discovery and protection of the various nationalities' "cultural traditions." The Soviets tried to spread a socialist interpretation of these "traditions," and used "nationality" as an administrative principle in order to achieve socialist societal and economic goals.[39]

Precisely because nationality was only an administrative principle aimed at the effective government of the socialist state, it was deemed to have been depoliticized: "Collective identity linked to nationality did not matter, as Soviet power obviated its politicization and limited the range of possible public representations and interpretations of this identity."[40] In this sense "Sovietization"—the creation of a collective identity for the multinational Soviet state—was deemed to have overridden and neutralized the appeals of alternative identities. "Culture" was actively encouraged, but only as a subordinate and supportive facet of state identity; culture as acculturation to a greater, composite identity was permitted, but culture as an alternative, subsidiary one was not. The three forms that alternative identity might take in Central Asia were locality, being urban or clan; ethnicity; and religion. Each of these then had to be repressed and politically neutered for the sake of state building.

In the 1950s era of China's alliance with Moscow, there was not only an adoption of Soviet doctrine on nationalities by China but also a very real "Sovietization" of the problems of local, ethnic, and religious identity in Xinjiang. The clearest example of this was the naming of the Xinjiang Uyghur Autonomous Region. Up until the late nineteenth century, "Uyghur" was a historical term that related to the Turks who had migrated from Mongolia in the tenth century and settled in the oasis cities of the Tarim. The term fell into disuse from the early sixteenth century as the last of the peoples of Eastern Turkestan were converted to Islam, and Uyghur was shunned as an appellation of a pre-Islamic people.[41]

However, from the time of Yaqub Beg in the nineteenth century through the ill-fated Turkestan republics of the 1930s and 1940s, Uyghur was to return as the denomination of both a historic people and a modern national identity. As elsewhere in the Turkic and Arab worlds, the relationship between this emergent national identity and Islam remained complex. Some felt that Turkic modernity must involve a rejection of traditional identity, of which religion was one part; others felt that the religious question provoked internal divisions that had to be suppressed to allow a national identity to emerge. In following these lines of development, the modern Uyghur identity took a path that was comparable to the rest of the Islamic world in the postcolonial era. Lapidus describes this:

> With independence nationalism was diffused from the elites to the masses. For these masses, now subject to new regimes bent on social and economic transformation of their societies, nationalism served, just as did universalist versions of Islam, to replace loyalties to parochial family, village and religious associations, and committed people to a broader concept of political identity. The masses began to see themselves in ethnic, national, and state political terms. Nonetheless, Islam remained of covert importance. For most Muslims identity has never been fully secularized. What makes Turks Turkish in the eyes of many is Islam. What makes one an Arab, for many Arabs, is being Muslim. Much of the emotional power of nationalism in the Muslim world comes from the capacity of national movements to parochialize Islam and channel the force of Muslim faith into national commitments. Nationalism becomes the bearer of Islam.[42]

Some specialists have cautioned against overascription of Islam as a factor in Uyghur identity, because it seems to have a character that separates it from Islamic "orthodoxy." But Bellér-Hann argues that Islam in Xinjiang is not an inferior marker of identity to that experienced in other Islamic societies but rather a distinctive variation of it:

> A hundred years ago, the integration of Islamic and non-Islamic practices was already deep enough to be indiscernible for practitioners. Instead of contrasting local beliefs in a "peripheral" region with an idealized "pure" or "high" Islam of the "center" (the local Little Tradition with a central Great Tradition), I am more impressed by the similarities of many small details in ritual and daily practice between regions situated far apart geo-

graphically, with other Turkic and Iranian speakers of the new Central Asian republics, the Middle East and South Asia.⁴³

In this sense, the modern Uyghur identity has followed a path common to other Islamic societies where there has had to be a negotiation between tradition and modernity, and between a variety of centers and margins. Within the context of political incorporation into a socialist China, Islam remains, along with land and language, one of the foundational aspects of that identity, where "each marker of identity takes on salience and enhanced meaningfulness in the context of significant oppositions."⁴⁴ In following the Soviet model of "creating and breaking nations," the Chinese state both helped to call into existence a modern Uyghur identity, of which Islam remained an integral part, at the same time it sought to subordinate this identity to the demands of building a multiethnic socialist country. One example of these paradoxes was to be language reform.

Until the 1920s, Uyghurs had used Chaghatay script (Arabic modified for Turkic linguistics) continuously, but Turkey had adopted Latin in 1928 and the Soviet Union imposed Cyrillic on its Turkic populations in 1937—at least partly due to a concern with Pan-Turkism; so by the 1950s, the Uyghurs were the last Turkic people still using Chaghatay. China considered several methods of reform, including in 1956 moving all the Turkic peoples of Xinjiang to Cyrillic.⁴⁵ By 1959 this was abandoned, and for the next twenty years a modified Pinyin script was the only authorized script for Uyghur and Kazakh. The reinstatement of Chaghatay in 1982 represented a significant reversal of state-led acculturation, in which the primary factor was Uyghur resistance to what was perceived as assimilation toward China and away from their cultural and religious heritage in Central Asia:

> The Arabic script represented a link with the religious tradition and the cultural past for many Uyghurs who were reluctant to part with their identity and resented the reform as one more step towards assimilation and a loss of their linguistic autonomy.⁴⁶

The period in question—1958–80—represented a more widespread attempt to integrate Xinjiang into China driven by a mix of internal and international politics. This era saw many revolutionary campaigns, notably the Great Leap Forward and the Great Proletarian Cultural Revolution; and it also saw the emergence of the Sino-Soviet and Sino-Indian cold wars. Under the "United Front Policy" of 1953, a China Islamic Association had been formed as a "patriotic religious association," but this was abolished under the National Religious Reforms of 1958, which instituted much tighter controls on religious practice. The combination of ideological fervor and economic crisis during the Great Leap Forward saw as many as 100,000 Uyghurs and Kazakhs displaced from Xinjiang to Soviet Central Asia by 1962, where they joined older communities that had made the journey in the Qing and Republican eras.[47] Thereafter, the border was closed and not reopened for twenty years.

There was also very significant inward migration into Xinjiang in these years. The 1953 census recorded a Han population of 330,000 in the region, or 7 percent of the total population; by 1964, this had increased to 2.5 million, or 33 percent of the total,[48] many of whom were the soldier-farmers (*bingtuan*) of the Xinjiang Production and Construction Corps. During the Cultural Revolution, Islam, like other religions, was targeted as one of the "four olds," and most mosques across China were closed and religious practice was confined within households.[49]

The turn to greater toleration of religious practice that began in 1980 was welcomed by China's Muslims, who look upon the decade as a period of relative calm in their relations with the Chinese state. Mosques were reopened, *hajj* resumed, and the Chinese Islamic Association was revived, with its role defined in a law of 1982 as assisting "the Party and the government to implement the policy of freedom of religious belief" and "to help the broad mass of religious believers and persons in religious circles to raise their patriotic and socialist consciousness."[50]

The politics of the period was also strongly shaped by the deterioration of China's security in Central Eurasia. Of the countries on China's western periphery, Beijing enjoyed a favorable relationship with only one, Pakistan, driven by the strategic alignment between Moscow and Delhi after 1962. As for participation in the international politics of the wider Middle East, China found itself largely excluded, as Halliday suggests:

> China had for decades maintained a rhetorical and remote stance on the Middle East that only matured into strategic and commercial engagement in the 1990s. Much as it postured on Middle Eastern issues, above all to discredit the Russians, China had no significant impact on any regional country or issue; indeed, for most of the period up to the 1990s at the earliest, the modern history of the Middle East could be written without any reference to it.[51]

Clearly, therefore, something had gone badly awry in the external strategy of New China since Zhou Enlai traveled to Bandung in 1955 and embraced Jawaharlal Nehru and Jamal 'Abd al-Nasir as the standard-bearers of modern Asian nationalism. If the failure of Tianxia China lay in its inability to take issues of geopolitics seriously and its flawed belief that virtue alone would govern the frontiers of the empire, then Sovereign China had clearly reversed these priorities. Geopolitics became the order of the day, and though a new form of All-under-Heaven was advanced under the banner of "the East Is Red," this won few adherents to Beijing's side. As a result, the twenty years from the Great Leap Forward to the beginning of the reform era bear some resemblance to past patterns in which the Chinese frontier was quarantined by state mobilization and migration controls. The main difference was that acculturation and transformation could no longer be left to virtue but had become a matter of ideological enforcement.

Thirty years after the first moves to reform and opening in China, it can be seen that this has resulted primarily in a return to Asia policy that has taken on considerable momentum since the 1990s. Among other changes, this has allowed China to make its first moves toward becoming a regionalist power. China calls this strategy its *zhoubian zhengce*—neighborhood policy—where the approach to the peripheral "neighborhoods" in Asia is strongly shaped by the interaction between internal and external modernizations. This creates a transnational sphere in which internal and external margins merge around a permeable frontier. China has to manage several types of these open margins at the same time, though the foundational example remains Greater China, as Callahan suggests:

> "Greater China" is the prominent site where the borders between East and West, nation and state, self and Other are continually drawn, erased and reasserted. Further, Greater China is an optimum site for an exploration of boundary production, because it does not exist as a legal or institutional body.... It is a fantasy, a dream, and a nightmare, created through symbolic exchange both between East and West and within East Asia.[52]

The existence of these transnational frontiers of China's neighborhoods indicates the continued relationship between Tianxia China and Sovereign China: between a China that is a temporal-historical project that still aspires to govern by principles of virtue and a spatial-political China that is ordered around the uncompromising rules of geopolitics. China may be confident that it has got the balance between virtue and geopolitics right in Greater China; but at the Inner Asian margins of China, virtue and geopolitics operate under different dynamics. Here, we find a boundary that has some geopolitical predictability following border agreements with the countries of the former Soviet Union and some fluctuating progress toward this with India. But China also encounters processes of frontier production that still shift between fantasy, dream, and nightmare. The fantasy is the cycle of Chinese films portraying the Inner Asia of Han and Tang times, where Chinese heroes and villains act out dramas of virtue, romance, and superheroic skills. The dream is of a Central Asia, and perhaps beyond it a Central Eurasia, where China is secure, influential, and respected—that is, a great power. The nightmare lies in the claim of Tibetans and Uyghurs to escape from China into their own modern nations of Tibet and East Turkestan.

In the final section, I turn to contemporary Chinese policy, examining China's efforts at government and governance across its frontiers with the Islamic world.

China and Islam in the Twenty-First Century: Harmony through Diversity?

The permeability of the frontier between China and Islamic societies has risen dramatically in recent years due to three forces: the emergence of a sovereign Central Asia, and with it mobilization around Central Asian national and regional consciousness; the policy of reform and opening on China's periphery, and the resulting construction of new kinds of relations across the boundaries of Central Eurasia; and the growth of a diasporic frontier community, of Uyghurs and Kazakhs in particular, in Central Asia but also globally. China is contributing to this permeability across frontiers with its strategy of the Xibu Da Kaifa Zhanlüe—the Great Western Development and Opening Strategy—internally; and its international diplomacy toward Central Asia and the Islamic world beyond, externally. Taken together, these may be considered yet another attempt to bring the benefits of Chinese civilization westward and make China a power in Central Eurasia. But here China meets many challenges.

China presents itself as a modernizing force—just as every other rising power, such as Britain or the United States, has done. Reform and opening lead the long march to the West; but Chinese modernity is resolutely materialist. The Xibu Da Kaifa may be an attempt to bind Western China into a modern Chinese state, but it is a philosophy of national construction that is "built" on concrete, steel, and migrant workers and cadres. The core issue may be, as I have noted, that with each emanation of its power China reinscribes difference alongside uniformity, and especially at its margins. The uniformity that China now proposes is that of the modernist China with its doctrine of peaceful emergence after thirty years of reform and opening; but alongside this, China generates a corresponding response from its frontiers, both internal and international.

Internally, modernist China both produces and consumes nationalism,[53] and though most of this symbolic circulation relates to the fast-evolving relationship between the Chinese state and the Chinese majority (Hanzu) population, China also produces and consumes nationalism in its minorities. As I have noted, nothing like a Uyghur identity existed before the era of modern politics in Asia. Uyghur nationalism has therefore followed a course not dissimilar to that of other Asian societies, in which democratic and national consciousness have advanced together. It seems to bear most resemblance to the other "hidden" nations of Asia—the Kurds, Sikhs, or Tamils—who got left behind in the sovereignty revolutions of the nineteenth and twentieth centuries; and indeed, Dru Gladney employs a term from South Asian studies—subaltern nationalism—to account for the way the modernist construction of the Chinese geobody has driven the production of new politicized identities at the margin.[54] Examinations of the Chinese state's relations with its subaltern nationalities seem to fall into three categories. First, assimilation, in which subalternity is an imposed condition prior to full incorporation. Second, some mix of accommodation and segregation in which most of the subaltern group is excluded from the processes of the new society but certain political, economic, or cultural elites may seek an accommodation with the modernist project of the State. And third, rejectionism, in which the power of the state is resisted, including by force, resulting in various counterstrategies of punishment.[55] As argued elsewhere, the fact that Xinjiang's frontier remains highly transnationalized presents other possibilities.[56] Thus it is quite hard to say what leverage the Tibetan community can derive from transnational relations, beyond its exposure in the global media; but the context of the Uyghurs may be different. Thus if Uyghurs are being assimilated, is this inward assimilation toward China, or outward assimilation toward the society and politics of the Turkic and Islamic worlds? If accommodation/segregation is taking place, is this as a "national minority" within China, or as a globalized diaspora spread across several continents? And when, as in 2004, the Pentagon named Uyghurs the fourth-largest nationality (after Saudis, Afghans, and Pakistanis) held in its interrogation center for the "war on terror" at Guantánamo Bay, then clearly the cycle of rejectionism and punishment has also become significantly internationalized.[57] In this way, the governance of the frontier remains open and contested, and it retains its historical feature as both the Islamic margin of China and the Chinese margin of Islam.

In its new diplomacy for Central Asia, China clearly hopes to create international space for its emergence, and this leads it toward experimentation with new forms of cultural, economic, and political governance beyond its boundaries. As well as advancing the conventional sovereign politics of an emergent power (diplomacy, military relations, infrastructure development and logistical corridors, etc.), China stands to gain from developing relations that present it not as a geopolitical object with hard boundaries but as a spatial-historical force with movable frontiers. In asserting this Chinese model of regional governance in the West, China faces a number of problems, however, not least the continued commitment of Islamic communities to their own systems of allegiance and obligation; and resistance to attempts to impose alien notions of governance upon them. The core of this resistance is the notion of "Islamism," a term much employed but very little analysed. Islamism can, of course, mean the modern doctrinal equivalent of the Caliphal tradition discussed above, which holds that the relationship between faith and politics, and thus between faith and the state, is indivisible. This, for example, is part of the ideology of Hizb ut Tahrir, the organization that seems most to concern the Chinese authorities. But Islamist politics are also evident in Islamic societies that are secularist, and sustain the autonomy of politics and faith. In these cases, Islamism does not mean Caliphalism but rather the wedding of Islam to modern Asian nationalism—Islam as the bearer of nationalist consciousness, as argued by Lapidus in the quotation above.[58]

This context of the fluid relationship between political and faith identities in Islamic societies presents evident problems for China in setting a course for its strategy in Central Eurasia. On the one hand, it is a staunch sovereigntist and has been pleased to use the "war on terror" to join in a grand coalition against Caliphal politics. On the other hand, it regards itself as a leading, and perhaps the leading, champion of modern Asian nationalism, and thus as a supporter of resistance to hegemonic missions to impose solutions on Asian political development. It certainly rejected the doctrine of preemption promulgated by the administration of U.S. President George W. Bush, as was most authoritatively indicated in an article by the Chinese state councillor, and former foreign minister, Qian Qichen a year after the beginning of the Iraq war:

> To insist on uniformity will get nowhere, and hubris is an even worse choice. To rely on the military superiority of "preemption" though it may take cities and seize territory [*gongcheng luedi*] will not eliminate threats or even more win people's hearts; on the contrary, it will create tension in international relations and bring about shifts in the world situation. ... Faced with the changes in the international situation at the beginning of the new century, China advocates complying with the trends of history, strengthening international cooperation, establishing a new concept of security, and advancing the democracy of international relations as a fundamental interest.[59]

In asserting concepts such as the trends of history and the democracy of international relations, China made clear its differences with the Western strategy for Central Eurasia. It argued for the autonomy of Asian societies in organizing their relations and asserted the equality of sovereign governments. This was a message that many in the Islamic world were happy to embrace, allowing China to establish strategic partnerships with countries as diverse as Saudi Arabia, Kazakhstan, and Pakistan.

In discussing the problems of coexistence between the Islamic world and other societies, Chinese analysts have been particularly adamant in rejecting any notion of a "clash of civilizations."[60] But this still leaves China with the complex question of how it can establish its own preferences for governance in a region riven with contentious politics but unified in its skepticism about the helpfulness of external intervention. At the same time, China faces the question of how it should align its strategy of expanding international space with those of Central Eurasia's other littoral powers—Russia, India, and Europe—with each of which it is seeking to develop strategic partnerships.

One product of this complexity has been China's first attempt to develop a system of regional governance "with Chinese characteristics." In this regard, the Shanghai Cooperation Organization (SCO), founded in 2001 and currently with six members and four observers, is interesting for three main reasons. First, though China's involvement with East Asian regional governance has been much studied, it cannot be argued that this is "regionalism with Chinese characteristics." Rather, it is regionalism with characteristics of the Association of Southeast Asian Nations—within which, some argue, China is being "socialized."[61] The SCO, conversely, was advanced by, and has been significantly shaped by, Chinese interests and values. As far as there is a regionalism with Chinese characteristics, therefore, the SCO should be it. However, this leaves unanswered the question of why China's strategy of development and security requires a regional governance structure.

This points to the second line of questioning about the SCO—"What is its mission?"—indicating a functional ambiguity about the organization. Thus, if China is pursuing a developmental strategy, this will require the establishment of strategic corridors for the circulation of resources, commodities, investment, and labor between China and Central Eurasia; but most of these agreements are being conducted bilaterally, including through strategic partnerships, and thus do not require regional multilateralism. Similarly, if China is pursuing a security strategy, particularly against the transnational threats of Islamism and ethnoseparatism, then this can be conducted between the security agencies of the relevant countries and does not require the apparatus of formal regionalism. Clearly, then, China's regionalization of its strategy in the West through the SCO has functions beyond those nominally advanced in the name of security or development.

The main explanation for this may lie in China's traditions of governance that do not permit it to pursue a strategy of emergence without reference to a body of normative and legitimating doctrine, and this is the third and final noteworthy aspect of the SCO. As Callahan argues, China is intensely preoccupied with creating a narrative for itself as a responsible and rising great power, and because regionalism is part of what great powers do, it is also necessary for China to have a narrative for this.[62] So the SCO establishes a narrative framework for a region in which China has limited experience and not a great deal in common. The narrative of emergence as responsible regionalist power precedes and creates a space in which mission and purposes can be developed over time. The SCO seeks to promote a distinctively Chinese normative order expressed through multilateral channels. For example, at the SCO's 2001 founding summit, President Jiang Zemin put forward the core ideas of "mutual trust, mutual benefit, equality, consultation, respect to different civilizations and common prosperity."[63] A further notable delineation was advanced at the 2007 SCO summit in Bishkek. The Bishkek Declaration calls for the building a new international security architecture for Eurasia:

The SCO member states advocate creation of a security structure on the basis of generally accepted norms of the international law that will: reflect the balance of interests of all subjects of international relations; guarantee the right of every state to choose independently its way of development based on its unique historical experience and national features, to protect its state integrity and national dignity, to participate equally in international affairs; ensure the settlement of international and regional conflicts and crises through political and diplomatic means in strict accordance with principles and norms of the international law and with consideration of legitimate interests of all parties concerned; preserve the diversity of cultures and civilizations, encourage implementation of initiatives aimed at deepening of dialogue among civilizations and religions.[64]

This declaration blends China's traditional concerns with sovereignty, legality, and the UN system with the particularistic perception of the religious, ethnic, and historical-cultural diversity of the SCO members and observers. In this way, the Bishkek declaration defines Chinese normative strategy toward the Islamic world as an attempt to negotiate between universal principles of sovereign internationalism and the diversity of Asian civilizational and religious traditions and their modernizing social systems.

This notion of blending diversity under universalism has come to be known as the "Shanghai spirit." Chinese analysts see this as deriving from the traditional Chinese idea of achieving "harmony through diversity" (*he er butong*, 和而不同):

The practical cooperation of the SCO itself advances the significant spirit of "respect diverse cultures, strive for common development," which embodies the common attitude of the majority of post–Cold War countries and peoples confronted with the present assaults of globalization. Under precisely this guiding spirit, the member countries of the SCO are surmounting ethnic traditions, religious ideas, ideological, and political systems and other multifaceted social and cultural differences, in order to obtain the historic opportunity of common development and a favorable regional environment, and by way of equal consultation establishing political confidence, security coordination, mutual beneficial economic relations, so as to bring forth new ideas in international practice in answering the question posed to international society at century's end of the "clash of civilizations." The "Shanghai spirit" embodies the Eastern philosophical idea of "harmony through diversity" [*he er butong*]. The spirit is not only "already established as the source of each member country's foreign policy, conceptual values and criteria for behavior" but also "possesses more and more universal international significance."[65]

Clearly, then, China has many aspirations for its strategy in the Islamic world. This strategy aims to meet standard objectives in security and development; but must also cope with the specific geopolitical and civilizational contexts of Central Eurasia: the intensifying rivalry among internal and external powers and the need to negotiate around the ongoing struggles to shape the future of Islam under modernity. China is pursuing a dual strategy in this context. On the one hand, it is very strongly focused on conventional geopolitics—resources, boundaries, regimes, and the logistics of economic and military infrastructures. On the other hand, it aspires to its own normative agenda of "harmony through diversity." This seeks to establish not only an ascendancy but also transcendence—it points to a China that rises above contradictions between Asians, and between East and West. Yet these two projects, geopolitical and normative, may not align. China's strategy is far more focused on states than publics; China's "harmony through diversity" is a pluralism of sovereign Asian states, not a plurality of publics. In the struggle for geopolitical certainty and territorial integrity, China's fears for its own sovereignty are much more powerful than its dream of civilizational and religious harmony.

This became more apparent in the summer of 2009, when violence within Xinjiang saw a further acceleration. Up to 200 people were killed in ethnosectarian riots centered on Urumqi. Subsequently, Xinjiang saw the most intensive security lockdown to date, with unknown numbers of people taken into detention. As before, the Chinese government refused to accept that it may have got its nationalities or development strategy for the Western regions wrong; instead, it pointed to a conspiracy between internal and foreign elements that sought to undermine China's national unity.[66] The fact that the cycles of assimilation and resistance, accommodation and segregation, and rejection and punishment are intensifying inside Xinjiang suggest that China's commitment to dialogue and transcendence would be better demonstrated in its government of the frontier, before it was espoused in its foreign policy. In the next generation, China's diplomacy will mature quickly, allowing it to further advance its presence in Central Eurasia; and West China's permeability with Central Eurasia will similarly develop. The interface between China and Islam is set to be a permanent feature of international life in the new Asia, therefore. Yet in the interpretation of this chapter, a stable and beneficial mode of governance for relations between China and the Islamic world has yet to be achieved.

Conclusion: China, Islam and "Different Heavens"

This chapter has suggested that we can learn much about the nature of contemporary Chinese foreign policy from the way that it negotiates between the received sets of belief around tradition and modernity, and between the temporal and spatial boundaries of the Chinese and Islamic worlds. China is not the only contemporary sovereign power that has a problem with Islam, or with religious communities more generally, but it remains a highly distinctive variant of this problem. Part of the problem is located in the shift from traditional to modern society, which tears up and rebuilds collective identities. The other part is located in the uncertain temporal-spatial boundaries of China and Islam as national, regional, and even, to some extent global, communities are relocated. Habermas indicates the core of this question:

> Every religion is originally a "*world*view" or "comprehensive doctrine" in the sense that it claims authority to structure a form of life *in its entirety*. A religion must relinquish this claim within a secularized society marked by a pluralism of worldviews. With the functional differentiation of social subsystems, the life of the religious community also becomes detached from its social surroundings. The role of "member of the community" becomes differentiated from the "role of member of society." (emphasis in the original)[67]

Islam arguably goes further than asserting an authoritative worldview, but rather proposes an alternative sovereignty: that there is no such thing as a "member of political society" differentiated from the "member of the community of faith." Though a majority of Muslims do not adhere to the indivisibility of faith and state, there remains a tension, perhaps inevitable, between the Islamic comprehensive doctrine and the pluralized worldviews of modernity. This need not lead to overt contradiction of sovereignties; but resolution of this question does depend on specific political and international political contexts. In this regard, China's interaction with Islam has differed from that of other societies.

First, Chinese political thought treated government as a form of supermoral organization. The very terms Tianxia (天下), *Tianzi* (天子), and *Tianmin* (天民) all point to ways that natural, spiritual, and social orders were fused so that political and moral categories were indistinguishable. Defense of this supermoral order meant defense of the temporal-spatial boundaries of China, which in the traditional world meant defense against barbarism. The potential for confrontation between China and Islam was attenuated by distance and the pluralization of Islamic societies themselves. The incorporation of part of Turkestan—and Tibet and Mongolia—into the Qing Empire did require reformulations of the idea of China and its boundaries, including provisional delineation of cultural nations. But the fact that the Turkic world was so diverse in its social organization, language, and religious practices meant that it was easy for the Qing to designate this as "culture" rather than an alternative social order. This plural boundary in the West only began to harden under the impact of modern international politics; but even here, as I have noted, this arrived in waves so that there was not a single revolutionary shift from ethical to geopolitical governance, from Tianxia to sovereign China, but rather the steady erosion of the former by the latter, though clearly this reached a critical level with the collapse of the old order. With each stage, China shifted its mode of governance of the frontier, though there were persistent characteristics.

China's preferred method of governance was by transformation and acculturation, though punitive missions and quarantine were also employed. What varied most were assumptions about what it meant to be "Chinese." At some times, this could be quite cosmopolitan; at others, a more monochromatic understanding was enforced. This system of reinscription, in which a Chinese center and a non-Chinese margin contested uniformity and difference, is still incomplete. China employs the ambiguity of its open margins, but these vary dramatically around its perimeter in Asia. The strategy of transformation and acculturation that aspires to the reconstitution of Greater China has very different consequences when applied in West China, triggering cycles of assimilation, resistance, accommodation, and revolt. To explain these cycles, we need to look at both China and Islam as they negotiate between the comprehensive doctrines of the past and the pluralist worldviews that mark modernity. China, for example, still has a tendency to represent itself as a form of "comprehensive doctrine" even as it embraces modernity. Thus, President Hu Jintao concluded his speech to the Seventeenth Chinese Communist Party Congress in October 2007 as follows:

> We must reinforce unity, take heed of the overall situation, conscientiously safeguard the integrity and unity of the whole Party, preserve the organic relations [*xuerou guanxi*] between Party and masses, consolidate the great unity of the ethnic peoples of the whole country, strengthen the great unity of the sons and daughters of the Chinese nation at home and overseas, promote the great unity of the Chinese people with the people of all countries of the world, in order to provide the immense power to overcome all difficulties and obstructions and propel the cause of the party and people toward new and even greater triumphs.[68]

Of course, this doctrine of Chinese integrity and ascendancy cannot disguise the extent to which modernity is producing a plurality of centers and margins inside China, and between China and other centers and margins. The Islamic frontier is just one of these, but certainly one of the most problematic, precisely because of its own trajectory between tradition and modernity. The meeting between China and Islam does not represent a single reflexive movement—Islam old, China modern, as was espoused in the Cultural Revolution—but a dual reflexivity. China's negotiation between its own tradition and modernity intermeshes with Islam under tradition and modernity, producing paradoxes both temporal and spatial.

The most serious of these paradoxes must be between China's claim that it favors harmony through diversity between itself and Islam as civilizations, on one hand, and its inability to realize this ideal of governance within its own jurisdiction of government, on the other hand. China's drive for modernity at all costs does not generate harmony at the frontier but rather intensifies again the reinscription of difference. China calls for the self-strengthening of Asian nationalism as a mechanism of resistance to hegemonic missions; but this very dynamic of Asian modernity in Islamic communities is declared anathema when it occurs within the boundaries of China's own sovereigntist project. In Xinjiang, as elsewhere in the Turkic world, modernity does not mean leaving Islam behind, but rather according it a defining place in the movement toward modern national identities. Thus the Islamic identity of the past and the Islamic identity of the future collide with their Chinese equivalents, so that, at the new frontier, Chinese and Uyghur still look to "different Heavens."

Notes

1. I use the terms government and governance in this essay to refer to two different, if related, kinds of political relations: government is an organizational relationship and governance a practical relationship. While contemporary China has made some progress in regularizing government of its relations in the West, governance as mutual and agreed practice is still under negotiation. This points to the fact that the agreement of boundaries is invariably an act of government; whereas frontiers refer to the places where different practices of governance meet. We should also note that other societies —e.g., India or Russia—have found the establishment of frontiers of governance with the Islamic world difficult.

2. Jürgen Habermas, *The Theory of Communicative Action*, vol. 2 (Cambridge: Polity Press, 1987), 56.

3. *Lun Yu*, translated by Arthur Waley (London: Everyman, 2000), 5.12, 17.19.

4. Benjamin I. Schwartz, *The World of Thought in Ancient China* (Harvard: Belknap Press, 1985), 123.

5. We should be clear that this is a disputed point. Fung Yu-lan argued: "There are many people who say that Chinese philosophy is a this-worldly philosophy. It is difficult to state that these people are entirely right or entirely wrong. Taking a superficial view, people who hold this view cannot be said to be wrong, because according to their view, Chinese philosophy, regardless of its different schools of thought, is directly or indirectly concerned with government and ethics. On the surface, therefore it is concerned chiefly with society and not with the universe; with the daily functions of human relations, not hell or heaven; with man's present life, but not his life in the world to come. . . . This, however, is only a surface view of the matter." Fung Yu-lan, *A Short History of Chinese Philosophy* (New York: Free Press, 1976), 7. Fung's answer was that Chinese philosophy was as much concerned with supermoral values as moral values; with universal, as much as relative, goods. The ideal Chinese citizen was *'Tian-min'*, who performs "not only as a citizen of society, but also as a 'citizen of the universe,' . . . otherwise his deeds would not have super-moral value." (p. 9). Yet I note that the definition of this supermoral citizen was in the classic texts not in scripture; that goodness was a matter of ethics not commandment; and universal citizens adjusted their deeds to the super-moral order, they did not adjust the world so that it conformed to revelation.

6. *The Qur'ān*, translated by M. A. S. Abdel Haleem (Oxford: Oxford University Press, 2005), vol. 2, 213.

7. Abdulaziz Sachedina, "The Qur'ān and Other Religions," in *The Cambridge Companion to the Qur'ān*, edited by Jane Dammen McAuliffe (Cambridge: Cambridge University Press, 2006), 294.

8. Qur'ān, 16:2.

9. Ibid., 39:6.

10. The translation of the term *ren* here as civility, rather than the conventional humanity or benevolence, requires justification. The Confucian notion of civility is clearly composite containing humanity, right, virtue, ritual, and loyalty (ren ,yi, de, li, zhong), but it is clear that Confucius intends *ren* to mean a human society that has been raised above the dominance of nature and is governed by civilized forms of behavior and intercourse. One way of identifying the significance of *ren* is to ask if barbarians have *ren*? Rather, we see that the definition of barbarian is very much the absence of *ren*: they are dominated by base human nature and lack forms of civilized intercourse. Hence the

famous exchange in *Lun Yu*, 9:13. For further discussion, see Wing-Tsit Chan, *A Source Book in Chinese Philosophy* (Princeton, N.J.: Princeton University Press, 1963), 14–17; and Schwartz, *World of Thought*, 75–85.

11. *Lun Yu*, 12.7.
12. Ibid., 16.2.
13. Ira M. Lapidus, *A History of Islamic Societies* (Cambridge: Cambridge University Press, 2002), 816.
14. Mu-chou Poo, *Enemies of Civilization: Attitudes to Foreigners in Ancient Mesopotamia, Egypt, and China* (Albany: State University of New York Press, 2005), 124.
15. Marc Samuel Abramson, "Deep Eyes and High Noses: Physiognomy and the Depiction of Barbarians in Tang China," in *Political Frontiers, Ethnic Boundaries, and Human Geographies in Chinese History*, edited by Nicola di Cosmo and Don J. Wyatt (London: RoutledgeCurzon, 2003), 123.
16. Chih-yu Shih, *Negotiating Ethnicity in China: Citizenship as a Response to the State* (London: Routledge, 2002), 70.
17. Poo, *Enemies of Civilization*, 153.
18. Richard Bonney, *Jihād: From Qurān to bin Laden* (Basingstoke: Palgrave, 2004), 8–9.
19. Qur'ān, 190–91.
20. Ibid., 193.
21. Mohammed Arkoun, *Islam: to Reform or Subvert?* (London: Saqi Books, 2006), 258.
22. Carter Vaughn Findley, *The Turks in World History* (Oxford: Oxford University Press, 2005), 18.
23. Transoxania stretched from the shores of the Caspian to the Pamirs, broadly in line with contemporary Uzbekistan. The Orkhon is in what is now Northern Mongolia.
24. Svat Soucek, *A History of Inner Asia* (Cambridge: Cambridge University Press, 2000), 70.
25. Isaac Mason, "How Islam Entered China," *The Muslim World* 19, no. 3 (2007): 249–63, at 256–57.
26. James Millward, *Eurasian Crossroads: A History of Xinjiang* (London: Hurst, 2007), 35–37.
27. Richard N. Frye, *The Heritage of Central Asia* (Princeton, N.J.: Marcus Wiener Press, 1996), 203.
28. Findley, *Turks in World History*, 14.
29. Lapidus, *History of Islamic Societies*, 338.
30. Soucek, *History of Inner Asia*, 117–18.
31. Zhao Gang, "Reinventing China: Imperial Qing Ideology and the Rise of Modern Chinese National Identity in the Early Twentieth Century," *Modern China* 32 (2006): 3–30, at 4; emphasis in the original.
32. Peter C. Perdue, *China Marches West: The Qing Conquest of Central Eurasia* (Cambridge, Mass.: Belknap Press, 2005), 285.
33. Ibid., 286.
34. Laura Newby, "The Chinese Literary Conquest of Xinjiang," *Modern China* 25 (1999): 451–74, at 459.
35. Ibid., 460.
36. Hu Zhenhua, "ZongYa yu ZhongYa yanjiu" [Central Asia and Central Asian studies], *ZhongYang Minzu Daxue Xuebao*, no. 5 (2005): 47–53, at 51.

37. Shih, *Negotiating Ethnicity*, 5.
38. Perdue, *China Marches West*, 338; emphasis added.
39. Paul Georg Geiss, *Pre-Tsarist and Tsarist Central Asia: Communal Commitment and Political Order in Change* (London: RoutledgeCurzon, 2004), 239–40.
40. Geiss, *Pre-Tsarist and Tsarist Central Asia*, 246.
41. Dru C. Gladney, *Dislocating China: Muslims, Minorities and Other Subaltern Subjects* (London: Hurst, 2004), 214.
42. Ira M. Lapidus, "Between Universalism and Particularism: The Historical Bases of Muslim Communal, National and Global Identities," *Global Networks* 1, no. 1 (2001): 37–55, at 48.
43. Ildikó Bellér-Hann, "'Making the Oil Fragrant': Dealings with the Supernatural among the Uyghurs in Xinjiang," *Asian Ethnicity* 2, no. 1 (2001): 9–23, at 10.
44. Gladney, *Dislocating China*, 219.
45. Jean Rahman Duval and Waris Abdulkerim Janbaz, "An Introduction to Latin Script Uyghur," paper presented at Middle East and Central Asia Politics, Economics, and Society conference, University of Utah, Salt Lake City, 2006, 2.
46. Ibid., 3.
47. William Clark and Ablet Kamalov, "Uighur Migration across Central Asian Frontiers," *Central Asian Survey* 23, no. 2 (2004): 167–82, at 177.
48. Colin Mackerras, "Xinjiang at the Turn of the Century: The Causes of Separatism," *Central Asian Survey* 20, no. 3 (2001): 289–303, at 293.
49. Edmund Waite, "The Impact of the State on Islam amongst the Uyghurs: Religious Knowledge and Authority in the Kashgar Oasis," *Central Asian Survey* 25, no. 3 (2006): 251–65, at 253–55.
50. Ibid., 255.
51. Fred Halliday, *The Middle East in International Relations: Power, Politics and Ideology* (Cambridge: Cambridge University Press, 2005), 98.
52. William A. Callahan, *Contingent States: Greater China and Transnational Relations* (Minneapolis: University of Minnesota, 2004), xviii–xix.
53. William A. Callahan, "History, Identity, and Security: Producing and Consuming Nationalism in China," *Critical Asian Studies* 38, no. 2 (2006): 179–208.
54. Gladney, *Dislocating China*.
55. See Abigail Sines, "Civilizing the Middle Kingdom's Wild West," *Central Asian Survey* 21, no. 1 (2002): 5–18; Herbert S. Yee, "Ethnic Relations in Xinjiang: A Survey of Uighur-Han Relations in Urumqi," *Journal of Contemporary China* 12, no. 36 (2003): 431–52.
56. David Kerr with Laura C. Swinton, "China, Xinjiang and the Transnational Security of Central Asia," *Critical Asian Studies* 40, no. 1 (2008): 113–42.
57. Dru C. Gladney, "China's 'Uyghur Problem' and the Shanghai Cooperation Organization," paper prepared for U.S.-China Economic and Security Review Commission Hearing, Washington, 2006, 1.
58. Lapidus, "Between Universalism and Particularism." For further discussion on the politics of Islamism, see Michel Hoebink, "Thinking about Renewal in Islam: Towards a History of Islamic Ideas on Modernization and Secularization," *Arabica* 46 (1999): 29–62.
59. Qian Qichen, "Meiguo guoji anquan zhanlüe tiaozheng yu xin shiji chu de guoji guanxi" [Revision in the U.S. international security strategy and international relations at the beginning of the new century], *Guoji Wenti Yanjiu* no. 1 (2004): 1–3, at 3.

60. See, e.g., Jin Liangxiang, "Xifang yu Yisilan: Gaidao yu yingdui" [The West and Islam: transformation and reaction], *Alabo Shijie*, no. 4 (2007): 18–24.

61. Alastair Iain Johnston, *Social States: China in International Institutions, 1980–2000* (Princeton, N.J.: Princeton University Press, 2008), 155–96.

62. William A. Callahan, "The Cartography of National Humiliation and the Emergence of China's Geobody," *Public Culture* 21, no. 1 (2009): 149.

63. Cited by Pan Guang, "A Chinese Perspective on the Shanghai Cooperation Organization," in *The Shanghai Cooperation Organization*, edited by A. J. K. Bailes et al., SIPRI Policy Paper 17 (Stockholm: Stockholm International Peace Research Institute, 2007), 49.

64. Shanghai Cooperation Organization, "Bishkek Declaration of the Heads of the Member States of the Shanghai Cooperation Organization," August 16, 2007.

65. Hu Jintao, speech to Sixth Shanghai Cooperation Organization Head of State Summit, June 2006, cited by Xu Tao "Gou jian diqu hezuo anquan de changshi: Jian lun Shanghai Hezuo Zuzhi anquan de hezuo de xin wenti" [Trying to build regional security cooperation: New problems in SCO security cooperation], *Eluosi ZhongYa DongOu Yanjiu* no. 1 (2007): 69–74, at 74.

66. The State Council's paper on Xinjiang of September 2009 says the events were due to internal and external forces of terrorism, splittism, and extremism (*you jing neiwai kongbuzhuyi shili, fenliezhuyi shili, jiduanzhuyi shili*). See Zhonghua Renmin Gongheguo Zhongyang Renmin Zhengfu, "Xinjiang de fazhan he jinbu" [Xinjiang's development and progress], September 2009.

67. Jürgen Habermas, *Between Naturalism and Religion* (Cambridge: Polity Press, 2008), 307–8.

68. Hu Jintao, "Hu Jintao zai Zhongguo gongchandang dishiqici quanguo daibiao dahui shang de baogao" [Hu Jintao's report at the 17th CCP National Congress], October 17, 2007, http://cpc.people.com.cn/GB/64093/67507/6429857.html.

Part III

Tradition and Modernity in Popular and State Discourse

Chapter 8

Beyond World Order: Change in China's Negotiations over the World

Elena Barabantseva

The chapters in the first and second parts of this book show the magnitude and variety of scholarly examinations of how China perceives its role and place in the world and how it conceptualizes the world. Many of these studies consider aspects of Chinese politics and identity, "strategic" culture, or official rhetoric as they examine the interplay between traditional and modern Chinese political practices.[1] Many look at how China's premodern history and traditional worldview affect China's foreign policy and engagements with the world today. Fairbank, in his classical edited volume, *The Chinese World Order: Traditional China's Foreign Relations*, stated that the "Chinese tribute system . . . has some indeterminate relevance to the world's China problem of today."[2] He added that "modern China's difficulty of adjustment to the international order of nation-states in the nineteenth and twentieth centuries has come partly from the great tradition of the Chinese world order."[3] Similarly, Kornberg and Faust argue that "one can better understand China's external relations, even today, by turning back the pages of history to ancient times."[4] Most recently, Scott echoes that "China's past is very much at play in the present, concerning Chinese attitudes and world view on war and peace."[5]

These approaches each utilize a particular interpretation of the history of China to explain China's behavior today. Chinese history is neatly divorced

This is an updated version of the article "Change vs. Order: Shijie meets Tianxia in China's Interactions with the World," *Alternatives: Global, Local, Political* 34, no. 2 (2009): 129–56. I would like to thank the British Inter-University China Centre for enabling me to do research presented in this chapter.

from the present and treated as a natural course of development that has informed China's interactions with the outside world. It is true that China's distant and recent history influences the construction and current orientations of its national identities. For instance, its experiences and memory of the "century of humiliation" inform much of current Chinese state-led and popular nationalism.[6] But the concrete uses of history in China are part of the present Chinese condition; they both reflect and create the present. These historical references are shaped by present-day circumstances and help construct a particular picture of the present.

Rather than contemplating how the past influences China's perception of its role in the world today, this chapter examines how China constantly negotiates its relationships with the world. It treats China not as a unitary actor but as a construct made up of multifarious identities at different levels. It calls into question the oppositions—between tradition and modernity, the past and the present, China and the West—which are often presumed or reproduced in our thinking about China's place in the world. The chapter illustrates that China's relationship with the world cannot be grasped by simply projecting Chinese history onto the present. One can only understand the interplay between history and the present by examining particular uses of history in practice.

Rather than focusing on the realm of "high politics," this chapter looks to the field of culture and visual politics as mediums through which China's negotiations with the world take place. In recent years, international relations scholars in the West started stressing the importance of taking the visual language seriously for our understanding of how global politics works.[7] Visual expressions are an important aspect of contemporary everyday life and politics in China and elsewhere. Visual language appeals to wider audiences than the language of texts because it is attractive and comprehensible to people outside policymaking and scholarly circles. Visual representations are components of politics and frame identities just like political practices and texts do.

The chapter analyzes how images of the ever-changing world are depicted in two visual narratives: a promotional video for the Confucius Institute and the film *The World* (*Shijie*, 世界). These two officially endorsed cultural products are significant because their emergence in China symbolizes an important moment of change. As if announcing China's imminent march of "soft power" around the world, both films were released in 2004, one year before the official pronouncement of the "harmonious world" vision by the Chinese leaders discussed by William Callahan in chapter 1 of this book. The promotional video was produced to accompany the opening ceremonies of China's Confucius Institutes around the world. It was one of the first visual expressions of China's global image making to circulate together with the burgeoning numbers of the Chinese language and cultural centers. *The World* is the first film approved by censors by the previously underground film director Jia Zhangke. The release of this film was the crucial moment in the director's relationship with the authorities, earning him high acclaim among officials and popularity among Chinese viewers. Since the successful relaunch of his career with the film, Jia has become a truly global Chinese cultural figure. He won the top prize at the Venice Festival in 2008 and directed a commissioned film for the 2010 Shanghai World Expo. Thus, the promotional video for the Confucius Institute and the film *The World* represent a certain turning point in China's negotiations of its place in the world. They offer an opportunity to examine through a different set of parameters how China speaks for itself and its role in the world to domestic and global audiences.

The visually narrated worlds of the film and the promotional video cannot be grasped by tracing historical continuities to the present or by drawing a line between history and the present. Nor can they be explained by counterposing China's traditional view of the world against the Western interpretation of international relations premised on state sovereignty. The fictional world that the characters of *The World* inhabit and the world for which China's leaders attempt to gain support by promoting Chinese language and culture have common properties: They each exhibit an interplay between the modern and traditional, the Chinese and non-Chinese, and the personal and universal. The world portrayed in the film and the world where China's official aspirations are presented, created, performed, and experienced through a spontaneous flow of images, practices, and relationships. China's engagements with the world and its interpretations of it take place at many levels involving a multitude of actors. Most notably, the visual narratives in the promotional video and the film reflect perceptions of a world that is always changing and lacks features predetermined by history or other factors.

The first section of this chapter discusses the etymological distinction between the Chinese notions of Tianxia (天下) and *shijie* (世界). The predominant discussions of China's engagement with the world focus on China's inability to apply its surviving traces of traditional culture (including the traditional vision of the world, Tianxia) to the Western-imposed world order, and China's failure to adapt to the established world order due to historical and cultural factors.[8] These discussions reflect two well-defined and predetermined visions of the world: China's cultural Tianxia and the Western-imposed territorial world order composed of sovereign nation-states. Neither vision includes the notion of an ever-changing, multidimensional, and relational world, to which *shijie* refers.

The second section analyses the Confucius Institute's promotional video. The video's effort to promote Chinese language and culture abroad combines elements of traditional cultural notions with modern and widely recognizable messages. It capitalizes on the changing nature of the world and presents China in the most favorable light. China is touted as a modern and important culture, and mastering the Chinese language is claimed to be timely for achieving professional and personal success. The marketing strategy of the Confucius Institute blurs the distinction between traditional and modern to produce a readily comprehensible message (at least in the West), with the name of Confucius appearing over the image of a dove in the center of the Institute's official logo.

The third section explores the film *The World*. It examines how the film expresses China's renegotiation of its place in the world. By analyzing the stories of the main characters against the background of the main attractions of the world, I demonstrate how the world outside China is presented for the consumption of the Chinese public and how the characters perceive and experience the changing nature of the world through their work and life in the World Park, an amusement venue in Beijing. The film features the World Park, but through its references to the world and China along with Beijing, it produces a complex spatial narrative that is both China-specific and characteristic of the contemporary world outside China.

The chapter's fourth and fifth sections examine the aspects of the modern world depicted in the film, namely mobility and the virtues and vices of the modern world. Despite the quick pace of transition of Chinese society and the proliferation of mobility as an aspect of modern living, for many workers in China the park in Beijing is the furthest out into the world that they will get to glimpse and experience modernity with all its ills and merits. Intimate relations with the multifaceted and complex world, integral to the notion of *shijie*, are daily experiences for the protagonists of the film.

The chapter's sixth and last section discuss how China performs an instructive role through projecting a particular vision of the world in the park and by actively advancing a certain version of China through the teaching of the language and introduction of Chinese culture to foreign audiences. The film *The World* shows how the world is interpreted in Chinese society with the help and active participation of the authorities. Yet, as the film vividly shows, the world, including within China, is an incoherent, diffused formation with different meanings for people making a living in it.

Both visual narratives discussed in this chapter exhibit China's use of informal and visual politics, which appeal to ordinary people, to shape perceptions of China (in the case of the Confucius Institute) and the outside world (in the case of the World Park). These narratives illuminate how China desires to be viewed by the outside world and how the outside world is represented in China. They highlight the intricacies and complexities of such representations, which often escape attention when analyzed through the lenses of either China's "traditional" worldview or the dominant world-order perspective. Rather than attributing Chinese views of the world's meaning and China's place in it solely to China's history and the contemporary international order, the chapter attributes them to an interplay of interrelated factors.

Tianxia versus *Shijie*

China's relationship with the world, its images of the world, and its contributions to the world have become matters of concern among scholars, the media, and policymakers. Many academic debates both in China and the West have paid particular attention to the role that China's premodern image of the world plays in shaping China's engagements with the contemporary world. Among the many traditional Chinese notions, the concept of Tianxia has been invoked as the one that best represents China's traditional worldview. In this view, the territory covered by the conquests of Imperial China constituted the whole world. It has become common historic knowledge that Tianxia constituted the Chinese premodern cosmological view of the world, which was starkly different from the world order established by the European empires.[9] The primary rationales for evoking the notion of Tianxia in contemporary scholarship have been to suggest that the way China operates cannot be solely understood by applying Western concepts and principles,[10] and, more recently in Zhao Tingyang's writings, that Tianxia can offer an alternative model to the largely dysfunctional organization of the world today.[11] Tianxia, as an abstraction, is employed to underline China's peculiar historic position and the influence in the world to which it aspires not only economically but also as a generator of new ideas and norms. These interpretations of Tianxia endow China with qualities that make it a distinct and special place in the world, one that cannot be grasped through Western concepts. These analyses interpret and construct China's present by appealing to certain historical readings of China's traditional worldview.

Following the publication of Zhao's book, three different meanings of Tianxia were identified by Callahan, as discussed in chapter 5 of this book.[12] In all of them, Tianxia does not presuppose definite spatial or temporal dimensions. Indeed, the Tianxia order does not have spatial limits; it can expand as far as Confucian principles and the imperial conquests. During the imperial period of China's history, the temporal dimension of Tianxia had a cyclical pattern; the rule of a new dynasty marked the beginning of a new era in the Chinese calendar, which Chih-yu Shih calls the heavenly order.[13] The temporal aspect of Tianxia was dominated by an emphasis on the internal (the greatest and highest) order and hierarchy, and did not welcome—and eventually could not survive—the changes brought about by the clashes with the Western imperial powers.

In his more recent discussion of the "bad world" (*huai shijie*, 坏世界), Zhao Tingyang juxtaposes the Chinese concept of Tianxia with what he perceives as the Western notion of the world (*shijie*). He argues that although Tianxia is a broader and more complex concept, encompassing natural, social, and political elements, the Western understanding of the world is essentially "thin" (*danbo*, 单薄), because it is restricted by its territorially driven language of interest and power.[14] He attributes the Western "bad" practices of hegemony and colonialism to the territorial perception of the world. Although he concludes that there are conceptual limitations in the Western understanding of the world, he does not explain the etymology of the English word "world" or any other Western notions of the "world." It is not clear why and how he traces the "thin" understanding of the world to the Western origins. He also overlooks the fact that there are etymological origins of the word "world" (*shijie*) in the Chinese, albeit not Confucian, tradition, which are discussed below.

In his critique of Zhao's thesis, Callahan observes that Zhao's interpretation of China's traditional worldview has a top-down perspective, which is preoccupied with maintaining the internal order and hierarchy within the Tianxia system (see chapter 5). Zhao's proposed adaptation of Tianxia for the twenty-first century presupposes a particular organization of relationships between people, within families, and between nations. According to this interpretation of Tianxia, priority should be given to the members of a family and community over outsiders.[15] Tianxia here is concerned with order, hierarchy, and stability, whereby Heaven grants the exclusive right of rule to the emperor. Tianxia is represented as an inward-looking system of values and governance that looked to Confucianism and the emperor as the highest authority in running the internal order. This vision of the world is essentially static, because it prioritizes maintenance of the order imposed from above over change, spontaneity, and contingency, and it ignores a multiplicity of formulations of the world and China's place in it. Though change was present in the strategic thinking of ancient Chinese rulers, as evident in the Chinese classic *Yi Jing* (The Book of Changes), the presumption of change within the Chinese system of cosmology was based on the ideal of preserving the reign of the emperor and his domain, Tianxia, for as long as possible.[16] This preoccupation with the preservation of stability and order implied by the dominant interpretations of Tianxia is echoed in current expressions of official nationalism in China, which stress that the existing political structure of the Chinese state, one-party rule, is essential for achieving the socioeconomic goals set by the leadership. According to this stance, only the ruling Communist Party can guarantee stability, so no substantial change in the organization of the state is welcome.[17]

Some academic attempts to reconcile China's traditional view of the world with its foreign policy orientations stress that the territorial-sovereign mode of the world order was imposed on China by the West and Japan in the late nineteenth century, and that China has had problems subscribing to and operating within it.[18] Scholars have also suggested that China's worldview (*shijie guan*, 世界观) is one of the more stable influences on China's foreign policy orientations.[19] This line of argument, which is found in many scholarly analyses, is premised on China's distinctness and unique character throughout its history. This postulation leads to the assertion that it is somewhat futile to try to analyze and understand China by applying Western norms and concepts. Yet China's alleged inadaptability to the territorial-sovereign mode of the world system is belied by its leadership's own formulations of its standards in foreign policy, which are consistently positioned within the state sovereignty framework.

China remains one of the most outspoken advocates of the principles of state sovereignty and territorial integrity in international relations. It has not only accepted these norms but has also become their ardent advocate.[20] China's leadership regards the realm of culture as inseparable from its sovereignty and requiring protection by the party-state from the potentially harmful effects of globalization. More recently, this priority to protect the national culture has been transformed into the active promotion of Chinese culture around the world. As for the thesis that China's vision of the world order has been relatively stable, its images of the world and its role in it are subject to constant negotiation and dispute at different levels. The very fashion whereby China attempts to protect and promote its culture blurs the distinctions between traditional and universal elements, and fusing and blending them. Through these practices, China's visions of the world and engagement with it are constructed, contested, and negotiated.

The concept of Tianxia, as a system of governance valuing order, stability, and hierarchy, might reflect (though not without reservations) the Chinese government's official take on how the country should be organized and governed domestically. However, Tianxia does not account for the tensions, inconsistencies, and struggles which take place in China at multiple levels as an integral part of its interactions with the modern world. In fact, the Chinese vocabulary evinces relational and dynamic views of the world, as exemplified by the word *shijie*, which comprises two characters: *shi* (世)—age, era, generate; and *jie* (界)—boundary, circles. Having originated in Buddhist thought and deriving from the Sanskrit term *loka-dhatu*, *shijie* in its original use perceives the world as ever changing and destroyable.[21] It refers to both spatial and temporal dimensions of the processes taking place at a particular time and within certain physical confinements. Tianxia is generally, but not exclusively,[22] understood as preoccupied with maintaining hierarchy, order, and unity, and the central role of the Confucian principles is to organize the civilized core of the system and ameliorate difference through acculturation. *Shijie* does not have the same connotations. *Shijie* does not presuppose a division of the system into civilized and barbarian components and the acculturation of barbarian subjects. It emphasizes temporal, ever-changing processes within physical spaces, whether they are confined to one person, a family, a social group, a city or particular part of it, or the whole planet. As such, *shijie* promotes a vision of the world from the point of view of its current affairs, developments, relationships, and experiences that will unavoidably come to an end. It stresses the interactions of people and social groups with the world surrounding them and suggests a dynamic and relational understanding of the world.

It is notable that "cosmopolitanism" is normally translated into Chinese as *shijie zhuyi* (世界主义), emphasizing an outward-looking and never-finished process, in opposition to China's purported historical perception of the world as an order-preoccupied Tianxia. Cosmopolitanism here could be understood as "no longer merely an ideal project but a variety of actually existing practical stances."[23] The classical interpretation of cosmopolitanism put forward originally by Kant opposed not nationalism, as often presented in academia, but the absolutist statism of eighteenth-century Europe.[24] The notions of Tianxia and *shijie* could perhaps also be seen as complementary opposites representing the values of stability versus openness to change, where Tianxia is seen as hierarchical and orderly and *shijie* stands for change in an ever-changing world. At the same time, Tianxia and *shijie* visions of the world should not be seen as dichotomous, because they coexist and complement each other in reflecting particular engagements with the world. In other words, *shijie* does not replace Tianxia but helps shift the focus to processes and developments that would otherwise remain concealed and unaccounted for. It offers a more nuanced perspective on China's complex perceptions and relationships with the world.

Now let us look at China's initiatives and visual representations expressing a dynamic view of the world in relation to the etymology of *shijie*. Different visual representations of China's relations with the world present the country as part of an evolving world and a site for developments engaging the world. The complexity and inconclusiveness of China's relations with the world cannot be grasped through opposing its traditional worldview to the Western-dominated organization of the world. The officially endorsed visual images present China as a modern and dynamic nation worthy of close study by the world. At the same time, China is portrayed as a space where the world in its many dimensions is manifested. The order-preoccupied discourse of Tianxia and the argument that China cannot adapt to the West-imposed order overlook the reality that China is part of the dynamically changing *shijie*.

The contemporary processes and relationships that are characteristic of the world and concern it at multiple levels shape China's outlook. *Shijie* is a world of relations always in the making, where people experience the world in a variety of ways. A certain place within China, such as the World Park, can be the ultimate place where people come into contact and experience the world in its many expressions (albeit with significant intervention from the authorities). The ever-changing world embraces China, reorganizing its social life and influencing its perceptions and relationships with the world. China's outlook is reflected in the short video produced to accompany the opening ceremonies of Confucius Institutes around the world.

With Confucius Out into the World

The Chinese authorities have called for a greater cultural presence of China worldwide to accompany the country's growing political and economic power, echoing Zhao's argument that it needs to match its economic assertiveness with the generation of new ideas for the world.[25] One of the most telling examples of this mode of thinking in policymaking is the 2004 initiation of the establishment of a chain of Confucius Institutes around the world. The mission of these institutes, as formulated in the official document disseminated by the government, is to promote "friendly relationships with other countries and enhance understanding of the Chinese language and culture."[26]

The activities of the institutes are coordinated by the central Confucius Institute headquarters in Beijing, which is subordinate to the central government's National Office for Teaching Chinese as a Foreign Language. The institutes have mushroomed around the world since the first one was established in Seoul in 2004. Initially, it was anticipated that there would be at least one institute on each continent, and that 100 Confucius Institutes would be set up around the world before 2010. However, the initiative was enthusiastically supported by governments and institutions worldwide so that by July 2010 there were already 316 Confucius Institutes established in more than 90 countries and regions around the world.[27]

Although the idea of a network of cultural institutions abroad is not new—China here follows the long-standing traditions of other similar initiatives—such the Alliance Française, the British Council, the Japan Foundation, the Goethe Institute, and so forth—the format that China has adopted in promoting its language and culture abroad is very distinct. Confucius Institutes are established in close association with local institutions of higher education, often on their premises where the head of the institute is also a senior member of the university faculty. In addition to the language training and introduction to Chinese culture, the institutes are aimed to "acquaint students with traditional values such as benevolence, righteousness and harmony."[28] As an official agent to promote Chinese culture and language abroad, the institutes take a very informal shape. For instance, they are deeply embedded in the structures of universities around the world, relying on their outreach to students and the general public.

Given the University of Manchester's recent strategy of investing more in research and teaching on China, as well as the city's populous and vibrant Chinese community, Manchester naturally became one of the proposed locations for a Confucius Institute. At the ceremonious launch of the Manchester Confucius Institute in October 2006, the audience was shown a promotional trailer of the institutes in which one of the characters proclaimed that institute students would be taught in the spirit of Confucius to know and understand China better. The video was very brief, but the narrative was effective in communicating its central ideas.

According to the video, the institutes not only serve as a basis for learning about China through teaching the Chinese language. They also offer courses on different aspects of Chinese culture: calligraphy, cuisine, tai chi, kung fu, traditional music and singing, fan dancing, and the art of paper cutting. The long list of aspects of traditional Chinese culture is complemented by a short reference to the success of Chinese sports, with a close-up image of the Chinese professional basketball player Yao Ming. The video also makes references to China's recent developmental initiatives, with the image of a Chinese engineer engaged in a conversation with a young Westerner against the backdrop of the Three Gorges Dam. At the same time, the video emphasizes that China is not ethnically homogeneous by zooming in on images of the Mongolian grasslands and their inhabitants. This introductory part of the video concludes with snapshots of the headquarters of the Confucius Institute in Beijing and its offices around the world. White doves fly out from the headquarters around the world, one of which is captured in the official logo of the institute. This introductory part focuses on China's development path and its most important characteristics. It is followed by three short visual narratives illuminating the modern nature of Chinese language learning.

First, the video presents learning Mandarin as a practical and valuable activity that could create more career opportunities and success. The Chinese language itself is presented as the future medium for business. The first short video presents a young white Western man at an interview for a corporate job. In the first scene, he is picked from the numerous candidates waiting for an interview. He was the only one reading a Chinese newspaper, while the rest were absorbed in English-language papers. The interviewer, whose face we do not see (but the plate on his desk explicitly says "to be hired," meaning the selected candidate is his man), poses a question: "Who is your teacher?" The interviewee replies with a certain amount of confidence and pride and a winning smile: "My teacher is Confucius!" This episode suggests that knowing Chinese is an unbeatable advantage. The viewer is left with no doubt that this candidate was hired.

The video's next short scene takes place at the bottom of the Eiffel Tower in Paris. A young white man spots a girl on a bike and approaches her in a rather determined way, knocking her off the bike. A book falls out of her bag, which is a textbook for the Chinese language. The couple exchange looks of interest, and we next see them studying together and holding hands on their way to the Chinese class in the Confucius Institute in Paris. The message of this episode is that learning Chinese can not only bring people together through business relations but also serve as a medium of friendship and romance.

The video's last sequence starts at 9 a.m. in a classroom with background music from the French film *Amélie*. It then progresses backward in time to show the student leaving home, having breakfast, and in bed with the alarm going off at 8:30 a.m. and a female voice calling: "Jack, it is time for Chinese!" This is probably the central message of the entire promotional video. Chinese is presented as a pragmatic, useful, and *timely* language to learn. Its time has come, and it is prudent to master it. Doing so is a guarantee of success in business and a way to impress and earn admirers. The video also says that China is becoming more important in the world, and that learning Chinese is desirable if you want to keep pace with world developments.

This promotional video reflects China's efforts to popularize a particular image of itself and its culture internationally. It presents an image of a modern, dynamic, rational, business-oriented but romantic culture that promotes peace and informal politics through education and cultural exchange. Language teaching and culture promotion serve here as tools of public diplomacy. With this initiative of language instruction, China produces an alternative to previous sporadic attempts of Chinese communities worldwide to provide Chinese language training predominately to the members of the diaspora. The initiative can also be regarded as China's response to the concerns voiced by many Chinese in the early 1990s about the increasing and potentially destructive influence of Western "global" culture and the English language on Chinese culture and society.[29] The initiative also reflects an earlier desire to immunize Chinese culture against the unfavorable influences of Western-orchestrated globalization.

Now, however, the initiative has developed into a proactive way to popularize Chinese culture and language around the world. Confucius Institutes are oriented toward a foreign, predominately non-Chinese, audience, with a view toward reinforcing the presence of Chinese culture around the world. By promoting Chinese language and culture, the Chinese state is attempting to project a certain image of China to a foreign audience. This image is of a peace-loving, peace-seeking, harmonious China that engages with the world through informal means and culture. There has been at least one clear example of the initiative's diplomatic purpose and benefits. In Japan, a traditional competitor of China in the East Asian region, the first

Confucius Institute was symbolically established inside Ritsumeikan University's memorial hall for peace.

The Confucius Institute initiative raises a host of questions about China's motives and interests. How does this way of promoting China's culture and language relate to its growing economic and political relevance in the world? Is it driven by China's aspiration to play a more important role in the global arena or by its desire to further increase its economic presence? Or is it also motivated by China's political rivalry with Taiwan and its desire to have the exclusive rights to represent Chinese culture internationally? Whatever the precise combination of motives, through the Confucius Institutes, China is attempting to tell people around the world about a changing and dynamic China.

China's global promotion of Chinese culture and language through the Confucius Institutes calls into question the Tianxia outlook on the world. The Tianxia order is usually not seen as welcoming and accommodating change, and cannot fully adapt to the Western territorial-sovereign world order. China's engagement with the world through the Confucius Institutes is an alternative way for it to advance its initiatives among foreign audiences. Rather than acting through explicitly state-run organizations, China directly appeals in an almost informal and personal way to people on the ground. It reaches out to individuals, predominately of non-Chinese origins, overseas to influence their perceptions of China. The initiative is in part a response to the dynamic and changing nature of the world—with China at the forefront—and thus it reflects the *shijie* outlook. The Confucius Institutes hold up a mirror to new developments and engage with them in an upbeat way. China is presented as an important part of a changing world.

Multifaceted Confucius

China's presentation of itself as a Confucian nation involves an ideological shift. Since the June 4, 1989, massacre in Tiananmen Square, there has been a noticeable departure from Marxist ideology in favor of the popularization of Confucian values in public and official discourse in China.[30] Guo Yingjie suggests that the revival of Confucianism as orthodox ideology is one of the main tasks for the Chinese leadership in the twenty-first century; it will nurture and strengthen the national spirit and unite the nation.[31] Confucianism has been revived at different levels in Chinese society and is often referred to as a new moral code, one that has even been used to evaluate

Communist Party officials' performance.[32] Confucian ethics is vigorously popularized on Chinese television and in popular literature.[33] The acceptance of these new cultural products by the Chinese is often attributed to the increased "demand for order, social values and ethics" in a rapidly changing society.[34]

Until recently, the return to Confucian values has been characterized by its domestic objectives: It was proposed as a remedy for Chinese society's problems and the declining authority of Communism. However, China seems to increasingly present Confucian principles as guidelines for foreigners' perceptions of China, as evidenced by the name "Confucius Institute" and also by China's prominent references to its Confucian values in its globally visible moments, such as the 2008 Beijing Olympics opening ceremony. In 2006, the China Confucius Foundation published a standard portrait of Confucius "to give him a single, recognizable identity around the world."[35] By making the central principles of Confucianism—including peace, harmony, and virtue—essential to its international image, China has started a new global public relations campaign to establish itself as an influential cultural authority and a peaceful, benign power. However, it has not yet shown a willingness to abandon Communism as the guiding principle of its ruling party and leadership.[36] So, with the Confucius Institutes initiative, China is nonetheless ingeniously fusing traditional and particular aspects of its culture with modern and universally recognizable styles and images.

While conflating some aspects of Confucian thought with Communist ideology,[37] China cautiously ignores other important components of Confucianism in promoting its Confucian image. It is remarkable how the recent move of the Chinese authorities to promote Confucian ideas is mixed with the promotion of other modern ideas, such as mobility, adaptability, and affluence. These attributes seem not only incompatible with classical Confucian thought but also to go against its very grain. When China claimed to be ruled according to Confucian principles, emigration and trade were perceived by the Chinese rulers as undermining the stability of the Confucian order. Confucianism prioritized agriculture and regarded commerce as a dishonorable activity; it associated those engaged in commerce with exploitation and parasitism.[38] Trade was seen as corrupting of human morality. Emigration was suppressed and condemned as against the value of filial piety toward parents and ancestors, as emigrants could not dutifully pay their respects to older family members.[39]

China's move to promote its language and culture through the network of officially sponsored Confucius Institutes expands and transforms its

Figure 8.1. The Logo of the Confucius Institute

Source: Confucious Institute, University of Manchester.

strategy to popularize a particular version of its national culture outside China. In the early 2000s, Chinese intellectuals urged youth in China not to renounce their language in favor of English, given that "English, after all, is only a tool to know the world."[40] Now, however, Chinese is presented as a language in line with world developments. In its popularization, China combines very modern objectives with elements of what is claimed to be traditional Chinese. Most telling, perhaps, is the very non-Confucian look of the official logo of the Confucius Institute: a white dove with wings spread out to embrace the world, while the world extends an arm to embrace the dove (see figure 8.1).

China did not choose any supposedly Chinese images or mythical characters for the logo, such as the panda, the dragon, or even the sacred bird the phoenix, which is highly regarded in Chinese mythology. One possible explanation for China's choice of an internationally recognized image is that it sought to emphasize that China seeks to engage with the outside world in an informal, people-oriented manner, rather than through highly institutionalized, state-centric international organizations. The choice of imagery to accompany these initiatives seems to express a desire to persuade the world to peacefully welcome China's growing presence and influence. It is emphasized that China goes out into the world to educate the people of the world without them having to visit China. The promotional video says that Confucius was preoccupied with making "education available to all men" (in premodern China), and now by establishing Confucius Institutes, China is giving almost everybody in the world an opportunity to learn about China without leaving their countries.

The promotional video of the Confucius Institute and the state-endorsed discourses and imagery popularizing this initiative illustrate how official Beijing wants China to be perceived by audiences worldwide. They frame a particular image of China and can be seen as expressions of the Chinese state's soft power. What is important is that the initiative and the international public relations efforts associated with it cannot be grasped solely by reference to either the allegedly Chinese-history-rooted Tianxia vision of the world or to the West-dominated, statecentric international system. The imperative of change, which is not integral to the dominant interpretations of Tianxia and China's relationship with the Western world order, is built into China's Confucius Institute initiative and the international public relations campaign.

The Park, Beijing, and the World

As part of the "China at Manchester" festival that was tied to the launch of the Confucius Institute there, a number of films by the Chinese director Jia Zhangke were screened. Jia is often regarded as one of the best of the new (sixth) generation of Chinese filmmakers. His film *The World* in some ways echoes the promotional video of the Confucius Institute, but it also provides a different perspective on China's changing relationship with the world. The film looks at how ordinary people in China perceive and experience their relationships with the outside world. Though the promotional video was made with the close involvement of the state and therefore presents a visually codified official formulation of China's engagement with the world, the art of film is not directly related to the discourse of the state.

As Shapiro observes, the "contemporary cinema provides a mode of thought about time and events that encodes the peculiarities of the present."[41] Building on the work of Deleuze, Shapiro argues that cinematography through its "banal" visual representation of nationhood and its treatment of daily life is engaged in the cultural expression of a nation and is closely related to the projects of states.[42] That is even truer if a film receives the support and endorsement of the state.

Until 2004, Jia Zhangke was famous outside China mainly for his highly acclaimed films made without the permission of the Chinese government. His films were well received in the West. All his earlier works—such as *Xiao Wu* (1998), *Platform* (2000), and *Unknown Pleasures* (2002)—were "underground" creations that were awarded prestigious awards at film festivals in the West. *The World*, however, was destined to have a different life in China. It received approval from the Film Bureau and was the first film by Jia to be publicly shown in China. Moreover, it was generously funded by the authorities, and its premier took place on National Day, by far one of the most celebrated holidays in China. In Jia's own words, in recent years the environment for filmmaking and censorship in China has been slightly relaxed by the authorities.[43] Thus it is not his style of work that has changed but the climate for film, which became more receptive to "underground" work. He emphasizes the importance of access to the Chinese market and the ability of his films to be watched by wider circles of the Chinese public.[44] However, there are more political explanations for why *The World* received such active promotion from the authorities, and one needs to turn to the film's plot to explore them.

The film starts off with a lavish beauty-pageant-like performance of people in national costumes from around the world. The plot is set in the World Park in Beijing, which features small-scale replicas of famous sights from all over the world. The viewers follow the daily experiences of work, romance, drama, and friendship of the people who live and work in the park. None of the characters in the film are natives of Beijing. They came there from remote parts of the country and abroad in search of a better life and more stable income. The film's narrative focuses on security guards and performers, but it also includes other migrant workers in Beijing. "See the World without Ever Leaving Beijing" is the slogan of the park, as viewers are reminded several times throughout the course of the film.

The themes raised in the film are different from those in Jia's earlier works, which were all set in his hometown in Shanxi Province. Through the experiences of local people, his earlier films portrayed the changing conditions of life in China undergoing a buoyant economic transition. *The*

World, however, is set in Beijing, and although China's social problems are at its crux, they are softened by the prominent background setting of the park and its extravagant shows. The film focuses on the daily struggles of its characters, with Beijing and China reference points for developments in the world; China's social ills and troubles of transition are partly represented as part of the contemporary world. The ever-changing character of the world, including China and Beijing, is the main theme of *The World*. The film depicts a curious intersection of geoscapes perceived by its characters. The references to the world, China, and Beijing are intertwined to produce a narrative of complex spatiality that is both China-specific and characteristic of the contemporary world. For the characters, Beijing and its World Park embody the world. Love, drama, and various spectacles unfolding in the park are their only experiences of the contemporary world. They are the prisms through which the protagonists learn about the outside world, relate to it, and experience it in their daily life. The world embraces Beijing, which many people in China regard as the hub of their life.

Beijing constitutes the whole world, especially for all those who have not experienced the world outside China and who are forced to travel long distances from remote parts of China to fast-growing cities in search of jobs and higher living standards. In their encounters with the modern world, the characters' experiences of mobility, as a fundamental condition of modern life, become "postprogressive" (to borrow a term from Rofel):[45] They exercise mobility in search of a better life, but experience it as a movement without purposeful destination. Moreover, although mobility brings them into contact with the modern world, they are ultimately alienated from it.

Experiences and Perceptions of the World

The film *The World* vividly portrays the daily experiences of the modern world of the World Park's residents. This section turns to examining the aspects of modern living that feature most prominently in the film, namely mobility and the virtues and vices of the modern world.

Mobility without Destination

Practices of mobility are indispensable for experiencing the modern world, both within and outside China. The very act of mobility (as opposed to the traditional sedentary style of life) is a manifestation of coming into contact with modern life. "An obligation to mobility" is imposed on the characters of *The World* in their interactions with the contemporary world.[46] The characters had to undertake journeys to come into contact with the modern world in Beijing. Traveling short or long distances becomes an important component of joining modern citizens. In this way, the protagonists' experiences of the world are related to how they perceive the modern condition. Their perceptions of modernity and of the world are coconstitutive and mutually informing.

The mobility that the characters in the film undertake is restricted, however. There are only a limited number of physical destinations and means of traveling available to them. There are also substantial institutional barriers to their mobility. Their perceptions of the material world outside China are confined to how it is presented in the World Park, where their life journey has led them thus far. The ex-boyfriend of Zhao Xiaotao, the main female character, stops in Beijing to visit her on his way to Mongolia. She says, "Your mum was right. Breaking up with me was good for you." He replies: "And for you too! New world every day." She agrees, "That is right. I see the world without leaving Beijing." She thus utters the official slogan of the park as her own life motto. For her and other park dwellers, the park provides their only exposure to the outside world: "I am on the train to India," "Are you going to Japan?" They move from one spot in the park to another, participating in colorful performances, impersonating different nationalities, and living in the world through their shows. One day they are Indian dancers; another they are Japanese, American, African, and so forth. In their daily shows, they engage in a very cosmopolitan mode of living without leaving Beijing or taking a plane. They experience the world through costume performances, while beyond the stage they face the realities of life in present-day China. And so perceptions of the outside world and China's realities are intimately intertwined in the characters' daily routines. Their daily life in the park conditions their perceptions of the outside world, and China and the world are mutually constitutive. The park's design—which expresses the views of the Chinese state's cultural authorities—and the everyday manifestations of modernity in China are the prisms through which the film's protagonists perceive the world.

Airplanes are depicted as an idealized modern way of traveling, but almost nobody in the park has ever been on a plane. When asked, "Who flies on those planes?" Xiaotao is baffled: "Who knows? I don't know anybody who has ever been on a plane." Instead, visitors and employees of the park can fly on the "magical flying carpet,"[47] or by paying a visit to the site of an old plane they can experience flying with the guidance of park workers who welcome them with the very real voice of a flight attendant: "Our airline would like to welcome you on board. Before landing in our park, this plane made international flights. We have preserved its original appearance. The hostesses are all performers of the Five Continents Company. Everything is there for you to experience the beauty of air travel." An actual airplane flight is presented as a highly desirable but almost unattainable activity for the park's dwellers and visitors. They cannot afford the modern condition of experiencing the world through the air, though covering long distances is not only a meaningful but also a necessary condition for their interactions with the modern world. *The World*'s characters, in other words, are found on the periphery of the modern world, where taking planes is often presented as an inalienable attribute of modern living. The closest they can come to experiencing it is through rides on magical carpets or decommissioned planes at the state-sponsored tourist sites. Trains, however, are accessible and affordable means of travel. And a train journey is associated with bringing the modern dream of financial success closer to reality. Taisheng, Xiaotao's current boyfriend, recalls that on the first night of his stay in Beijing he slept in the hotel next to the train station, listened to the trains, and dreamt of becoming successful in Beijing.

A passport is also essential for visiting the foreign world. There are several references to its practicality in the film. The main protagonists, Xiaotao and Taisheng, do not seem to have passports, which in China you only need to travel abroad. When Xiaotao's ex-boyfriend stops in Beijing on his way to Mongolia, he shows his passport to Xiaotao. She does not understand why he needs it until he explains that he is going to Mongolia by train. A passport is also associated with freedom.[48] The only non-Chinese characters in the film are Russian women who are employed to perform in the park. When they arrive in Beijing, their manager insists on keeping their passports. They reluctantly hand them over to him. We later find out that Anna, one of the Russian dancers, had to take up prostitution to afford to visit her sister in Ulan Bator. She is the only employee in the park who is able to take a plane. Xiaotao gets on well with Anna, and they become closer without knowing each other's language by doing laundry together, drinking, sharing, and chatting. When Anna tells Xiaotao that she is going to change jobs, Xiaotao does not understand what she means but notices that she is worried and tries to cheer her up: "Christmas is coming. [There will be] fireworks in the park. It's beautiful. You should see it. I will take photos for you. I envy you. You can go abroad. You can go anywhere. What freedom!" Underlying Xiaotao's remark is the assumption that a person with a passport and thus the capacity to travel anywhere can be free.

Taisheng is attracted to Cun, the sister of one of his dubious friends. She hails from Wenzhou, and her husband has been living in Paris for many years. She wants to join him and recently applied for a French visa. Taisheng cannot understand why her husband left. Cun explains that Wenzhou people are "attracted to going abroad." Taisheng suggests that if she does not get her visa, she should come to the World Park, because they have all the French attractions there—the Eiffel Tower, Notre Dame, and the Arc de Triomphe. But as Cun observes, they do not have Belleville, the Parisian Chinatown, where her husband is supposedly based. In the end, Cun gets her visa, and Taisheng looks at her passport, curious about the visa, but he still cannot relate to her desire to leave China.

The narrative lines referred to above depict how the film's characters perceive the world and experience modern living. In their interactions with the world, the forms of mobility available to and exercised by the protagonists are essentially restricted. They come into contact with these forms without leaving Beijing. They only occasionally leave the premises of the park, the passers-by travel by train, and if they go abroad they are confined to their circles of relatives and friends in Chinatowns. Cosmopolitanism takes a domesticated character. The characters engage in a cosmopolitan mode of living without leaving their current homes, or if they do go abroad, they are confined to the spaces dominated by China. Restricted mobility without a clear destination stands out as a value and aspect of modern living. The act of moving is associated with bringing the ideal of modernity closer to reality, even if what constitutes being modern is not clear to the performer. Moving is a mark of the modern identity for the characters in *The World*. They are engaging in what Zigmunt Bauman metaphorically calls a "liquid life," a series of beginnings without a clear destination, where "the need . . . is to run with all one's strength just to stay in the same place."[49]

This indeterminate nature of modernity among the Chinese can also be linked to China's postsocialist transitional context, where "the struggles . . . over the meaning and ownership of modernity" are highly likely to occur.[50] This meaning for the protagonists of *The World* seems to be ambiguous, with no clear formulation or source. Like Rofel's young Chinese female interviewees, the characters in *The World* have "no sense of certainty about historical progress."[51] The only prominent aspects of their lives are restricted mobility, uncertainty, and precariousness. Mobility as an essential part of modern living does not grant them membership in the modern world, governed and dominated by multiple-passport holders and frequent travelers by plane. They are alienated from this world, though in many ways their very alienation makes the conditions for this modern world possible.[52]

The Vices and Virtues of the Modern World

Jia's films are celebrated for their exploration of the problems of China's post-Mao transition. They expose societal vices, troubles of development projects, and personal tragedies in the course of transformation. *The World* is no exception. The film exemplifies how the values celebrated in China during the reform period clash with traditional virtues, which are not presented as peculiar to China. The country's problems are presented as notoriously modern and partly credited to its engagement with the outside world. They are as much the modern world's problems as they are China's. The global and local intersect in the production of attributes that are shared at many levels by many societies today, irrespective of their geographical location. They are expressions of how the capitalist economy penetrates and conditions human lives in different parts of the world.

Among the qualities that are singled out as measures of success in the modern world and China is financial accomplishment. Many conversations in the film revolve around the subject of money or the lack of it. The characters talk about debts, salary levels, pay rates, compensation, and gambling. Money, rather than what it can buy, is depicted as the value that brings the realization of dreams closer. The blind pursuit of money goes hand in hand with tragedy. Taisheng's co-villager, nicknamed Little Sister, comes to Beijing in search of earnings and finds a job on the construction site near the park. To make extra money, he works all day and overtime at night, until one day a cable breaks, severely injuring him. Lying on his deathbed in the hospital, he scribbles his last message to Taisheng, which contains a list of people with the sums of debts he owes them. This is the tragic legacy that he leaves for his family to take care of. They will now have to face the reality of spending most of the compensation paid by the construction company for his death to cover his debts.

Only two characters in the film represent values that are not measured by financial success in the modern world. Anna, Xiaotao's Russian friend, came to China to earn money for her family in Russia, and although she has to take up prostitution, her cause is pure. She wants to save up money and visit her sister in Mongolia. She confesses that Xiaotao is her only friend and her song to her is a nonmaterial expression of friendship and affection. Xiaotao appears to be indifferent to money, status, and career growth. She refuses the advancements of a seemingly successful businessman, and is somewhat unenthusiastic about the role she is assigned in the daily performances in the park. When the new manager announces that she is going to perform an African dance, Xiaotao answers, "Whatever." The character of Xiaotao is an example of female goodness, humbleness, purity, loyalty, and modesty. She resists the vices of the modern world, many of which her boyfriend Taisheng possesses. At the same time, Xiaotao's character is intrinsically cosmopolitan, despite her necessary attachment to China and work in the park. The way Xiaotao relates to and cares for Anna, who is not only a foreigner but also a prostitute, points to Xiaotao's ability to rise above ethnocultural and social divisions in her relations with people. For her, the value of a human being is separate from any social and moral codes or affiliations.

Taisheng, conversely, is the mouthpiece of the values of individualism and self-reliance. Perhaps the epitome of his personal stance and views is expressed in an intimate scene in a hotel room when Xiaotao asks him to be faithful and never cheat on her: "If you ever cheat on me I will kill you. You are my whole life. If you are unfaithful, I will be left with nothing." Taisheng brings her back to what he considers today's reality: "Don't have so much faith in me. You can't count that much on anybody these days, including myself. You can only count on yourself." Taisheng's views on relationships are reminiscent of Bauman's observation about the character of romantic relationships in "liquid modernity," which are "light and loose" and avoid the promises of long-term commitments.[53]

The modern world of the protagonists is filled with both positive and negative features. The values of these features, however, cannot be determined, for it is not clear which of them can bring the protagonists closer to the realization of their dreams. The characters of the film represent millions of rural migrants in China who are estranged from the modern world and the benefits often associated with it. In China's promotion of the Confucius Institutes, the modern and traditional and the particular and global are in flux to produce desirable images of China for foreign consumption. Similarly, in the daily struggles and experiences of the outside world of the characters in *The World,* there is no clear distinction between what represents good and bad. There is no clear sense of what system of values constitutes moral guidance and what life aspirations are considered auspicious and therefore desirable.

Educating Intersecting Worlds

The promotional video of the Confucius Institute and the film *The World* produce visual accounts of the world for different purposes. However, they parallel and complement each other in their representations of the world and China's place in it. Both construct an interpretation of the world that is presented as the dynamically changing world of today. In these visual interpretations, the Chinese state plays the role of cultural authority.[54]

A visit to the World Park is presented as an educational activity that will introduce the visitors to the world's main attractions. It offers a particular perspective on and formulates prescribed knowledge of what constitute the world's major cultural sites. A visit to the park is not merely entertainment, as the tour guide of the park declares: "Good day, dear visitor. Welcome aboard the elevator of our own Eiffel Tower. We hope this panoramic view will heighten your knowledge of the world." The park offers a view of the world that for many visitors could be their only experience of the world's most famous sites.[55] The world is reproduced in snapshots: The park has its own Eiffel Tower that is 108 meters high, the Twin Towers of Manhattan in America (though the Twin Towers' images were jettisoned after 9/11), London's Tower Bridge and Big Ben, Italy's Leaning Tower of Pisa, the Egyptian Pyramids, the Taj Mahal, Saint Mark's Square, and so forth. The park's primary aim is to introduce visitors to the main attractions of the world outside China (see figure 8.2).

There are no references to Beijing's tourist sites in the World Park.[56] The park's main audience is China's domestic tourists. When I visited the park on the last Sunday of the May Holiday in 2007, I expectedly did not encounter any foreigners queuing to enter it. Most visitors were families and groups of tourists from other parts of China who had come to Beijing over the week-long holiday and were using the opportunity to visit the park. The world presented in the park caters to Chinese consumers, who come to rest, relax, and effortlessly take in a picture of the world. The choice of food on International Street (*guoji jie*, 国际街), adjacent to the park's main gate, is limited to varieties of Chinese cuisine, such as Sichuan, Hunan, Cantonese, and Shanghaiese (see figure 8.3). The park is presented as a place where visitors can learn about the outside world in one step. China serves as a stage, while Chinese people are the creators, performers, and consumers of the world.

Like the World Park, the Confucius Institutes have an educational dimension, but they are primarily directed at foreign audiences and overseas

Figure 8.2. Taking Photos in the World Park

Source: *The World*, author photo.

Figure 8.3. The Entrance to the World Park

Source: Author photo.

Chinese, with the slogan of learning about China without needing to enter it. The Confucius Institutes' promotional video offers carefully selected messages and materials detailing Chinese contemporary society and polity; the video highlights major and probably the best-known aspects of contemporary China. It also emphasizes that the initiative caters to the personal needs of people around the world, which will be met through qualified Chinese instructors. But the audiences targeted for educational purposes are not presented as a homogeneous group.

The intersection of global and local is especially evident in *The World*, where the world, reconstructed within a particular locality, is presented as a place of diverse cultures and contested identities. The film does not present China as possessing a uniform culture either. There are references to multiple dialects, which will only be overcome once migrants come together in Beijing and are forced to speak standardized Chinese to understand each other. There are also references to cultural stereotypes and diverse modes of living in different parts of China. Taisheng observes that Shanxi people are sour like vinegar, and Wenzhou people have a "traveling" gene in their blood and "rely on their hands to make money" (*kao shou chifan*, 靠手吃饭).

Toward the end of the film, the director of the World Park informs the troupe that the next Chinese New Year's CCTV concert will be broadcast from the park and that they "will be viewed by 1 billion people worldwide." Yet the Chinese population today is estimated to be more than 1.3 billion. The year's main TV program is closely watched by the Chinese overseas, who total more than 30 million. The director's underestimate of the potential audience of the concert not only excludes a vast number of people in China but also the officially highly regarded overseas Chinese. Thus, his remark delimits China's world to less than that presented in the official Chinese discourse.

By educating the world about China and telling the Chinese about the world, the Confucius Institutes' promotional video and the film *The World* produce multiple, intersecting images of the world. These images are multilayered, conflicting, heterogeneous, and in flux. The contemporary world depicted in the promotional video needs to show a better understanding of China to be in line with world developments. For the protagonists of *The World*, the world, China, Beijing, and the park are enmeshed, and they come to recognize this complex spatiality in their own unique ways in spite of the state's strong presence.

Conclusion

In *The World*, when Xiaotao finds the farewell text message from Cun on Taisheng's mobile phone, she leaves him and stays in the apartment of a friend from the World Park who got married and is away on her honeymoon. Taisheng, not realizing what he has done wrong, finds and confronts her: "What is wrong? You have left without saying good-bye—why?" Xiaotao responds with silence. In the next scene, we learn that there was a gas leak in the block of apartments, and Xiaotao and Taisheng are carried unconscious or dead outside and laid on the ground. The film is over, the screen goes blank, and the voice of Taisheng asks: "Are we dead?" Xiaotao's voice replies: "No, it is just the beginning."

It is the beginning of a new world, which they experience as a sequence of constant beginnings with no clear direction or end. Every day is a new world *(yi tian yi ge shijie,* 一天一个世界), although the setting for them is the same. The film's concluding remark expresses the vision of the modern world found in official and popular visual representations: a world always in the making through mutual influences and personal experiences.

The depictions of the world and China's place in it in *The World* and the Confucius Institute's promotional video challenge treatments of the world order that have been taken for granted. They also highlight the struggles and constant negotiations over the meaning of the world and China's place in it that take place in China at different levels. China's perceptions of and engagements with the world cannot be grasped by assuming that the only traditional notion of the world available to China is Tianxia and by examining how China adapts to the West-dominated international conventions imposed on it. China's interactions with the world are conditioned by the particular effects of time and space.

China's initiation of the Confucius Institutes around the world and its promotional video illustrate how China evokes universally recognized images, norms, and practices along with traditional concepts to construct and project a particular image of itself to foreign audiences. To make the modern world work to China's advantage and to produce a particular place for China in it, traditional and modern notions are conflated. The experiences of the world for the inhabitants of the World Park in Beijing are regulated and formalized by the park's design and its work routines, but they are not solely a product of how the park's architect and the shows' producers configure it. Despite the state-sponsored setting and its multiple limitations and restrictions, the park workers' experiences of the world are utterly personal, though conditioned by the sociopolitical and economic factors integral to China's participation in global processes. Though visitors to the park can only see aspects of the world that are selectively represented there, performers live through their daily performances and experiences at the park. Through their emotions, relationships, daily encounters, and shows, they not only imagine the world but also craft and live in it. And thus, even if the whole world is restricted to a particular place, it is performed differently and experienced in a variety of ways every day.

The visual narratives in both the promotional video and *The World* point to change as an essential aspect of the world experienced in China. The world is changing, and so is China's place in it. It is therefore important to learn more about and better understand China, as the promotional video tells us. Conversely, the interaction between global processes and domestic dynamics in China change the country's sociocultural conditions in profound ways. These changes, and China's closer engagement with the world, are made possible through the alienation of many at the very center of the changes, along with those who cannot or will not adapt to the ever-changing world.

Notes

1. See John K. Fairbank, ed., *The Chinese World Order: Traditional China's Foreign Relations* (Cambridge, Mass.: Harvard University Press, 1968), Mark Mancall, *China at the Center: 300 Years of Foreign Policy* (New York: Free Press, 1983); Lowell Dittmer and Samuel S. Kim, eds., *China's Quest for National Identity* (Ithaca, N.Y.: Cornell University Press, 1993); Lydia H. Liu, *The Clash of Empires: The Invention of China in Modern World Making* (Cambridge, Mass.: Harvard University Press, 2004); Judith F. Kornberg and John R. Faust, *China in World Politics*, 2nd ed. (London: Lynne Rienner, 2005); David Scott, *China Stands Up: The PRC and the International System* (London: Routledge, 2007); and Sujian Guo and Jean-Marc F. Blanchard, eds., *"Harmonious World" and China's New Foreign Policy* (Lanham, Md.: Lexington Books, 2008).

2. John K. Fairbank, "A Preliminary Framework," in *Chinese World Order*, ed. Fairbank, 1.

3. Ibid., 4.

4. Kornberg and Faust, *China in World Politics*, 7.

5. Scott, *China Stands Up*, 8 n. 1.

6. E.g., see William A. Callahan, "National Insecurities: Humiliation, Salvation, and Chinese Nationalism," *Alternatives* 29 (2004): 199–218; William A. Callahan, "History, Identity and Security: Producing and Consuming Nationalism in China," *Critical Asian Studies* 38, no. 2 (2006): 179–208; and Peter Hays Gries, *China's New Nationalism: Pride, Politics and Diplomacy* (Berkeley: University of California Press, 2004).

7. E.g., see Michael J. Shapiro, *Violent Cartographies* (Minneapolis: University of Minnesota Press, 1997); Cynthia Weber, "Popular Visual Language as Global Communication: The Remediation of United Airlines Flight 93," *Review of International Studies* 34 (2008): 137–53; and Elizabeth Dauphinee, "The Politics of the Body in Pain: Reading the Ethics of Imagery," *Security Dialogue* 38, no. 2 (2008): 139–55.

8. For debates on the persistence of traditional culture in China's foreign policy, see Michael Ng-Quinn, "National Identity in Premodern China: Formation and Role Enactment," in *China's Quest for National Identity*, ed. Dittmer and Kim, 32–61. For the argument on China's incongruity with the sovereign-territorial-based international system, see Chih-yu Shih, *Navigating Sovereignty: World Politics Lost in China* (New York: Palgrave Macmillan, 2003), 27.

9. Cosmology can be understood as "a way of acting, thinking, and creating a world, including distinctive ways of being and thinking what is human, of organizing space and of calibrating time." See Stephan Feuchtwang, "Between Civilizations: One Side of a Dialogue" *Social Identities* 12, no. 1 (2006): 79–94, at 85.

10. In addition to the studies mentioned in note 1, see Chih-yu Shih, *China's Just World: The Morality of Chinese Foreign Policy* (Boulder, Colo: Lynne Rienner, 1993) and Chih-yu Shih, *Navigating Sovereignty*, 7.

11. Zhao Tingyang, *Tianxia tixi: Shijie zhidu zhexue daolun* [The Tianxia system: A Philosophy for the World Institution] (Nanjing: Jiangsu jiaoyu chubanshe, 2005); and Zhao Tingyang, "Rethinking Empire from a Chinese Concept 'All-under-Heaven' (*Tianxia*)," *Social Identities* 12, no. 1 (2006): 29–41.

12. The first sense of "Tianxia" is geographical and refers to all the lands (that were known to the Chinese) under heaven. But the territory included in this sense did not have clear boundaries, as they could be extended and restricted in accordance with the victories and defeats of the Confucian rulers of the All-under-Heaven. The second sense of "Tianxia" is the popular sentiments of the people inhabiting the All-under-Heaven, which through their transformation and submission to the rule of the Confucian order bestowed legitimacy to the rulers. In the third, ethno-political sense, "Tianxia" is the system promoting family-like relationships which can eventually serve as a model for an alternative world international organization addressing the problems of the contemporary world.

13. Chih-yu Shih, *Navigating Sovereignty*, 29.

14. Zhao Tingyang, *Huai shijie yanjiu: Zuo wei diyi zhexue de zhengzhe zhexue* [Investigations of the bad world: Political philosophy as the first philosophy] (Beijing: Zhongguo renmin daxue chubanshe, 2009), 83–84.

15. Daniel A. Bell, *China's New Confucianism: Politics and Everyday Life in a Changing Society* (Princeton, N.J.: Princeton University Press, 2008), 29; Joseph Chan, "Territorial Boundaries and Confucianism" in *Confucian Political Ethics*, edited by Daniel A. Bell (Princeton, N.J.: Princeton University Press, 2008), 81.

16. Wang Gungwu, "China and the International Order: Some Historical Perspectives," in *China and the New International Order*, edited by Wang Gungwu and Zheng Yongnian (London: Routledge, 2008), 23.

17. Wu Guoguang, "From Post-imperial to Late Communist Nationalism: Historical Change in Chinese Nationalism from May Fourth to the Late 1990s," *Third World Quarterly* 29, no. 3 (2008): 467–82, at 473–74.

18. Kai-wing Chow, "Narrating Nation, Race, and National Culture: Imagining the Manzu Identity in Modern China," in *Constructing Nationhood in Modern East Asia*,

edited by Kai-Wing Chow, Kevin M. Doak, and Poshek Fu (Ann Arbor: University of Michigan Press, 2001), 49; Chih-yu Shih, *Navigating Sovereignty*, 27.

19. Samuel Kim lists four levels of variables composing China's foreign policy structure: "the top level, *policies* (most variable), the second level, *principles* (most vocal), the third level, *the basic line* (reaffirmed or revised every five years at the party congresses), and the fourth level, *worldview* (*shijie guan*) and *national identity* (most constant) [italics in the original]." Samuel S. Kim, "Chinese Foreign Policy in Theory and Practice," in *China and the World: Chinese Foreign Policy Faces the New Millennium*, edited by Samuel S. Kim, 10 (Boulder, Colo.: Westview Press, 1998)

20. *China Daily*, "Jiang Zemin Calls for Fair New World Order," April 13, 2000, http://english.people.com.cn/english/200004/13/eng20000413_38891.html. For more on China's approaches to sovereignty, see Allen Carlson, *Unifying China, Integrating with the World: Securing Chinese Sovereignty in the Reform Era* (Stanford, Calif.: Stanford University Press, 2005); and Allen Carlson, "More Than Just Saying No: China's Evolving Approach to Sovereignty and Intervention," in *New Directions in the Study of China's Foreign Policy*, edited by Alastair Iain Johnston and Robert S. Ross (Stanford, Calif.: Stanford University Press, 2006), 217–40.

21. For more on the origins and uses of the concept of *shijie*, see Chun-Mei Chuang, "The Translation and Construction of Shi-Jie: Several Cosmopolitanisms in the Discursive Field of Westernization in Early Twentieth Century China," *Soochow Journal of Sociology* 20 (2006): 59–108, at 76–77. I thank Wei Yin for directing me to this source.

22. The Chinese philosopher Tong Shijun refers to *tianxia* as "the sense of obligation to the most inclusive community under Heaven." See Tong Shijun, "Varieties of Universalism," *European Journal of Social Theory* 12, no. 4 (2009): 449–63, at 450.

23. James Clifford, cited by Pheng Cheah, "Introduction Part II: The Cosmopolitical-Today," in *Cosmopolitics: Thinking and Feeling beyond the Nation*, edited by Pheng Cheah and Bruce Robbins (Minneapolis: University of Minnesota Press, 1997), 21.

24. Cheah, "Introduction Part II," 23–24.

25. Other academics have expressed a similar opinion. E.g., Chinese-American new Confucian scholar Tu Weiming argues for universalization of Confucianism: "A global perspective is needed to universalise its (Confucianism) concerns"; Tu Weiming, "Towards a Third Epoch of Confucian Humanism," in *Way, Learning and Politics: Essays on the Confucian Intellectual*, edited by Tu Weiming (Singapore: Institute of East Asian Philosophies, 1989), 159. Similarly, Kang Xiaoguang, a professor at the People's University in Beijing, has strongly argued both for the Confucianization of Chinese society and political system and for exporting Confucianism. See Kang Xiaoguang, "Wo weishenme zhuzhang 'ruhua': Guanyu zhongguo weilai zhengzhi fazhan de baoshouzhuyi sikao" [Why do I support Confucianization: A conservative reflection on China's future political development], 2004, http://www.tecn.cn/data/detail.php?id=4908, 2.

26. China National Office for Teaching Chinese as a Foreign Language, "Introduction to the 'Confucius Institute' Project," n.d., http://www.edu-chinaembassy.org.uk/english/confucius.htm.

27. "No Need to Fuss over Confucius Institutes," *People's Daily*, August 12, 2010, http://english.peopledaily.com.cn/90001/90782/90873/7103027.html.

28. Ibid.

29. For a detailed overview of the intellectual debates in China on the impact of globalization on Chinese culture, see Nick Knight, "Reflecting on the Paradox of Glo-

balization: China's Search for Cultural Identity and Coherence," *China: An International Journal* 4, no. 1 (2006): 26–27.

30. Not only have Chinese leaders adopted Confucianism-inspired notions in their political lexicon—echoed in such terms as "harmonious society" and *xiaokang shehui*—it is now claimed that Mao was one of the practitioners of Confucianism. Kang Xiaoguang, "Why Do I Support Confucianization," refers to Lin Biao's following characteristic of Mao in the "Summary of Project 571": "Mao is wearing the skin of Marxism, practicing the doctrines of Confucianism, and applying the methods of Qin Shi Huang."

31. Guo Yingjie, *Cultural Nationalism in Contemporary China* (London: Routledge, 2004), 62.

32. Bell, *China's New Confucianism*, 9.

33. One of the examples of this trend is *Sentiments on the Analects of Confucius*, a book by Yu Dan that topped the list of best-selling books in China for two months in the summer of 2008. The book was based on Yu Dan's lectures broadcast in a popular television series on Chinese Central TV. See John Liu, "Confucius TV Spin-Off Leads China's Non-Fiction: Top 10 Books," Bloomberg News, July 17, 2008, http://www.bloomberg.com/apps/news?pid=20601088&sid=a2KZVfUqxteg&refer=muse.

34. Ibid., quoting Shuyu Kong.

35. "China Unveils Standard Portrait of Confucius," Xinhua, September 24, 2006, http://www.china.org.cn/english/2006/Sep/182087.htm.

36. The unshaken centrality of Communist thought in China was reaffirmed in April 2011 when the statue of Confucius erected near Tiananmen Square in January 2011 was suddenly moved to a "less prominent" position in the National Museum. See Andrew Jacobs, "Confucius Statue Vanishes Near Tiananmen Square," *New York Times*, April 22, 2011, http://www.nytimes.com/2011/04/23/world/asia/23confucius.html?_r=1.

37. The Communist rhetoric is especially evident in the materials distributed by the Chinese Communist Party. For an apt example, see *Hu Jintao's Report to the Seventeenth National Congress of the Communist Party of China*, Xinhua, October 15 2007, http://news.xinhuanet.com/english/2007-10/24/content_6938749.htm.

38. Yen Ching-Hwang, "Ch'ing Changing Images of the Overseas Chinese (1644–1912)," *Modern Asian Studies* 15, no. 2 (1981), 261–85, at 264.

39. Lu observes another collision of Confucian values with recently promoted modern norms. He notes that the term *xiaokang* (小康) society (moderately well-off society), which has recently been widely acclaimed in Chinese political rhetoric, was mentioned alongside the term *datong* (大同) in *The Book of Rites*. The book is attributed to Confucius, where *xiaokang* was considered inferior to *datong*. See Sheldon H. Lu, *Chinese Modernity and Global Biopolitics: Studies in Literature and Visual Culture* (Honolulu: University of Hawaii Press, 2007), 200.

40. "Protection of Chinese Language Urged," *People's Daily Online*, May 27, 2004, http://english.peopledaily.com.cn/200405/27/eng20040527_144542.html.

41. Michael J. Shapiro, *Cinematic Political Thought: Narrating Race, Nation and Gender* (New York: New York University Press, 1999), 15.

42. Michael J. Shapiro, *Methods and Nations: Cultural Governance and the Indigenous Subject* (New York: Routledge, 2004), 49.

43. Valerie Jaffee, "Interview with Jia Zhangke," *Senses of Cinema Online*, http://www.sensesofcinema.com/contents/04/32/jia_zhangke.html.

44. Ibid.

45. Lisa Rofel, *Desiring China: Experiments in Neoliberalism, Sexuality, and Public Culture* (Durham, N.C.: Duke University Press, 2007), 129.

46. Shapiro, *Cinematic Political Thought*, 33, evokes Virilio's characteristic of modernity as "obligation to mobility" in defining it as an "aspect of contemporary power."

47. The fictional flying carpet appears in epic stories of most prominently the Middle East, such as *One Thousand and One Nights* and others.

48. The link between holding a Chinese passport and freedom is especially apparent in the recently popularised case of Woeser, a Tibetan poet living in China who openly criticized the Chinese government for its treatment of Tibet and was repeatedly refused a passport allegedly to prevent her from engaging in anti-Chinese government activities abroad; Associated Press, July 23, 2008). Chinese authorities practice confiscation of passports of Chinese Muslims, especially Uyghurs, to stop them from going on Hajj to Mekka independently from the pilgrimage organized by the state. See "China Confiscates Muslims Passports," Radio Free Asia, June 27, 2007, http://www.rfa.org/english/uyghur/uyghur_passports-20070627.html.

49. Zygmunt Bauman, "On Living in a Liquid Modern World," in *The Contemporary Bauman*, edited by Anthony Elliott (London: Routledge, 2007), 108.

50. Susanne Brandtstädter, "Transitional Spaces: Postsocialism as a Cultural Process," *Critique of Anthropology* 27, no. 2 (2007): 135.

51. Rofel, *Desiring China*, 129.

52. Hannah Arendt elaborates on the condition of alienation from the modern world: "expropriation, the deprivation for certain groups of their place in the world and their naked exposure to the exigencies of life, created both the original accumulation of wealth and the possibility of transforming this wealth into capital through labor. These together constituted the conditions for the rise of a capitalist economy." See Hannah Arendt, *The Human Condition* (Chicago: University of Chicago Press, 1958), 254. I thank Pheng Cheah for directing me to this source.

53. Zygmunt Bauman, "Falling In and Out of Love" in *Contemporary Bauman*, ed. Elliott, 102.

54. For an analysis of the intricate relationship between migration and cultural authority in China, see Pal Nyiri, *Mobility and Cultural Authority in Contemporary China* (Seattle: University of Washington Press, 2010).

55. There was an intention to build several World Theme Parks around China to create an opportunity for Chinese people to get a glimpse of the world's attractions. The two surviving ones are Beijing's World Park and Shenzhen's Window of the World. Shenzhen and Beijing are also two of the main destinations for migrant workers in China. With the growing number of opportunities for Chinese people to travel abroad, these parks became less relevant. Such was the fate of the similar park initiative in Chengdu. I thank an anonymous participant at the Centre for International Politics Colloquium on April 22, 2009, for this information.

56. There is a small replica of a section of the Great Wall in the park in the section representing Asia.

Chapter 9

Confucianism, "Cultural Tradition," and Official Discourse in China at the Start of the New Century

Sébastien Billioud

For the last few years, the consonance suggested by the slogans and themes mobilized by China's leadership—particularly harmony (*hexie*, 和谐) and the rule of virtue (*yi de zhi guo*, 以德治国)—has led to speculation concerning their relationship to Confucianism or, more generally, to China's classical cultural tradition. What does the emergence of this new rhetoric mean? How does it fit with Marxist orthodoxy? Can it be explained in terms of a simple phenomenon of instrumentalization? What does this increasing reference to traditional culture indicate about the evolution of contemporary China?

The goal of this chapter is to contribute to the comprehension of this phenomenon on the basis of a body of discourse. It is necessary at the outset to clarify four methodological orientations and limits to this study. First, my interest is in discourse and not actions. Second, this discourse emanates from the central authorities and from semiofficial entities. Thus, here I do not explore the important interaction between an emergent popular Confucianism and authorities at the local level. Third, the category of "Confucianism" is complex and entails very different elements. In this chapter, I consider it in its largest sense, focusing on all possible direct (i.e., explicit use of the term *ru*, 儒, with reference to Confucian figures) and indirect

---

This chapter is a revised version of "Confucianism, 'Cultural Tradition,' and Official Discourse in China at the Start of the New Century," translated by Christopher Storey, *China Perspectives*, no. 3 (2007): 50–65.

(the use of concepts associated with Confucian writings) references. In addition, because it factors regularly into allusions made in official discourse, I am interested in another general and imprecise category: cultural tradition (*wenhua chuantong*, 文化传统) or traditional culture (*chuantong wenhua*, 传统文化).[1] However, I am excluding from the domain of this study the entire aspect of Chinese tradition that the authorities link with religious practices.[2] And fourth, the authorities' relationship with tradition at present appears to be intimately tied to the complex and changing relationship that both society and intellectuals also have with tradition. Thus, here I evoke this important context for this analysis without, unfortunately, being able to go into full detail.

The current renewed popular interest in classical culture, which has been quite significant since the beginning of the new century, constitutes the background matrix of this study. The phenomenon has taken on "religious" (Buddhism, Daoism, qigong, and, more generally, all self-cultivation practices),[3] educational (e.g., the major movement to get children to read classical literature),[4] patrimonial, economic, and touristic forms. It is also recognizable in terms of mass culture (the craze for historical shows on television, the return of traditional dress,[5] the multiplication of Internet sites devoted to classical culture, etc.). In this context, Confucianism, which during the classical era permeated more or less every area of life, is currently being referred to in a fragmented way.[6] In addition, this widespread interest in classical culture has been accompanied by a self-conscious discourse. There has been a profusion of articles and special issues of major national magazines focusing on identity, traditional culture and history, and religious and Confucian revival.[7]

At the popular level, China is currently undergoing an exceptional moment of rediscovery and reinvention of a traditional culture that was repressed for a long time. This rediscovery fits into the larger framework of the extremely rapid evolution of ways of thinking within a society that has only recently—a point often forgotten—emerged from totalitarianism. It is also powerful evidence of the progressive enlargement of experience and cultural references at both personal and collective levels during the past thirty years. Here, I am evoking a movement that extends beyond classical culture; China's fascination with the West (which was particularly strong during the 1980s) and the current rapid growth of Christianity, as well as a transformation of certain modes of sociability via the Internet, are other illustrations of this tendency. This expansion is intimately related to fundamental social change, particularly crises like the increasing sense of insecurity caused by the dislocation of previous structures of cohesion (*danwei*, 单位, or family), the rise of competition (i.e., for education, access to employment) or the impoverishment of specific segments of the population throughout the country. It also reflects the emergence of new aspirations that are far from being only material, despite what is often said.

In postrevolutionary China, the government must come to terms with a context that it creates and to which it also must adjust. Yves Chevrier has used the phrase "distended Communism" (*communisme distendu*) to describe how the government "allows social groups that it controls only indirectly a margin of liberty without granting them full recognition or complete autonomy."[8] This combination of relative social autonomy and government control appears to determine the reaction of the authorities toward the renewed interest in traditional culture. In loosening its grip, the government itself has created the necessary preconditions for the phenomenon. At the same time, as is made clear below, it is cautiously appropriating certain elements that mesh well with its own objectives and reinforce its legitimacy.

In the pages that follow, after a brief summary of the relationship between the Communist Party and Confucianism since China's opening, I examine the extent to which recent official discourse (the Five-Year Plan, speeches by Hu Jintao and Wen Jiabao) refers to traditional culture and Confucianism and which themes are privileged. I complete this investigation with a short analysis of the discourse emanating from "semiofficial" sources (Web sites closely linked to the government, ideological publications, etc.). And I seek to enhance the overall perspective of my observations by assessing the importance of Confucianism in current intellectual debates. I conclude by raising a few questions about the nature of contemporary China's relationship to time.

A Brief Summary of the Communist Party's Relationship with Confucianism since China's Opening

"Confucius, Thinker and Ardent Defender of Slavery," "Confucius, the Great Master of the Partisans of Counterrevolutionary Restoration"—the titles of brochures attacking Lin Biao and Confucius during the Cultural Revolution give a sense of the distance traveled in the past thirty years. The end of Maoism and the beginning of the policies of liberalization inaugurated a long process of reevaluating Confucianism. The question has clearly been a sensitive one given the Chinese Communist Party's (CCP's) history of antitraditionalism along with the role of Confucianism in Republican China and in Taiwan.[9] From the very beginning of the 1980s, traditional Chinese philosophy was featured again as the subject of conferences and articles, at the same time that official organizations were created, like the China Confucius Foundation in 1984.[10] At the end of 1986, in the context of the Seventh Five-Year Plan, the government authorized the formation of a large research group on the so-called Contemporary Confucianism movement directed by Fang Keli, a professor at Nankai University in Tianjin. The Contemporary Confucianism movement encompasses leading intellectuals, including several famous figures who fled to Hong Kong, Taiwan, and the United States when the Communists came to power.

These Confucian intellectuals have achieved prominence through their writings and, in certain cases, through their international activities (i.e., at the Parliament of the World's Religions or at UNESCO). Umberto Bresciani has highlighted two principal motivations for the government to support such a research project: its desire to better comprehend a philosophy that could easily be used as an anti-Marxist tool;[11] and its desire to integrate Confucianism, a source of positive economic values, into its narrative of China's long march toward socialist modernization. The 1980s were a time that saw the eruption of a very Weberian debate over "Asian values" and the development of the four "Asian Tigers." The CCP's renewed interest in Confucianism can be better understood if one takes into account the overall context of the 1980s and the policies of liberalization.

Economic liberalization and the imperative of modernizing the country need to be considered first. Historically, since the end of the dynastic era, both liberals and revolutionary Communists have blamed Confucianism and its "feudalism" for China's backwardness and inability to modernize. However, by the 1980s, this situation had obviously changed. Lao Siguang noted at the time that traditional Confucian culture no longer had any force (*wuli*, 无力),[12] and thus no harmful influence. A controlled and critical re-evaluation[13] was possible given that, on the one hand, the contemporary Confucian intellectuals were the children of the May 4th Movement,[14] and, on the other hand, values attributed to the tradition had paradoxically been emphasized abroad—especially in Singapore—as playing a key role in the process of economic modernization.

Another key form of liberalization was cultural, what became known as the "cultural fever" (*wenhua re*, 文化热). This popular enthusiasm for all things cultural was marked by two dominant tendencies: a prevailing aspiration toward Western modernity, symbolized by the television series, *River*

Elegy (*He Shang*, 河殇); and the rediscovery of traditional culture, especially among those on the most educated and urbane fringe of society.[15] Though this ambiguous interest in traditional culture was not orchestrated by the political authorities, it was nevertheless tolerated and was accompanied by a noticeable shift in tone toward Confucianism. In 1987, Gu Mu (谷牧), the vice prime minister, who was also instrumental to the creation of special economic zones, participated in a symposium on Confucianism in Qufu, the first of its kind since the founding of the People's Republic of China, where he spoke of Confucianism as "a crystallization of Chinese national culture."[16]

Shortly after the events of Tiananmen Square, Gu Mu participated in another symposium celebrating the birth of Confucius and emphasized his positive role in Chinese history,[17] where Jiang Zemin also met some of the symposium's speakers. On the basis of various speeches, Werner Meissner has asserted that "the political leadership clearly functionalized traditional concepts to broaden its dwindling legitimization after June 4th." He points to the following year's rehabilitation of Zhu Xi, the great Song Dynasty thinker. According to Meissner, Confucianism served a dual function for authorities in the 1990s: Its "authoritarian" aspects helped contribute to a "socialist spiritual civilization" and to social cohesion, while it also offered a cultural antidote to the threat of Westernization.[18]

As early as 1995, Jean Philippe Béja went so far as to evoke the establishment of "national-Confucianism." However, in his extremely well-documented study *Lost Soul*, John Makeham shows convincingly that the phenomenon should not be exaggerated and that there is in the end very little evidence supporting the thesis of any substantial endorsement by the party-state of *rujia* values.[19] One can simply note that during the 1990s, the government's attitude toward classical culture in general and Confucianism in particular evolved. Though definitely not reducible to a political strategy, the "fever" for national studies (*guoxue*) at the time could not have spread without the government's tolerance.[20] Thus, throughout this period, some high officials made positive passing remarks concerning Confucianism, although mostly in relatively informal circumstances.[21] All this nevertheless needs to be situated within the larger general context: Although direct references to Confucianism or to traditional culture were more frequent and more visible than during the preceding decade, they nevertheless remained very limited and were mostly restricted to the academic world. At the beginning of the new century, however, things appeared to take a new turn.

An Overview of Confucianism and Traditional Culture in Today's Official Discourse

Here, it is useful to give an overview of Confucianism and traditional culture in today's official discourse. My investigation is based on a body of official texts emanating from the highest levels of state: speeches by Hu Jintao or Wen Jiabao, the 2001 Action Plan for the Development of Civic Morality (hereafter PCM; *gongmin daode jianshe shishi gangyao*, 公民道德建设实施纲要), and especially the 2006 Plan for Cultural Development (hereafter PCD) that was incorporated into the Eleventh Five-Year Plan (2006–10) (*guojia "shiyiwu" shiqi wenhua fazhan guihua gangyao*, 国家"十一五"时期文化发展规划纲要). Two issues need to be explored together: on the one hand, the extent to which these texts make direct reference to traditional culture and Confucianism; and on the other hand, beyond any direct references, the overall nature of the discourse along with the new concepts it generates.

The partisans of a Confucian revival (*rujia fuxing*, 儒家复兴) hailed the Eleventh PCD as great step forward.[22] Although socialist references remained predominant in the text, references to traditional culture were prominent from the very first lines:

> Chinese culture, with over five thousand years of brilliance, has contributed immensely to the progress of human civilization. It is the spiritual bond of our national heritage, of our unceasing dynamism, the source of our power of resistance in the face of difficult challenges and a complex world.

The need to promote "the eminent national culture" (*youxiu minzu wenhua chuantong*, 优秀民族文化传统) is reaffirmed in several passages and constitutes one of the directing principles of the plan.[23] The concrete measures representing the implementation of this principle are enumerated in detail. Before reviewing them, it is worthwhile to note the essentially positive role that traditional culture has assumed in the public discourse of the top leadership.

In a speech delivered in February 2007 concerning the initial phase of socialism,[24] Wen Jiabao praised traditional culture and the excellence of some of its aspects: its philosophies of "harmony without uniformity" (*he er bu tong*, 和而不同, a Confucian concept that has subsequently become a common reference in that it opposes uniformity of thought), of "the people as the basis of the state" (*min wei bang ben*, 民为邦本),²⁵ and of "respecting teachers and valorizing studies."²⁶ In another speech by Wen Jiaobao, delivered at Harvard University in March 2007, and now often cited by advocates of Confucianism in China, the references are even more explicit:

> From Confucius to Sun Yat-sen,²⁷ the traditional culture of the Chinese nation consisted of large number of precious elements, of many positive things concerning the nature of a people and of democracy [*renminxing he minzhuxing*, 人民性和民主性]. It emphasized, for example, love and the sense of humanity [*ren'ai*, 仁爱], community [*qunti*, 群体], harmony and not uniformity, the fact that what is under Heaven is for all [*tianxia wei gong*, 天下为公].²⁸

Within an ensemble of still overwhelmingly socialist references, there is an essentially positive interpretation of traditional Chinese culture, even though the latter is pointed to in an extremely vague way.

Apart from a few scattered references to cultural tradition in a number of discourses, there has also been an increase in the use of slogans with a decidedly Confucian accent, like "harmonious socialist society" (*shehuizhuyi hexie shehui*, 社会主义和谐社会). How have the authorities integrated this new slogan into the standard body of ideological catchwords? A speech by Hu Jintao in 2005 provides a certain amount of insight because it attempts to provide the slogan with some historical grounding.²⁹ In the speech, the idea of harmony in classical thought is evoked in a paragraph in which Confucius, Mozi, Mencius, the Book of Rites, the leader of the Taiping Rebellion, Hong Xiuquan, and Kang Youwei are all jumbled together. The concretization of the ideas of these figures, Hu goes on to explain, was not possible in a feudal system of class oppression. Without ascribing too much importance to this point, it is nevertheless noteworthy how he makes the distinction between the potential resources that classical thought offers today and the former political system that must still be vigorously condemned.

In his speech, Hu also situates the notion of harmony within the history of socialism in order to establish its genealogy while at the same time acknowledging the opposing notions of contradiction and class struggle. The harmony extolled by utopian socialists (*kongxiang shehuizhuyi*, 空想社会主义) like Charles Fourier and Robert Owen in the nineteenth century did not, according to Hu, sufficiently take into consideration the contradictions at work in capitalism, which was precisely the remedy provided by the scientific socialism of Marx, Engels, and Lenin. As for China, Hu carefully demonstrates the contribution of each generation of leaders to the idea of harmony, even if the Maoist record on this score was rather mixed. The primacy of contradiction for the Great Helmsman is hinted at through a commentary on the second generation of leadership (that of Deng Xiaoping), which "abandoned the erroneous line that consisted of attributing a central role to class struggle" (*yi jieji douzheng wei gang de cuowu fangzhen*, 以阶级斗争为纲的错误方针). Advocating a harmonious society today, the text makes clear, is not a matter of denying the existence of contradictions within society but one of "resolving them in the appropriate fashion" (*tuoshan chuli*, 妥善处理).

Various studies have highlighted the CCP's historical ambivalence toward the concept of contradiction and of class struggle. Arif Dirlik has pointed out the existence of a profound ambiguity at the heart of Chinese socialism throughout the twentieth century, characterized by a tug of war between promoting the interests of the working class and avoiding class conflict.[30] Kalpana Misra—who refers to Dirlik's work, but also to that of Li Yuming and of Joseph Levenson, has demonstrated how the hard line Maoism of the 1960s and 1970s clashed with a preference for harmony among elites, a conflict that revealed itself, at various times and contexts in different guises, like the United Front, the "collaboration of the four classes," and "the democratic dictatorship of the people."[31] Hu's speech, despite its careful effort to recall various episodes in the evolution of Marxist theory,[32] overwhelmingly gives the impression that the idea of contradiction, once stripped of all philosophical underpinning (as a law of development or a principle of epistemology),[33] boils down to simply describing concrete problems that can be resolved through the appropriate policy. It is true that the mystique of contradiction (and its most obvious avatar, class struggle) has been off center stage for some time. Nevertheless, its absorption/dissolution into the concept of harmony—a concept with which it has always been in opposition—might indicate an interesting turning point in official discourse. It is of course a pragmatic shift that opens the door—at least in theory—to reconciling the interests of the emerging bourgeoisie with a commitment to fighting against social cleavages; but it is also a clever theoretical innovation that preserves a certain ideological continuity while at the same time evoking "tradition" in a highly vague manner.

Assuring the unity of the people is one of the principal functions of culture as outlined in the Eleventh PCD.[34] Culture must provide the "spiritual resources" for constructing a harmonious socialist society and achieving a "moderately prosperous society" (*xiaokang shehui*, 小康社会).³⁵ From this standpoint, traditional culture is particularly vital in three domains: morality, education, and social cohesion.

The Question of Morality

The second section of the Eleventh PCD takes up the question of morality under the heading "Reinforcing Socialist Morality."³⁶ Like the billboards put up in the past few years by neighborhood committees across the country, the text emphasizes from the outset the necessity of both the rule of law (*yi fa zhi guo*, 以法治国) and the rule of virtue (*yi de zhi guo*, 以德治国). The general tone of the text reflects an attempt to find the proper balance between or synthesis of references to socialism and references to the national spirit (or to traditional culture), while at the same time insisting on the importance of being in sync with the zeitgeist (*shidai jingshen*, 时代精神), as if to defuse any temptation toward exclusive reference to tradition.

Three key elements are highlighted. First, there is the necessity to work toward raising the "moral level of the people" (*gongmin de daode sushi*, 公民的道德素质). Here I find the continuation of the arguments of the PCM written five years earlier.³⁷ Next comes the (socialist) conception of "honors and shames" (*rongruguan*, 荣辱观), popularized by the slogan "eight honors and eight disgraces" (*ba rong ba chi*, 八荣八耻).³⁸ Many promoters of a Confucian revival consider this recourse to shame in the slogan as a direct reference to traditional moral philosophy.³⁹ The Eleventh PCD calls for the integration of *ba rong ba chi* into school textbooks, where, in fact, the amount of space and the pedagogical role assigned to traditional culture has evolved in the last few years. The last of the three elements is the moral and patriotic indoctrination of youth.

This moral indoctrination campaign seeks to get to the root of a set of clearly identified problems.⁴⁰ Though peppered with Confucian elements, it fits into a certain historical continuity. Before 1949, despite the antitraditionalist bent of the May 4th Movement, the governments in place actively contributed to the promotion of Confucian-inspired moral education. Emblematic of this kind of educational policy was the use of Dai Jitao's (戴季陶) theories linking Confucianism and Sun Yat-sen's Three Principles of the People by the government of Chiang Kai-shek.⁴¹ Once the Communists came to power, the discourse changed radically, but certain structures of thought persisted. Numerous studies have drawn attention to this continuity.⁴² In a work on Marxism in China, Li Zehou (李泽厚) demonstrates the extent to which Chinese Communism, far from limiting itself to the system of socialist ethics that is discernible in some Western currents of Marxism, is impregnated with the tradition of self-cultivation (*xiuyang*, 修养) and "inner sainthood" (*neisheng*, 内圣), under the guise of "a moralism aiming at reforming individual thought."[43] Jin Guantao has used the phrase "the Confucianization of Marxism" to describe this phenomenon, which he claims began during the Republican Era.[44] He points to an essay written by Liu Shaoqi that was first published in 1940 as a good illustration of the evolution in question":[45] "On the Self-Cultivation of Chinese Communist Party Members" (Lun Gongchandangyuan de xiuyang).[46] The Marxist project of social transformation is linked to the necessity of personal transformation (*gaizao ziji*, 改造自己), with Marx and Lenin serving as examples. Having incorporated a certain élan associated with the question of self-cultivation, Marxism evolves and by the 1950s, according to Jin Guantao, becomes for the Chinese a form of moral idealism. Li Zehou, in the work cited above, compares the CCP under Mao with the Confucian tradition, identifying in both cases a "trinity" (*san he yi*, 三合一) involving religion (*zongjiao*, 宗教), ethics (*lunli*, 伦理), and politics (*zhengzhi*, 政治).[47] For Li, CCP rule finally embodied a kind of theologico-political (*zhengzhi zongjiao*, 政治宗教) power.[48]

Of course, the situation in China today is no longer the same, but it is important to keep in mind a certain historical continuity. Mass mobilization campaigns have mostly disappeared with the onset of liberalization; any remnants have been on a more limited scale.[49] Individuals have carved out a considerably larger sphere of autonomy. However, the discourse of moral indoctrination continues to play a role of varying importance and, at present, it gives the impression of reclaiming, at least to a certain extent, an ambiguous Confucian inspiration. In a way, the core Marxist orthodoxy, already significantly Sinicized, appears, at least on the surface, to be undergoing a partial and careful process of re-Confucianization.

The promotion, based on moral indoctrination, of a highly ethical and political conception of education relies to a large extent on articulating some form of philosophical justification. The clear affirmation of the availability of a knowledge (concerning humanity, society, history, etc.) both legitimates a certain type of indoctrination and establishes its contours. In her analysis of the foundations of the Chinese regime's legitimacy, Vivienne Shue has identified three factors (access to truth, benevolence toward the people, glory) that she traces historically back to the end of the Imperial Era while emphasizing their pertinence throughout the Maoist years and up to the present.⁵⁰ The "truth" that particularly concerns us here is no longer a Confucian one; it is, based on the primacy of scientific empiricism, a teleological conception of modernity, one that is a source of positive and transcendent ethical values (progress, etc.).⁵¹ As far as this study is concerned, the actual details of this truth matter less than the fact that it has been clearly recognized as available and consequently may constitute a basis for ethical and political indoctrination.⁵²

To some extent, Shue's analysis matches that of another important recent work, Thomas Metzger's *A Cloud across the Pacific*, which focuses not on official discourse but on that of intellectuals.⁵³ Analyzing major works of political theory in contemporary China, the book identifies a constant beyond the different schools of thought distinguished in the text (Marxism, Sunnism, liberalism, Confucian humanism): the existence of a recurrent "epistemological optimism"—in other words, a conviction that a system that can explain reality (history, values, etc.) is available.⁵⁴ Metzger goes on to show how this epistemological optimism coincides with the promotion of a form of *paideia* or a conception of children's education imbued with a strong ethical and political dimension.⁵⁵ Shue undertakes a fairly comprehensive analysis of the political and its sources of legitimacy. Metzger dissects contemporary political theory. Though their studies differ in focus, both authors place epistemology at the center of their political reflection.

Another author whose conclusions somehow echo those mentioned above is Yves Chevrier, who outlines the CCP's objective of "situating the legal order within a higher normative order," a (Communist) morality historically constituted.⁵⁶ Aside from the question of a possible "Confucian or traditional turn" to the current moral education campaign, what is clear is the persist link between the primacy of a state-affirmed vision of the world and the state's continued commitment to fashioning individuals.⁵⁷

The Promotion of Traditional Culture in the Schools

Having examined the question of morality, I continue this study of official discourse and the Eleventh PCD by taking into consideration the document's seventh part, which is devoted to the preservation of national culture. Of particular interest in this part of the text is the campaign to promote traditional culture in the schools, whose objective is not outlined in the second section on morality analyzed above.⁵⁸ Two points draw one's attention immediately: first (in section 28), the call for the reissuing of major classical texts. Edition work on Qing history, as well as "the important and great project" of "preserving and protecting national classics," figure in this section of the document. The publication of classic texts of minority groups is also mentioned. Section 30 goes on to stress the importance of education in the domain of "China's remarkable traditional culture" (*zhonghua youxiu chuantong wenhua*, 中华优秀传统文化) and classical literature. Explicitly stipulated is the following:

> In those schools where it is possible classes in calligraphy, painting, and other classical arts should be established. At the middle school level, the proportion of compositions on poetry and the classics must be increased during Chinese classes. In primary schools and middle schools, links between the specificities of the various disciplines instructed and traditional Chinese culture need to be emphasized.

Moreover, the plan calls for the promotion of classical culture at the postsecondary level and in society.

Within the "Confucian revival movement," those interlocutors whom I have been able to meet during field study have all stressed the innovative nature of these measures. It will be interesting during the years to come to observe the changes in school curricula as a measure of the "turn" with regard to classical culture currently taking place. Which classical texts will be privileged (and which ones will not be discussed)? How will they be read (or memorized) and explained? How will teachers be trained? I can provide no answers here. However, I must insist once again on a fundamental contextual element. This interest for traditional literature and culture in all its forms—beyond just Confucianism—can in no case be analyzed only in terms of top-down instrumentalization. It reflects a much larger popular aspiration. After years of gestation, the craze for traditional culture that has become more and more apparent in the last few years goes way beyond any political framework and is rooted as well in popular practice. Examples of this phenomenon at the grassroots level in today's China are manifold: the rapid spread of a movement to encourage children to read classical literature (*shao er du jing*, 少儿读经);[59] an enthusiastic rediscovery of the major canonical texts;[60] an interest on the part of many entrepreneurs in Confucianism;[61] the opening of private schools where studying the classics once again has taken on a special importance (*sishu*, 私塾; *xuetang*, 学堂; *shuyuan*, 书院); a return to traditional styles of dress; a craze for television shows with historical themes; and a multiplication of Web sites on classical culture and the like—not to mention the massive return of religion, especially Buddhism. These few examples testify to the profound changes that Chinese society is undergoing.[62]

It is precisely in this context that the political usage of culture and the policy of promoting traditional culture in the schools need to be situated. Government policy, in this sense, is more a matter of dynamic interaction with an ongoing and widespread cultural phenomenon than a directive from on high. It makes possible an expansion of the range of experience for individuals, and a deepening of their relationship with certain aspects of their own history and culture (a point that may be problematic). At the same time, policy adapts and responds to the demand made possible, producing a tradition that serves the interests of the state and reinforces social cohesion.

Mobilizing Strong Symbols of Cohesion

The Eleventh PCD explicitly stipulates (part 7, section 29) the need to encourage the potentially positive role of important holidays and customs "with careful attention to the reorganization of their content and rituals, festivals and popular traditions that embody a strong national character need to be fostered." The plan goes on to cite a large number of major festivals like *chunjie* (春节), *yuanxiaojie* (元宵节), and *qingmingjie* (清明节). The key condition governing their celebration, which the plan stresses repeatedly, is that they reflect the spirit of the present era. New forms must be found to which celebration can be adapted. On this point, the document does not provide more details. These traditional festivals, which were celebrated in the past in a diverse fashion depending upon the region, were all intimately linked to popular religion (which is currently undergoing a spectacular revival, even though it is technically illegal because the state officially only recognizes five main religions), and thus to a whole body of beliefs deemed to be "superstitions" by today's authorities. In addition, these festivals were often an occasion to ask for an increase of descendants (*qiuzi*, 求子), something that was basically incompatible with current family planning policies. In any case, the CCP faces the challenge of reappropriating these traditions without losing sight of the fact that its own history is intrinsically rooted in the fight against "feudalism." We have here a textbook case of what Eric Hobsbawm means when he evokes "the use of ancient materials to construct invented traditions of a novel type for quite novel purposes."[63] It must be emphasized, however, that, in the case of the PCD, the reinvention of tradition is made explicit and is clearly articulated in such terms; above all, it is an effort to reactivate elements of the cultural patrimony considered to be of use for today's purposes.

The PCD also explicitly makes provisions for the "continued amelioration of activities and ceremonies in honor of the ancestors of the Chinese nation." In the end, "it is essential to reinforce the cohesion of the Chinese nation and further the creation of a harmonious society." This section also mentions national holidays celebrating labor and the CCP; however, interestingly enough, those holidays are discussed as a secondary matter. The document nevertheless reflects a clear concern that elements of traditional culture must be integrated with the socialist heritage. The ceremonies associated with the cults devoted to great mythical and tutelary figures like Yu the Great (大禹; in Shaoxing, Zhejiang Province) and Huangdi (黄帝), the Yellow Emperor (in Huangling, Shaanxi Province) have increasingly become the object of extensive media coverage.[64] Moreover, the Ministry of Culture has even decreed these two cults that honor figures featured in the canonical texts associated with Confucianism to be "national cults" (*guoji*, 国祭, as the cult of Yu the Great has been defined since 2007).[65]

In his study of the cult devoted to Huangdi, Térence Billeter has highlighted the continuity in the homage paid to the Yellow Emperor throughout the twentieth century (except during the Cultural Revolution) as well as the evolution of the discourse involved in his veneration.[66] Building up on his research on Huangdi, he defends a broader thesis concerning contemporary Chinese nationalism and explains to what extent the utilization of the past aims at strengthening an autocratic power.[67] I need to highlight here the fact that the figure of the "ancestor" is probably easier to be made instrumental than many other ones. In this respect, Confucius, because he is considered first as a master and not as an ancestor, might be much more subversive a figure than the Yellow Emperor, even though his birthday is celebrated each year in Qufu (Shandong Province) with great pomp and government support.[68]

Finally, in recent years many cities have sponsored their own projects to preserve local sites of archaeological and mythological importance.[69] It is not possible in this context to go into this phenomenon in any detail. It is clear, nevertheless, that further studies would probably reveal that pointing only to ideological instrumentalization on the part of the government (even though such an instrumentalization clearly exists) is not sufficient to explain the diversity of ceremonies and practices in question. Instead, it is a matter of the intersection of many factors (political, economic, touristic, religious, cultural, etc.) at both the central and local levels, forming what Mauss described as "total social facts."[70]

The political use of traditional culture, to reinforce either the stability of the country or its social cohesion, is clearly outlined in the PCD. Far from being a form of covert instrumentalization, the effort is openly promoted as a key element of a cultural policy that seeks to blend the socialist legacy with a sense of historical continuity. At the same time, this policy is in no way "unidirectional"—is not simply a directive from on high—but appears instead to be driven by close interaction with a changing society. The schema here is not a matter of an all-pervasive party disseminating culture but instead one of an orientation by a regime that is increasingly allowing a greater of margin of autonomy to "civil society" while at the same time profiting from the evolution set in motion. However, the autonomy granted is closely controlled to the point of ruthless action when a threat is perceived, as was the case with Falungong, which originally enjoyed the support of the government.[71]

Confucius in Official and "Semiofficial" Discourse

Up to this point, I have repeatedly referred to Confucianism in "official discourse," even though most of the time the references are in fact not explicit. I have approached the question from the margins, noting the increasingly frequent appearance in official discourse of Confucian notions and themes. I have also been drawn to expand the field of my interrogation to "tradition," and to "traditional culture," while emphasizing the need to be careful in using such terms. The difficulty posed by an interest in Confucianism today is that one is confronted with an ensemble of scattered "fragments" (in this sense, Yu Yingshi has referred to a "wandering soul") that obviously in no way approach the hegemonic dimension of Confucianism during imperial times (even if different époques were not homogenous). In any case, it must be stated that in a document as fundamental as the Eleventh PCD, the term *ru* (儒), which corresponds to what I call Confucianism, does not appear at all. It is periodically cited in other texts, but always with the greatest prudence. Though everything that I have considered so far suggests that China is currently undergoing some kind of critical reevaluation of its traditional culture, there remains the question of Confucianism as a direct reference and of Confucius himself.

To explain the difficulty that any direct reference to Confucius entails, I must first remind the reader that the legitimacy of Communism in China has always been rooted in its rejection of all forms of "feudalism." Moreover, what makes the question particularly sensitive is the manner in which the Kuomintang and the regime in Taiwan have made use of Confucianism. Finally, it is necessary again to focus my analysis on the most recent context, one that has seen a widespread propagation of "elements" of or references to Confucianism, for it is this development that differs significantly from what was prevalent in the 1990s.[72] While the CCP is indeed interested in using all available resources to reinforce its legitimacy, it is not prepared to lose control or to let its agenda be dictated by what could be perceived as radical forms of cultural conservatism.

Visiting official and semiofficial Web sites (especially online forums and message boards)[73] makes it possible to "take the temperature" of the situation in 2007 and to examine the kind of discussion currently taking place as well as the semiofficial positions circulating (opinions of CCP school professors, high-ranking civil servants, et al.). These discussions are interesting because they are often more spontaneous and less carefully prepared than the official discourses and texts that I have analyzed above. While considering them, however, it is all the more important to be prudent in attempting to link such pronouncements with the official position toward Confucianism. What follows is just an example of the kind of discussion that could be found on official sites in 2007. It by no means reflects an exhaustive survey of the enormous mass of information available online.

The first point to be emphasized is that the question of Confucianism's role is sometimes directly discussed. For example, this clarification concerning "national studies" (*guoxue*, 国学) was posted on the Web site of the Central Party School (CPS) at the beginning of 2007:

> As for those intent on using Confucian doctrine [*rujiao*, 儒教] as a way to replace Marxism, to Confucianize China [*ruhua Zhongguo*, 儒化中国] or Confucianize the Communist Party, Professor Wang Jie (an instructor at the school) has formulated a set of critiques, estimating that the academic world must seriously reflect upon and criticize such completely erroneous positions. Professor Wang also suggested that given the current fever for national studies, it is necessary to remain vigilant toward all tendencies to return to the past [*fuguzhuyi*, 复古主义] and toward radical nationalism [*jiduan minzuzhuyi*, 极端民族主义].[74]

This article appears, in fact, in a semiofficial discussion space where the subject of Confucianism is broached directly and sometimes defended. The following passages appeared in an article published at the end of 2006 on the Web site "Study Times" and were written by a high-ranking military official, Xu Zhizin, a general based in Xinjiang, with the title "Leaders and Cadres Must Also Study a Little Classical Culture:"

> Confucian culture is a cultural resource which we cannot distance ourselves from in the construction of a harmonious socialist society. . . . As cadres and leaders, we must nourish ourselves with Confucian culture. . . . Every Communist Party cadre must contribute to the radiance of the spiritual specificities of Confucian culture by aspiring to the highest moral qualities and behavior.[75]

Reacting to this article, the "Professor Wang" mentioned in the quotation two paragraphs above estimates that it reflects the opinion of many students (who are also cadres) at the CPS.[76] Though his position is rather orthodox, as exhibited in his strong criticism of the idea of any institutional role for Confucianism, he nevertheless defines a double mission for the CPS: promoting both Marxism and Chinese traditional culture. Moreover, he launches into an interesting criticism of the institution that, in his opinion, reacted too slowly (with a lag time of ten to twenty years) "to the problem of traditional culture that has absorbed the attention of the whole of society." At that point, I need to add that courses on Chinese traditional culture are now extremely popular within the CPS. Apart from providing basic content to cadres who some times know little about the topic, they also aim at "linking Marxism to traditional culture" and at showing how these traditional resources may be useful in today's society. An example quoted to me was how the CCP's ideas of "scientific development" and "ecological civilization" (*shengtai wenming*) could be associated with "the ecological philosophy of Confucianism." The question of whether such a theoretical exercise can translate into anything practical remains open. However, as far as ideological production is concerned, the CPS is probably now instrumental in promoting some sort of hybrid "Marxist-traditional" rhetoric.[77]

In addition to Web sites, the semiofficial literature provides other resources from which one can gain an idea of the authorities' interest in Confucianism. More often than not, they stress the importance of a selective and critical appropriation of traditional resources, including Confucian ones.[78] Using such literature and the kinds of examples cited above,[79] I can emphasize two elements: on the one hand, it appears as though the role of "Confucianism" in the more formal sense of the term can be discussed directly and, as a consequence, that an internal debate is occurring, if only informally among CCP cadres; on the other hand, the positions that appear to be emerging in these circles oscillate between extreme prudence and critical reappropriation, as if the time might have come to reevaluate Master Confucius and his influence.

A Political Use of Confucianism Today?
The Issue in Intellectual Circles

For the past few years, within China's official discourse there has been a multiplication of slogans with Confucian overtones without any explicit or exclusive reference to Confucianism or traditional culture. In fact, the desire to blend these slogans with China's socialist and Marxist legacy has been evident, which is not too surprising, given that the very legitimacy of the regime stems from this heritage. Particularly in the domains of culture, morality, education, and other means of solidifying national cohesion, the role of Chinese "tradition" has been affirmed, without the actual content of this category being precise. However, does this "tradition" offer something additional to the practice of power, to the defining of public policy, or, indeed, to the regime's institutional evolution?

A debate on these kinds of questions is currently taking place within intellectual circles in China. In and of itself, this phenomenon is extremely interesting. My goal here is simply to point out its existence because it constitutes a part of the general context within which the official discourse I have been analyzing emerges. I have already mentioned the interaction between the authorities and society at large. Intellectuals—and more specifically, "public intellectuals"—collectively form the third side of a triangle, even if it is difficult to discern the actual influence—which is probably still very modest—that their debates on this subject have on the top leadership.[80]

The existence within intellectual circles of discussion about Confucianism is, of course, not a new phenomenon. However, the way in which Confucianism is viewed has evolved considerably in the last thirty years.

Though in the 1980s, the country's problems were still often blamed on the subsistence of "feudalism," today Confucianism is often seen in a favorable light. An examination of certain scholars' intellectual itineraries illustrates this phenomenon. One example is Gan Yang (甘阳), a talented and influential thinker who is considered to be one of the main representatives of the "New Left." His view of Confucianism, which once was consistent with the dominant perspective of the 1980s as described above, has evolved. In a recent article, he goes so far as to advocate a "Chinese way," which could take the form of a "Confucian socialist republic" (*rujia shehuizhuyi gongheguo,* 儒家社会主义共和国).[81]

In Gan's opinion, the political reality in China must take into account a triple heritage, in which each of three main elements is important. The first element corresponds in some way to the policy of liberalization launched thirty years ago and oriented toward market forces, "which also includes several concepts that have become familiar, like freedom and rights." The second element is the Maoist heritage, which for Gan is important not to forget—"it is a tradition that embodies equality and justice" that is reasserted in the current slogan "harmonious society." Third and finally, the "Confucian tradition" must be assimilated. By "Confucian tradition," he means most of all a collection of practices inherited from the past that structure "daily life," notably family relations.[82]

Naturally, Gan does not embrace "Confucianism" uncritically—to the contrary, one can see that he relies on a very reduced meaning of the term. But what is particularly interesting is his intellectual evolution, as well as the fact that Confucianism has become for him a concept that is sufficiently promising as to merit being promoted. During the 1990s, the position of a considerable number of former liberals of the 1980s shifted toward the New Left or toward forms of conservatism. The current decade has seen many of the same intellectuals engage in a critical reappropriation of aspects of tradition.[83]

The debate concerning Confucianism has been nurtured by a group of intellectuals who have more openly claimed a strong institutional role for it on the Mainland. They have differentiated themselves from a highly speculative "philosophical Confucianism" still embodied during the 1990s in the writings of thinkers in Taiwan, Hong Kong, and the United States. Among these "activist intellectuals" figures Jiang Qing (蒋庆), the author of a book in 2003 titled *Zhengzhi ruxue* (Political Confucianism, 政治儒学) as well as other works in which he proposes concrete measures to institutionalize Confucianism. For Jiang, the legitimacy of political authority stems from three sources: Heaven (*tian*, 天), which is the incarnation of a certain transcendence; Earth (*di*, 地), which represents culture and history; and finally humanity, (*ren*, 人), which reflects notion of the will of the people. This conception of things leads, in his case, to concrete proposals for institutional reform, notably the establishment of a tricameral parliament reflecting the three sources.[84] Jiang is the leader of a group of intellectuals in various disciplines, including the "Confucian economist" Sheng Hong (盛洪). Another well-known "scholar-activist" close to this group of Confucians is Kang Xiaoguang (康晓光), a sociologist and former adviser to Zhu Rongji. Like Jiang, Kang advocates that Confucianism should become an official religion, and even a state religion.[85] Such proposals have sparked considerable debate and polemics outside strictly academic circles. Proof of this development is the amount of discussion about the "Confucianization of China" within the semiofficial discourse analyzed above.

Given the overall context, the Confucian positions put forth by Jiang and these other activist intellectual writers cannot fail to generate strong reactions, especially among liberal writers. Thus, for example, Qin Hui (秦晖), a writer and public intellectual whose political preferences lean toward social democracy, has denounced in both books and conferences those political practices that have historically claimed Confucian inspiration. He argues that in reality they have reflected a fundamentally legalist spirit (*ru biao fa li*, 儒表法里, which means "Confucian on the outside, legalist on the inside") or a pernicious interaction between authoritarianism and the interests of casts of people using their positions to plunder the country. However, Qin Hui also identified a lineage of "true Confucians," from Huang Zongxi to Tan Sitong, whose critique of power remains inspiring for a modern age.[86] Paradoxically, even the most pointed criticism contributes to Confucianism's presence in intellectual debate at the moment.[87]

Without doubt, the true influence of Confucian intellectuals or those inspired by that tradition on the regime remains very weak, despite the fact that some, like Kang Xiaogang, actively lobby for their cause. Nevertheless, the notion of a Confucian renaissance (*ruxue fuxing*, 儒学复兴) has been echoed in both semiofficial quarters (including in actual debates) and in the mass media (where there is less of an emphasis on politics). The intellectual debates and the emergence of a "popular Confucianism" together add to the framework within which the regime's own discourse operates, a framework the regime both makes possible and tightly controls.

Conclusion: A Breach in Time?

This chapter's central arguments can be summarized in three points. First, the nature of the relationship between the CCP and "Chinese tradition" (understood in the largest sense) is complex, because the regime's legitimacy stems from a rupture with the old order, even though certain aspects of this order—notably in epistemology and the moralization of politics, what is often call the "Sinicization of Marxism—have been somehow perpetuated.

Second, in the past thirty years, there has been an evident shift in the Chinese regime's attitude toward this "tradition." Confucian-sounding references figure into the regime's overall political orientation, although great care is taken to provide a Marxist justification for the new concepts and to avoid breaking the thread of ideological continuity. Therefore, the importance of the shift should not be overplayed. However, in certain domains, such as culture and education, a turning point appears to have been reached, whereby classical culture and popular traditions once again enjoy a place of honor or are being reinvented and students are being encouraged to take an interest in them. Thus the regime seems to have entered a new period of careful and critical reassessment of "traditional culture" that involves designating some of its elements as compatible with the socialist legacy.[88]

And third, although this reevaluation certainly serves clear political purposes (legitimation, fortifying national cohesion), it is not a simple matter of an authoritarian, top-down, cultural instrumentalism; it is a phenomenon that can be linked to a more general evolution of perspectives on classical culture (and Confucianism) at both the level of society as a whole and within more limited intellectual spheres. In this sense, it reflects a style of rule in which the CCP no longer seeks to impose its will directly at all levels of society but instead allows for a certain degree of autonomy while tightly controlling the changes thereby unleashed.[89]

I conclude by briefly pointing to a larger question that is important in China today: that of the society's relationship to time. This theme of society and time is addressed in an important work by the historian François Hartog, who explores a concept that he calls the "historicity regime" (*régime d'historicité*), described as "a heuristic tool that aids in better apprehending . . . mostly moments of temporal crisis that occur, here and there, when the connections between the past, the present and the future come to lose their sense of obviousness."[90] This concept is a sort of intermediary between the long duration (*la longue durée*) and the momentary (*l'événement*) and thus, according to Hartog, allows us to elucidate the tension between the field of experience and the horizon of expectation.[91]

Hartog's book provides several examples of moments in which a shift to a new historicity regime took place. Thus, using the writings of Chateaubriand and Tocqueville, he demonstrates how at the end of the eighteenth and beginning of the nineteenth centuries, in the wake of the American and French revolutions, a new order of time emerged, "in which lessons are to come from the future.... The former historicity regime, in which the past illuminates the future, is definitively nullified."[92] The end of the twentieth century, a bit before and after 1989, marks the arrival of yet another historicity regime that Hartog, through a study of memory and patrimony, characterizes via the idea of the dominance of "presentism" (*le présentisme*). The future no longer illuminates the present; instead, it is the present that gets hypertrophied and overwhelms the horizon through information, globalization, consumption, ephemera, and so on. According to Hartog, the present now manufactures the past and the future that it needs on a daily basis.[93]

Lacking the perspective of a lengthier stretch of time by which to judge, it would be both overambitious and premature to suggest that China has entered into a new historicity regime. Nevertheless Hartog's work invites us to consider to what extent China—given the examples analyzed above of the changing relationship toward "tradition" in general and "Confucianism" in particular—might be undergoing a "time crisis" leading to a new organization of the link between past, present, and future. Though insufficient on their own to provide an answer to such a question, the elements mentioned in this chapter (official and intellectual discourses and, above all, the emergence of a popular reference to fragments of the Confucian heritage) at least invite us to ponder this issue. They suggest, in effect, that China is currently discovering, on a much larger scale than in the 1980s and 1990s, that its classical tradition—whether real, idealized, or reinvented—is perhaps once again becoming a source that is capable of informing the present or the future.[94] At the very least, it is escaping from its previous "museumification" to expand the field of experience and collective references.[95] In doing so, it may become a resource for producing memory and identity.

However, it must be stressed that this reactivation of the past in China, at a variety of levels, is by no means determined by a monopoly of any given tradition. Indeed, it is characterized by pluralism (as typified by the renewal of interest in religion) and fragmentariness.[96] Moreover, one also needs to keep in mind that this major return and "production" of the past are taking place in a context still limited by huge areas of collective amnesia. In any case, this situation reflects an increasingly acute collective awareness that contemporary China, far from being just "new," is actually the product more than anything else of the telescoping of many traditions.

Notes

1. In avoiding a precise definition, I am using these two categories of Confucianism and cultural tradition in a provisory manner, as, following the Buddhist notion, a convenience (*fangbian*, 方便); in other words, as categories established at a certain moment because of their usefulness (in this case, as a way to better understand the relationship of authorities to aspects of the pre-Republican past) while recognizing at the same time their eminently problematic character and limitations.

2. Confucianism is not considered to be a religion in Mainland China. In Hong Kong, however, it is one of the official religions.

3. David A. Palmer, *Qigong Fever, Body, Science and Utopia in China* (New York: Columbia University Press, 2007).

4. Also see Sébastien Billioud and Joël Thoraval, "*Jiaohua*: The Confucian Revival Today as an Educative Project," *China Perspectives*, no. 4 (2007): 4–20; and Ji Zhe, "Traditional Education in China: Conservative and/or Liberal?" *Chinese Cross Currents* 2, no. 3 (2005): 32–41.

5. The most spectacular example of this phenomenon is the "Han Dress Movement" (*Hanfu yundong*, 汉服运动), which has inspired tens of thousands of young people to march through China's large cities dressed in traditional clothing. In another register (the *qipao*), also see Matthew Chew, "On the Contemporary Re-emergence of the Qipao—Contemporary Re-emergence of the Qipao; Political Nationalism, Cultural Production and Popular Consumption of a Traditional Chinese Dress," *China Quarterly*, no. 189 (2007): 144–61.

6. For a general mapping of the situation, see Billioud and Thoraval, "*Jiaohua*"; Sébastien Billioud and Joël Thoraval, "*Anshen Liming*, or the Religious Dimension of Confucianism," *China Perspectives*, no. 3 (2008): 88–106; and Sébastien Billioud and Joël Thoraval, "*Lijiao*: The Reinvention of Confucian Ceremonies at the Start of the New Century," *China Perspectives*, no. 4 (2009).

7. A few recent examples suffice to illustrate the extent of the phenomenon: The *Liaowang dongfang zhoukan*, one of the leading national weeklies, mentions *guoxue re* (国学热, the fever for national studies) as one of key phrases of 2006; *Liaowang dongfang zhoukan*, January 4, 2007, 64–65. In another issue, the same magazine dedicates a special feature to the official sacrifices to the great ancestors of Chinese civilization; *Liaowang dongfang zhoukan*, June 21, 2007, 10–23. *Zhongguo xinwen zhoukan* [China Newsweek], no. 42 (2006), dedicates a special feature to "the Dignity of China" (Zunyan Zhongguo), emphasizing the role of Confucianism. *Zhongguo xinwen zhoukan*, no. 40 (2006), made its headlines with the question "Who Are We?" [*women shi shui*, 我们是谁] in a special dossier featuring articles on the issues of rites, Han dress, traditional education, Chinese medicine, etc. Another national magazine, *Xin zhoukan*,

no. 238 (November 1, 2006), proposed to its readers several articles on the utilization of history that analyzed, among other topics, the craze for historical television shows on television.

8. Yves Chevrier, "De la révolution à l'Etat par le communisme," *Le Débat*, no. 117 (November–December 2001): 109–10.

9. See Jennifer Oldstone-Moore, "The New Life Movement of Nationalist China: Confucianism, State Authority and Moral Formation," PhD thesis, University of Chicago, 2000; Frederic Wakeman Jr., "A Revisionist View of the Nanjing Decade: Confucian Fascism," *China Quarterly*, no. 150 (1997): 394–432; Zheng Yuan, "The Status of Confucianism in Modern Chinese Education, 1901–1949," in *Education, Culture and Identity in Twentieth-Century China*, edited by G. Peterson, R. Haynoe, and Yongling Lu (Hong Kong: Hong Kong University Press, 2001), 193–216. Let me also emphasize that at the very time when the People's Republic of China launched the Cultural Revolution, the Kuomintang authorities replicated by initiating in Taiwan a movement of revival of traditional culture largely based on the active promotion of a Confucian ethos. See Huang Chun-chieh, "Confucianism in Postwar Taiwan," in *Norms and the State in China*, edited by Chun-chieh Huang and Erik Zürcher (Leiden: Brill, 1993), 162–65.

10. Concerning this reactivation of Confucianism in the 1990s, particularly in academic circles, see Umberto Bresciani, *Reinventing Confucianism, The New Confucian Movement* (Taipei: Taipei Ricci Institute, 2001), 419ff.

11. His argument is based on Fang Keli's analysis. The argument strikes us as only moderately convincing because it is hard to see why this research project resulted in so many publications.

12. Lao Siguang, "Shilun dangdai fan rujia sichao," in *Rujia fashan de hongguan toushi*, edited by Tu Weiming (Taipei: Zhengzhong shuju, 1988), 7.

13. This is using a Marxist perspective and methodology.

14. As a group, these intellectuals refer to Confucian thought while maintaining an extremely critical perspective on the history of certain practices, particularly imperial ones. Major thinkers like Xu Fuguan, Mou Zongsan, and Tang Junyi are democrats (i.e., democracy and science for them are universal). Contrary to what certain intellectuals are doing more and more today, they do not advocate a political system directly inspired by Confucianism. From their perspective, Chinese tradition could only contribute to the improvement and correction of a previously established Western-style democracy. During the 1980s, it was above all the moral and metaphysical writings of these thinkers that were studied rather than their political texts. In the case of Mou Zongsan, it was not until 2007 that his landmark political work, *Zhengdao yu zhidao*, was published on the Mainland.

15. See Joël Thoraval, "La 'fièvre culturelle chinoise': De la stratégie à la théorie," *Critique*, August–September 1989, 558–72; and Joël Thoraval, "La tradition rêvée: Réflexions sur l'Elégie du fleuve de Su Xiaokang," *L'infini*, 1990, 146–68.

16. See Song Xianlin, "Reconstructing the Confucian Ideal in 1980s China: The 'Culture Craze' and New Confucianism," in *New Confucianism*, edited by John Makeham (New York: Palgrave Macmillan, 2003), 86–87.

17. Ibid., 87.

18. Werner Meissner, "China's Search for Cultural and National Identity from the Nineteenth Century to the Present," *China Perspectives*, no. 68 (November–December 2006): 48.

19. Jean Philippe Béja, "Naissance d'un national Confucianisme?" *Perspectives chinoises*, no. 2 (November–December 1995): 6–11; John Makeham, *Lost Soul: Confucianism in Contemporary Academic discourses* (Cambridge, Mass.: Harvard University Asia Center, 2008), 55–73, 333–44.

20. Chen Yan explores this question; see Chen Yan, *L'Eveil de la Chine: Les bouleversements intellectuals après Mao (1976–2002)* (Paris: Éditions de l'Aube, 2002). He cites articles in *Renmin ribao* from 1993 and 1995 attesting to the government's support of the resurrection of national studies (p. 304 n. 286). He also explains that other parameters (academic strategizing or, in some cases, genuine conviction) have also contributed to the "craze" for national studies (*guoxue*) (p. 198). Let me emphasize here that it might be necessary to study this so-called craze to assess to what extent it was not largely overplayed by the mass media. See Peng Guoxiang, "Inside the Revival of Confucianism in Mainland China," paper presented at Confucianism for the twenty-first-century conference, University of Hamburg, Hamburg, September 21–23, 2009. Among the landmarks of the 1990s regarding the authorities' interest in Confucianism, one can also point to the creation of the International Confucian Association (*Guoji ruxue lianhehui*) in 1994.

21. This is notably the case with Li Ruihuan, who was the president of the Chinese People's Political Consultative Congress and a longtime member of the Politburo of the Central Committee before retiring during the Sixteenth Party Congress. At the end of 2005, he published a two-volume collection of his major speeches since the 1980s. Li Ruihuan, *Xue zhewue, yong zhexue* [Studying philosophy, using philosophy], 2 vols. (Beijing: Zhongguo renmin daxue chubanshe, 2006). In one speech of 1999 he stated: "More than 2,000 years of history have proven that the teachings of Confucianism can inspire us as means to resolve the problems confronting human societies. We must adopt toward these teachings a scientific method and attitude—we must study them, systematize them, synthesize them, keep what is best and reject the rest" (vol. 2, 681). This was a speech specifically tailored to an assembly of specialists. More interesting is the fact that this speech was included in a widely disseminated anthology published in 2005. Willy Wo-Lap Lam has pointed out that Li Ruihuan, Gu Mu, and the former governor of Guangdong, Ye Xuanping, have all called for a reevaluation of Confucianism. See Willy Wo-Lap Lam, *Chinese Politics in the Hu Jintao Era: New Leaders, New Challenges* (Armonk, N.Y.: M. E. Sharpe, 2007), 280.

22. I refer here to Confucian activists that I met during my fieldwork on Confucian revival in China today. Some of these activists are intellectuals but many are not and work in a variety of different sectors.

23. However, the promotion of traditional culture is very often accompanied with reminders that China must also absorb the excellent aspects of other cultures. There is a clear desire to find the right balance to avoid unleashing cultural nationalism. The idea of promoting traditional culture already appears in some of the documents contained in previous plans, but the importance accorded this notion is, at least on paper, much more pronounced in the eleventh plan which for the first time contains such a large section devoted to culture.

24. This notion was officially adopted by Zhao Ziyang in his report to the National Party Congress in October 1987 and was taken up again by Jiang Zemin in 1997. For Zhao Suisheng, "the primary stage concept conveyed an old mixture of pride and humility: It simultaneously celebrated the historical achievement of China's socialist revolution and recognized the flaws in China's economy and its underdevelopment." Today,

it is the imbalances of development that are often referred to. Suisheng Zhao, *A Nation-State by Construction* (Stanford, Calif.: Stanford University Press, 2004), 225.

25. The aphorism *Min wei bang ben* (民为邦本) first appears in the *Book of Documents* (Shangshu 尚书). It also commonly appears in a condensed version as *minben* (民本). Wang Enbao and Reina F. Titunik have studied its usage (notably by Confucius, Mencius, and Huang Zongxi) and indexed various studies from the past devoted to the concept, including one by Liang Qichao. They have also made the connection between the notion of *minben* and Sun Yatsen's Three Principles of the People (as well as Sun's notion that "what is under heaven is for all," *tian xia wei gong*), which is also used in contemporary political discourse. They explain that concept of minben has become fashionable within circles close to the top leadership since the 1990s. Enbao Wang and Regina F. Titunik, "Democracy in China, The Theory and Practice of Minben," in *China and Democracy*, edited by Suisheng Zhao (New York, Routledge, 2000), 73–83. This essay is another in a long-standing line of works that attempt to find within Chinese tradition concepts that are susceptible to facilitating the combination of that tradition with Western-style democracy.

26. Wen Jiabao, "Guanyu shehuizhuyi chuji jieduan de lishi renwu he wo guo dui wai zhengce de ji ge wenti" [Concerning a few questions relative to the historic duty of the initial phase of socialism and our country's foreign policy], http://news.xinhuanet.com/lianzheng/2007-02/26/content 5775737.htm.

27. The comparison of Confucius with Sun Yat-sen is linked indirectly to a quotation from a text by Mao from 1938: "Zhongguo gongchandang zai minzuzhanzheng zhong diwei" [The role of the Chinese Communist Party in the national war]; see Wang Xingguo, "Chengnian Mao Zedong yu ruxue" [Mao as an adult and Confucianism], http://www.mzdlib.com/xsyj/display.asp?Reco_ID=2992.

28. Wen Jiabao, "Ba mugang toushexiang Zhongguo" [A look at China], http://news.phoenixtv.com/special/wenzong/waijiaofengcai/200703/0301 764 81517.shtml. In the same speech, Wen Jiabao mentions a visit with the philosopher Ji Xianlin. Ji Xianlin, who is a "consultant on artistic matters" (*yishu guwen*, 艺术顾问) for the 2008 Olympic Games in Beijing, has proposed including a special reference to Confucius during the opening ceremonies. See http://news.cctv.com/sports/aoyun/other/20070830/101574.shtml.

29. Speech of February 19, 2005: "Hu Jintao guanyu goujian shehuizhuyi hexie shehui jianghua quanwen" [The complete text of Hu Jintao's speech on the establishment of a harmonious socialist society], http://www.china.com.cn/chinese/news/899546.htm.

30. Arif Dirlik, *The Origins of Chinese Communism* (Oxford: Oxford University Press, 1989), 64. In some ways, the spectre of harmony has always haunted Chinese socialism, even during those periods in which contradiction and class struggle were at the forefront of ideological theorizing.

31. Kaplana Misra, *From Post-Maoism to Post-Marxism: The Erosion of Official Ideology in Deng's China* (New York: Routledge, 1998), 148–50.

32. In one passage, Hu makes an explicit allusion to contradiction as the fundamental motor of social development.

33. By epistemology, we mean the way in which contradiction has been able to be thought of as an instrument for the discovery of the truth. On the philosophical foundations of the idea of contradiction, see Frederic Wakeman Jr., *History and Will: Philosophical Perspectives of Mao Tse-Tung's Thought* (Berkeley: University of California Press, 1973), 295–301.

34. PCD, "Introduction."

35. The notion itself is of Confucian inspiration. It is found in the part of the *Book of Rites* (*Liji* 礼记) concerned with "the evolution of rites" (*Liyun* 礼运), in which three ages are distinguished: the age of Great Unity (*Datong*, 大同), which refers to the idealized golden age of those paragons of virtue, Yao and Shun; that of relative peace (which is how in this context *xiaokang*, 小康, can be translated), an intermediate stage of the enlightened rule of the sovereigns of late antiquity; and finally the troubled age of Confucius when the Sage asserts that the Way has been forgotten. Dividing history into ages will become a recurring practice, one most notably taken up during the Han dynasty by He Xiu (何休) (AD 129–182) and at the end of the nineteenth century by Kang Youwei (康有为) (1858–1927), who reverses the historical logic: the age of *xiaokang* is embodied by the West at the time of Kang's writing whereas the Great Unity becomes a utopian dream of the future, developed in his *Datong shu* (大同书), of a united humanity.

36. In part 6, *Jiaqiang shehuizhuyi sixiang daode jianshe*; literally, it is a question of the "morality of socialist thought."

37. "Gongmin daode jianshe shishi gangyao" [Draft plan for the building up of public morality], http://news.sina.com.cn/c/2001-10-24/385297.html. There is a long historical precedent for discourse on public morality. This is a point made by Pierre-Etienne Will in the introduction to *La Chine et la démocratie*. In line with Philip Kuhn's arguments, Will emphasizes how this conservative approach, rooted in the classical era, continues "to dominate modern Chinese history, including the most recent history" and generate a discourse that is opposed to democracy. Pierre-Etienne Will, "L'histoire n'a pas de fin," in *La Chine et la démocratie*, edited by Mireille Delmas-Marty and Pierre-Etienne Will (Paris: Fayard, 2007), 14–15.

38. This "notion of eight honors and eight disgraces" was the subject of a speech by Hu Jintao in March 2006; see http://news.tom.com/2006-03-08/000N/39000992.html. The slogan is often transformed into an object of ridicule on the part of the general public (I thank Daniel A. Bell for having drawn my attention to this point).

39. Concerning the question of Confucianism and shame, see the chapter by Bryan Van Norden, "The Virtue of Righteousness in Mencius," in *Confucian Ethics: A Comparative Study of Self, Autonomy, and Community*, edited by Kwong-loi Shun and David B. Wong (Cambridge: Cambridge University Press, 2004). In exploring the very "Mencian" virtue of righteousness, which is likely to make itself known in ordinary life as the feeling of shame, Van Norden shows that the question of shame was a more important factor to life in ancient China than in ancient Greece and that this had significant implications later on.

40. It is interesting to observe which terms are used to describe these problems. For example, in PCM (section 1, subsection 2): the cult of money (*baijinzhuyi*, 拜金主义); the cult of pleasure (*xianglezhuyi*, 享乐主义); unbridled individualism (*jiduan gerenzhuyi*, 极端个人主义); the putting of personal interest above all sense of justice (*jian li wang yi*, 见利忘义, with the classic opposition between *li* 利 and *yi* 义); of private interest above the common good (*sun gong fei si*, 损公肥私), directed at problems of corruption and influence peddling; the inability to distinguish between good and evil (*shan*, 善, and *e*, 恶) or truth and falsehood (*shi*, 是, and *fei*, 非—understood as targeting Falungong). Finally, as a kind of echo to the theme of a crisis of confidence (*chengxin weiji*, 诚信危机), there is the question of confidence (in terms of relations between individuals (*xinyong*, 信用). Patriotic and moral indoctrination campaigns responding to different situations are a constant of the Chinese regime. E.g., after the

Tiananmen Square movement, a major patriotic indoctrination campaign (reasserting control over students and workers, *guoqing jiaoyu*, 国情教育), was launched resulting in a directive in 1994. *Guoqing* (国情) corresponds to the situation of the country or its "intrinsic circumstances." For more on this concept of *guoqing*, see Geremie R. Barmé, *In the Red: On Contemporary Chinese Culture* (New York: Columbia University Press), 257, 446–47 nn. 15–18. The ancient term *guoqing* (which appears in the Warring States Records, *Zhanguo ce*) has had a rich and complex history since the nineteenth century. Barmé focuses on all the literature on the subject since the 1980s. The term still frequently appears in speeches today.

41. Zheng, "Status of Confucianism," 193–216. The new regulations put in place in 1912 significantly weakened the place of Confucian moral education in school curricula. However, by 1915, with Yuan Shikai, and even more so with Chiang Kai-shek, Confucianism-inspired moral education came back in force.

42. On this point see Misra, *From Post-Maoism to Post-Marxism*, 204.

43. Li Zehou, *Makesizhuyi zai Zhongguo* [Marxism in China] (Hong Kong: Mingbao chubanshe, 2006), 44. This text is a reprint of a 1987 text, *Shitan Makesizhuyi zai Zhongguo* [An attempt to discuss Marxism in China], supplemented with a long interview from 2006, *Zai tan Makesizhuyi zai Zhongguo* [A second discussion of Marxism in China], and five annexes, including one that is a long interview with Frederic Jameson, who is extremely influential in China, particularly among thinkers in the New Left. Terms like *daode xiuyang* continue to be widely used today. For an example, see PCM, section two, subsection 10.

44. Jin Guantao, "Dangdai Zhongguo Makesizhuyi de rujiahua" [The Confucianization of Marxism in contemporary China], in *Rujia fazhan de hongguan toushi*, edited by Tu Wei-ming (Taipei: Zhengzhong shuju, 1988), 152–83. According to Jin, the sinicization (which in this context means Confucianization) of Marxism began in the 1930s, when a number of important intellectuals joined the Communist Party, motivated primarily by the desire to fight the Japanese and save the country. They did not share the same outlook as the first Marxists who were attracted by historical and dialectical materialisms (pp. 156–57). Though a distinction between the two groups remains valid, the set of reasons that China's first Marxists were attracted to Marxism is probably more complex than what is argued by Jin. E.g., Artif Dirlik has pointed out the important role of anarchism among the intellectuals of the May 4th Movement; Dirlik, *Origins of Chinese Communism*.

45. Jin, "Confucianization of Marxism," 158.

46. This text is better known in English under the title *How to Be a Good Communist*, which does not reflect the traditional idea of *xiuyang* (self-cultivation) found in the Chinese title.

47. Li, *Marxism in China*, 97.

48. Ibid., 105.

49. The campaign against Falungong is a recent example of mass mobilization (press, work units, schools, neighborhood committees, etc.) but it has not taken on the massive proportions of Maoist China.

50. Vivienne Shue, "Legitimacy Crisis in China?" in *State and Society in 21st-Century China: Crisis, Contention and Legitimation*, edited by Peter Gries and Stanley Rosen (New York, Routledge, 2004), 24–49, at 33.

51. Shue, "Legitimacy Crisis?" 33. It is also in this context that the campaign promoting a Conception of scientific development (*kexue fashan guan*) can be also situated,

even though its implications are both much broader and practical as well. On this point, see Heike Holbig, "Wissenschaftliches Entwicklungskonzept, Harmonische Gesellschaft und Eigenstaendige Innovation: Neue parteipolitische Prioritaeten unter Hu Jintao" *China acktuel*, no. 6 (2005): 16. *Kexue fazhan guan* (科学发展观) made its appearance in official discourse in 2004. It was incorporated into the Communist Party's Constitution during its Seventeenth Congress in October 2007.

52. It is interesting to compare the importance of ethical and political education in China with the situation in the West. Using France as an example, C. Lefort, C. Castoriadis, and M. Gauchet have all written of the decline of such a dimension to education. See Sébastien Billioud, "De l'art de dissiper les nuages: Réflexions à partir de la théorie politique de Thomas Metzger," *Etudes Chinoises* 26 (2007): 191–234.

53. Thomas Metzger, *A Cloud across the Pacific: Essays on the Clash between Chinese and Western Political Theories Today* (Hong Kong: Chinese University Press, 2005).

54. Metzger's thesis is supported by Kalpana Misra, who points to the existence of a faith in a "capitalist telos," which has replaced the socialist one among the partisans of neoauthoritarianism or neoconservatism.

55. For a critical analysis of Metzger's work, see Billioud, "De l'art de dissiper les nuages." This article focuses on the problems and limits of the notion of "epistemological optimism," with a particular interest in the questions of elitism and paideia.

56. Yves Chevrier, "De la révolution," 111. Moreover, Chevrier emphasises that "the rule of virtue" (*yi de zhi guo*, 以德治国) represents "a borrowing from the past completely devoid of any meaning associated with the past."

57. As classical literature and Confucian references increasingly become key elements of school curricula, it will be interesting to determine to what extent there is a real evolution in the system of values promoted. At present, it is still too early to discern any significant change.

58. During the Republican Era, courses in which classical literature was studied (*dujing*, 读经) were already distinct from those devoted to moral perfection (*xiushen*, 修身). Gan Chunsong, *Zhiduhua rujia ji qi jieti* [Institutionalized Confucianism and its dismantlement] (Beijing, Zhongguo remin daxue chubanshe, 2003), 220–42.

59. This movement might currently involve tens of millions of children. See Ji Zhe, "Traditional Education in China: Conservative and/or Liberal?" *Chinese Cross Currents* 2, no. 3 (2005): 32–41.

60. Perhaps the most spectacular example of this craze is the great success of a television show about the Analects of Confucius, which features the very charismatic Yu Dan and her lively and topical interpretations of the sayings of the great sage. A book based on the show has also been a big hit, with almost 4 million copies sold. Yu Dan has also interpreted texts by Zhuangzi.

61. Two phenomena attest to this fact. On the one hand, a growing number of entrepreneurs are enrolling in special programmes offered by universities throughout the country that feature instruction on aspects of classical culture; on the other hand, the ideal-type of "the Confucian entrepreneur" (*rushang*, 儒商), who simultaneously strives for moral cultivation and to fulfill his responsibility to society (and his employees), has emerged.

62. The fourth-quarter 2007 issue of *China Perspectives* considers the rapid growth of a movement aiming to rejuvenate traditional education and the study of the classics.

63. Eric Hobsbawm and Terence Ranger, eds., *The Invention of Tradition* (Cambridge: Cambridge University Press, 2003), 6.

64. See, e.g., a recent issue of a major weekly (*Liaowang dongfang zhoukan*, owned by the Xinhua News Agency) dedicated a series of articles and a cover to the rites associated with and the ceremonies devoted to the Yellow Emperor, "Jitan zhi shang, jizu xianxiang de zhengzhi jingjixue" [On sacrificial space, the political economy of the phenomenon of the major rites of ancestor cults], *Liaowang dongfang zhoukan*, June 21, 2007, 10–23. The articles contain several examples of ceremonies, while paying a special attention to the cult of the Yellow Emperor. Along with their political dimension, the magazine highlights the significant economic and touristic dimensions of the ceremonies.

65. Ceremonies in honor of Yu the Great have been held in Shaoxing, in Zhejiang Province, since 1995. In 2007 the ceremonies took place on April 27 and were jointly sponsored by the Zhejiang Provincial Ministry of Culture and the Ministry of Culture in Beijing, thus conferring a national character (*guojia ji*, 国家祭) on the celebration. see http://zjnews.zjol.com.cn/05zjnews/system/2007/04/10/008323624.shtml. I am not able to comment further on the meaning of such a "national character."

66. Térence Billeter, "Chinese Nationalism Falls Back on Legendary Ancestor," *China Perspectives*, no. 18 (July–August 1998): 44. See also the doctoral thesis that Billeter wrote on the subject at the Institut d'Etudes Politiques de Paris, whicht has been published: Térence Billeter, *L'Empereur jaune. Une tradition politique chinoise* (Paris: Les Indes savantes, 2007). Also see the speech by Li Ruihuan, "Zhengxiu baohu hao Huangdi ling" [A call for the restoration and preservation of Huangdi's tomb], in *Xue zhexue, yong zhexue*, 689.

67. The book by Térence Billeter is reviewed in the fourth-quarter 2007 issue of *China Perspectives*. This remarkable work constitutes an important study of the relationship between power and the past. Its main limitation (actually acknowledged by the author himself) is nevertheless to focus almost exclusively on a top-down analysis. I believe that ascribing totally the initiative to power (and then playing down the importance of society) makes it difficult to understand what is currently happening around the issue of traditional culture in China. The reappropriation of "fragments" of the past/ traditional culture, both by the people at a grassroots level and by the intellectuals, needs to be taken into account in order to understand the dynamic interaction between the authorities and a society now enjoying some large degree of autonomy (even though this autonomy remains limited and controlled).

68. At present, the cult devoted to Confucius does not have official status. As argued below, the direct relationship between the regime and the figure of Confucius is maybe still too sensitive for such an embrace to occur. For background on the cult of Confucius, see Thomas A. Wilson, ed., *On Sacred Grounds: Culture, Society, Politics and the Formation of the Cult of Confucius* (Cambridge, Mass.: Harvard University Asia Center, 2002). For a detailed analysis of the current cult of Confucius, see Billioud and Thoraval, "*Lijiao*: The Reinvention of Confucian Ceremonies."

69. E.g., I could observe during a field research that the city of Bangbu in Anhui Province has completed a major urban development and renewal project in the city center, remodeling the vast central park while erecting a group of statues representing the major ancestors of Chinese civilization, including Yu the Great.

70. The extent of this phenomenon became apparent during fieldwork conducted in Bangbu in Anhui Province and Qufu in Shandong Province. The urban renewal project in Bangbu (see n. 69 above) was driven by a combination of economic, touristic, cultural, and political factors.

71. See Chevrier, "De la revolution," 109.

72. The actual extent of this phenomenon remains difficult to evaluate, but evidence suggests that it is significant.

73. See, e.g., Zhonggong zhongyang dangxiao, the site of the Central Party School, www.ccps.gov.cn, or Xuexi shibao, www.studytimes.com.cn. Given the quantity of information, we looked at several Web sites using the following keywords: *guoxue, ruxue, rujia, rujiao, chuantong wenhua*, etc.

74. See Zhongyang dangxiao yanjiusheng zhexue luntan shou jiang guoxue, http://www.ccsp.gov.cn/xinwen.jsp?daohang_name=%BD%FC%.

75. Xu Zhuxin, "Lingdao ganbu ye yao xue yidian chuantong wenhua" [Leaders and cadres must also study a little classical culture], on the Xuexi shibao Web site, http://www.china.com.cn/xxsb/txt/2006-06/20/content_6249063.html.

76. Wang Jie, "Dongxiao yao zhongshi dui youxiu chuantong wenhua de xuanchuan he hongyang shibao," on the Xuexi shibao Web site, http://www.china.com.cn/xxsb/txt/2006-10/24/cotent_7271511.html.

77. Wang, "Dangxiao yao zhongshi dui youxiu chuantong wenhua de xuanchuan he hongyang." The remarks about the courses within the party school result from interviews with senior professors at this institution. In 2007, the course titled "The Fundamental Spirit of Traditional Chinese philosophy" was ranked by students the best course of the year. A series of courses on traditional culture (*chuantong wenhua xilie*) is now taught at the party school. Even though it is not limited to Confucianism, the latter nevertheless has a pivotal importance in the curriculum.

78. Numerous semiofficial theoretical works, written by teams of researchers working for major state organs, have recently been published. One book worth citing has been written by a team of the Academy of Social Sciences in Shanghai: Wang Ronghua and Tong Shijun, eds., *Duoxueke shiye zhong de hexie shehui* [The Harmonious Society from a Multidisciplinary Perspective] (Shanghai: Xuelin chubanshe, 2006). In this work, it is affirmed that a new inventory of Confucianism needs to be taken. Certain aspects judged positive—ideals (great unity, *Datong*, 大同) and values—are deemed useful, while others are designated as meriting rejection (particularly the conception of interpersonal relations illustrated by the *san gang*, 三纲) (pp. 326–29, 402). Certain other works travel down the path of positive evaluation far less. See, e.g., Leng Rong and Xia Chuntao, eds., *Kexue fazhan guan yu goujian shehuizhuyi hexie shehui* [The concept of scientific development and the construction of a harmonious socialist society] (Beijing: Shehui kexue wenxuan chubanshe, 2007). This book, published by the Center for Studies of Deng Xiaoping Theory and "Three Represents" Thought of the Chinese Academy of Social Sciences, upholds the standard line of the Marxist vulgate, while dwelling on the question of xiuyang (self-cultivation, 208ff), socialist morality, and the "theory of honors and shames" (*rongruguan*, 荣辱观) (examined in terms of its relation to scientific development, 225ff). For a more thorough discussion on the idea of "critical inheritance" of the cultural tradition / Confucianism, see Makeham, *Lost Soul*, 234–56.

79. These examples were chosen because they are fairly representative of what can be found on official Web sites.

80. Chen Ming, one of the representatives of the so-called *Dalu xinrujia* (continental neo-Confucianism) and an advocate of cultural conservatism explains that one might have the feeling that there is some sort of tacit understanding between Confucian intellectuals and the authorities. Nevertheless, direct relations between the two are in fact

nonexistent. Gan Chunsong and Chen Ming, "Xinrujia duihua: Ziyouzhuyi yu xinzuopai dou you duanban," *Nandou zhoukan*, August 10, 2007, http://hi.baidu.com/acd5968/blog/item/254cbe6da73afcf84216940c.html.

81. Gan Yang, "Zhongguo daolu, sanshi nian yu liushi nian," http://www.wyzxwyzx.com/Article/Class17/200704/17083.html. The article also appeared in *Dushu*, no. 6 (June 2007): 3–13.

82. This text by Gan Yang has provoked both considerable debate and severe criticism. See Yi Quan, "Xin gaige gongshi bu neng zou rujia shehuizhuyi daolu" [The new reform consensus can not lead to Confucian socialism], *Gaige neican*, no. 16 (2006): 43–45; and Yang Jisheng, "Xiandai minzhu zhidu: Yi ge bu neng bei paichu de gaige gongshi [The contemporary democratic system: A consensus on reform which cannot be put aside], *Gaige neican*, no. 16 (2006): 45. These two authors denounce Gan Yang's idealized vision of Maoism and his notion that the Cultural Revolution was an example of "creative destruction" (*chuangzaoxing pohuai* 创造性破坏). Yi Quan asserts that Confucianism has nothing to do with socialism and likens Gan Yang's proposals to Chang Kai-shek's New Life Movement (*Xin shenghuo yundong*, 新生活运动), an effort to unite Confucian values with the Three Principles of the People. Yang Jisheng argues that the kind of social relations promoted by Confucianism is incompatible with the very idea of a republic.

83. In a recent dialogue, two specialists of Confucianism, Gan Chunsong and Chen Ming, express very similar views. Indeed, they depict an important switch in the discourses of both the Chinese liberals and the New Left. They notice that the New Left increasingly refers to "Chinese tradition" in its thinking about modernity ("Chen Ming, Gan Chunsong duihua lu, Zhujian qie ru shenghuo de ruxue").

84. According to Jiang Qing, the *tongruyuan* (通儒院) representatives, those embodying Confucian wisdom, would be recruited by examination or by recommendation, whereas the *guojiyuan* (国体院) representatives (history and culture) would be, e.g., descendants of Confucius. Finally, the *shuminyuan* (庶民院) representatives, representing the people, would be elected as in a Western-style democracy. Jiang Qing, *Shengming xinyang yu wangdao zhengzhi* (Taipei: Yangzhengtang wenhua shiye gufen youxian gongsi, 2004). However, one needs to emphasize that these ideas remain highly sensitive and do not appear in Jiang Qing's most famous work published in the People's Republic of China: *Zhengzhi ruxue: Dangdai ruxue de zhuanxiang, tezhe yu fazhan* [Political Confucianism: Development, characteristics, and orientations of contemporary Confucianism] (Beijing: Sanlian shudian, 2003). For a recent analysis of Jiang Qing's work, see Daniel A. Bell, *China's New Confucianism* (Princeton, N.J.: Princeton University Press, 2008), 174–91.

85. Kang Xiaoguang, *Renzheng: Zhongguo zhengzhi fazhan de di san jiao daolu* [The sense of humanity as a basis for politics: The third way of Chinese political development] (Singapore: Global Publishing, 2005). The positions of Jiang Qing and Kang Xiaoguang cannot be completely assimilated with those of the "Confucian camp." The Confucian "liberals" (often inspired by the movement referred to as "contemporary Confucianism") reject them, along with certain specialists of Confucianism more influenced by Marxism. Thus, the propagation of an institutional Confucianism is vigorously opposed by Fang Keli, who in the 1980s was commissioned by the government to conduct the first research on contemporary Confucianism, which he concluded was an anti-Marxist offensive attempting to Confucianize the Communist Party or China. See *Bulletin of the International Confucian League*, March 30, 2007, in which there is

a letter by Fang Keli. A research group spearheaded by Fang has just written a combative book denouncing cultural conservatives like Kang Xiaoguang, Jiang Qing, Shen Hong, and Chen Ming. They openly deride the project to "Confucianize China" (ruhua Zhongguo): Zhang Shibao, ed., *Dalu sinrujia pinglun* [Critical analysis of contemporary Mainland China] (Beijing: Xianzhuang shuju, 2007).

86. Qin Hui, *Chuantong shi lun* [Ten essays on tradition] (Shanghai: Fudan daxue chubanshe, 2003), 167. Qin Hui is not critical of Confucianism as a system of thought but condemns it as a set of political practices. As an illustration of the Confucian influence on liberal thinking in Mainland China, I can point to the presence of some of their representatives, like Liu Juning, at the tenth anniversary celebration of the founding of the journal *Yuan Dao*, hosted by Chen Ming, a leading cultural conservative. Joël Thoraval provided this information.

87. On the situation of Confucianism in intellectual discourses in the 2000s, see Sébastien Billioud and Joël Thoraval, eds., *Perspectives on the Political in China Today*, special issue of *Extrême-Orient Extrême-Occident* 31 (Presses Universitaires de Vincennes, 2009). Three remarks: (1) As emphasized above, Confucianism was an object of study during precedent periods. But, in my opinion, there is a definite shift at work. It has taken on a much greater importance than it previously enjoyed. The amount of controversy it generates is testimony to this new standing; in particular, I am thinking of a debate concerning the work of a Confucian specialist, Li Ling, who has been highly critical of rejuvenated Confucianism, or of another very recent debate, which has spilled a lot of ink, on the need for a new renaissance (*wenyifuxing*, 文艺复兴) or moral reconstruction (*daode jianshe*, 道德建设). (2) Confucianism, throughout Chinese history, has consisted of a variety of elements (philosophy, practices, crystallization of habits and modes of thought) and has included, to limit ourselves to intellectual production, a wide range of authors, to the point that it is not at all surprising that it has engendered a multiplicity of contemporary reappropriations. Some believe that it is perfectly compatible with liberal democracy (notably the thesis of "contemporary neo-Confucians," often inspired by Song and Ming Confucianism); others with an "illiberal" democracy (e.g., Jiang Qing and Kang Xiaoguang); others stitch it together with American pragmatism (Roger T. Ames), others with communitarianism (Daniel A. Bell), while a yet another tradition—which appropriates some of the arguments of the others—draws a comparison with socialism (Gan Yang is an example but another we could cite is Li Zehou). The comparison made between noncommunist socialism and Confucianism could also prove to be very fruitful at a time when, on the one hand, tradition has taken on a new attraction, and, on the other, there is a growing interest in European experiments with social democracy, especially in Sweden (see the recent debate around Xie Tao, a Chinese Communist Party veteran whose call for the institution of social democracy in the review *Yanhuang Chunqiu* generated significant debate and a public counterattack by conservatives). During the Republican Era, there was a faction of socialist Confucians that included Zhang Junmai and his project for a "third way." See Roger B. Jeans Jr., *Democracy and Socialism in Republican China: The Politics of Zhang Junmai (Carsun Chang), 1906–1941* (Lanham, Md.: Rowman & Littlefield, 1997). (3) The political world has also engaged in its own diverse appropriation of Confucianism. Confucianism has not solely served as a means to justify authoritarianism. Thus both Kim Dae-jung in South Korea and Lee Teng-hui in Taiwan have judged Confucianism to be compatible with liberal democracy. It is another element to take into account when considering the relationship between politics and culture in China. I thank Jean-Pierre

Cabestan for having drawn my attention to this point. The renewed interest in Confucianism is ripe with tensions.

88. Here we are only interested in the nondirectly religious dimensions of classical culture.

89. For a more extensive analysis of this evolution of the regime, see the article by Chevrier, "De la revolution," 92–113.

90. François Hartog, *Régimes d'historicité: Présentisme et experiences du temps* (Paris: Éditions du Seuil, 2003).

91. Ibid., 28. A historicity regime, Hartog writes, "is simply the expression of a dominant order of time. Weaving together different regimes of temporality, it is, in the end, a way of translating and ordering experiences of time—manners of articulating the past, present and future—and giving them meaning." He goes on to add a few pages later that "contested as soon as it is established, in fact, never fully established, . . . a historicity regimen settles into place slowly and lasts a long time." He specifies that there are periods of overlap between different regimes (pp 119–19).

92. Ibid., 107.

93. Ibid., 200. Hartog provides an illuminating example of the transition from the former historicity regime (dominated by the future) and the current one (under the yoke of the present) through urban planning in Paris. In 1971, the Baltard Pavilions at Les Halles were razed. A few years later (and Hartog cites the preservation of the Orsay train station as an analogy), such destruction would have been impossible, and Les Halles would have been preserved as part of the heritage of the nineteenth century."

94. For a perspective on the 1980s and 1990s, see the interview with Joël Thoraval in "Conscience historique et imaginaire social, le débat intellectuel des décennies 1980 et 1990," *Esprit*, February 2004, 171–83. Thoraval shows how the perspective on the imperial heritage evolved during the 1990s.

95. This is not to say that it leaves the museum. On the contrary, it will be interesting to see in the years to come how the return of tradition will translate itself into heritage, commemorations, and expositions of all sorts. The notion of the "museumification" of Confucianism has been coined by Joseph Levenson. In 1958, in a well-known manifesto, four major intellectuals—Mou Zongsan, Tang Junyi, Zhang Junmai, and Xu Fuguan—who were all very isolated at the time, denounced such a vision of a fossilized Chinese culture.

96. As mentioned above, there remain major zones of collective and highly problematic amnesia. However, the phenomenon under way has little to do with historical objectivity but mainly consists in a "production of past" deemed meaningful for the present and the future.

Chapter 10

Conclusion: World Harmony or Harmonizing the World?

William A. Callahan

The chapters in this book demonstrate the richness of the discussion of Chinese philosophy and international theory in China. They show how Chinese thought presents us with a diversity of ideas, concepts, and norms. The critical engagement found in these chapters shows how seriously scholars are taking the new influence of Chinese culture and foreign policy.

Although each chapter takes a unique approach to explaining Chinese theory and foreign policy, a number of shared themes emerge: exceptionalism/syncretism, hierarchy/equality, Westphalian system/Chinese School of international relations (IR) theory, perfect world/contingent worlds, epistemological optimism/epistemological skepticism, theory/policy, and great harmony/harmony-with-difference. In this conclusion, I examine these themes first as a way of summarizing the book's collective analysis, and second because they can serve as a lens for understanding the emerging role of Chinese-style global norms, specifically Beijing's new foreign policy of building a harmonious world.

Because much discussion of Chinese norms is Sinocentric, this conclusion seeks to decenter analysis in style as well as content. It offers a series of interrelated commentaries that do not necessary follow a single narrative strand. Although this is a strange way to write a conclusion in English, it is perhaps appropriate because it appeals to the decentered rhetorical style of classical Chinese thought. Likewise, the goal here is not to draw hard-and-fast conclusions that would prove or disprove the "Chinese School of IR theory"; rather than provide final answers, the aim is to raise a new set of questions about China's soft power, norms, and foreign policy.

Exceptionalism/Syncretism

Although historians have been engaging in a nuanced critical analysis of China's imperial and international history,[1] many IR scholars still take for granted that China's traditional world order was a peaceful hierarchical system that linked the imperial center with tributary states. This singular view of the Chinese world order tends to limit the vibrant possibilities of Chinese thought to an essentialized expression of "the Chinese Perspective."

This argument is part of a Chinese exceptionalism, which sees China's ethical system as the solution to the problems of the current international system. According to many scholars, imperial China's Tianxia system of governance worked very well—until it was challenged by Western imperialism. Thus, in modern times, China was forced to build a nation-state to defend itself from these foreign challenges. Though China had to submit to the violent world order of nation-states when it was weak in the nineteenth century, Zhao Tingyang and Yan Xuetong are among the many Chinese intellectuals who think that Beijing should now use its current strength to reassert China's traditional moral world order, for the benefit of the world and Zhao and Yan convey these views in, respectively, chapters 2 and 4.

This approach to China's role in the world parallels arguments for "American exceptionalism";[2] but rather than criticizing the "exceptionalism" part of this formula, such texts seek to replace a moralized America with a morally superior China.[3] As Barabantseva shows in chapter 8, the spread of Confucian Institutes around the world has shown that China has its own missionary urge. Sinocentrism likewise replaces Eurocentrism because the central teleological narrative is not seen as problematic; rather than seeking to decenter analysis, the goal is to recenter it as part of the rejuvenation of the Chinese nation.

But this book also shows how other Chinese intellectuals are expanding beyond this "Confucian pacifist" view of China's cultural heritage. Thus, in chapter 3 Qin Yaqing is interested in the tributary system, but it only constitutes one source of his Chinese School of IR theory. He argues that one also needs to include theories from China's modern experience of revolution and reform.

Sinocentric exceptionalism relies on Chinese tradition being unique, separate, and different from other traditions. Yet Christopher R. Hughes shows in chapter 6 how Chinese thought is most successful when it abandons the search for cultural purity to syncretically combine various contradictory discourses—East and West, tradition and modern, and, most recently, "scientific development" and "harmonious society / harmonious world." The result of this synthesis is not the ideals of Confucian universalism but the popular politics of Chinese nationalism. In chapter 7, David Kerr likewise argues how Chinese politics involves a dynamic that joins similarities and differences in a contingent unity. This resonates with Qin's method for combining tradition/modernity and reform/revolution in his Chinese-style IR theory. The diversity of views presented here as "Chinese tradition" thus underlines one of Qin's main points: that China's relation with the world is not so much a security dilemma as an "identity dilemma." Barabantseva pushes the identity dilemma in new directions by arguing that we need to look beyond the hegemonic Tianxia/Westphalia debate to appreciate other Chinese expressions of "the world."

Hierarchy/Equality

A hierarchy/equality dynamic runs parallel to the exceptionalism/syncretism theme. Zhao and Yan explore the possibilities of using Chinese thought to institute a hierarchical world order, whereas Qin Yaqing and William A. Callahan (in chapter 5) wonder how Chinese tradition could promote a more egalitarian international society. Though most IR studies of "empire" frame it as a problem, Zhao and Yan see a *Chinese* empire as the solution to the world's global governance ills. As we have seen, Zhao seeks to discard Roman, British, and American empires as a way of promoting Tianxia as the "acceptable empire" that is "reasonable and commendable." Yan pursues a similar analytical strategy when he argues that the Chinese world order is superior because it involves "voluntary submission" to an international power that "owns the world" (*you* Tianxia, 有天下). This is part of the "the rejuvenation of China," where the goal, according to Yan, is to "restore China's power status to the prosperity enjoyed during the prime of the Han, Tang, and early Qing dynasties," when it was at the center of a hierarchical world order.[4] Though Yan concentrates on the "voluntariness" of submission in this hierarchy, it seems odd that one would design a utopia around the negative practice of "submission" rather than around "equality," "emancipation," or other positive values.

Qin is confident that a close study of concepts like Tianxia can separate negative hierarchical aspects from positive ideas that could promote a more egalitarian world order. Callahan, conversely, wonders if it is possible to separate the positive from the negative because they are intertwined in the Tianxia system's holistic world order. He thus concludes that discussions of Chinese world order present a cautionary tale for critical IR theorists: In their search for diversity beyond Euro-America, they often recycle updated versions of empire for the twenty-first century. More to the point, Hughes argues that in the early twentieth century, syncretic Confucianism shifted from being a universal creed of imperial order to become a mode of Chinese national identity that *resisted* the hierarchy of imperialism.

Westphalian World System / Chinese School of IR Theory

A grand distinction between the current Westphalian world system and the Chinese School of IR theory is another theme that runs throughout the book. In chapter 2, Zhao argues that the Westphalian world system is a failure. Qin very directly argues that a Chinese School of IR theory is the best possible solution to the world's problems.[5] In some ways, this call for a Chinese School is an outgrowth from China's domestic political trends. To explain away the contradictions of a socialist market economy, Deng Xiaoping declared that the goal of reform was to "build socialism with Chinese characteristics."[6] Since then, scholars in many disciplines, including international studies, have responded to the call for "having Chinese characteristics" (*you Zhongguo tese*, 有中国特色) in their research.[7]

There is a feeling among many in China, and some the West, that Chinese IR theory is a natural extension of Beijing's growing global political influence. In other words, to be a great power, a state must have its own theory for world order.[8] According to this view, because the United States promotes ideas like "democratic peace" and the United Kingdom talks about "international society," it is only natural for China to promote ideas like "Tianxia" and "harmonious world" as its contribution to world civilization and global order.[9] The soft power of IR theory is thus seen as an outgrowth of hard power; China needs to cash in its new economic power for enduring political, cultural, and normative power.

Even so, Yan has questioned the value of creating a Chinese School of IR theory, arguing that one cannot name a theory before it exists. But his current project actually presents an alternative vision of Chinese-style IR theory.[10] He is a prominent public intellectual in China who is well known for his Realist understanding of national security and international politics. But in the mid-1990s, he questioned the Realist dismissal of cultural matters as epiphenomenal to refigure culture (including traditional culture) as an important factor in China's national interest.[11] Since 2005, he has encouraged many scholars to examine classical Chinese texts and to develop alternative approaches to international studies.

Building a Chinese School of IR theory involves more than reviving and reinterpreting ancient concepts. As Qin and Yan show, it also involves building methodology and building institutions. In addition to their own research, they have been laying the foundation for a new school of IR in China. Rather than just combing the classics for evocative passages, they are taking a more structural view of building Chinese-style IR theory that includes defining the proper methodology, publishing collections of primary sources, and organizing national conferences for networking.[12] Most important, Yan is using the resources of Tsinghua's Institute for International Studies to train PhD students, hire new staff, and edit national and international journals to produce and distribute the results of this research project in both Chinese and English.[13] It is likely that Yan's project, which is not yet called the Chinese School, will have an enduring impact on scholarship in China and abroad.

Thus far, the Chinese School of IR is primarily used to criticize the Westphalia system, Eurocentrism, and American foreign policy, rather than offer a critical view of Chinese politics and policy.[14] For example, some celebrate how Chinese bloggers used Mencius to criticize the U.S.-UK invasion of Iraq in 2003 as a sign of the growing power of Confucianism in Chinese society.[15] But in China, being against the Iraq war was not a controversial position, and thus does not provide a hard case for assessing the global utility of Chinese ideals and norms. Until the Chinese School can critically discuss China's own policies, it will be hard to judge its utility—and its limits.

Perfect World / Contingent Worlds

People generally analyze Chinese IR theory as part of two quite different research agendas. One group sees Chinese philosophy as an alternative to the neoliberal Western world order. Chinese and Western writers who promote this research agenda thus look to tradition for cultural resources to solve the world's problems in a new and different way. The goal is to find a complete system, a silver bullet, that can solve all the world's problems once and for all. We can see this in Zhao and Qin's writing most clearly.

But this utopianism is a common theme among Chinese intellectuals who feel that it is their duty to search for the "perfect world."[16]

Other scholars treat Chinese utopia less as an exceptional model of a perfect world that is above politics and more as a different system of thought that has its own power dynamics. Rather than treating Chinese IR theory as a ready-made alternative, many of the book's chapters critically examine Chinese norms as new sites of political contention that empower and disempower different communities. This critical engagement shows how scholars are taking the Chinese theory very seriously as one of the many ways of thinking about global politics and world order.

David Kerr, Elena Barabantseva, and Sébastien Billioud develop this theme by considering the temporal dimension of utopia and world politics (in chapters 7, 8, and 9, respectively). The perfect world proposed by many scholars suggests that we are on a linear historical trajectory that is heading toward one unified future, with the goal being, as the 2008 Olympics slogan promised, "One World, One Dream" (see figure 10.1). Kerr and Barabantseva take a critical view of this organic timeless world order to see how we can shift from one future to the many futures that develop in contingent plural worlds. Billioud concludes that we are now in a new era where

Figure 10.1. Olympic Slogan Sign at Beijing's Airport

the past is again seen as meaningful by different groups in China, which are producing and reinventing Chinese tradition according to their various current needs. Barabantseva likewise suggests that China's debates over memory and identity are not just about the past or future; they are actually creating a pluralistic present.

Epistemological Optimism/Skepticism

The epistemologically optimistic and skeptical approaches to Chinese thought of course reflect different theories of knowledge. In their analyses of Chinese intellectual discourse, Thomas Metzger and Gloria Davies both note its strong normative character. "China" is seen as a "problem" that needs to be solved: "Worrying about the problems that prevent China from attaining perfection, not only as a nation but also as an enduring civilization, is the kind of patriotic sentiment that one commonly encounters in the essays of Chinese intellectuals."[17] This "patriotic worrying" (*youhuan*, 忧患) gives intellectuals the moral obligation to frame problems and solutions in terms of China's national and civilizational perfection. Debates about Chinese culture and politics thus characteristically discuss what China can and should be rather than what it is; a recent Chinese PhD dissertation, for example, confidently declares that "history will show that the notion of a 'harmonious world' is a rational banner guiding human civilization in the twenty-first century" because there will be "inevitable progress from ideal to real."[18]

Although different thinkers take different approaches, they are all united in the project of perfecting China. This quest entails what Metzger calls an "epistemological optimism," which sees the world in terms of grand systems, like classes or civilizations, that evolve according to internal structures with inherent laws. If worrying intellectuals can find the correct theory and method for explaining the world's logic of development, then all of China's problems will be solved once and for all.[19] Thus critical inquiry in China is both normative and positivistic, with a "linguistic certitude" that the truth is out there. The moral obligation of intellectuals is to discover this truth, save China from its imperfections, and thus reestablish China as the moral center of the world. Davies points out that patriotic worrying's sharp focus on China as the problem means that intellectuals rarely frame their considerations in terms of wider issues of humanity.[20]

This analysis of China's domestic intellectual discourse can help us better understand the normative discourse of Chinese-style IR theory. But this book's chapters show how the horizons of patriotic worrying are expanding: The perfection of China is now closely linked to the perfection of the world. Qin, for example, employs this epistemological optimism to argue that a Chinese School of IR theory is not only necessary but also "inevitable."

Likewise, the sharp focus on methodology in discussions of Chinese IR theory reflects this epistemological optimism. Song Xinning, one of the pioneers of Chinese-style IR theory, concludes that Chinese scholars need to work harder on methodological issues.[21] Zhao offers Tianxia not just as the model for the superior world order but also as a method for thinking about global problems; to prove this thesis, he often appeals to game theory. Qin and Yan spend much effort discussing the proper scientific method for building theory and analyzing texts. A Chinese PhD student likewise describes the methodological value of harmonious world: "The concept of harmonious world provides an excellent world view and methodology for human beings to realize ultimately the magnificent ideal of everlasting peace and mutual prosperity."[22] This is not simply a traditional Chinese research style that is completely different from the West; rather, it combines the patriotic worrying of Confucian scholar-officials with the high-modernist positivism that China's social scientists learned from their training in Marxian scientific socialism.

Although this Chinese discourse employs a positivistic social science methodology that seeks universal truth, many of this book's chapters employ a more skeptical epistemology that questions such foundationalist arguments. Rather than searching for laws of history, many chapters examine the contingencies of Chinese history, culture, and philosophy, as well as the politics of the party-state. Thus, while Zhao, Qin, and Yan consider how China can help the world, Callahan, Hughes, Kerr, Barabantseva, and Billioud focus more on what Chinese articulations of "tradition" and "the world" can tell us about identity politics in the People's Republic of China (PRC).

Theory/Policy

There is a strong interplay between theory and policy in China, which can help us expand from thinking about the chapters in this book to consider the theoretical aspects of Chinese foreign policy. Alongside the call for Chinese-style IR theory from scholars, China's leaders have been employing similar discursive strategies to frame foreign policy in terms of the "goal of building a harmonious world of sustained peace and common prosperity." This goal was initially set by Hu Jintao at his UN speech in 2005, and then was elaborated on in the "China's Peaceful Development Road" white paper (2005). A harmonious world will be built, according to the white paper, through "mutual dialogues, exchanges, and cooperation" that lead to "mutual benefit and common development." It explains that "upholding tolerance and opening to achieve dialogue among civilizations" is necessary because the "diversity of civilizations is a basic feature of human society, and an important driving force for the progress of mankind." China will lead this dialogue because "opening, tolerance, and all-embracing are important features of Chinese civilization." The goal is to build a harmonious world that is peaceful, equal, and fair with common development and common security shared by all.[23]

China's foreign policy, according to the white paper, is more than simply policy. It is also an example of epistemological optimism that presents a new way of thinking about the world: "Peace, opening-up, cooperation, harmony and win-win are our policy, our idea, our principle and our pursuit." Hence, scholars are increasingly influential in Beijing's system for making foreign policy,[24] and the state is also quite interested in using philosophical concepts like harmony to build world order.

The use of harmony to explain contemporary issues actually preceded Hu Jintao's call to build a harmonious society and harmonious world. Under Jiang Zemin's leadership, the discussion of harmony and policy mushroomed in the fields of sociology, politics, cross-Strait relations, and IR, as well as in Jiang Zemin's speeches and the 1998 "National Defense White Paper."[25]

Chinese scholars have now become quite interested in developing the idea of harmonious world. Thus, the China Knowledge Resource Integrated Database shows that before Hu promulgated the policy in 2005, there were only three articles that discussed "harmonious world"—none of which was about international relations. But in the four years following Hu's announcement of this foreign policy narrative (2005–9), more than 750 articles on harmonious world were published, and at least five PhDs were granted on the subject. In addition to a high quantity of publications, the site of this research activity in the Chinese Communist Party's (CCP's) Central Party School and university party history departments underlines that the party-state thinks harmonious world is an important topic.[26]

The authors of this book's chapters also have made important contributions to this mix of theory and policy. Yan used the harmonious world concept to analyze China's foreign affairs in 2006; Qin's academic articles on harmonious world have been condensed for a popular audience; and Zhao wrote an editorial for the top international studies journal, *World Economics and Politics*, exploring the philosophical implications of Beijing's harmonious world policy.[27]

Great Harmony / Harmony-with-Difference

The debates over world order and China's future go far beyond the intellectual debates discussed in this book. The term "harmony" (*hexie*, 和谐) is quite common in China's popular discourse; "Building a Harmonious Neighborhood/City/Society/World" is a popular slogan on many billboards and notice boards in the PRC. The international Olympic Torch Relay was called the "Journey of Harmony," China's national railroad now has a special class of "Harmonious Trains" (*hexie hao*) for fast intercity travel, and the Shanghai World Expo's China Pavilion is peppered with references to harmony.

Scholars and officials likewise use a set of classical terms—Tianxia (天下, All-under-Heaven), *he* (和, harmony), *Datong* (大同, great harmony), and *he er butong* (和而不同, harmony-with-difference)—to assert a commonsense notion of harmony that is clear to all.[28] Yet a closer examination reveals that what we now call "harmony" can have two quite different meanings.[29]

Great harmony describes an overarching unity; the *"tong"* in *Datong* also means sameness. This sameness is seen as harmonious because it describes a universal utopia. The main source of the ideal of great harmony is a famous passage from the *Book of Rites* (*Liji*, 礼记):

> When the Great Way prevails, the world will belong to all [*tianxia wei gong*, 天下为公]. They chose people of talent and ability whose words were sincere, and they cultivated harmony. Thus people did not only love their own parents, not only nurture their own children. . . . In this way selfish schemes did not arise. Robbers, thieves, rebels, and traitors had no place, and thus outer doors were not closed. This is called the Great Harmony [*Datong*].[30]

This passage is one of Chinese philosophy's key visions of a perfect world; it is still invoked in the twentieth and twenty-first centuries in the utopian dreams of Chinese scholars and activists.[31] Guo Moruo wrote a short story, for example, where Marx and Confucius discuss their shared utopian goal of great harmony.[32]

Although great harmony creates perfection through a unified order, "harmony-with-difference" questions the utility of sameness. In the famous passage that gives us the phrase "harmony-with-difference," Confucius discusses the harmony/sameness (*he/tong*, 和/同) distinction that is found throughout classical Chinese literature: "The exemplary person harmonizes with others, but does not necessarily agree with them (*he er butong*); the small person agrees with others, but is not harmonious with them (*tong er buhe*, 同而不和)."[33] Confucius tells us that agreeing with people means that you are the same as them, here uncritically the same: sameness-without-harmony (*tong er buhe*). Harmony-with-difference, conversely, allows us to encourage different opinions, norms, and models.

Rather than describing the same thing, great harmony and harmony-with-difference present very different notions of social order and world order; one appeals to the benefits of overarching unity, whereas the other seeks to preserve opportunities for difference. In this way, these two senses of harmony are similar to the two research agendas and epistemologies discussed above. Great harmony describes an essential and perfect China, whereas harmony-with-difference is a contingent and open social grammar that can encourages multiple political possibilities.

It is common to distinguish normative Chinese thought from more self-critical Western philosophy.[34] But we need to think beyond this East/West figuration of political thought because the tension between great harmony and harmony-with-difference shows that there are different epistemological, methodological, and political agendas *within* Chinese tradition.

We should be careful, however, not to romanticize harmony-with-difference. This notion of harmony is not free from political calculations either. As the "Doctrine of the Mean" (*Zhong Yong*, 中庸) states: "Harmony is the workable way of the Empire-Tianxia."[35] The politics of harmony is described in classical discussions that argue that cooking delicious food is similar to building political harmony. David Hall and Roger Ames thus argue that "harmony is the art of combining and blending two or more foodstuffs so they come together with mutual benefit and enhancement without losing their separate and particular identities, and yet with the effect of constituting a frictionless whole."[36]

A famous passage from the *Lüshi chunqiu* (呂氏春秋) applies the culinary metaphor as a political lesson. The goal, however, is not a decentered harmony of difference or a "frictionless whole." The aim, as the minister in this story explains to his king, is to build empire: "Your state is too small and is inadequate to have the full complement of the necessary ingredients. It is only once you are the Emperor that you would have the full complement."[37] Harmony thus is not a natural organic state. It is built through an active political process, and judged from a particular perspective—in this case the king's perspective. As Yan points out in chapter 4, Tianxia is likewise possessed; the successful emperor "has the empire" (*you* Tianxia, 有天下). Hence even in classical texts, harmony does not lead to an ultimate solution and a perfect world; it merely generates a different political dynamic that empowers some and disempowers others.

Building a Harmonious Society / Building a Harmonious World

Beijing is currently implementing a raft of policies to build a harmonious society and to build a harmonious world. How do these classical and modern understandings of harmony inform policy formulation and policy implementation? Do they resonate with past practices of building empire?

Harmonious society appeared as a policy narrative in 2004 to address the fallout from China's spectacular economic growth. As in many rapidly developing countries, China's dramatic transition to a market economy created a new set of winners and losers. Urban areas on the East Coast benefited much more than rural areas and the interior; educated people benefited much more than less educated people. Though Deng Xiaoping's economic reform policies have lifted more than 400 million people out of absolute poverty since 1979, China has become increasingly polarized between wealthy urban elites and impoverished people in rural areas. One of the CCP's enduring concerns is national unity, and these economic reforms risked tearing the country apart at the seams.

Harmonious society therefore describes a set of government policies that seek to "rebalance" China's economic and social polarization. There are new funds, for example, to provide free public education and subsidized health care to disadvantaged people, especially in rural areas. Hu's domestic harmonious society policy seeks to "close the wealth divide and ease growing social tensions."[38] Harmonious society thus looks to the party-state to solve China's economic and social problems.

We could see how Beijing is building a harmonious society in a positive way at the Opening Ceremony of the 2008 Olympics. Multiethnic China's harmony-with-difference was illustrated at the beginning of the festivities when the procession of children wearing the traditional costumes from China's fifty-six ethnic groups carried the national flag across the stadium floor. The harmony of this united multicultural group was not completely natural, however. The People's Liberation Army was deployed to harmonize the fifty-six cute kids by standing guard over their cultural procession; later, it was revealed that these "ethnic" children were in fact all Han Chinese.

This hierarchical harmonizing helps explain Beijing's more negative response to unrest in Tibet in 2008 and Xinjiang in 2009. Beijing criticized the Dalai Lama for not being a "harmony promoter," while it dispatched more than 7,000 "harmony workers" to deal with a series of riots in Urumqi.[39] Harmony here is judged according the CCP's standards of unity, legitimacy, and stability. As Billioud points out in chapter 9, harmonious society is known as harmonious socialist society in Chinese-language texts. Harmonious society in both its positive and negative expressions thus resonates with the hierarchical political dynamic of great harmony.

What can Beijing's experience of building harmonious society in the PRC tell us about China's goal to build a harmonious world on a global scale? A strong state is necessary to build China's harmonious society at home. Although it is common for Chinese writers to proclaim "harmonious society to be model for the world,"[40] it is not entirely clear if a strong state—either the PRC or Zhao's Tianxia system—is necessary to build a harmonious world abroad. Though Beijing generally describes its harmonious world policy in vague platitudes, others want China to take a more active role in building this new world order. The Hong Kong newspaper *Wen Wei Po* expects Beijing to take the lead as the "'formulator, participant and defender of world order,' in order push the entire world toward harmony."[41] Conversely, most of the discussion of Tianxia and Chinese-style IR theory is resoundingly silent on the role of the CCP and the PRC in world ordering.

To explain the workings of harmonious world policy, it is necessary to see what examples Chinese scholars and officials point to. As Kerr explains in chapter 7, many Chinese commentators see the Shanghai Cooperation Organization (SCO) as an example of Chinese-style regionalism that epitomizes, as Hu Jintao told the 2006 SCO meeting, the Shanghai spirit of "harmony-with-difference" (*he er butong*). Other commentators thus argue that the SCO best illustrates Beijing's project of building a harmonious world.[42]

Yet the diversity here is among nation-states, rather than among people in domestic and transnational space. Indeed, one of the functions of the SCO, which has been dubbed "the club for autocrats and dictators,"[43] is to extend Beijing's domestic ethnic policies into Central Eurasia as a way to better control the movements of transnational ethnic groups.

The question is whether China plans to treat the two hundred nation-states of the world the way Beijing treats China's fifty-five national minority groups. Does *hexie shijie* refer to a relatively benign egalitarian harmonious world, or to a more ominous hierarchical "harmonizing the world"?[44]

Strength/Weakness of Ambiguity

The influence of Chinese philosophy is growing, especially as the party-state searches for norms to justify its domestic and foreign policies as a "ruling party" rather than a revolutionary party. But it also has limits. The details and contours of harmonious world policy need to be elaborated if this concept is to become a powerful global norm and one China's soft power assets.

This brings up the same problem raised in Callahan's discussion of Tianxia in chapter 5: Ambiguity is one of the keys of harmonious world's success. This is much like the secret of Yu Dan's success as a Confucian TV star. Yu is deliberately (and thus politically) apolitical, discussing individual happiness rather than probing structural contradictions. Harmonious world is likewise popular, because who could argue against global peace and prosperity?

But ambiguity is also the key weakness of harmonious world. After more than five years of implementation, we still know little about how China plans to build a harmonious world. As we saw in the last section, the more Beijing clarifies its vision of a harmonious world, the more this policy concept will necessarily exclude nation-states and peoples that have different ideals of world order. Harmonious world thus seems stuck somewhere between being a bland slogan and constituting a new global norm. It will be telling to see if Hu Jintao's concept survives after he retires in 2012.

Yet even if it fades into China's ideological mists, "harmonious world" is already having an impact on China's view of the world and itself. The very vagueness of "harmonious world" has created discursive space for debate about a range of strategic concepts, including Tianxia, many of which challenge Beijing's official policy of peacefully rising within the existing international system.

Resisting Harmony

Slogans like "building a harmonious society" and "building a harmonious world" also provide an opportunity for resistance within China. As we often see in the West, when politicians piously promote moral order and family values, they open themselves up to charges of hypocrisy. In China, with its rich literary tradition, wordplay is a popular mode of resistance—especially because the party-state still maintains control over most public space. Soon after Hu Jintao unveiled his "Eight Honors and Eight Shames" campaign (discussed in chapters 6 and 9 by Hughes and Billioud, respectively), the prominent social critic, and future Nobel Laureate, Liu Xiaobo not only criticized the CCP for treating Chinese citizens "like kids in kindergarten." He also lampooned this moral campaign with alternative lists of honors and shames.[45] One counter-list includes:

> Spreading social values is an honor, and spreading totalitarianism is a shame.
> Respecting humanity is an honor, and stealing freedom is a shame....
> Protecting human rights is an honor, protecting special privileges is a shame.
> Allowing different opinions is an honor, repressing public opinion is a shame.

Or as a saucy list by a frustrated student declares:

> Cadres in the Ministry of Education: Getting a young and beautiful date for the dance is an honor, staying with your old wife is a shame....
> Graduate school admission: Admission to children of high-ranking officials and beautiful women is an honor, admitting only outstanding students is a shame.
> Professor's outstanding achievements: Working less, gaining a lot, and deceiving people is an honor; seeking the truth and refusing to plagiarize is a shame....
> PhD evaluations: Wisely bribing is an honor, being evaluated on one's real strengths is a shame....
> The whole education system: Earning money is an honor, being honest and upright is a shame.

Lists like these show how parody is a time-honored method of resistance in China, where "only by replicating or mimicking the formal qualities of the discourse of the state can critics of the state make their voices heard."[46]

Hu Jintao's harmony discourse was mocked more directly as a reaction to a relaunch of the party-state's antipornography campaign in early 2009. China's Web community was incensed because Beijing used the campaign to—again—censor political discussion. A clever Netizen thus made a YouTube video about a grand battle between Grass Mud Horses and River Crabs; Grass Mud Horse (*cao ni ma*, 草泥马) is a homonym for the popular Chinese oath "fuck your mother," and River Crab (*hexie*, 河蟹) is a homonym for "harmony."[47] Thus Netizens mocked the censorship campaign by using one of the Chinese language's most graphic curses to defeat the party-state's latest slogan of choice. This entertaining episode underlined how for many in China "harmony" actually means "censorship"; indeed, "harmonizing" is now slang for state censorship on the Web.

The struggle over the meaning of harmony suggests two things: Chinese intellectuals take harmony seriously as a policy narrative; but they are not always convinced of its utility, and have now turned this mode of cultural governance into a site of resistance. Harmony thus is no longer simply another political slogan; this concept has become an arena of political interpretation and ideological battle—which is very interesting for both IR theory and international studies.

Indeed, as part of this trend, the contributors to this volume seem to be taking a cue from the *Zhuangzi*'s (庄子) final chapter, "Tianxia," which outlines a number of different approaches to political philosophy, and thus different views of what is "under Heaven."[48]

The main conclusion of this book, then, is that we need to stop talking about Chinese philosophy as if it were a singular coherent whole—for example, "the Chinese Tradition"—and allow different understandings of Chinese identity and politics to thrive. The rich diversity of Chinese culture, which includes both ancient ideals and new concepts, is what makes the PRC's normative soft power and new foreign policy interesting and important topics of study.

Notes

1. Peter C. Perdue, *China Marches West: The Qing Conquest of Central Eurasia* (Cambridge, Mass.: Harvard University Press, 2004); Kirk W. Larsen, *Tradition, Treaties, and Trade: Qing Imperialism and Choson Korea, 1850–1910* (Cambridge, Mass.: Harvard University Press, 2008); Li Dalong, "Chuantong Yi-Xia guanyu Zhongguo jiangyu de xingcheng" [The traditional barbarian-civilization view and the formation of China's territory], *Zhongguo bianjiang shidi yanjiu* 14, no. 1 (2004): 1–14; Emma Jin-

hua Teng, *Taiwan's Imagined Geography: Chinese Colonial Travel Writing and Pictures, 1683–1895* (Cambridge, Mass.: Harvard University Press, 2004); Chen Liankai, "Zhongguo, huayi, fanhan, zhonghua, zhonghua minzu: Yige neizai lianxi fazhan bei renshi de guocheng" [One method for recognizing the developmental relations between the terms Zhongguo, Huayi, Fanhan, Zhonghua, Zhonghua minzu], in *Zhonghua minzu de duoyuan yiti geju* [The pluralistic unity structure of Chinese nationalism], edited by Fei Xiaotong (Beijing: Zhongyang minzu xueyuan chubanshe, 1989), 72–113.

2. See Godfrey Hodgson, *The Myth of American Exceptionalism*, (New Haven, Conn.: Yale University Press, 2009); and Robert Kagan, *Of Paradise and Power: America and Europe in the New World Order* (New York: Alfred A. Knopf, 2003).

3. See Feng Zhang, "The Rise of Chinese Exceptionalism in International Relations," paper presented at "Global Politics of China" conference, British Inter-University China Centre, London and Manchester, November 2009.

4. Yan Xuetong, "The Rise of China and Its Power Status," *Chinese Journal of International Politics* 1 (2006): 5–33, at 13.

5. See Qin Yaqing, "Why Is There No Chinese International Relations Theory?" *International Relations of the Asia-Pacific* 7 (2007): 313–40.

6. Deng Xiaoping, *Selected Works of Deng Xiaoping*, vol. 3 (1982–92) (Beijing: Foreign Languages Press, 1994), 72–75.

7. See Shi Bin, "Guoji guanxi yanjiu 'Zhongguo hua' de lunzheng" [The debate over Sinicization in international relations research], in *Zhongguo gouji guanxi yanjiu (1995–2005)* [International Relations Research in China (1995–2005)], edited by Wang Yizhou and Yuan Zhengqing (Beijiing: Beijing daxue chubanshe, 2006), 518–45; Liang Shoude, "Constructing an International Relations Theory with 'Chinese Characteristics,'" *Political Science* 49, no. 1 (1997): 23–49; Liang Shoude and Hong Yinxian, *Guoji zhengzhixue lilun* [International Politics Theory] (Beijing: Beijing daxue chubanshe, 2000); and Song Xinning, "Building International Relations Theory with Chinese Characteristics," *Journal of Contemporary China* 10, no. 26 (2001): 61–74.

8. See Qin Yaqing, ed., *Zhongguo xuezhi kan shijie: Guoji zhixu chuan* [Chinese scholars view the world: International order] (Beijing: Xin shijie chubanshe, 2007); and Tang Shiping, "Coming Intellectual Power," *China Security* 4, no. 2 (2008): 14–15.

9. See William A. Callahan, "Nationalizing International Theory: Race, Class and the English School," *Global Society* 18, no. 4 (2004): 305–23.

10. For another discussion of theory building, see Yan Xuetong, "Bianzhe de hua" (Editor's preface), in *Wangba tianxia sixiang ji qiyou* [Thoughts on world leadership and implications], edited by Yan Xuetong and Xu Jin (Beijing: Shijie zhishi chubanshe, 2009), 1–3; Yan Xuetong, "Guoji guanxi lilun shi pushixing de" [International relations theory is universalistic], in *Wangba tianxia sixiang ji qiyou* [Thoughts on world leadership and implications], edited by Yan Xuetong and Xu Jin (Beijing: Shijie zhishi chubanshe, 2009), 292–93; and Yan Xuetong, "Why Is There No Chinese School of IR Theories?" in *Wangba tianxia sixiang ji qiyou* [Thoughts on world leadership and implications], edited by Yan Xuetong and Xu Jin (Beijing: Shijie zhishi chubanshe, 2009), 294–301.

11. See Yan Xuetong, *Zhongguo guojia liyi fenxi* [An analysis of China's national interest] (Tianjin: Renmin chubanshe, 1995), 232–35, 249–52; and Yan Xuetong, "The Rise of China in Chinese Eyes," *Journal of Contemporary China* 10, no. 26 (2000): 33–40.

12. For the sourcebook, see Yan Xuetong and Xu Jin, *Zhongguo xianQin guojiajian*

zhengzhi sexiang xuandu [Pre-Qin thoughts on foreign relations] (Shanghai: Fudan daxue chubanshe, 2008).

13. Interviews with Yan Xuetong and others at the Institute for International Studies, Tsinghua University, Beijing, May 2009. The Institute for International Studies issues two journals: the *Chinese Journal of International Politics* in English, published by Oxford University Press, beginning in 2007; and *Guoji zhengzhi kexue* [International Political Science], published in Chinese, beginning in 2005.

14. For an example typical of using Chinese norms to criticize U.S. policy, see Liu Jianfei, "Sino-U.S. Relations and Building a Harmonious World," *Journal of Contemporary China* 18, no. 60 (2009): 479–90. The only article I found that recognized that China might have problems with its foreign policy was published in English rather than Chinese: Shi Yinhong, "China's Peaceful Development, Harmonious World and International Responsibility: Achievements and Challenges," *Global Review* (Shanghai), no. 1 (2008): 19–28, at 25.

15. See Daniel A. Bell, *China's New Confucianism: Politics and Everyday Life in a Changing Society* (Princeton, N.J.: Princeton University Press, 2008), 28.

16. See Shiping Hua, "A Perfect World," *Wilson Quarterly*, Autumn 2005, 62–67; and Shiping Hua, *Chinese Utopianism: A Comparative Study of Reformist Thought with Japan and Russia, 1989–1997)* (Stanford, Calif.: Stanford University Press, 2008).

17. Gloria Davies, *Worrying about China: The Language of Chinese Critical Inquiry* (Cambridge, Mass.: Harvard University Press, 2007), 1.

18. See Zhou Shuchun, *Quanqiu zhili mubiao jiangou de xin fanshi: "Hexie shijie" lilun jichu tanxi* [Global governance and the goal of building a new model: A analysis of "harmonous world" theory], PhD dissertation, Central [Communist] Party School, June 2008, iv; and Gao Zugui, *Constructive Involvement and Harmonious World: China's Evolving Outlook on Sovereignty in the Twenty-First Century*, Friedrich Ebert Stiftung Briefing Paper 13 (Bonn: Friedrich Ebert Stiftung, 2008).

19. Thomas Metzger, *Clouds across the Pacific: Essays on the Clash between Chinese and Western Political Theories Today* (Hong Kong: Chinese University Press, 2005), 21–31, 295; Davies, *Worrying about China*, 23.

20. Davies, *Worrying about China*, 7.

21. Song, "Building International Relations Theory with Chinese Characteristics."

22. See Wang Yanzhi, "Zhongguo de hexie shijie linian ji shixian jizhi yanjiu" [China's harmonious world concept and research on mechanisms for bringing it about], PhD dissertation, Fudan University, January 2009, iii; and Huang Renwei, "Cong 'hexie shehui' dao 'hexie shijie'" [From "harmonious society" to "harmonious world"], *Wenhui bao*, November 13, 2006, 3.

23. See State Council, "China's Peaceful Development Road," Xinhua, December 22, 2005; Shi, "China's Peaceful Development"; Dong Yaping and Zhao Qiong, "Shizong buyu zou heping fazhan daolu, tuidong hexie shijie jianshe" [Unswervingly take the road of peaceful development, promote the construction of a harmonious world], *Qiushi*, no. 2 (2009): 73–75; and Ruan Zongze, "Goujian hexie shijie de Zhongguo waijiao" [China's foreign policy of building a harmonious society], *Liaowang*, no. 46 (November 14, 2005): 13–15.

24. Linda Jakobson and Dean Knox, *New Foreign Policy Actors in China*, SIPRI Policy Paper 26 (Stockholm: Stockholm International Peace Research Institute, 2010); Bonnie S. Glaser and Evan S. Medeiros, "The Changing Ecology of Foreign Policy-

Making in China: The Ascension and Demise of the Theory of 'Peaceful Rise,'" *China Quarterly*, no. 190 (2007): 291–310.

25. Jing Tiankui, ed., *Zhongguo shehui fazhanguan* [Chinese views of social development] (Kunming: Yunnan renmin chubanshe, 1997), 41; Tian Guangqing, *Hexie lun: Rujia wenming yu dangdai shehui* [On harmony: Confucian civilization and contemporary society] (Beijing: Zhongguo huaqiao chubanshe, 1998); Hu Fagui, *Rujia wenhua yu aigou chuantong* [Confucian culture and patriotic tradition] (Shanghai: Shanghai shehui kexue chubanshe, 1998); Lou Jie, *Zhonghua wenhua yu zuguo heping tongyi* [Chinese culture and the peaceful unification of the motherland] (Wuhan: Wuhan chubanshe, 1998); Liu Zhiguang, *Dongfang heping zhuyi: yuanqi, liubian ji zouxiang* [Oriental pacificism: Its origins, development and future] (Changsha, Hunan: Hunan chubanshe, 1992), 221–33; Jiang Zemin, "Enhance Mutual Understanding and Build Stronger Ties of Friendship and Cooperation," speech delivered at Harvard University, November 1, 1997; State Council, "White Paper on China's National Defense," Xinhua, July 27, 1998.

26. See Liu, "Sino-U.S. Relations"; Zhou, *Quanqiu zhili mubiao jiangou de xin fanshi*; Gao Yingdan, "Hexie shijie linian xia Zhongguo gongchangdang duiwai zhanlue yanjiu" [Researching the role of the harmonious world concept in the Chinese Communist Party's international strategy], PhD dissertation, Northeast Normal University, CCP Party History Department, March 2008; and Dong and Zhao, "Shizong buyu zou heping fazhan daolu."

27. See Yan Xuetong, "China implementing harmonious diplomacy," *China Daily*, January 19, 2007; Qin Yaqing, "Hexie shijie: Zhongguo waijiao xin linian" [Harmonious world: China's new foreign relations concept], *Xuezhi luntan* no. 5 (2007): 22–23; and Zhao Tingyang, "Guanyu hexie shijie de sekao" [Some thoughts about the harmonious world], *Shijie jingji yu zhengzhi*, no. 9 (2006): 1.

28. See "Harmonious World: China's Ancient Philosophy for New International Order," *People's Daily*, October 2, 2007; and Yu Keping, "We Must Work to Create a Harmonious World," *China Daily*, May 10, 2007.

29. This argument is developed by William A. Callahan, "Remembering the Future: Utopia, Empire and Harmony in 21st-Century International Theory," *European Journal of International Relations* 10, no. 4 (2004): 569–601.

30. See W. T. de Bary, ed., *Sources of Chinese Tradition*, vol. 1 (New York: Columbia University Press, 1960), 176.

31. See K'ang Yu-wei, *Ta T'ung Shu: The One-World Philosophy of K'ang Yu-wei*, translated by Lawrence G. Thompson (London: Allen & Unwin, 1958); and Hua, *Chinese Utopianism*.

32. See Guo Moruo, "Makese jin wenmiao" [Marx enters the Confucian temple], in *Guo Moruo zuopin jingdian*, vol. 3 [Guo Moruo's classic works, vol. 3] (Beijing: Zhongguo huaqiao chubanshe, 1997), 394–402; and Hua, *Chinese Utopianism*, 19.

33. Confucius, *The Analects*, translated by D. C. Lau (London: Penguin, 1979), 13/23. I have modified this translation.

34. See Davies, *Worrying about China*.

35. See "The Doctrine of the Mean," chapter 1.4, in *Confucian Analects, The Great Learning and The Doctrine of the Mean*, by Confucius, translated by James Legge (New York: Dover Publications, 1971), 384–85. I have modified the translation.

36. David L. Hall and Roger T. Ames, *Thinking from the Han: Self, Truth, and*

Transcendence in Chinese and Western Culture (Albany: State University of New York Press,1998), 181.

37. See *Lüshi chunqiu* (Shanghai: Shanghai guji chubanshe, 1996), 210; and James D. Sellmann, *Timing and Rulership in Master Lü's Spring and Autumn Annals (Lüshi chunqiu)* (Albany: State University of New York Press, 2002).

38. "Harmonious World: China's Ancient Philosophy for New Int'l Order (1)," *People's Daily*, October 2, 2007.

39. "Chinese Political Advisors: Dalai Lama Not Harmony Promoter but Trouble Maker," Xinhua, March 11, 2009; "Thousands of Harmony Makers Sent to Urumqi Communities while Authorities Vow Harsh Punishment against Syringe Attackers," Xinhua, September 7, 2009.

40. Qin Xiaoying, "Harmonious Society to Be Model for the World," *China Daily*, October 13, 2006.

41. The *Wen Wei Po* is a Hong Kong newspaper that is close to the CCP. Cited by Melissa Murphy, *Decoding Chinese Politics: Intellectual Debates and Why They Matter* (Washington, D.C.: Center for Strategic and International Studies, 2008), 22. Also see Gao, "Hexie shijie linian xia Zhongguo gongchangdang duiwai zhanlue yanjiu," 7–8; and Dong and Zhao, "Dong and Zhao, "Shizong buyu zou heping fazhan daolu," 75.

42. See Qin, "Hexie shijie," 23; Wang, "Zhongguo de hexie shijie linian," 108–34; and Gao, "Hexie shijie linian xia Zhongguo gongchangdang duiwai zhanlue yanjiu," 119–21.

43. David Wall of Chatham House's Asia program, cited by Simon Tisdall, "Irresistible Rise of the Dictator's Club," *The Guardian*, June 6, 2006.

44. See Zhao, ""Guanyu hexie"; and Xiang Lanxin, "Jieyan quqi, shenyan hexie" [Stop talking about China's rise, be careful discussing world harmony], *Lianhe zaobao* (Singapore), March 26, 2006.

45. Liu Xiaobo, "Bei xixue de qinding rongchi guan" [The joke of the imperial edict on honor and shame], Independent Chinese Pen Center, March 23, 2006, http://www.boxun.com/hero/liuxb/532_1.shtml.

46. Michael Schoenhals, *Doing Things with Words in Chinese Politics: Five Studies* (Berkeley: Institute of East Asian Studies, University of California, 1992), 21.

47. For the video with a translation, see "Song of the Mud-Grass Horse (Cao Ni Ma)," http://www.youtube.com/watch?v=wKx1aenJK08. Also see Michael Wines, "A Dirty Pun Tweaks China's Online Censors," *New York Times*, March 11, 2009.

48. See *Chuang-tzu: The Seven Inner Chapters and Other Writings from the Book "Chuang-tzu*," translated by A. C. Graham (London: George Allen & Unwin, 1981), 274–85.

Contributors

Elena Barabantseva is a British Inter-University China Centre research fellow and lecturer in Chinese politics at the University of Manchester. She received her PhD in politics from the University of Manchester in 2006. Her research focuses on Chinese identity politics, nationalism, transnationalism, and cultural citizenship. Her publications include the book *Overseas Chinese, Ethnic Minorities and Nationalism: De-Centering China* (Routledge, 2010); and a number of articles in the *Journal of Contemporary China*; *Asien: The German Journal on Contemporary Asia*; *Critical Asian Studies*; *Alternatives: Global, Local, Political*; and *Asian Ethnicity*.

Sébastien Billioud is associate professor of Chinese civilization at the University Paris Diderot, Sorbonne Paris Cité. His work focuses on Confucianism in contemporary China, with a cross-disciplinary approach primarily in anthropology and intellectual history. He is the author of *Thinking Through Confucian Modernity: A Study of Mou Zongsan's Moral Metaphysics* (Brill, 2011); and in collaboration with Joël Thoraval, he is completing a book manuscript on the current Confucian revival.

William A. Callahan is professor of international politics and Chinese studies at the University of Manchester, and codirector of the British Inter-University China Centre in Oxford. His research examines the nexus of identity and security in China and East Asia. His books include *China: The Pessoptimist Nation* (Oxford University Press, 2010); *Contingent States: Greater China and Transnational Relations* (University of Minnesota Press, 2004); and *Cultural Governance and Resistance in Pacific Asia* (Routledge,

2006). His articles have been published in many journals, including *International Organization*, the *Journal of Strategic Studies*, *Critical Asian Studies*, and the *Journal of Contemporary China*.

Kelvin Chi-kin Cheung, who translated chapter 3, is a British Inter-University China Centre postdoctoral fellow at the University of Manchester. His PhD dissertation is "Chinese Nationalism: A Critical Understanding of Chinese Identity in a Transnational Context," a chapter of which has been published as "Modernity, History, and the Negotiation of Chinese Identity: Revisiting the Liberals / New Left Debate," in *China in Search of a Harmonious Society* (Rowman & Littlefield, 2008).

Christopher R. Hughes is professor of international relations at the London School of Economics and Political Science, where he also previously served as director of the Asia Research Centre. He has written widely on Chinese foreign policy, with a special focus on the impact of nationalism and the Taiwan issue. His most recent monograph is *Chinese Nationalism in the Global Era* (Routledge, 2006).

David Kerr is lecturer on the international relations of China and director of the Centre for Contemporary Chinese Studies at Durham University. His publications have appeared in journals such as *Europe-Asia Studies*, *International Studies Quarterly*, *Critical Asian Studies*, *Review of International Political Economy*, and *The International Spectator*.

Qin Yaqing is the vice president of China Foreign Affairs University, Beijing, where he is professor of English and international studies. He has published many books and articles, including *Power, Institutions, and Cultures* (2005); and *China's New Diplomacy* (2008). In addition to his own original research, he translated Alexander Wendt's *Social Theory of International Politics* into Chinese.

Yan Xuetong is the director of the Institute for International Studies at Tsinghua University in Beijing. He is a well-known security studies expert, and his publications include *Thoughts on World Leadership and Implications* (coedited, 2009); *Pre-Qin Thoughts on Foreign Relations* (coedited, 2008); *International Politics and China* (2005); *An Analysis of China's National Interest* (1995); and numerous articles in English and Chinese.

Zhao Tingyang is based at the Institute of Philosophy of the Chinese Academy of Social Sciences. His books include *Investigations of the Bad World: Political Philosophy as First Philosophy* (2009); *The Tianxia System* (2005); and *The Non-World World* (2003, 2005). He has also published numerous journal articles in English.

Index

Abramson, Mark, 149
Academia Sinica, 130
Action Plan for the Development of Civic Morality, 220
alienation, 204, 210, 214 n. 52
All-under-Heaven, 7, 9, 22–23, 29–30, 33–34, 35 n. 11, 94, 158, 165, 211 n. 12; legitimacy of, 24–27; system, 31. *See also* Tianxia; tributary system
ambiguity, 170, 174, 222, 262
Amélie, 194
Ames, Roger, 259
An Lushan, 152
Annotated Catalogue of the Imperial Library, 123
ASEAN, 84, 170
Asian Values, 218

Bachelard, Gaston, 101
Bandung, 165
Barabantseva, Elena, 12, 250, 254, 255, 256
barbarians, 6, 48, 77, 121, 138, 149, 157. *See also* periphery
Bauman, Zygmunt, 203, 205
Beijing city, 186, 199–201
Beijing Consensus, 2, 80
Bell, Daniel, 138
Bellér-Hann, Ildikó, 162
Billeter, Térence, 228, 244 n. 67

Billioud, Sébastien, 12, 254, 256, 261, 263
Bishkek Declaration, 170–71
Book of Rites, 258. See also *Interpretations of Rites*
boundary, 174, 190; between China and barbarianism, 149–50; between China and Islam, 144, 153; civilizational, 147; Inner Asian, 158, 165–66; of the state, 159. *See also* frontiers
Boxer Rebellion, 126, 135
Buddhism, 122, 123, 127, 132, 227
Bull, Hedley, 43
Bush, George W., 5, 70, 81, 169

Callahan, William A., 10, 165, 170, 184, 188, 251, 256, 262
Campbell, David, 8
Central Asia, 1, 151, 157, 166, 168; Soviet, 161, 164. *See also* Inner Asia
Central Eurasia, 11, 155, 169, 170, 172–73, 262
Central Party School, 230, 245 n. 73, 257
Chaghatay, 153; khanate, 154; script, 163
Chevrier, Yves, 217, 225. *See also* Communism
Chiang Kai-shek, 121, 131, 223
China-Africa Forum, 82
China Central Television, 7, 208

273

China Merchants' Steam Navigation Company, 124
Chinese Communist Party, 47, 80–81, 189, 196, 224, 257; cadre, 231; Confucianism, 217–18; congress, 175; and *ti/yong,* 119
Christianity, 123, 128, 146, 216
civil society, 97, 229
civility (*ren*), 28–29, 41, 44, 147, 148, 176 n. 10
civilization, 45, 110–11, 148; and barbarism, 103, 159; Chinese, 106, 145–48, 150, 166, 257; ecological, 231; frontiers of, 149, 158; Han, 93; human, 220; and Islam, 146; Islamic, 11, 144, 155; socialist spiritual, 134, 136, 219; Western, 48; world, 6, 252
civilizing mission, 105,160
clash of civilizations, 5, 6, 109, 169, 172
Cold War, 40, 42, 46, 79, 84, 163; post–, 5, 110, 171
Communism, 130, 131, 133, 196, 224; distended, 217. *See also* Chevrier, Yves; legitimacy of, 230
Confucianism, 11, 12, 28, 41, 119, 121, 127–28, 139, 145, 215–16, 218–19, 228–31, 252; and communism, 133, 196, 232; in discourse, 220–23, 247 n. 87; Gan Yang on, 233; Jiang Qing on, 233–34; Kang Xiaoguang on, 234; movement, 218; national-Confucianism, 219; neo-Confucianism, 122–23, 125, 132, 138, 146; and the Party, 131, 217; power of, 253; representations of, 129; revival of, 195; Yuan Shikai on, 129
Confucius, 3, 7, 13, 24, 126, 133, 145, 198, 196, 217, 228–30, 259; Foundation, 218; on government, 147; Mao on, 134; and Sun Yat-sen, 240 n. 27; teachings of, 127; the worship of, 129, 219
Confucius Institute, 3, 6, 7, 192, 195–98, 205–6, 209; promotional video of, 11, 185–86, 193–94, 206, 208
Connolly, William, 101

cosmopolitanism, 9, 92, 93, 102, 111, 129, 130, 139, 149, 190, 203
Cultural Revolution, 81, 132–33, 163–64, 175; and Confucianism, 217; pre–, 134
culture, 5, 39–40, 43, 49 103, 161, 184, 208, 222; Chinese, 3, 9, 93, 106, 119, 186, 192–93, 194–95, 249, 255, 264; Confucian, 41, 153, 218, 231; critique of, 45, 48; Mao on, 132; of modern science, 135; national, 7, 197; promotion of, 190, 225–27; and sovereignty, 189; superior, 127–28; traditional, 50, 185, 215–17, 219–21, 223, 228–29, 235, 253; Turkic-Muslim, 157, 174; usage of, 227; Xunzi on, 58–59
culture/cultural fever, 6, 218

Dai Jitao, 223
Dalai Lama, 261
Dao (Way), 25, 145–46, 147
Daode jing, 95, 100. *See also* Laozi
Davies, Gloria, 255
democracy, 24, 26, 31, 96–97, 103, 169, 221, 247 n. 87; cosmopolitan, 102; liberal, 97, 133; social, 234
Deng Xiaoping, 1, 46, 134, 222, 252, 260
development: China's path of, 170, 193; economic, 47, 62, 80, 83; model of, 2, 5; national, 77; peaceful, 1, 3, 80, 257; Shanghai Cooperation Organization on, 171; scientific, 118, 138, 160, 231, 242–43 n. 51, 251; theories of, 6. *See also* modernization
diplomacy, 166, 168, 172
Dirlik, Arif, 222, 242 n. 44

East Turkestan, 124, 143, 154, 161, 166. *See also* New Frontier; Xinjiang
empire, 5, 21, 32–33, 93–94, 260; Abbasid, 152; Arab, 151, 153; Chinese, 6, 27–29, 35 n. 11, 92, 104, 111, 251–52; Chinese concept of, 22, 28, 60, 68–69; Eurasian, 155; European, 187; and frontiers, 149, 159, 165; multiethnic, 155–56; new, 97–98;

Qing, 124–25, 157, 174; studies of, 251; and Tianxia, 107, 259; Turkic, 152–54; Western, 105; Xunzi on, 70; Zhang Zhidong on, 126. *See also* imperialism
end of history, 5
Enlightenment, 41, 44, 132
epistemological optimism and skepticism, 12, 225, 249, 255–57
equality, 12, 26, 44–45, 169; and hierarchy, 12, 249, 251–52; social, 153; of states, 43, 49, 84
ethics, 29, 56, 80, 128; Confucian, 132, 138, 196, 224; domestic, 73; of Tianxia, 101; Xunzi on, 62
European Union, 32, 82, 95, 97
exceptionalism, 11; and syncretism, 12, 249–50

Fairbank, John King, 6, 42, 183
Falungong, 229, 242 n. 49
familyship, 25–26, 27, 30, 35 n. 13
Fang Lizhi, 136
Fei Xiaotong, 42
Ferghana, 152
foreign policy, 1–2, 5, 8–9, 11–12, 67, 92–93, 101, 107, 119, 121; American, 253; Chinese, 63, 109–11, 158, 172, 173, 183, 189, 212 n. 19, 249, 256–57; harmonious, 4, 10, 106, 262; new, 80; realist style of, 138;
Foucault, Michel, 100, 120, 137. *See also* power/knowledge
frontiers, 8, 32, 104, 143–44, 148, 165, 168, 176 n. 1; between China and Islam, 11, 151; of civilization, 149, 158–59; Inner Asian, 160; permeability of, 166; in Qur'ān, 150
Frye, Richard, 153
future, 1, 3, 12, 135, 236, 254; China's, 106; China's/world's, 2, 91, 109–10, 258; of global politics, 4; of Islam, 172, 175; world order, 4

Gang Zhao, 155
Geiss, Paul, 161

Geopolitics, 165, 166, 172
Giddens, Anthony, 31
God, 145, 146, 147–48, 150, 151. *See also* religion
governance, 43–44, 54, 57, 143, 160, 166, 175, 176 n.1; in Afghanistan, 69; of All-under-Heaven, 25; centralized, 28; cultural, 264; elite, 99; global, 2, 10, 21, 33, 97, 251; in Inner Asia, 159; Mirror of (Sima Guang), 132; mode of, 102, 111, 174; 106, 189–90, 250; regional, 168–69, 170; Xunzi on, 65, 75
Gladney, Dru, 167
globalization, 5–6, 11, 21, 31–33, 94, 98, 118, 136–37, 194; effects of, 18
Great Leap Forward, 81, 163–65
Greater China, 93, 165–66
Grotius, Hugo, 42
Gu Mu, 219
Guo Moruo, 259
Guo Yingjie, 195

Habermas, Jürgen, 98, 109, 144–45; on energy of social solidarity and moral authority of institutions, 147; on religion, 173
Hall, David, 259
Halliday, Fred, 164
harmonious: society, 1, 80, 108, 118–19, 136, 138, 228, 233, 251, 260–61; world, 1, 2, 4–6, 10, 12, 80, 106, 108–9, 110, 138, 184, 249, 252, 256–58, 260–62
harmony, 1, 25–26, 29, 215, 222, 257, 260; in classical thought, 221; and contradiction, 222; through diversity, 166, 171–72, 175; great, 7, 12, 126, 258–59, 261; resisting, 263–4; revival of, 138; socialist, 7, 221–22, 231; in Tianxia, 108; -with-difference, 259
Hartog, François, 235–6
hegemony, 7, 10, 105, 188; new, 10, 105, 109, 111; US, 33, 40, 48; in Xunzi, 55–56, 70–72, 79, 86 n. 2

hierarchy, 9, 10, 42–43, 76–79, 84, 93, 100, 103; Confucian, 127; hierarchy/equality, 12, 249, 251; of imperialism, 252; social, 77, 127; in Tianxia, 190
history, 39, 103, 148, 184–85, 250; of antitraditionalism, 217–18; Chinese, 30, 48, 50, 104, 128, 132, 149, 183–84, 187–89, 219, 250, 256; Chinese intellectual, 119; diplomatic, 40; of international relations, 84; Qing, 122, 225
Hobsbawm, Eric, 227
Hoffman, Stanley, 40
Hong Xiuquan, 123, 221
Hu Jintao, 1, 2, 4–5, 138, 175, 221–22, 257, 261–63
Hua Guofeng, 134
Hughes, Christopher, 11, 250, 252, 256
Hundred Days Reform, 44–45, 49, 120
Huntington, Samuel, 109–10

identity, 5, 12; Chinese, 48, 106, 118–19, 123, 155–57, 252, 264; collective, 148, 161; dilemma, 8, 47, 49, 251; Islamic, 175; modern, 203; politics, 124, 256; of Tianxia, 102; Uyghur, 162–63, 167
imperialism, 21, 30, 32–33, 97–98, 118, 125, 157–59; Western, 104, 106. See also empire
Inner Asia, 152, 153–55, 159, 166. See also Central Asia
intellectuals, 3, 8, 99, 110, 197, 232–34, 248 n. 95, 254–55; Confucian, 138, 218, 238 n. 14; establishment, 136; public, 7, 8, 91–92, 106
International Monetary Fund, 77
international relations, 59, 79, 101, 159, 169, 171, 185, 189; China's, 6, 44–45, 159; Chinese School of, 2, 4, 7, 9–10, 12, 37, 41–42, 45, 47–50, 91–92, 108, 249, 252–53; English School of, 40–42; of Islamic world, 144; power in, 65; public, 198; realist, 11, 41, 57, 73–74, 79, 102; theory, 4, 37–38, 52 n. 12, 54–57, 67, 249, 257; ti/yong in, 137

International Society, 2, 3, 26, 40, 43, 48, 50, 84, 171, 251
Interpretations of Rites, 28–29. See also *Book of Rites*
Iraq: invasion of, 5, 67, 253; war, 81, 98, 138, 169
Islam, 11, 127, 143–44, 146, 147–48, 151–52, 154, 163–64, 165; and China, 153, 166, 173–75; and modernity, 172; in Qing, 157; and Uyghur identity, 161–62
Islamism, 168, 170

Japan, 64, 84, 135, 194; invasion by, 131; Meiji, 62, 121; war against, 133
Jia Zhangke, 11, 185, 198–99
Jiang Zemin, 137, 170, 219, 257
Jin Guantao, 224
Johnston, Alastair Iain, 104, 138
Judaism, 146

Kalpana, Misra, 222
Kang Youwei, 44, 121, 124, 126, 130, 190–91, 221
Kant, 32, 102, 190,
Keohane, Robert, 76
Kerr, David, 11, 251, 254, 256, 261
Kornberg, Judith, and John Faust, 183
Kuomintang, 129, 230

Lakatos, 47, 48
language: Chinese, 6, 186, 192, 193–95, 197, 264; reform, 163; visual, 184
Lao Siguang, 218
Laozi, 25, 95, 100. See also *Daode jing*
Lapidus, Ira, 162, 168; on Islam, 154
League of Nations, 73
legitimacy, 133, 137, 147, 119, 217, 224, 225; of communist regime, 230, 232, 235; political, 25, 33, 129, 151; popular, 12, 24, 103, 234; of Tianxia, 97, 105; and *ti/yong,* 129
Levenson, Joseph, 118, 119, 125, 222, 248 n. 95

Leviathan, 147
Levinas, Emmanuel, 101
Li Zehou, 135, 223, 224
Liang Qichao, 120, 122, 125, 126
Liberalization, 135, 217–18, 233, 244,
liquid life, 203, 205
Liu Binyan, 136
Liu Shaoqi, 133, 134, 224
Liu Xiaobo, 263
Lost Soul (John Makeham), 219
Lun Yu, 145, 149

Mao Zedong, 82–83, 119, 121, 131–32, 135; on Confucius, 134; thought, 133, 136
Maoism, 217, 222
Marx, 39, 45, 259
Marxism, 131, 223, 224, 230–31, 235; in China, 223
medicine: Chinese and Western, 39
Meissner, Werner, 219
Mencius, 23, 74, 129, 221, 253
Metzger, Thomas, 225, 255
Ministry of Culture, 228
mobility, 186, 196, 200–201, 203–4; and passport, 202
modernity, 11, 31, 160, 175, 186, 203, 225; and airplanes, 201–2, 144, 163, 173, 184, 251; Chinese, 119–20, 128–29, 160, 167; liquid, 205; of nation-state, 21; and tradition, 99; Turkic, 162
modernization, 5–6, 45, 49, 121, 135, 218. *See also* development
Mongolia, 131, 152, 174, 201–2, 204
morality, 44, 73, 97, 146, 223, 225, 241 n. 37; civic, 220; Confucian, 131, 134
Morgenthau, Hans J., 59, 73
Muhammad, 146, 150, 151, 152

national humiliation, 119, 125–26, 131, 136, 138; century of, 157, 184
national interest, 11, 33, 76, 253
National Religious Reforms, 164

national studies, 219, 230
nationalism, 119, 124–25, 129, 167, 184, 189; Asian, 165, 168, 175; Chinese, 228, 251; and Islam, 162; subaltern, 167
nationality, 161
Nation-state, 22, 23, 27, 31–33, 43, 97–98, 106–7, 186, 250; system, 21, 41
NATO, 84
New Frontier, 11, 143–44, 151, 157, 175. *See also* East Turkestan; Xinjiang
Newby, Laura, 157
norms, 6–7, 187; Chinese, 4, 9, 10–11, 249, 253–54; international, 55, 67, 70, 84; of international law, 171; social, 73, 75–76; Western, 189
Nye, Joseph, 5, 76, 98

Olympic Games, Beijing, 3, 119, 131, 196, 254, 260
ontology, 26–27, 48; political, 22
order, 42–43, 165, 256; international, 55–56, 73, 77, 157, 160; Tianxia, 26, 41–42, 94, 97, 99, 158, 188, 190–91, 195; Turkic, 152. *See also* world order
overseas Chinese, 93, 106, 131, 208

Pakistan, 164, 169
Pax Sinica, 7, 102, 105
People's Liberation Army, 261
Perdue, Peter, 156, 160
periphery, 6, 103, 150, 164, 166. *See also* barbarians
philosophy, 218; Chinese, 23–24, 26–27, 29, 44, 54, 93, 96, 176 n. 5, 218, 249, 253, 262; Platonic, 22; Western, 29, 259
Plan for Cultural Development (PCD), 220, 222–23, 225, 228–29; on national character, 227
Poo, Mu-chou, 149
power/knowledge, 100. *See also* Foucault, Michael

Qian Qichen, 169
Qianlong, 156, 157

Qin Hui, 234, 247 n. 86
Qin Yaqing, 8, 9, 250–51, 256, 257–58
Qing Dynasty, 104, 119, 120, 122–23, 129, 130, 152, 155–56, 160, 174; and New Frontier, 157–58
Qur'ān, 146–47, 150

race, 103–4, 130, 149; Chinese, 127, 139
Realism, 11, 41–42, 44, 73–74, 102
reciprocity, 28
reform and opening, 9, 46–47, 50, 63, 80–81, 134, 136, 160, 165–75; and *ti/yong,* 133, 136
religion, 123, 143, 162, 224; Habermas on, 173; popular, 227. *See also* Buddhism; Christianity; God; Islam
ren (benevolence). *See also* civility
resistance, 44, 125, 168, 175, 263–64; Uyghur, 163
responsible China, 107–8
revolution, 9, 25, 44–45, 122, 123, 132, 158; dual, 159. *See also* Cultural Revolution
rise of China, 3, 5, 9, 47, 49, 79, 82–83, 85
River Elegy, 218–19
Roosevelt, Franklin, 70

Sachedina, Abdulaziz, 146
Schmitt, Carl, 27, 96
Schwartz, Benjamin, 145
Scott, David, 183
security, 2, 66, 85, 150, 169–70, 172; China's, 164; dilemma, 8, 251; and identity, 12; national, 63, 67, 252. *See also* identity
Shanghai Cooperation Organization, 169–170, 171, 261
Shapiro, Michael, 104, 199
Shih, Chih-yu, 149, 158, 159, 188
Shijie (The World), 11, 185–86, 187–88, 190–91. *See also* world
Shue, Vivienne, 224, 225
Sinocentrism, 150, 250
skepticism, 12, 169, 249–50
social science, 37–40, 41, 50, 256

soft power, 5–8, 12, 81, 98, 109, 184, 198, 262; of IR theory, 252
Son of Heaven, 23, 25, 61. *See also* Yellow Emperor
Song Xinning, 256
sovereignty, 44, 155, 158–60, 171, 172–73, 185, 189; cultural, 108
Soviet Union, 62–63, 81, 84, 130, 163, 166
Sovietization, 161
Stalin, 82
state, 12, 45, 72, 79–80, 84, 97, 118, 147, 159, 252; Chinese, 9, 105, 155, 163, 164, 167, 189, 206; Indian Moslem, 83; in IR theory, 65; Islamic, 66, 148; nation-, 21–23, 31–33, 43, 49, 183, 186, 250, 262; Pre-Islamic Turkic, 152; in Shanghai Cooperation Organization, 171; socialist, 161; sub–, 27, 28; Xunzi on, 55–56, 59–62, 64, 67, 69–71, 75, 85; Zhang Zhidong on, 127
status quo, 1–2, 5; power, 12, 91
Sun Yatsen, 129, 130, 223
syncretism, 119, 122–23; exceptionalism/, 12, 249–51

Taiping Rebellion, 123, 221
Taiwan, 104, 124–25, 131–32, 138, 160, 186, 195, 230
Talas, Battle of, 152–53
Tan Sitong, 121, 126, 234
theory/policy, 12, 249, 256–57
Three Principles of the People (Sun Yatsen), 129, 130, 131, 223, 240 n. 25
Tianxia, 7, 9, 10–11, 22–23, 39–40, 41–42, 46, 51 n. 11, 68–69, 79, 92, 94–95, 101, 103–4, 106–7, 111, 130, 159–60, 165, 174, 195, 209, 251, 259–60, 262; in *Daode jing,* 100; model, 98, 105; /*shijie,* 185, 187–91, 198; system, 43–44, 99–101, 108–10, 261. *See also* All-under-Heaven; world
Tibet, 104–5, 131, 166, 174, 261

time, 235–37; and space, 27, 38–39, 42, 190, 209
ti/yong, 11, 118–19, 126, 132, 136–38; Deng Xiaoping on, 134; in Marxism, 131, 133, 135; in nationalist discourse, 120–22, 129–31
Todorov, Tzvetan, 101
tradition, 222, 229, 236; and CCP, 235; Chinese, 4, 7–10, 12, 61, 100–101, 161, 171, 232, 250, 264; Confucian, 224, 233; cultural, 215–16, 221; and modernity, 11, 99, 144, 159–60, 163, 173, 175, 184–85, 251; revival of, 134, 136, 141 n. 42, 227
transition, China's, 2–3, 45, 119, 112 n. 7, 199–200, 204, 260
tributary system, 28, 42, 45–46, 48, 50, 84, 103, 250. *See also* All-under-Heaven; Tianxia
truth, 3, 75, 100, 136, 146, 224–25, 240 n. 33, 255–56
Turks, 152–53, 154, 161, 162

unequal treaties, 121
Unger, Jonathan, 133
United Front, 132, 222
United Nations, 1–2, 30–32, 64, 70, 77, 95, 97, 108
United States, 3, 5, 40–41, 48, 62–64, 73, 79, 81–84, 92, 98, 120, 124, 218, 233, 252
universalism, 30–32, 171; Confucian, 119, 251
Uyghurs, 161–64, 166–68

Vietnam, 63

Wæver, Ole, 4
Walker, R.B.J., 101
Waltz, Kenneth, 59
Wang Gungwu, 92
Wang Hui, 102
Wang Ruowang, 136
war on terror, 168–69
Warsaw Pact, 84
Washington consensus, 80

Weber, Max, 38
Wen Jiabao, 138, on traditional culture, 220–21
Wendt, Alexander, 52 n. 12, 41, 57–58
West, 3, 44–5, 96, 216; /China, 101–2, 184; as function, 120, 128
Western learning, 123, 125, 128, 136. See also *Annotated Catalogue of the Imperial Library*
Westphalia system, 11, 41, 95, 98–99, 102, 111, 249, 252–53; treaty, 84
Wilson, Woodrow, 73
Wolf Totem (Lang tuteng), 139
world, 22–23, 25–28, 31–33, 93–96, 99–100, 105, 107, 130, 183–84, 187, 195; China's perceptions of, 184, 186–87, 189–90; failed, 33, 93, 188; future, 2, 91, 110; globalized, 41; Islamic, 143–44, 148, 150–53, 162, 166, 169, 171–73; modern, 186, 202, 204–5; natural and social, 37–38; Park, 186, 191, 201, 206, 208–9; perfect/contingent, 12, 253–54; postprogressive, 200; Sinocentric, 127; theory, 34; Turkic, 174–75; War I, 72; War II, 33, 40, 42, 48, 69, 70; Xunzi on, 56, 67. *See also* All-under-Heaven; harmonious world; *shijie;* Tianxia
World, The, 184–5, 198–99, 200, 202, 205, 208, 210
World Expo Shanghai, 3, 185, 258
world order, 8, 11, 92, 95, 102, 124, 159; Chinese, 4, 6, 7, 10, 92, 183, 250; hierarchical, 9, 41, 99; post-western, 2, 8, 9, 93, 186; Westphalian, 6, 12, 95, 111, 252. *See also* order
World Trade Organization, 77, 137
worldview, 23, 32–33, 93, 97, 101, 105, 111, 144, 173–74, 183, 187–89; China's, 42, 46, 107, 212 n. 19
Wu Zetian, 123

Xibu Da Kaifa Zhanlüe (Great Western Development and Opening Strategy), 166, 167

Xinjiang, 11, 104, 105, 143–44, 158, 162–63, 172, 175, 231, 261; migration into, 164; Sovietization in, 161. *See also* New Frontier; East Turkestan
Xu Zhizin, 231
Xunzi, 9, 22, 54; on foreign relations, 63; on hegemony, 70–71; on hierarchical order, 76–79; on human nature, 74–75; on moral principles, 69, 81; on rising strategy, 82–83, 85; on ruler, 57–58; on state, 55–56, 60–61; on state power, 61–65, 69, 72–73; on Tianxia, 68–69, 79

Yan Fu, 119
Yan Xuetong, 2, 7, 8, 9, 250, 252–53, 257–58, 260
Yaqub Beg, 156, 162
Yellow Emperor (*Huangdi*), 228. See also Son of Heaven
yellow man's burden, 102
Yellow river, 152

Yi Jing (The Book of Changes), 189
Yu Dan, 7, 213 n. 33, 243 n. 60, 262
Yu Keping, 109

Zen Guofan, 131
Zhang Yesui, 6
Zhang Yimou, 106, 119, 131
Zhang Zhidong, 120–22, 125–26, 131–32, 136, 138; on international system, 127; on studying the West, 128; on Tianxia, 130
Zhao Tingyang, 5, 8, 9, 10, 92, 258; on Tianxia, 111, 187–88, 250
Zheng He, 6
Zhou Enlai, 165
Zhoubian zhengce (neighborhood policy), 165
Zhu Xi, 122, 123, 219
*Zhuang*zi, 264
Zhungharia, 104, 152, 156
Zongli Yamen (Office for the General Management of Affairs and Trade with Every Country), 124